SEAT YOURSELF

Published with the assistance of the Borne Fund

Published by Louisiana State University Press
Copyright © 2016 by Louisiana State University Press
All rights reserved
Manufactured in the United States of America
LSU Press Paperback Original
First printing

DESIGNER: Mandy McDonald Scallan
TYPEFACES: Cassia, text; Cabrito Sans, display
PRINTER AND BINDER: Maple Digital

All photographs are by Alex Cook.

"Boudin in Krotz Springs" and pieces on ABear's Café, the Creole Lunch House, Hot Tails, Louie's Café, the Olde Tyme Grocery, St. Rose Tavern, and Tiger Deaux-Nuts first appeared, in different form, in *Country Roads* magazine and are reproduced with permission of the editor. The piece on Calandro's Supermarket first appeared in different form as "Ode to King Cake" in *Oxford American: Best of the South 2012*.

Library of Congress Cataloging-in-Publication Data
Names: Cook, Alex V., author.
Title: Seat yourself : the best of South Louisiana's local diners, lunch houses, and roadside stops / Alex V. Cook.
Description: Baton Rouge : Louisiana State University Press, [2016] | Includes index.
Identifiers: LCCN 2015035406| ISBN 978-0-8071-6253-8 (pbk. : alk. paper) | ISBN 978-0-8071-6254-5 (pdf) | ISBN 978-0-8071-6255-2 (epub) | ISBN 978-0-8071-6256-9 (mobi)
Subjects: LCSH: Restaurants—Louisiana—Guidebooks.
Classification: LCC TX907.3.L8 C66 2016 | DDC 647.95763—dc23 LC record available at http://lccn.loc.gov/2015035406

The paper in this book meets the guidelines for permanence and durability of the Committee on Production Guidelines for Book Longevity of the Council on Library Resources. ∞

To Maya,
    my favorite dinner companion

CONTENTS

ACKNOWLEDGMENTS ix

Prologue: The Silver Moon Café   1

BATON ROUGE AND ENVIRONS   5

Calandro's Supermarket, *Baton Rouge*   7
Fleur de Lis Pizza, *Baton Rouge*   10
Frank's Restaurant and Smokehouse, *Baton Rouge*   13
Jerry Lee's Cajun Foods, *Baton Rouge*   16
Lindsey's Diner, *Baton Rouge*   19
Louie's Café, *Baton Rouge,*   22
Tiger Deaux-Nuts, *Baton Rouge*   24
Zeeland Street Market, *Baton Rouge*   27
Hot Tails, *New Roads*   29
Magnolia Café, *St. Francisville*   32

CAJUN COUNTRY   35

Glenda's Creole Kitchen, *Breaux Bridge*   37
Kelly Citgo, *Bunkie*   41
Hymel's Restaurant, *Convent*   43
Stump's Shell, *Gramercy*   46
Boudin in Krotz Springs
  • Kartchner's Grocery and Specialty Meats   48
  • Billy's Diner   51
  • Cajun Corner Café and Krotz Springs Canal   53

Creole Lunch House, *Lafayette*   55
Don's Seafood Hut Restaurant and Oyster Bar, *Lafayette*   59
Olde Tyme Grocery, *Lafayette*   62
Lea's Lunchroom, *Lecompte*   66
Mr. Francis, *St. Martinville*   69
The Best Stop Supermarket, *Scott*   73

GULFWARDS   77

Sportsman's Paradise, *Chauvin*   79
Starfish Restaurant, *Grand Isle*   82
ABear's Café, *Houma*   86
Griffin's Poboy and Grille, *Houma*   89

NEW ORLEANS AND NORTHSHORE   93

Middendorf's Seafood Restaurant, *Akers*   95
Rocky & Carlo's Restaurant & Bar, *Chalmette*   98
Crabby Jack's, *New Orleans*   101
Dong Phuong Bakery & Restaurant, *New Orleans*   106
Hansen's Sno-Bliz, *New Orleans*   109
Manchu Food Store, *New Orleans*   112
Parasol's Bar and Restaurant, *New Orleans*   116
Parkway Bakery & Tavern, *New Orleans*   118
Verti Marte, *New Orleans*   122

Epilogue: St. Rose Tavern, *New Sarpy*   124

INDEX   129

ACKNOWLEDGMENTS

There are so many people to thank for this book. First and foremost are my wife, Jerri, and my daughter, Maya, who not only tolerate having a writer in the family but also encourage it. I am grateful to my mother, Martha, for instilling in me that food is more than fuel for the body; it's a manifestation of who we are. At LSU Press, this book would not have been possible without the encouraging and then stern hands of Alisa Plant and Catherine Kadair. I want to thank every person who told me of a place I should go and maybe even took me there. *Country Roads* magazine is the finest publication a culture writer could work with, and I thank its editors for letting me appear in its pages all these years.

The food experience I always go back to, though, the one that made me want to tell people about what I ate, was when my dear departed mother-in-law Frances told me about eating poke salat growing up in Mississippi. I said, "I've always wanted poke salat," and she marched me right out into the yard and picked some sprouting up on the fence line. She cooked it down "to get the poison out" and cracked into it a guinea hen egg, also from the yard. She put it on a plate with two of her little sour handmade biscuits and I have been chasing after that taste ever since.

SEAT YOURSELF

Prologue
THE SILVER MOON CAFÉ

"Let me take you to this one place."

That simple phrase speaks volumes. It says that you have someone in your life, whether permanently or just-met, who wants to guide you through the mystery of life. That person has considered all the places one could go and all the people you are and has made a match. Going to the place—"this one place"—is a singular experience, something you have never experienced before or will henceforth, but can experience right now.

Your host will take you there, go with you, let you into his or her life, not to show off but because that is how you live life; you bring others into it.

If I could, I would take you right now to the Silver Moon Café. Since we are dealing with the intangibles, I'd take you to their old location on Oleson Street, in a shack of a house in a weedy lot just over the train tracks that run parallel to Nicholson Drive in Baton Rouge. The lights were dim inside—sometimes it felt like the place wasn't really open—but hungry college students and professors and factory workers would be gathered around four-top tables preparing themselves for the culinary onslaught of Mama's cooking.

Mama is Seabell White Thomas, stewer of meats, alchemist of gravy, purveyor of food comas for decades in Baton Rouge. I only went to the old location a few times; I was more familiar with the one on State Street, which runs across the northeast edge of the LSU campus. That location was only marginally more civilized. You still got your soft drinks out of the cooler and hopefully found a table strung throughout the space.

What to get: You got the lunch special. Smothered chicken or smothered pork chops or smothered anything—whatever meat was reduced to a pure succulent form and ladled over rice, but for me, the real star was the rice and gravy that came with every meal. Often, it was indistinguishable from the main entrée, and you were treated like Henry VIII with two steaming bowls of dark brown deliciousness. People like to say they never finished their meal at Silver Moon, but I know their dark secrets. I have seen people lift the first and then the second bowl to their lips so as to not let a drop of Mama's love go to waste.

Eating at Silver Moon was not without its consequences. My office at that time was across the street in a stately art deco university building that contrasted as much as it could from the rudiments of Silver Moon, and often I was lucky to make it up the steps as the overpowering malaise of that heavy gravy kicked in. You would find wherever you were supposed to be, pretend to do whatever it was you were supposed to be doing, as your brain turned to its own gravy, stewed in this home away from home.

Silver Moon is no more. The building was ravaged by fire in 2007. Thomas has a cookbook available online, but otherwise this one place is gone and I cannot take you there.

What I can do is take you to the places that *are* here in south Louisiana, a culinary anomaly that is, in itself, that one place. South Louisiana food is praised far and wide, the gumbos and jambalayas and crawfish of myth and song, the dreams of stepping through time into a posh New Orleans restaurant still holding its polish after a decade, or attending a boucherie, where every part of a slain hog is put to a delicious purpose.

Louisiana food deserves that praise, for it is singular and songworthy, and there are any number of celebrated places I could take you, but I want to take you to that one place. The place the concierge of your hotel won't likely tell you about, but he or she might actually eat there. The reason is that for all its magic and charm, Louisiana is a real place with real people conducting their daily lives in this culture. I want to take you to the places where those people eat.

One thing you may notice is that the restaurants featured here are spread across the I-10 corridor, the simplest route for exploring Louisiana's culinary nature, but that I have not included more than a handful of places in New Orleans.

New Orleans food is well documented, and you could easily spend a lifetime trying to eat every great dish in the city. As of this writing, my favorite is the fresh pasta in cream sauce with guanciale topped with a golden deep-fried poached egg from Herbsaint, but that fine establishment is not in this book because it is pricey. Herbsaint is a special-occasion restaurant, and where I want to take you is the culinary everyday of south Louisiana, the place where fifteen dollars or less will buy you some dish you will taste in your memory forever. It might be the smoked duck poboy at Crabby Jack's. It might be a softshell crab at the end of the road in Chauvin.

Chances are, I'm going to want to stop at a gas station somewhere along I-10 to get a boudin link, not just because it is delicious and a little weird to be getting homemade sausage from a gas station, but because that link contains the truth of south Louisiana food. It is made of rice and pork in a natural casing, not separated by much from the origins of the ingredients. Gas station boudin is made not by chefs per se, but by people who learned how to make it from their relatives and loved ones. And they sell it at the gas station. And it will be the best thing you ever ate.

So, let me take you to this one place . . .

BATON ROUGE
and ENVIRONS

CALANDRO'S SUPERMARKET

4142 Government St.
Baton Rouge, LA 70806
(225) 383-7815
calandros.com

Mississippi mud and other delectable king cakes

"I go back there and tell them I want half peanut butter and jelly, half apple," growled Miss Beverly from her cashier station when I asked what kind of king cake she gets. "Some people at the house like peanut butter and jelly and some people like apple." It seems a reasonable enough solution if you are like me and Miss Beverly, a fan of Calandro's king cakes. There are two Calandro's in Baton Rouge now—a while back, they built another store out south for the suburban set—but my Calandro's will always be the original Government Street store, a little more quirky than its sibling.

Starting the morning after Epiphany, the table by the deli in the back of this beloved Baton Rouge supermarket is stacked high with this perverse bounty, rings of sugared dough filled with cream cheese and jelly and whatever else that might give the Mardi Gras purist the vapors. One such keeper of the flame announced with considerable histrionics on Facebook that her secret engagement was over because her boyfriend had mistakenly brought home a filled cake rather than one of the magnificent cinnamon rings of wonder from Randazzo's in New Orleans. I bit into a generous wedge of the red velvet cream cheese number on the plate before me, smearing a little sugar across my iPad and thinking, "Maybe it's best they find out now."

A delectable selection of king cakes at Calandro's, Baton Rouge

I do understand that my predilection for off-message king cakes could upset the precarious balance between the tradition that keeps Louisiana interesting and the monoculture that threatens it. Louisiana's charms derive from clinging to idiosyncrasy in deference to "progress." The king cake is less a confection than it is a shoring up of our defining wall. That ring of dough becomes a symbolic arena in which, for a month or so, the great social olympiad that is Mardi Gras is enacted. It rankles me that many bakeries no longer dare to hide the little plastic baby Jesus in the cake, lest some uninformed visitor choke on the Lord while wondering when all these drunk women are going to start bearing their breasts already. Baby Jesus now rolls around loose in the box like a throwaway child.

So yes, the addition of fillings to a king cake is unnecessary, an abomination, maybe. But Mardi Gras is abomination, a loosening of acceptability, a personal parade of excess that culminates in an actual parade of more excess. In that spirit, I deem the Calandro's king cake to be so good it transcends the appropriate.

One discerns what sort of madness is playing out in any particular cake by the little checked-off squares pre-printed on the side of the box. Check for cream cheese, check for fruit filling, check for cinnamon, etc. There are specialties like the aforementioned red velvet or the "Better than Sex" (I don't know if "better" is correct, but it is stickier), but the king of the freaks, the two-headed monkey god reigning over king cake island, is the Mississippi mud cake. A pecan-encrusted, cream cheese and pudding–filled, caramel-drizzled loop that defies all sense of propriety. They should put the Marquis de Sade in this one instead of baby Jesus.

An aspect almost on a par with the cake itself is how the bakery staff draws in extra boxes labeled "Oreo" and "Marshmallow-based," and then checks them off. This is a profound act of grassroots conceptual art, a melding of folk pragmatism and cerebral gamesmanship. This cake should be offered at the next Whitney Biennial, and visitors should be allowed to eat a slice as they ponder what stands before them. Pierce the membrane of spectacle with ad hoc Sharpie taxonomy and chocolate pudding.

Calandro's is so fast and loose with tradition that come Mardi Gras day, when festivalgoers leave Baton Rouge for its wilder neighbors (our last parade is the Spanish Town parade the Saturday before), I am stunned to see the cake table empty when I saunter in on my way out of town. SORRY, KING CAKES ARE OVER says a hastily scrawled sign. It's when I know Mardi Gras season has come to a close, and I am cast back into the insufficiently spangled, less-drunken slog of reality. "I could get a king cake from somewhere else, but what's the point," I glumly admit, slumping back to my car.

Miss Beverly no longer works at Calandro's; fate has drawn her elsewhere. But come every Mardi Gras season, when I contemplate which ring of fire will send me into a sugar coma, I'm tempted to order a half peanut butter and jelly, half apple—partly in tribute, and partly to see how far I am willing to push it this year.

FLEUR DE LIS PIZZA

5655 Government St.
Baton Rouge, LA 70806
(225) 924-2904
fleurdelispizza.com
No credit cards

Rectangular anchovy pizza and cold beer in tiny glasses together make a culinary time machine.

If the end of the world happens like it does in the movies, where buildings are suddenly emptied and cities become vacant husks populated by the occasional roving band of cannibals, I have a loose plan. I'll draw the shades to hide from marauders—I live on a quiet street, so it's unlikely they'll make it this way—and then when everyone I love is secure, I will wind my way a few blocks down Jefferson Highway with a ladder and wrench so I can take the TELEPHONE TAKE-OUT neon sign on top of Fleur de Lis Pizza that, in civilized times, blazed out in red neon as you pulled into the gravel lot. I love that sign.

Fleur de Lis is a pink stucco relic from a lost era. The current owners bought the cocktail lounge in 1946 when that stretch of Government Street was a gravel road. The neon on the front boasts "Air Conditioning" and "Cocktails"—the two things people need to get through a Louisiana summer. They still steadfastly refuse to take credit cards, as if they are waiting for this whole plastic money phase to pass. It is often the only check I write anymore.

My embrace of Fleur de Lis extends beyond nostalgia, though. I am drawn to their rectangular pizzas and little beer glasses like I am drawn to very little else in the world. Fleur de Lis has the details down.

The inside of the restaurant is dark red faux leather and wood paneling. An old jukebox holds court by the windows that likely haven't had the shades drawn in half a century. The bar juts out into the tangled glut of tables, as does the old phone booth where they take the aforementioned telephone takeout orders. On a busy night, you may wait thirty minutes, standing there like a lost soul for a table and then even longer for a pizza because it is worth it.

What to get: It seems foolish to suggest that you get a beer—what else do you get with pizza?—but get a beer. They have a standard selection with a few local microbrew products, but whatever your poison, they bring you the bottle and a little juice glass to pour it in. It seems like such a simple thing, but that glass elevates the whole experience. I've watched countless children in there, including my own, dazzle at getting a Sprite in a glass bottle and pouring it into a glass, instead of the standard paper cup. They hardly know what to do.

The rest is easy; all they have is pizza in two sizes, a circular personal pizza or a rectangular large. Don't be coy; get the large. It feeds two reasonable people or one rabid gourmand.

Theirs is a soft, saturated dough that takes the cheese and sauce and grease through a process akin to folding heated metal to become a sword. There are standard toppings, but my suggestion is to go past pepperoni and go for a salami pizza. The Italian sausage and green pepper is an umami joy. I know people who swear by the shrimp pizza there.

The menu sign has not changed for decades, and neither has the "Round the World" menu item:

Anchovy, Italian Sausage, Mushrooms, Pepperoni, Salami, Onions
No Substitutions

They will concede if you insist that you don't like anchovies, but I'd do things their way. The large Round the World is a magic carpet of flavors, a raft sent to rescue you from a fast-casual culinary oblivion, ready to take you on the high seas of delicious pizza. Salty and savory and dense, each little square of pizza is scientifically calibrated to complement a little juice glass of chilly domestic beer and old country 45 plays on the jukebox. It's the kind of thing that will transport you from a digital omniconnectivity to one where having air-conditioning is a thrill, where things are worth the wait and time slows to a halt around you.

The alternative is to phone in your order—it can take an hour on a busy night—just so you can pull up to that TELEPHONE TAKE-OUT sign, the glowing heart of a Baton Rouge that was. They finally added an ATM machine inside by the phone booth, but it is a bit of a glowing eyesore in the dim past manifest inside Fleur de Lis. I suggest you fish out your checkbook and a pen and go old school with it. It will seem like a whole new world to you.

FRANK'S RESTAURANT and SMOKEHOUSE

8353 Airline Hwy.
Baton Rouge, LA 70815
(225) 926-5977
franksrestaurantla.net

A good biscuit speaks volumes.

My mother-in-law could make some biscuits. The first time I met her, she had biscuits already made for us: tight little balls of fluffy dough, buttermilk sour and resplendent. We started talking about what she and her family ate growing up as sharecroppers in northern Mississippi, and when the conversation turned to poke salat—the best conversation turn ever—I mentioned I'd never had it but always wanted to try it.

She took me straight out to the yard, unsteady on her feet from the first stages of the cancer that took her life, and pointed out which weeds on the fence were pokeweeds and which were just weeds. There was a particularly good patch near a place where, the week before, she'd killed a snake with a hoe. We gathered up a colander-full and she cooked them down for a protracted amount of time, "to cook the poison out," she said. Poke salat contains phytolaccatoxin, which can produce symptoms from muscle spasms to seizures if it isn't cooked down right, and even when it is, there remains a thrilling little tingle of it. Our bounty was reduced to a small bowl of dark greens. She got a guinea hen egg from the yard, fried it and put it on top of the poke salat, and accompanied my impromptu snack with a pair of those biscuits. That right there is my all-time favorite biscuit experience, one that sadly cannot be replicated.

Fortunately, I can replicate my second-favorite any day of the week at Frank's on Airline Highway in Baton Rouge, just north of the down-at-the-heels Cortana Mall. There is a second Frank's location on Airline, about twenty miles to the south in Prairieville, and it's a fine place, but in my opinion it doesn't quite stack up to the original location. I'll vouch for the boast on the sign that they have the world's greatest biscuits. In late 2013, in a move to ensure consistency, Frank's started using its own commercially produced biscuit mix—the same one it now sells to the public—but I can't tell the difference.

The kitchen is flanked by two dining rooms, crowded with knick-knacks and happy diners in the know. I love to bring people to Frank's, preferably on their first morning in Baton Rouge. My friend Traci Jean was visiting us from Macon, Georgia, and said she wanted some of those biscuits I posted about on Facebook. "I will dip those in so many things," she said. Our table was near a windowsill festooned with a rack of 45s—Percy Sledge's minor hit "Cover Me" poking up at the end—and an antique shipping scale with a brown-papered package atop. We pondered what was in it: Cocaine? Government secrets? Poke salat antidote?

What to get: Biscuits. It was determined early on that we were to get biscuits, but what permutation? Traci was starting to get overwhelmed by the meat choices. Frank's has its own smokehouse on the property where the owners make their own sausage—hot, patty, smoked Italian, alligator, turkey, and green onion—as well as a respectable boudin. They also do turduckens, a Cajun poultry orgy involving a boneless duck stuffed in a boneless chicken stuffed in a boneless turkey, as well as one of the finest fried turkeys available anywhere.

Traci went the safe route with patty sausage biscuits, my wife got her usual order of biscuits with white sausage gravy on the side, and I filled in all possible culinary gaps with a boudin breakfast platter with eggs over easy, grits, and biscuits. Frank's will realign what you think patty sausage tastes like, giving it a complex density and juiciness that makes you wonder how a McDonald's sausage patty ever passes muster.

The sausage gravy is near magical. South Louisiana is not big on milk gravies except on chicken-fried steak—you can get a chicken-fried steak breakfast platter at Frank's, by the way—and the salty, rich lava floe of sausage is a welcome sight.

I like the boudin breakfast platter because it is a laboratory of specific breakfast alchemy. No egg is better than the thousandth over-easy egg a fry cook has made that day, the spatula technique almost transparent in the cooking. Frank's boudin is tightly packed and juicy, with a slight tartness to it, and almost no trace of liver, which is how I prefer it. I like to cut the links up into coins, dredge a piece through the egg yolk, dip the golden forkful into my grits, and then deposit it on one of their fluffy biscuits.

In that bite, you understand the great synergy of the universe, how all things arose from an explosion of matter and will one day converge back into a singularity. Traci is saying something about how she likes to pack any kind of food into a biscuit but I am for a moment a rude host, enrapt in my own breakfast.

Boudin can be a dodgy prospect to a newcomer to our shores. Frank's version is an excellent gateway drug. All of their sausage is. Their hot links are just sharp enough to bring you to the verge of a tear, but not to spoil your meal. The smoked sausage is solid, snapping crisp in its casing, and the green onion variety has a delightful vegetal spark to it. The boudin, however, is their smartest sausage move.

Traci described the boudin democratically as "ricey" but was more evocative about the sausage biscuits. "Oh my god, it is so perfect. You know when you are eating patty sausage and you bite into a random chunk of something? There is none of that. It's just the perfect size for those big-ass biscuits."

When I go to Frank's with just my daughter, I like to sit at the counter and watch the congenial, efficient chaos of the kitchen unfold. The waitress demographic skews toward, let's say, the seasoned coffee slinger, women who know at an almost pheromonal level when a cup needs refilling or when a platter is emerging from the window to the kitchen. In full swing on Saturday mornings or on Sunday after church, it is like attending a master class on juggling. How they get all that food out that quickly, all those biscuits still hot, is beyond me. Cirque du Soleil could learn a thing or two about choreography from Frank's.

At the end of that first visit with my mother-in-law, she packed us some little biscuits filled with fried ham for the road. I still think about those biscuits as a manifestation of the person who made them, as an extension of love lingering past that person's time with us. They were supposed to tide us over on the trip back to Baton Rouge, but I'm pretty sure we killed them off before hitting the state line. I'll never be able to re-create those biscuits, but will rely on the virtues of a most-reliable substitute.

JERRY LEE'S CAJUN FOODS

12181 Greenwell Springs Rd.
Baton Rouge, LA 70814
(225) 272-0739
jerryleescajunfoods.com

Home of the boudin poboy

I took a reporter from the *New York Times* out to Jerry Lee's once. He mentioned he was eager to try boudin, and while my instinct was to take him to Lafayette or better, to Scott, the purview of his piece was Baton Rouge. Plus, Jerry Lee's is actually one of my favorites.

It is hubris to declare something the best, or even a favorite, because when you do, the gods that govern the objective and subjective measurements of the universe laugh and throw something in your way to quickly make your declarations seem foolish.

Immediately you'll rattle off any number of places with better boudin, and maybe you are right. Jerry Lee's boudin is tight in the casing, lending the link a nice snap. Not too heavy on the liver, but still possessing some of the needed tang, with just the right amount of cayenne to make you consider it in the rankings of Best Boudin. It is likely heresy to think a Baton Rouge joint might ever contend with the likes of the Best Stop in Scott or Deshotels in Ville Platte, but then I have always found good company in heretics.

A favorite boudin place is a product of merchandise and proximity, being just far enough to feel like you are accomplishing a mission but close enough that you can jet out on a whim, and Jerry Lee's location—ten minutes out of downtown Baton Rouge—puts it right on the sweet spot. The stretch of

Greenwell Springs Road sings the haunting melody of north Baton Rouge's onetime place of prominence. A desolate lot at the intersection with Airline Highway occupies the space where the grand Bellemont Hotel once stood. The massive yellow carcass of the Real Superstore lingers as a defiance against time among any number of industrial buildings given over to rust.

In their shadow are Mexican groceries and little churches, the kinds of places that seem to thrive in the cracks of society. Then Baton Rouge peters out altogether, and before it becomes the white-flight promised land of Denham Springs, there is Jerry Lee's. A pretentious person might deem it a liminal place, resting between states of being.

Jerry Lee's is a convenience store with a meat market, tucked into an unremarkable strip of Greenwell Springs Road. No tables, not much to see, really, unless you are like me and can gaze into the glass of a meat counter all day. They sell boudin, cracklins, head cheese, Italian sausage, andouille, pork skins, and beef jerky. What else could one really need?

They also sell loose boudin, something you don't see on offer in every south Louisiana sausage stop. The deeply savory mix of pork, spices, and rice makes an excellent stuffing for peppers, chicken, turkey—whatever you need stuffed. It also happens to be delicious eaten directly out of the pan with a spoon.

What to get: The boudin poboy. I'm sure there are other boudin poboys out there, but none hold my fascination like those from Jerry Lee's. The boudin is squeezed from its casing—well, I like to imagine it is squeezed from its casing. I'm sure the pork-and-rice mixture is just spooned onto the soft buns they use (a far cry from the chewy/crunchy poboy bread required by purists) and then slathered with American or Jack pepper cheese. It is all wrong but so right.

Jerry Lee's makes some damn fine hogshead cheese, the gelled and sliced terrine of pig face meat and spices that is to some tastes the outlying border of appreciable Cajun delicacies. Theirs has the requisite saltiness and density, yet it is also delicate. There is an earthiness to it that one finds in Indian food; maybe they put some mustard seed and cumin in the mix.

Head cheese comes about by boiling all the meat off the head and whatever other scraps you have once a hog is butchered, and then cooking it down with a gelling agent so it can be poured into molds to be refrigerated and, once set, sliced to be eaten cold. In haute cuisine terms, it is a terrine. Put in more vernacular terms, meat jelly.

Like boudin, the tradition of making head cheese stems from stretching

Boudin at Jerry Lee's, Baton Rouge

the use of a butchered animal as far as one can go. For those who rarely venture past the basic cuts, this is a little far out, but if you only eat one slice of head cheese in your life, get some from Jerry Lee's.

We split the poboy and slices of head cheese and ate them in the car, careening back toward civilization. I was going to take the reporter to a funky antique mall (Circa 1857, in the Garden District) that he needed for his story, but I could see he was feeling a transformation. This slender Brooklynite was picking up what we were laying down.

He was all over Jerry Lee's offerings and, by extension, all over Louisiana. He now had a favorite boudin place, one of the steps required to be a part of what it means to be here.

LINDSEY'S DINER

2502 N. Acadian Thwy. E
Baton Rouge, LA 70805
(225) 355-5050

The best soul food in north Baton Rouge

I asked my buddy Don where the best soul food in north Baton Rouge is and he said, without question, Lindsey's Diner. Don would know; he's a produce delivery driver in the area and the brother of Teddy Johnson, owner of Teddy's Juke Joint in Zachary. We were drinking beers on Teddy's front patio when Don broke it down. "You want to go on Monday when there is spaghetti and meatballs, or Friday when there's catfish." He adds with a chuckle, "And you want to get there while they still have chitlins."

I tried not to blanch. When it comes to southern food, chitlins will separate the men from the boys and I will admit to my seat at the kids' table. I get the tradition that keeps it on the menu; when you are poor, you eat anything that can be eaten on a pig, even the intestines—or, as they are called, chitterlings or chitlins. I want to have a taste for it.

My first chitlins experience was at Tabby's Blues Box, the long-defunct Baton Rouge blues club, one drunken night. My roommate tried to warn me that the romance around it might not meet the reality, but I took a heaping bowl. I don't know if it was the blinking holiday lights, or Lil' Jimmy Reed's blistering solo filling the air, or the previous six or nine beers, but I had what could be considered a psychedelic reaction to them. Colors smeared, lines blurred, and then time got away from me. I don't actually know how it played out; I just know there is a lingering voice in my consciousness that warns, NO MORE CHITLINS.

Voices be damned, I headed to Lindsey's for catfish and maybe some enlightenment. I've passed this corner of Acadian and Choctaw dozens of times—in my less financially sound youth, I would get my power turned back on at the Winn-Dixie out there—but I never noticed that this nondescript building was an actual open business.

The interior possesses a glorious diner patina, the kind of wear in a restaurant that is largely lost to the fast-food landscape increasingly occupying many of the corners in this part of town. North Baton Rouge—the north-south dividing line generally being Florida Boulevard—was once the suburbs for state government and the plants along the river, but with decades of white flight and economic struggle, its history seems to be slipping away.

There were four older African American women scurrying about behind the counter filling Styrofoam clamshells from steam trays and smoothing the buttercream frosting on the homemade cakes they offer on order. I'm a little lost in a dream of buttercream when a woman named Gladys asks what I want.

What to get: I take Don's suggestion and get the fried catfish with sides of greens and red beans. The catfish is exactly how you want soul food catfish to be: crisp cornmeal batter against flaky planks of catfish. The mustard greens are surprisingly subdued; one gets used to the saltiness or acidity by which many cooks will try to dress up the plant. This was what mustard greens taste like: a rich vegetal tang with a substantial texture. Soul food red beans, if one may categorize them, are a soupier thing than the thick, creamy creole-style red beans one associates with New Orleans, and I think this distinction about Louisiana cuisine is important. Something as humble as red beans is a radically different dish depending on where you hold your bowl. It's a product of the people making it, the people ordering it. Red beans and rice is just too basic a dish to put on airs.

While I'm making my order, I scan the steam tray and there they are. The chitlins. Little white rings smothered down in a yellowish juice. I'd spoken to a friend about chitlins and he said that among enthusiasts, there are two schools of thought about extruding the contents of that which becomes chitlins: they are either squeezed clean or they are "stump beat," basically pounded clear of their original purpose while maintaining their integrity. I don't have it in me to ask Gladys which method she prefers, but I do get a small cup.

"You want rice?" she asks, and I say, "Lots."

"You want juice?" she asks, and I make a small pinch gesture with my fingers. I suggested to my dining companion that we take the booth farthest from the counter, just in case I am not able to eat this sweet lady's chitlins. I peer into the cup and am delighted to see a healthy population of onions and green onions in the mix, the rice absorbing whatever the juice is. Lifting a forkful, I think maybe this bite of chitlins will turn me around, but that flabby texture, something like thin rubber, stops me short, and then that voice returns: I TOLD YOU. And I take heed. I want to be at one with this little cup of history made by this sweet old lady who puts the same care into it as she does her buttercream frosting, but I'm just not there yet.

Outside, I snap a few shots of the building and a young man emerges from a really nice truck to ask me what I am doing. I thought about saying that I often ask myself that very question, but I keep it simple. "I'm writing a book about good places to eat, and this is one of them." My answer seems to satisfy us both.

LOUIE'S CAFÉ

3322 Lake Street
Baton Rouge, LA 70802
(225) 346-8221
louiescafe.org

Home cooking for generations of Baton Rougeans

Every college town has that place you went to late at night, early in the morning, as a default. It was a place where you or someone you know worked, a crappy waitressing or dishwashing job being a rite of passage in that town. It's a place you went on first dates and where breakups were enacted, its familiarity a buffer to life's and love's harrowing transitions. It's that place you think about when you finally leave that town in adulthood and eat at nicer places with healthier food. It is the first place you go when you get back to town. In Baton Rouge, that place is Louie's Café.

"I don't know if it's going to be the same," I said to a dining companion as we descended the hill from LSU's campus to Louie's in its new location on Lake Street. Louie's has occupied a number of sites on the outskirts of LSU since 1941, but it had remained at its State Street residence for over a quarter of a century until this last move, down the block to the site of an old Wendy's. How could a place everyone has eaten at for so long be the same in a new spot?

My first impression on taking a seat at the counter was that it is like the old Louie's but brighter. Gone is the curious beach mural that graced the old location's walls, replaced by windows on all sides. But otherwise, the red swiveling barstools, the tables, the black-and-white tile, the ubiquitous Louie's T-shirt on every waitress, each bearing the place's mustachioed mascot... it's all still there.

And then there is Frenchie. Marcus "Frenchie" Cox is the long-running chef and central character to the cast that is Louie's, carrying on multiple conversations between customers and prep chefs, rattling off a ceaseless patter at the grill. A Joycean deluge of half-jokes, local references, and caterwauled songs is a complimentary side dish with your veggie omelet. I've asked a couple of staff members over the years how they can withstand the cracked glossolalia issuing from this man and they all claim that after two shifts you don't hear it anymore, and by your tenth, it becomes the mad, cheery telegraph pulse of your consciousness, the engine that gets you through your shift. But a favorite restaurant is not had on the merits of a motormouth spatula jockey; it is on the food. And as greasy spoons go, Louie's is peerless.

What to get: Everyone has their thing. Many swear by the Big Cheesy Lou, deeming it the best hamburger in town (a contender, I'll say). In my heady vegetarian years, I swore by the Phyllis—the same veggie mix that goes into the omelets, here topped with melted Swiss on a poboy bun—but now it's a BEST (bacon, egg, sprouts, tomato) plus jalapeños on rye. It's an earthy upgrade on a BLT, the umami of sprouts meeting the richness of the egg head-on and the bacon and chilled tomato keeping the battle corralled. The jalapeños add a little danger and the rye a layer of gritty sobriety.

If that sounds overthought, well, I've spent a lot of time at Louie's mulling over this and countless other life choices while perched on one of those little barstools, as has every regular. I suspect every Louie's customer has their own sandwich or omelet permutation as equally identifiable as their genome. The one thing I'll say to any customer of Louie's, longterm or newcomer, is to get a side of hash browns. Louie's hash browns are chunks of potatoes fried up on the grill with green and white onions and butter and the shimmer of everything else cooked there. Salty and savory and complex, a conflation of the myriad personalities that eat there.

So is the new Louie's the same? Or better? The experience is more for me like when your family moves to a new house. The physical pathways need adjustment, the little details are for a time askew... but ultimately, the thing that made it home comes along for a ride.

TIGER DEAUX-NUTS

5162 Government St.
Baton Rouge, LA 70806
(225) 421-1091

Fry it and they will come.

I show up around six in the morning, but Jeff Herman of Tiger Deaux-Nuts has been at work for two hours already. Because he has a dream about donuts.

Herman counts off the unglazed donuts on his racks, figuring out how many of each kind to make this morning. Tiger Deaux-Nuts doesn't just specialize in gourmet donuts—it's all he makes. Currently that includes maple bacon, bananas Foster, chocolate mint, chocolate peanut butter, s'mores, apple pie, key lime pie, and, my favorite, vanilla-jalapeño.

These are the best donuts within a hundred miles. The donut itself has a heft and crispness you simply are not going to find in a place that has to deal in volume, and each one is hand-decorated to ensure a culinary experience to its fullest. I know this for a fact because after I confessed to a stint working in a donut shop in high school, Herman ordered me to scrub up and put me to work.

Herman exhorted me to work fast: the vanilla glaze hardens quickly. I start plugging the centers with marinated apple chunks for the apple pie donuts and then drizzling them with the thick juice of the marinade. Donut making is a weirdly antiquarian business, one where you apprentice with a donut cutter before you are left to work the dough and the fryer and the icing bags yourself.

Maple bacon donuts at Tiger Deaux-Nuts, Baton Rouge

Herman learned his way by watching every YouTube video he could find on the subject and then hanging out in area donut shops, peeking through the kitchen door to glean what he could.

He went to places like Voodoo Doughnut in Portland, places where the foodies' hunger for the next thing meets the eagerness of the entrepreneur. He doesn't want to be in the donut business; he wants to be in the business-starting business.

That said, there are donuts to fill. I am tasked with pushing jalapeño slivers into vanilla icing while Herman's sister Nicole steps in to spread melted marshmallow on the s'more versions. Herman is off to the side, carefully tending a commercial-grade mixer. "I think I have a perfect meringue going here," he crooned. He wields an icing bag, pushing the perfect meringue into holes in the side of the donut shells destined for the key lime variety.

His donuts are amazing, and not in a way that subs for clever or inventive, but straight up amazing. There is the tiniest crunch to the donut holes, the glaze carrying a toothiness that you just don't find elsewhere.

Herman's maple bacon donut is the big seller, a tag team of rich sweetness with just a nod of salt from the bacon. The chocolate mint and peanut butter varieties are exercises in restraint. There is just enough filling piped in these to get the flavor across without becoming too much.

The apple pie, bananas Foster, and key lime donuts are architectural feats. "I like to think of them as deconstructions," Herman offers as he balances chocolate graham crackers with lime slices fresh from the mandolin. Almost as much thought goes into them as does work.

The vanilla-jalapeño variety is probably the simplest in structure, but to my taste, the most inventive of the bunch. The peppers are seeded and cut into moons, offering a twinge of heat to bounce off the vanilla icing, tickling every flavor profile on the rebound. The heat comes on quickly and disappears before you get the burn.

Eight a.m. rolls around just as the last of the peanut butter has been piped and the final row of apple pie pastries has been dusted with crumble. Herman changes into a light purple Oxford.

He sets up a tray on the counter displaying samples of the day's ornate, dream-filled bounty; he updates Facebook to tell the world he's open. Then, with a slight exhale, he unlocks the door, ready for whatever opportunity comes through.

ZEELAND STREET MARKET

2031 Perkins Rd.
Baton Rouge, LA 70808
(225) 387-4546
zeelandstreet.squarespace.com

Answer the siren call of the pot roast.

A bad day has no chance with Stephanie. All she has to do is yell, "Hayyy Alex!" in her girlish singsong while taking orders or running the kitchen or just coordinating the life of Zeeland Street Market, a bustling lunch joint in the Garden District neighborhood of Baton Rouge. "How you doin'? Where's your wife at? How's that girl doin'?" is the line of questioning that I get in there—that everybody gets in there. Stephanie knows everybody.

Stephanie owns and runs the restaurant with her ex-husband Hayden, but the impetus of the restaurant is all Stephanie.

With its array of freestanding booths, Zeeland Street is eminently comfortable. It's a neighborly place, where folks want to see what people are getting. Local art dots the walls, punctuating the chatty din of the lunch rush.

My favorite thing about Zeeland Street, though, is the staff and, at heart, Stephanie's staffing philosophy. For lack of a better word, Stephanie takes in strays—people who have fallen through the cracks somewhere in society—teaches them a skill, and makes them part of her family.

What to get: There really isn't a bad dish on the menu, but my go-to is Mama's pot roast. The beef roast pulls apart as easy as the pages of a diary you shouldn't be reading, and is just as tantalizing. There is a peppery tartness to the gravy that really gets me. If they don't have pot roast that day (as the specials rotate on a frequent basis), the beef brisket will do. Tender as the night without any overly sweet barbecue sauce that mars most briskets, it's the kind of dish I try to show some restraint with, hoping to save some for the next day to make sandwiches, but I never do.

Zeeland Street Market has an elaborate sandwich menu named for streets in the Garden District. My buddy Lance, who lives around the corner, swears by the Reymond, which is pot roast, gravy, and coleslaw on a kaiser roll. I've been known to dabble with a Pericles, a heroic name for pot roast, sauteed green peppers, and cheddar. Vegetarian friends love the Arlington Grilled, a heady mix of pecans, Swiss cheese, avocado, tomato, alfalfa sprouts, and Italian vinaigrette.

If you are going to deny yourself the pleasures of Zeeland Street's pot roast for whatever reason, the vegetable sides are the real stars of the meal, especially the turnip greens. They are likely the most balanced turnip greens you will ever have in a restaurant, the perfect mix of earthy, sweet, and sour, smothered to just the right texture to eschew any stringiness but still to hold their shape. You get two sides with any plate lunch, and Zeeland Street's cabbage, lima beans, and okra with stewed tomatoes are all amazing. I always want to opt for a veggie plate of four sides, but the siren call of the pot roast gets me every time.

HOT TAILS

1113 Hospital Rd.
New Roads, LA 70760
(225) 638-4676
hottailsrestaurant.com

Young rock-star chef couple makes the best fish sandwich you will ever eat.

New Roads might be as close as south Louisiana gets to a resort community. Pricey vacation homes line the banks of False River, an oxbow lake left over from one of the Mississippi River's many migrations over the millennia. The place is a haven for water sports of every stripe or just watching the Jet Skis go by from the deck of your second-mortgage camp, beer in hand, not a care in the world.

New Roads also has its share of great restaurants. Satterfield's sits at what once was the St. Francisville ferry landing before the Audubon Bridge connected the Pointe Coupee Parish town to its neighbor across the way. Morel's offers fine dining on the main drag and a coveted place to watch the New Roads Mardi Gras parades if you can score a table. But just off the beaten path on Hospital Road lies an unassuming joint called Hot Tails, where the Louisiana cuisine that has informed this little bend of Pointe Coupee is being rejuvenated by the married chef team of Cody and Samantha Carroll.

Now, you'd be hard pressed to have a bad fried seafood meal anywhere in New Roads, but the Carrolls are not your average chefs. In April 2010, just a few months after they both graduated from the Louisiana Culinary Institute in Baton Rouge, they opened Hot Tails on Hospital Road, and in the short time since have become rather celebrated chefs in south Louisiana. Their numerous awards fill a china cabinet in one corner of their homey restaurant, among them a silver platter from the 2013 New Orleans Wine & Food Experience's Grand Tasting, naming Cody "King of Seafood." Cody edged out some legendary competition with a Louisiana Speckled Trout Perdu and Red Swamp Crawfish, accompanied by sweet corn and blue crab callas, whipped creole potato salad, house-pickled banana pepper, charred green onion and sassafras, and Tabasco sabayon.

Cody grew up in the tiny community of Batchelor, just a few miles north of New Roads. Before entering culinary school, he worked the local crawfish ponds, fishing them himself and establishing relationships with his buyers. In deciding where to start his first restaurant, it made sense to return to the area where he had already built up a name.

Samantha and Cody met in culinary school, and the restaurant is a manifestation of their lives. One wall of the dining room is made from wooden pallets that came from the grain co-op Cody has done business with his whole life. Elements of the dining room come from the beachhead of a plantation that his family farms. The tin is from the roof of an old barn on a friend's property. Some of the light fixtures came from the Caterie Restaurant in Baton Rouge when it burned down. Cody's daddy, brother, and Cody himself killed all the deer mounted on the wall.

The Hot Tails menu is drawn from the familiar: poboys, gumbo, burgers—all given a chef's spin. All ingredients are locally sourced and everything is made in house, down to the pickles and condiments. They make their own salt pork and pickled peppers. Until you try them at Hot Tails, you may not know how good your favorite Louisiana dishes can taste.

What to get: Cody and Samantha bring out some gumbo as a demonstration of their ideals. The dark chunky broth sits in a small individual cast-iron pan on a wooden serving board, a sphere of rice adrift in a dark lake of okra and fat juicy shrimp. The flavor transcends the typical cocktail of roux and okra—there is at first a lingering smokiness, followed by a quick spicy bite. The vegetables are neither too chunky nor have they disappeared in the smothering, but instead coalesce into the rare gumbo that is actually better than what you'll find cooked at any of the hundred camps lining False River.

Also, anything you get, go for a side of their white remoulade topped with pickled mustard seeds. It operates as a deconstructed creole dressing and is a central flavoring to their finest creation: The Sangwich. One of their chefs would fix himself what he called a fish "sangwich," Samantha explained to me, and it was so good that they added it to the menu.

The Sangwich is a mountain of flavors and textures, stabbed in the top by a steak knife with a side order of thick home fries in a little metal bucket. It encapsulates and intensifies that which is great about a fried fish sandwich. It is at once tangy and savory, crunchy and delicate, rich and airy. I have eaten my weight in fish sandwiches over the years, and this one is singular in how advanced it tastes. Cody explains that he and Samantha make their own tartar sauce and their own blue cheese-and-pecan cole slaw that gives a spiciness and nuttiness. "If we can't get it, we don't serve it," he says. I'm thankful they can get whatever they need to keep the Sangwiches rolling and give New Roads food a chef's touch. Each bite makes me think, "Maybe I do need a camp out here . . ."

MAGNOLIA CAFÉ

5689 Commerce St.
St. Francisville, LA 70775
(225) 635-6528
themagnoliacafe.net

Great restaurant and cozy screened-in porch with live Cajun and roots music

I forget how flat the land of south Louisiana is until I drive up into the mild hills of the Felicianas, where the landscape starts to hint of what awaits for endless miles through Mississippi, all deep green pine and loping highways. St. Francisville sits as a final outpost of south Louisiana, in a way. It is tucked away from the road, rife with the Victorian quaintness that defines so many river towns. It had one of the few remaining ferry crossings until the gleaming Audubon Bridge connected the town with New Roads across the river. With selfish motives, I wonder if such connectivity to the rest of the world will sully some of St. Francisville's charms.

Thankfully, the Magnolia Café still acts as a cultural and ideological anchor to St. Francisville. The place is a marriage of fine dining and back-porch drinking, of country congeniality and revelry. Locals still refer to the building it occupies as the "new location." The original building burned down in 2003, and the café relocated to the building behind it.

The town of St. Francisville revolves around the restaurant and its adorable cadre of businesses. I always try to find an excuse to stay in one of the tiny, lovingly restored 3-V Tourist Court rooms that have lined the edge of the Magnolia's parking lot since 1938. There is no hangout better suited to my temperament than Birdman Coffee and Books, its pastry and ice cream

counter as carefully curated as its bookshelves. But the Magnolia holds the central place in orbit.

What to get: The Magnolia's menu is heavy on salads and sandwiches. For the former, you will be remiss if you pass through this life without sampling their sensation salad. The origins of this salad go back to the old Bob & Jake's Restaurant in Baton Rouge, which hit on just the right mixture of garlic, Romano cheese, vinegar, parsley, pepper, and lemon juice; it's now the signature salad of much of the region. In some ways, a sensation salad has a similar flavor profile to a muffaletta, without relying on chopped olives for acidity.

The Magnolia's version is one of the best. An abundance of onions gives the salad an earthy bite, and adding shrimp or grilled chicken makes it a substantial meal unto itself. But I like to leave a little room for my favorite, the spicy shrimp poboy.

Most shrimp poboys are battered and deep-fried, but these fat, juicy shrimp are sautéed in garlic butter and then loaded onto dense, chewy French bread with jack cheese, grilled bellpeppers, onions, and tomatoes. The bread gets fully saturated with spicy butter as do the peppers, creating a perfect synergy of garlic wonder.

Magnolia's soup du jour offerings are always on point, but try to get there for their bisquelike crawfish and artichoke soup or their surprising combination of butterbean and shrimp. The Magnolia also makes its own pizza dough every morning, and the chicken, pesto, spinach, and feta pizza comes highly recommended.

All this garlic would lend one to think the Magnolia is not the best place to have an intimate conversation, which couldn't be further from the truth. At lunch, every milligram of town gossip passes across the wooden tables in its cozy dining rooms. In the evenings, the action is out on the screened-in porch, a fork in one hand and a beer in the other. On Friday nights the Magnolia has live music—but really, any night finds the place buzzing with talk, a human counterpoint to the cicada din of the country. Conversations spill over from table to table like they do in crowded New Orleans restaurants, yet you are there with the trees and the stars and all the right people of one of the most charming towns in the South.

CAJUN COUNTRY

GLENDA'S CREOLE KITCHEN

3232 Main Hwy (LA 31)
Breaux Bridge, LA 70517
(337) 332-0294
glendascreolekitchen.biz

The epitome of down-home cooking

In the portion of Breaux Bridge running north of I-10, standing guard over the neat rows of a soybean field, stands a metal state highway sign pointing the way to Camp Bon Temps, "Camp Good Times." The sign is riddled with buckshot. A friendlier, hand-painted sign leans against an oak tree in front of Glenda's Creole Kitchen across the street, promising "plate lunches daily, catering available, old-fashioned hamburgers, sweet-dough pies." Maybe the locals just want everything hand-done around here.

If they grew up on Glenda Broussard's food, I can see why. Glenda's Creole Kitchen opened in 2000 on a tidy square of land that boasts a modest parking lot, and that lot is filled to capacity seven days a week for breakfast and lunch. A truck towing a horse trailer finds some real estate on the side as I get there.

Glenda's is the epitome of down-home cooking. The place has about five tables total and the daily specials are set up in steam trays, cafeteria style. Removing the lids reveals a detailed study in the art of gravy: a mysterious, glistening deep brown next to a peppery red, adjacent to a tray of turkey wings half-submerged in their own concoction. It is the kind of tableau that will have you rethinking the color wheel, happily replacing the prismatic rainbow of life with this parade of gravy brown.

According to Broussard's niece, Kayla Rossyion, the food itself brought the restaurant into being. Glenda once worked as a dispatcher at the sheriff's office, and when she brought her own cooked food for lunch, everyone wanted some. She started selling her cooked food at work, and the restaurant took off from there.

Broussard owned the property out here on LA 31, but to city dwellers like me who define location by what off-ramp a thing is near, it seems a remote locale for a restaurant. Poche's Meat Market, about a mile back at the turnoff, already seems out of the way. But according to Rossyion, this is a busy highway for the area.

What to get: anything with gravy, which is easy, since everything comes with gravy.

Gravy is the nucleus of the creole food world, the juice in which the real alchemy happens. Creole gravy is thinner than most, not the thickened sauce of a Cajun étouffée or the milky concoction one gets ladled over biscuits, but an extension of the food cooked in it, a literal essence. You could take gravy from any one of the dishes offered up, put it over a little rice, and know from whence it came.

My top suggestion would be the catfish coubillion. Elsewhere, you might find the dish spelled "courtbouillon," "courtbullion," or even "couvillion," but I will here defer to Glenda's spelling, as it is the best representative of the dish that I have ever eaten. A Cajun-style courtboullion is generally a roux thickened with tomato puree in which a fish seasoned with aromatic herbs, garlic, and lemon is allowed to simmer down, but that doesn't begin to describe the complexity of the coubillion at Glenda's.

The catfish has taken on a saturated, glowing orange hue, having become one with the gravy. The stuff is spicy, enough to require a refill of the peach tea they have on hand instead of the usual syrupy sweet tea. A hint of lemon offers a tart edge that then gives way to a slight sweetness in the gravy, maybe from the puree, maybe from pure magic. Attempts to pry the formula for it go nowhere. "She might kill us if we tell her secret," Rossyion laughs.

Glenda's take on smothered okra is a thing to behold as well. Usually, you can find okra cooked down with Italian sausage and tomatoes as a side dish in any Cajun restaurant, but here it is okra, shrimp, and crabmeat in their own beguiling gravy. The fat, juicy Gulf shrimp meet the soft okra halfway, and the crabmeat disappears into the complex sauce. One is tempted to say

Catfish coubillion at Glenda's Creole Kitchen, Breaux Bridge

that smothering food is cooking it down to nothing, but I'd counter you are really cooking it down into everything.

Another take on smothering is Thursday's smothered fresh sausages. Slow-cooking plump, homemade sausages in that tangy tomato gravy releases the salty richness from within the casings, permeating the rice with a pork essence you just are not going to get any other way.

The staff greeted a couple that had moved away from the area years ago and were coming back for a visit. "The first thing he wanted was one of those stuffed turkey wings," said the woman as she sat down. It was what I suddenly wanted as well.

In creole cooking, "stuffed" doesn't mean a rice or cornbread stuffing, but instead making a cut in the meat and packing it with aromatic spices and garlic. Glenda's offers stuffed pork chops, stuffed fried chicken, and stuffed brisket depending on the day, but they have a batch of stuffed turkey wings going every weekday.

Turkey wings have their own innate wildness. There is no delicate way to dig into the savory dark meat hanging on hefty bones. Again, the star is the gravy, a translucent maple brown dotted with pockets of spices and hot sauce. The heat is just at the right balance to bring out the complex tenor of dark-meat turkey. You might never go back to white meat again.

Should you find yourself traversing the backroads of Acadiana during Lent (the forty days after Mardi Gras until Easter Sunday, when most Louisiana Catholics give up something dear like chocolate or soft drinks and, as a whole, swear off meat on Fridays), get yourself some of Glenda's garfish balls—if you can, since they run out fast. For some of us, garfish balls can replace meatballs anytime, not just in Lent. Glenda smothers them in a gravy with onions, much like her étouffée.

Glenda's sweet-dough pies are a thing of local legend, coming in a variety of flavors. Should the creole cooking gods be smiling upon you, they will have either delicious sweet potato pies on hand or, for the true and good of heart, delicate fig pies. You might want to call ahead to ensure the gods' favor.

KELLY CITGO

8667 U.S. 71 S
Bunkie, LA 71322
(337) 623-4796

An analog boudin experience for a digital world

I pulled into the gas station hoping for a cheap fill-up, not a horrible cup of coffee to counteract an afternoon eating my way through Evangeline Parish, when I saw the magic word "boudin" on a sign on a Citgo station at the opposite corner. I want to think the mechanical pumps were a good sign, the lever action and the little dial spinning like a slot machine through the tenths of a gallon, 10, 20, 30, and so on. Last time I used a pump like this, my bill wasn't quite as high. I wonder if there are pumps that lock up after $99.99, having not been manufactured to handle that impossibility.

A hunter pulled up in the kind of truck that racks up that kind of bill, he and his son still in hunting gear, and I followed them in. They went past the wooden shelf of motor oil and the general candy chaos at the register, straight to the deli counter in the back, like this is where they always go after a day firing at rabbits or squirrels. The counter is little more than a couple of metal trays with heat lamps. The place is a mess, frankly, but I feel committed after standing in line. The boy opted for chicken fingers, the guy wants a hot link, but the bored fry cook in the steamy little kitchenette declares they are out of them. I saw fried pigtails on the menu, a placard seemingly ambitious for what's on offer. I don't particularly like fried pigtails, their toughness makes them more an occupation for your mouth than something to eat, but when the possibility is broached, you want it fulfilled. It's a puzzle-piece kind of thing.

With adventure trumping caution, I asked for a boudin link, and the bored young man handed me a boudin link wrapped in foil. This happens a lot in the boudin game. Just one link? he seemed to ask, opening up the larger unanswered question of why are we here having this transaction in the middle of nowhere for just one link of boudin. Sitting in the driver's seat with the door open to the gravel dust of the parking lot and the growing heat of the day, I went through the timeless ritual of unwrapping and biting in. It will probably say something about unwrapping and biting in on my tombstone.

The natural casing was whisper thin, the filling easy on the liver but still letting the earthy bit of the orange meat come through. This humble half-wanted link possessed the right amount of salt, the right amount of greasiness—it was shaping up to be a perfectly satisfactory but average boudin experience.

Then, when the hunter peeled out in his gas guzzler, sending a spray of gravel into the air, a wave of spice hit me. A twinge of cayenne, maybe a bitter kiss of cumin, I'm not sure what it was because it was so surprising. It's why I stop, not just at gas stations or hole-in-the-wall restaurants, but anywhere. I want my meter to tick by like an old analog gas pump and then when I hit that mark, I want to hear that old gas station bell go off, something alerting whoever is there to hear it that I am here, ready to do business. I pulled into the right place.

I don't think I heard an actual bell when the heat of the link took hold, but it jolted me awake to the here and now when it did. I knew the secret that the hunter was revealing to his son, the same secret hidden in the unyielding countenance of the teenage clerk, likely unaware that the thing he was dealing is solid gold.

HYMEL'S RESTAURANT

8740 LA 44
Convent, LA 70723
(225) 562-9910
hymelseafood.com

Family-style seafood joint that will put you in touch with the actual Mississippi River

We all know the main reason the world ever came to Louisiana is because of the Mississippi River, a tangled umbilicus that links the heart of the continent to the rest of the world. We know about the forts and battles, the Huck Finn mythic allure of Big Muddy, but for most of us, the River is just a water feature as we motor about the state. With the gradual dismantling of the ferry system, the Mississippi is mostly something we drive over on a bridge.

But, if you take your little land boat down River Road, you'll see that the Mississippi is still essential to who we are culturally and economically. Dozens of chemical and processing plants sit amid the checkerboard of restored plantations and ruins. Weird brackets of pipe work and conveyor belts arch the road so that raw materials and final products can be channeled to rusted barge arrays hidden from view by the ever-present levee that our finest minds and greatest hubris erected to keep the Mississippi in check.

It is easy to get mesmerized on River Road with all this past and present knotted up together against the contours of the River that defines us. Fortunately, Hymel's sits out there amidst all this in the town of Convent, like an oasis.

Hymel's doesn't seem like much from the outside: a busted gas pump,

a brick bar and restaurant next to an aging, whitewashed warehouse, but inside it is one of the homiest seafood joints in the region.

My daughter and I arrived post-lunch rush after a protracted trek down from Baton Rouge, and I thought I had her talked into trying raw oysters.

What to get: The sign outside boasts "Crabs, shrimp, oysters," and that's what they have in abundance. We started out with an old-school shrimp cocktail and a half-dozen raw oysters. Now, there are more storied places to get oysters dressed up to be revered, but here at Hymel's they are served up straight with but a cup of horseradish and cocktail sauce.

My daughter's will blanched at the gray juicy specimens before her, so the plate was slid to me. I understand. It took me years to finally come around to raw oysters. "They are so good smoked or grilled or stewed or fried," I'd think, but I get it. Putting a raw oyster in your mouth is the most direct culinary connection we can have with the water that defines us. Filter feeders they are. Everything we are as a state seeps through that little oyster, and we take it back in. Maybe that kind of thinking might lead us to be more conscientious of what we put in the water.

Just about everywhere else, seafood is special-occasion food, but Hymel's is about how quotidian fresh seafood is to south Louisiana. Were I with other drivers, I'd opt for the fishbowl goblet of Abita beer, but in this case, a can of Bud will do.

My daughter gets fried catfish, which Hymel's does a fine job of: crispy breading on thick planks of catfish fried just short of being at all greasy.

A friend of mine sings the praises of Hymel's turtle soup, served with a little sherry on the side, but I go for a soft-shell crab poboy, which is, in my opinion, the most Louisiana thing you can eat this side of boiled crawfish (which they also serve, as well as boiled crabs and shrimp).

Delicately breaded and fried whole, a soft-shell crab is a brass-tacks thing to eat. Like a raw oyster, there is little distance between the animal and the meal. It is understandable why most people savor lump crabmeat; it bears the richness of the sea in every morsel. Soft-shell crab is the real thing, though. Not a particular species as one might think, a soft-shell crab is one that has recently molted its exoskeleton—something a crab must do to grow—but has yet to create a hardened exterior. The crab is battered and fried whole, except for the gills and abdomen—every part of it combining into something strikingly real.

The main taste is still the buttery density of the white crabmeat, but then there is a twang of the rest. Something vaguely fibrous, a whisper of sourness to it. It is complex and delicious, the kind of culinary journey one expects to take with haute cuisine.

Instead, you are at Hymel's. A family nearby might be having a birthday party. A little-league team may be celebrating a victory. Or, as on this lazy afternoon, you are there in the dining room with the staff on break, watching TV court dramas while sipping Bud from the can. The early shift of Saturday night partiers takes to their stools in the adjacent bar. Light lazily pours in through the glass brick as you contemplate oyster shells, whole crabs, little containers of cocktail sauce, and the truly calm state of being that culminates from it all.

If this all sounds too docile, wind your way to Hymel's on a Thursday or Saturday night and hope you can find a parking spot. Thursday nights are country music open mic and Saturday has regional country bands playing in the bar, with the sound pouring out into the packed dining room. It's on these nights that Hymel's embodies a reality of Louisiana, where people converge in the middle of nowhere to drink and eat and spend time with family and friends and cut up and say grace and live the whole of their lives in the same spot, one little dot on a bend in the giant river that is the reason any of us are here in the first place.

STUMP'S SHELL

220 E. Airline Hwy
Gramercy, LA 70052
(225) 869-8611

The weirdest gas station in south Louisiana

Of all the gas stations in south Louisiana, Stump's in Gramercy might be the most curious, and thus my favorite. It is perched on a bend in Highway 61 at the end of an exasperatingly empty eight miles from the I-10 exit, right across from the unassuming but, from a Louisiana culinary standpoint, important Zapp's potato-chip plant. The rest of Gramercy/Lutcher is tucked away on back streets closer to the river. One generally arrives at Stump's with a mixture of relief that there is actually a gas station off Exit 187, and some initial dismay that this is it.

Stump's has not been upgraded to in-pump credit card machines, forcing you to enter the age-old dance of trust that is handing your credit card over to the clerk. I wonder if younger generations of drivers actually know how to negotiate this social transaction. You might as well have them write out a check. There is a mural of a Middle Eastern man smoking a hookah next to the window of D's Corner, the little bar attached, where the words "you are beautiful" are scrawled over a dim interior collage of beer signs. Next to the pump itself is a frayed, cock-eyed poster of "Old Doorways of Jerusalem." It is beautiful.

The interior of Stump's is classic gas station chaos with a utilitarian twist. This humble outpost serves a number of plants along the river, and so the back part of the store is given over to heaps of work jeans and uniform shirts. I take note that the next time I need Wranglers with a carpenter loop, I'm coming here.

There is also the caged gray parrot, basking in the sun during the warmer months just outside the entrance, adding to the chaos inside during the winter. The bird does a killer impression of various cellular ringtones and walkie-talkie chirps from the plant workers, so well executed that every person in line reaches for their phone. I wonder if behind those cold avian eyes, the parrot is having an endless laugh.

What to get: Stump's has a ramshackle take-out lunch counter offering oyster poboys, fries, and the like, but I've spent a couple of weeks teaching classes at a nearby aluminum plant, and the workers told me to get the boudin. They have three varieties: regular, shrimp, and crawfish, each wrapped in tight foil like cigars in the self-serve tray. Normally, I would advise against crawfish boudin—it often comes off as a mutant love child that misses the best attributes of its parents—but the crawfish boudin at Stump's is right on.

My aunt Dodie remarked on my Facebook post about the crawfish boudin that it looked to her like a pumpkin Icee, which is as good a way as any to describe the peculiar dense orangeness of the link. It is packed tight in the casing, giving it a good bite when you eat it on the run and a rich cayenne and vaguely curried after-tang that hangs with you. The regular pork boudin is a fine representative of the form, but when you are at someplace as weird as Stump's, go weird. And say hi to the parrot.

BOUDIN in KROTZ SPRINGS

A mile of boudin and dreams

Krotz Springs is a sliver of a town known largely for one thing: the speeding ticket you will eventually get coming over that double bridge on Highway 190. Outside of that legacy, the other thing the scrappy little outpost has going for it is a mile-long row of boudin and cracklin shops, and within them, a panoply of pork-and-meat sausage delivered with heart, spirit, and dreams. The fine sausage entrepreneurs of Krotz Springs have some ideas.

In boudin circles, Krotz Springs rests in the shadow of the titans in Scott, Breaux Bridge, and Lafayette. Ever the intrepid explorer, willing to risk the unknown and a burgeoning waistline to find what Louisiana has to offer, my faithful running partner Clarke and I set off to sample the mile of boudin in Krotz Springs.

KARTCHNER'S GROCERY AND SPECIALTY MEATS

24562 U.S. 190
Krotz Springs, LA 70750
(337) 566-0529
kartchnersspecialtymeats.com

As I suggest above, there are only three things to get in Krotz Springs: boudin, cracklins (fried pork skin), and speeding tickets. The last speeding ticket I got was just off the base of the twin span bridge over the Atchafalaya River. It was a training ambush; a team of rookie cops ran me through the full cycle of vehicular law enforcement. Once I submitted to the unnecessary field sobriety test—I hadn't been drinking, just driving over the allegedly posted 45 mph limit—the training officer thanked me for my good attitude and handed me a ticket. I was hoping he'd hand over my license as well, but that involved a stop at an ATM across the street and then the Krotz Springs police station. That ATM was my first visit to Kartchner's.

This second visit, it was to take in the sights. I can be endlessly entertained by freezer cases of meat. If there was a program on cable TV where they just slowly scanned meat cases, I'd take the batteries out of the remote, having found the perfect station. As it happens, this visit also coincided with my first official research trip for the volume you hold, and I needed a ceremonial purchase to seed the quest. Every epic journey starts with a single boudin ball. I saw a sign over the warming tray of cracklins: NO HANDS IN THE CRACKLIN! THANK YOU! Maybe there had been an unsanitary incident in the past, but whatever the reason, I was happy for this assurance.

This place is full of meat, a classic gallery of refrigerated cases that can hold their own against the displays at Poche's in Breaux Bridge and Bergeron's in Port Allen. It is a dazzling demonstration of monochromatic power, the rich rainbow contained in the red-brown hue of smoked sausage. I'm eyeing the sausage infiltrated with crab-boil seasoning and a full-sized crawfish pie. My buddy Clarke is looking at a chicken stuffed with boudin wrapped in house bacon and pricing ice chests.

Kartchner's makes everything on the premises: head cheese, boudin, cracklins, beef jerky. According to manager Jordan Leger, they make and sell three hundred pounds of boudin a day—some hot, some cold, some frozen in five-pound boxes that are shipped all over the country. Kartchner's has been here for only four years, taking over the spot once held by T-Belle's Meat Market.

Leger reveals what sets their meat apart: They use no liver and no extra rice; theirs is a meatier boudin. And it's mild enough for people here and up north to like it. In some boudin circles, this is heresy, but his goal is to appeal to the masses.

We sat out on the front porch with a grand tour of their offerings: links of smoked and hot boudin; three kinds of boudin balls—crawfish, pork, and pork with jalapeño and cream cheese—and a sizzling paper tray of cracklins.

It seems positively civilized, with cars whizzing off to who knows where on the majestic bridges, the "Welcome to Krotz Springs" banners flapping in the breeze.

What to get: Kartchner's smoked boudin is the thing. True to Leger's claim, it is denser than a lot of boudin, and it has a nice snap to it. One of the biggest hurdles newbies can face in their boudin experiences is when the sausage and rice mixture comes loose from the casing. It can feel like you are sucking stuffing from a balloon.

All the boudin balls at Kartchner's (and in Krotz Springs in general) have one thing in common—a slight flour coating holding the piece together, as opposed to a deep-fried cornmeal batter that leaves the thing tough, somewhere between a burnt hush puppy and a racquetball. Kartchner's crawfish boudin is a fine representative of the form, and the pork boudin has a pleasing meaty texture with a mild afterbite, but the ones embedded with cream cheese and jalapeños are a wonder. The cream cheese highlights the tang of the pepper but also bridges the flavor back to the pork and the rice.

Most remarkable are the cracklins. I can only eat so many cracklins before I fear breaking a tooth or breaking a treaty with my digestive system, but I could eat these all day. They are popped fresh—Leger installed an intercom system to call for fresh ones to be thrown in the fryer for each order. Clarke filled his ice chest with wonders like sausage embedded with Steen's cane syrup and some fresh backstrap bacon, and we braved the beautiful day, wondering how we were going to eat any more. But we had decided to hit all the boudin joints Krotz Springs had to offer, so we continued on.

BILLY'S DINER

24467 U.S. 190
Krotz Springs, LA 70750
(337) 566-2080

When people talk boudin, Billy's name is said in hushed tones. Based in Lafayette (where he ingeniously has a drive-thru) and with outposts in Opelousas and Krotz Springs, Billy's is considered the go-to link joint. We pop into the restaurant adjoining the convenience store hoping this was the place where the boudin could be sampled sitting down, but we were directed over to the store.

This is when you know you are at the right place to get boudin: the line of customers snakes all the way to the back of the convenience store, around the candy island back to the drink case. The procession files past a steamy glass meat case.

It's a great moment for eavesdropping. One fellow tells a couple of women from his church that he's just been to New Orleans, where "those bloodsuckers get you on the parking." The women recoil with the sought-after amount of horror.

Usually there are a couple of pro-grade crockpots going, with a semi-frenzied staff trying to keep them filled with boudin links. By the time you reach the cashier, both of you are sweating. The process results in your being handed a paper sack, usually with a quickly spreading grease stain at the bottom, and you are off to enjoy your bounty wherever the day takes you.

What to get: The cracklins were the meatiest of the day, juicier, more filling, and not as spicy. The boudin balls had a bready softness to them.

Cracklins, boudin, and boudin balls from Billy's in Krotz Springs, splayed out on the hood of my car

The meat was shredded finely, making a loose mortar around the rice. The pepperjack variety had a great twang to it, the hit from the cheese working well with the green onions in the pork and rice mixture. I found Billy's to be one of the more vegetable-y examples of boudin I've tried. It made me wonder how you could work boudin meatballs into a gumbo.

The boudin links, glistening from the steamer, were textbook examples, down to the loose bond between the meat and the casing. The liver was definitely apparent in this one, but not to the point that you felt like you were licking an iron skillet. I found the boudin mixture had a richness to it that you don't always find. Remembering that their boudin is made at the Lafayette location and brought in, I made a mental note to find out if boudin gets better when it travels.

The pickings are slimmer here than at Kartchner's—boudin links, cracklins, and balls—so we order one of each and partake of our bounty in a classic setting: on the hood of my car. I note on my recorder app: "My hands are so greasy I can hardly operate my phone. Boudin is fixing to slide down my hood."

Given that we had another stop to go and were already feeling the effects of our excesses, coupled with the fact that Krotz Springs is really only a mile long, we left the car behind and walked.

CAJUN CORNER CAFÉ AND KROTZ SPRINGS CANAL

24386 U.S. 190
Krotz Springs, LA 70750
(337) 566-8003
www.cajuncornercafe.com

The first thing you notice at the Canal gas station is the massive mural by local folk artist Bobby Soileau that depicts an alligator named Pierre, as it says on his shirt. Pierre is also wearing white shrimp boots. One foot is cocked on the prow of a pirogue; the other holds a net of crawfish. I like this kind of thing; it transcends kitsch in its homey, unabashed appreciation of itself. And before co-owner Toby Kimball even tells me his name, he points out the alligator logo on their T-shirts and shows me an artist's rendering of his restaurant idea.

"We didn't show up here on no goddamn 747. We walked carrying black iron pots," says Kimball of his Cajun heritage and his fierce love for the food he makes. His wife Denise announces they are low on cracklins, so we follow him back to the kitchen to check if the oil is smoking yet. We have a few minutes, so I ask about the thin breading in the boudin balls of Krotz Springs, and the conversation turns philosophical. He stresses quality and consistency as the reasons for his restaurant's success.

This impromptu business seminar is cut short as the iron pot of hog lard in the kitchen gets to the right temperature. Kimball sprinkles a bit of his seasoning in my hand so I can taste its lemony tones, its sweetness, but most importantly, to see that it's not too salty. He gingerly drops a bin of cooked cracklins into the oil to "pop" them, allowing the 400-degree grease to fluff them up and give the skin that important blistered quality. It takes just about a minute before they are back on the work table getting seasoned. We then follow him out to the front, where customers are already waiting.

The afternoon's third paper sack of cracklins gives us the chewiest and

Fresh cracklins at Cajun Corner Café, Krotz Springs

densest of the bunch. They are crispy yet without that enamel-chipping hardness that a heat lamp can bring. These taste like meat, like pork rinds, like fresh seasonings. Each place in Krotz Springs has its nuances, each owner their own idea of how things should really be done. My stomach was glad we'd exhausted the boudin and cracklin offerings of Krotz Springs, but it left me wondering about the town's potential. What if it was two miles long? What dreams would be cooked up in its back kitchens then?

CREOLE LUNCH HOUSE

713 12th St.
Lafayette, LA 70501
(337) 232-9929
Cash only

The plate lunch perfected

One wants to make the right choice, so I consulted the wisdom of the ancients (Facebook, in this case) to see where I should spend an errant luncheon in Lafayette. It opened up the floodgates. One contingent of online foodies was dead-set on Laura's II or Creole Lunch House. Another was lobbying so hard for Johnson's Boucanière that I was afraid it was going to come to blows should the factions meet in the real world. Yet another recommended I watch the documentary *Raised on Rice and Gravy,* about the Lafayette plate lunch scene, if only to confound my choices. Finally a coin toss set my target on Creole Lunch House. A friend of mine that grew up in Lafayette had been monitoring the decision process and cooed, "Ooh, that creole stuffed bread." Good ol' coin toss.

I shot over the Atchafalaya as quickly as I could on a Friday afternoon, accounting for the fact that I almost always get lost in Lafayette's warped grid of French-named thoroughfares, pulling into the gravel parking lot of Creole Lunch House just at the tail end of the lunch shift, only to discover it was a cash-only business. Circling for the nearest gas station with an ATM sign, I passed three more plate lunch spots, ones that even my Facebook cadre didn't know about. The ATM was broken at the place boasting frog legs on their sign, and the boudin balls were beckoning me at the next convenience store. I considered abandoning my original quest and just snacking my way through the convenience store scene, but I had a goal.

I was further thwarted when I got back to Creole Lunch House; the last of the creole stuffed bread had been sold, though a fried pork chop plate with greens, red beans, and rice and gravy did a lot to console my heart. Breading and deep-frying a pork chop might be considered overkill, but then so might the fins on a classic Cadillac, or the lapels on a zoot suit. The greens were expertly seasoned, not too salty nor too tangy; they were left with enough earthy twinge to counter the richness of the pork chop. The red beans performed a similar balancing act. These weren't the rich, creamy New Orleans–style creole red beans, but thinner, almost soupy.

The star of the show, with the stuffed bread in absentia, was the rice and gravy. The gravy in question was left over from chicken fricassée, but I suspect this gravy finds itself in a lot of dishes at Creole Lunch House. Rice and gravy is a magic dish to me. It's so simple, left over from the main meal even, yet something about the alchemy of the starch in the rich pot liquor of stewed meat creates culinary gold, warming the heart, filling the belly, clogging the arteries, all of it. It is a complete thing. My friend that cooed about the stuffed bread told me that during her college vegetarian days, she'd steal over to Creole Lunch House just for the rice and gravy, a fix that at least approximately allowed her to maintain her resolve for the rest of the week.

The exterior of Creole Lunch House is just that, a house indistinguishable on the block except for the bright yellow sign out front. The interior is a soft sunlit-pink room speckled with framed pictures and accolades from newspapers and magazines over the years. The beauty of these places that stick around for decades is that they can be perpetually discovered. They are waiting there for you. Each first plate of rice and gravy is like a personal moon landing.

Raymond came around from behind the counter to check on me; evidently I appeared more dismayed about the stuffed bread situation than I actually was. "Thee Heavenly Donut in Baton Rouge carries them," he reassured me. "They buy them directly from us." Raymond is the son of Merline Herbert, who opened this plate lunch spot in in 1983 after retiring from teaching school. She first opened the restaurant in a little building in the parking lot and then in 1986 purchased the house and renovated it into a restaurant. Raymond claimed that he and his dad were the willing guinea

pigs for his mother's recipes; he has worked in the restaurant pretty much since it opened.

I asked about the difference between the creole cuisine of New Orleans and that of Acadiana. "This is traditional Louisiana home cooking that you would find at someone's house, where someone is going to take the time to prepare it," Raymond offered. "In New Orleans, it's a little more commercial or chef-oriented. Here you want to get filled up, you want to feel happy, and hopefully can go back to work after."

I had to do exactly that, so I bid my adieu to the sweet, shady house on 12th Street, making a mental appointment to hit up Thee Heavenly Donut on the way back, followed by another to come back to Creole Lunch House the next week to score the stuffed bread from the source. But, as always, life got in the way and I just didn't make it back in time. Too many choices, too many deadlines got in the way.

I found myself at the second-to-last day of Jazz Fest in New Orleans, thinking about how I was going to finish all the projects I had before me, which, as usual for me, coincides with me figuring out what to eat. Honestly, I go to Jazz Fest for the food as much as I do the music, and the food stands were stretching out to the vanishing point before me. I'd already had my requisite cochon de lait poboy from Love at First Bite, the famous WWOZ mango freeze, a greens plate from Bennachin the weekend before, and a United Houma Nation fry-bread taco that morning. I'd eaten the world yet was determined to find something new, some culinary hole in my life that needed to be filled, looking for a sign and lo, I turn my head and see an actual massive sign reading CREOLE LUNCH HOUSE—CREOLE STUFFED BREAD.

There was Mrs. Herbert handing them out as fast as a Red Cross relief worker. I tried to explain to her the serendipity of finding the stand, but my excitement turned my story into gibberish, so I just handed over my four dollars and pointed.

It was worth the wait. The small pod of brown bread fit perfectly in my hand, each bite revealed the strata of pork and rice and jalapeños and Italian sausage. The bread became its own pocket, holding in the splash of verde chili sauce on offer—Raymond's Hot Sauce to be precise. It was the perfect Jazz Fest food. I wanted to proclaim this find to the gathered masses. This is what you've been searching for! I know the Raymond that made the sauce! The sausage! The bread! The stuffing!

But I didn't. I realized I have more effective pulpits from which to radiate my praise and besides, we are all on our own journeys, culinary or otherwise. We have our own choices to make, and in the making do we find which one is the right one for us.

DON'S SEAFOOD HUT RESTAURANT and OYSTER BAR

4309 Johnston St.
Lafayette, LA 70503
(337) 981-1141
donsseafoodonline.com/lafayette/

Ask for an old-fashioned from Mr. Cliff, and a Seafood Bouquet.

Sweet old dizzying Lafayette. I never know where I am or what to do there, but it always comes through. Lafayette is somewhat unnavigable to me; I never really know where I am in its dense grid of French-named streets, but then maybe I don't have to. I can just ride the tide in the ocean of Cajun charm, ready to pull me out past the breakers.

For instance, one Saturday I was in town for a book signing at a particular big-box bookstore. These occasions are sometimes a dubious honor—an author stranded at a couple of café tables, guilt-tripping shoppers with smiling, quiet desperation—but thanks to a slow news day in Acadiana, my book signing was announced on the front page of the city paper, the *Advertiser*, above the fold. My signing pen ran out of ink!

I had an evening to kill until my next stop, and my friend Alli said the most Lafayette thing I could do is go to Don's, the venerable downtown flagship of the steak-and-seafood empire. Specifically, I was instructed to go to the bar, ask for an old-fashioned from Mr. Cliff, and get a Seafood Bouquet. "We call it the seafood bucket," Alli said, catching the attention of her young son Sammy. "Oh man, I love the seafood bucket!" he added. I need no more ringing endorsement.

I enlisted my buddy Dave for this mission. Dave is a mixologist, one who looks at a cocktail the way a geneticist studies a double helix. I like cocktails, but I do not possess the deep knowledge to measure the truth in its making. We place our request for a round of Mr. Cliff's old-fashioneds with the young woman holding down the bar, and she rolls her eyes. "Do you really want to wait? I can make it and it's the same drink."

Alli said she'd waited 45 minutes for Mr. Cliff before, but I'm ready to get on with this, and before us are placed two light amber highballs that have that familiar tincture of the old-fashioned: bourbon, Angostura bitters, and a maraschino cherry. I'm won over by the sugar-encrusted swizzle stick, but I look over to Dave for his expert opinion. "Yep. A proper old-fashioned."

What to get: the Seafood Bouquet—a wide tray of fried crab fingers, catfish nuggets, delicately battered golden oysters, and bacon-wrapped shrimp. There is harness racing on the TV behind the bar, and we make our way around the tray apace with the horses, each with a jockey hanging way back, their view limited to the back end of their steed. I'm starting to feel this drink hanging off of me. Sometimes I wonder whether I really like cocktails all that much. They strike me as affectations half the time, an attempt to make more out of a thing than is really there.

An older bartender arrives as we polish off the last of the bacon-wrapped shrimp. "See now, bacon and shrimp—that is a cocktail I can get behind," I slur through the veil of bourbon. The bar is starting to fill up. It is the University of Louisiana's graduation and the monthly Artwalk at once, so we need to make active use of our spots at the bar. Dave addresses Mr. Cliff in his gentlemanly manner. "I'm told to get an old-fashioned from Mr. Cliff. Are you he?"

"That's me, but the girl makes the drinks," he grumbles, his attention on the harness race. It strikes me that he perhaps has money on this. Who watches harness racing otherwise? The finish line gets crossed, and there is no indication of whether it was a good finish or not when he looks at our desperate little faces. "Okay, I'll make 'em. Bourbon or rye?" I look to Dave. Even I know an old-fashioned is supposed to be bourbon, but this guy is the expert. "You're the expert. What do you suggest?" I counter.

"Well, the traditional one is rye . . ."

"Rye it is!" we shout with perhaps too much excitement. This is the other problem I have with cocktails. I always feel like I'm putting on a Frank Sinatra act when I get to the second one, like I'm a sip away from talking about the ponies or dames or something.

The new drinks look like the last ones but with a slight aura about them that I'm not sure is attributable to this drink or the previous. The swizzle stick looks like a crystal cave formation trapped in amber, the cherry a bubble of primordial magma. One sip, and the alchemy takes hold. Everything goes amber. I remember the rest of Alli's recommendation: "It will F you up."

I no longer require any expert opinion to know this is a superior cocktail, the kind of thing that replaces your body's dull juices with itself. I feel like my spine is a sugar-encrusted swizzle stick, my brain a fat, red cherry. "This is a good drink," is all Dave can muster, and I nod.

This all sets the stage for the Seafood Bouquet. Each morsel of fried catfish, fried crawfish, and crab claw is a delight. Don's knows its way around fried seafood, having served it in downtown Lafayette for generations. Its massive fried seafood platters are a thing of legend, but here, the epic proportions are broken down into finger food and thus even feel like a party.

Nestled into this celebration are a handful of shrimp and oysters *en brochette,* a specialty at Don's. Gulf shrimp and oysters are wrapped in bacon and fried until crisp and then broiled on the grill to attain a *soupçon* of smoke. A few folks are enjoying some raw oysters down the bar from us, and they look amazing until Dave and I are left to the few oysters remaining in the bouquet. Thankfully there was an even number so we didn't have to have a duel or anything.

Glancing up at the TV in the bar, I see a jockey being hailed and roses hung on a horse's neck. I can't tell by the look on Mr. Cliff's face whether his horse has won or not. I rescue my swizzle stick from the drained glass and crunch on the last crystal of sugar, secure in my own little victory.

OLDE TYME GROCERY

218 West St. Mary Blvd
Lafayette, LA 70506
(337) 235-8165
oldetymegrocery.com

There are a million poboys to be eaten; this place serves some of the best.

For those of us who teach, there is a delicious downshift right before the semester kicks into gear: a frantic run of preparation ends with the sudden realization that there is no more ready one can become. In that limbo, one is left wondering what to do. Unless the professor is your humble author, who has a default way to kill an idle stretch during the day: go get a poboy.

There are a million poboys to be eaten, or at least that's how I cut my way through life; but on the precipice of what looked to be a busy semester, I needed the best—at any cost, any distance. That meant I needed a quick drive across the Atchafalaya Basin to Olde Tyme Grocery in Lafayette.

My Lafayette friends have the small convenience store resting just off the U-of-L campus as their go-to eatery, so I hit them up on Facebook for what to get. They unanimously hollered back, "SHRIMP! IN THE NAME OF ALL THAT'S HOLY, GET THE SHRIMP!" You could hear the desperate cry bellowing out of my monitor. I posited, how special can a shrimp poboy be? I mean, fried shrimp, bread—it's a classic that leaves little room for error.

I parked around the corner, starving after a hungry hour on rainy I-10. The waft of undifferentiated "fry" smell hit me from down the block. I wondered if they pumped it into the air to tempt the neighbors. I wondered, like

I do about many little neighborhood joints like this, how one could bear to cook at home when this was but a hop away.

It was the tail end of the lunch rush, with customers lined up around the chip display waiting for their order. In the great Louisiana convenience store tradition, there is a meat counter where you make your order. I chose a half shrimp/half oyster to eat there, a half sausage to have on the way back, and a roast beef to drop off for my wife at home. I like to cover my bases.

There was a bit of a delay—I milled with the usual customers, apparently in the way of the drink machine. I like being in a dining establishment that is cozy as mama's kitchen to the regulars but somewhat foreign territory to interlopers. It's where you get to experience the soul of such an operation.

For instance, there was a long line of T-shirts mounted on the wall near the ceiling. I assumed that Olde Tyme Grocery sponsored a Little League team or something like that until I peered closer. They were at least two dozen custom-designed shirts celebrating Lent, the forty-day Catholic season when the devout must give up something dear for the duration and abstain from meat on Fridays—all in the service of considering the suffering of the Lord.

Setting the moral good aside, Lent is a great season for seafood restaurants—shrimp and oyster poboys are exempt from Lenten restrictions. The T-shirts have images like a crawfish and shrimp decrying from the fryer, "Though you cried & we nearly fried—Still alive for '95." According to the restaurant's website, they are awarded to the hard-working staff at the end of Lent and are "some of the most coveted shirts in Lafayette and are only worn by those that have put in blood, sweat, and tears." I question the true suffering one goes through, limping along on shrimp poboy Fridays, but then it's one of the great things about Louisiana culture that manifests in its food. It's a tradition rooted in faith and observance; yet we manage to have fun with it.

Lost in these philosophical musings over novelty T-shirts, I almost fail to hear the cashier holler out, "Anyone want to pay now?" She is looking at me.

Poboys are not always the most photogenic dishes, unless you are really into lengths of bread; but Olde Tyme knows how to dress an old standard up. Deep golden fried shrimp and fat juicy oysters hang off the bun like a shapely bare leg dangling coyly off the mattress. A drizzle of hot sauce across a stray lettuce strand, the tomato just cold enough, mayo just tangy enough, the bread with just enough tack that it doesn't pull out your fillings—the poboy dressing is the perfect stage for their oyster-and-shrimp star attraction.

Shrimp poboy at Olde Tyme Grocery, Lafayette

When confronted with the idea that a poboy is just another name for a hoagie or a sub or bomber or what-have-you, I'm compelled to disagree, not from a sentimental Louisian-ista stance but from an ideological one. The right poboy is a synergy of ingredients; they reflect one another and become one new delicious thing, and Olde Tyme might be the best at it. The whole thing tastes like a magnification of oysters or poboy, a larger taste that seafood cannot muster on its own.

I polished off the shrimp and oyster halves in the name of journalistic thoroughness, but took to the sausage poboy out of pure gluttony. There was no way it was going to last even the ride back to Baton Rouge. A dense Polish sausage with a rich brown skin, slight cayenne and black pepper profile, and Olympic-precision snap to its bite: again, all resting in a perfect setting. I killed it off and, with a bleary gaze, cast eyes on the roast beef wrapped up to take home. "Don't," warned a stern, resolute voice in my stomach, muffled from the damage I'd just done.

The contractors at the next table were detailing the fallout from jobs around the Atchafalaya region. A couple of high school students took up a table in the corner, a last gasp before school commenced—just like mine, perhaps. I made my way out of the homey dining room and through the divine riot of the convenience store, to-go poboy in hand. A few hours later, my wife declared it the best roast beef poboy she's ever had, even slightly cold and carried across a swamp and a river to get to her. "I KNOW," I texted back, suddenly echoing the all-caps zealotry that confronted my Facebook inquiry earlier that day. But I get it now. I know.

LEA'S LUNCHROOM

1810 U.S. 71
Lecompte, LA 71346
(318) 776-5178
leaslunchroom.com

The pie and ham sandwich capital of south Louisiana

Sitting one booth over from me at Lea's was a sweet retired couple who'd ridden in from parts unknown on a Honda Gold Wing. The Gold Wing excursion is how retirees flaunt their life of making good choices: not only did love sustain them long enough that they'd both be willing to straddle the same motorcycle for hours at a stretch, but they worked out the financials to allow it. They'd polished off ham sandwiches, and the gentleman pulled from his pocket a deck of cards and started shuffling them. So adorable! I felt I was in the presence of life geniuses. Then she asked him what kind of pie he wanted, and he grunted, "Oh, I don't know. Whatever." And I thought, "God, what an idiot."

I'm just saying, Lea's is famous. So much so that in 1989, Lea Johnson was invited as a guest on *The Tonight Show* with Johnny Carson and occupied the guest chair for a full eleven minutes of airtime. Johnson greeted the famed talk show host with "I declare! Which one of those wives did you eat dinner with tonight?" That wily spirit infuses the place, informs the gleaming pie counter with recipes that haven't changed since the Great Depression. You don't want to go into this kind of dining experience willy-nilly.

What to get: Lea's has a full country menu with affordable plate lunches, but there are two things to get here. Written on the side of the building is

LEA'S PIES AND BAKED HAM. It's the menu that Lea Johnson came up with in 1928 when he opened the restaurant. He'd grown up on his family's plantation raising hogs. Johnson eventually found work as an auto mechanic and traded an automobile for the first furnishings of his lunchroom, catering a simple menu to tourists.

The ham sandwich is exquisite in its simplicity, a mixture of sliced and chopped ham on a bun with lettuce, tomatoes, pickles, and mayo. Normally, a ham sandwich is the kind of thing you have at home instead of going out, but I've known people that have driven up from New Orleans for the experience. Carefully layered, it is a perfect ham sandwich. Don't mess with a proven formula.

The pie situation is going to entail some decision making on your part. Lea's Lunchroom is the center of the Louisiana pie vortex, so much so that I can't think of a place that comes as a close second. Lecompte, perched in the boot of the state equidistant between the sweaty insole and the sturdy upper, is on the way to nowhere, except for maybe Alexandria. The town signs all have pies on them because of Lea's. It is a town whose entire identity is built on light doughy crust and expert meringue.

The pie case, which extends half the length of the dining room, is a testament to the virtues of free will. You are confronted with perfect flattened domes of meringue obscuring the lemon, coconut, banana pudding, and chocolate filling underneath. Then there is a full range of fruit pies: peach, blackberry, apple, and if in season, sweet potato and pumpkin pies. And finally, the crown jewel: the pecan pie, glimmering with cane syrup from behind the plexiglass.

I understand the gentleman's reticence to pick: there are a lot of options. What if his dining companion picks something better than him, and he is left to suffer? Or maybe the secret to his success is not rocking the boat, letting her make the decisions. I get that. Plus, how can the inexperienced or the timid make a sturdy decision when confronted with such bounty? It's tough, but when you are set with such an important choice as what kind of pie to get from Lea's, it's time to man up and get decisive.

A friend of mine swears by the cherry pie, while I contend their chocolate pie is a perfect yin-yang balance of neutral crust, mind-altering sweet pudding, and the singular texture and flavor of expert meringue. My daughter was taken aback by the frothy, lightly sweetened fluff, expecting something more like Cool Whip or marshmallow. She was not yet nuanced enough in life to accept the divine singularity of meringue.

The intoxicatingly sweet depths of Lea's pecan pie are mitigated by the almost cracker-like crust and the savory earthiness of toasted nuts. Having an unsweetened dough is crucial to the pie flavor detente. The same pie with a graham cracker crust would be just an invitation to diabetes, while here, it is like a Fabergé egg allowed its filigree diamond glow, resting atop an unadorned silk cushion. A Picasso in an elegant but simple frame. A blazing sunset against the calm of a bay. I fear I am underselling their pecan pie with these analogies.

That said, I go for the sweet potato pie when they have it. Sweet potato pie is not my favorite pie in general—often it is a soufflé or mousse masquerading as a pie. The way Lea's does sweet potato, it is as if the pie is the dream that sweet potatoes long to attain all those months in the Acadiana soil. You can feel the heft of the yam in each forkful, which is what you want in a pie. Heft is what separates pie from more fleeting confectionery. It has just enough sweetness to keep it humble, but not so much to become candy. It is what you want every other sweet potato pie in life to have tasted like, regret mitigated by the assurance that sweet potato pies will taste like this from now on because you will always get them from Lea's.

So, yes, knowing your pie cocktail is key, even if it takes some road trips and research. Bring an ice chest with you to Lecompte if you want to conduct further studies at home, or have them shipped if the open road is not the canvas upon which your longing is painted. By whatever means necessary, get a pie from Lea's, but take your choice seriously. Letting the entropy of "whatever" guide your way is like riding a motorcycle just to follow the line in the road. At some point you need to steer life's journey using both sound judgment and lustful daring to its golden, flaky, meringue-topped destination. "Whatever." You might as well sell the Gold Wing with that attitude.

MR. FRANCIS

720 S. Main St.
St. Martinville, LA 70582
(337) 394-6226

Fragrant smoked meat in a clamshell

The elusive sliver of perfect spring weather is the optimum time to take in the sleepiness of small-town Acadiana. My buddy Clarke and I had a plan that fell through in Henderson, and at the last minute we pulled out of Lafayette's magnetic draw to veer off and see what there was to do in St. Martinville on a Saturday.

The way into St. Martinville is the flat fields that surround every Louisiana prairie town. What separates St. Martinville from the rest is the quaintness initiative on display in its downtown. Banked by a white-columned courthouse that gleamed with justice in the summer glare, the line of old-timey storefronts with whitewashed verandas reminds me a bit of the square in Oxford, Mississippi, the queen of Dixie civic quaintness. St. Martinville is a duchess by comparison, but I'll take it.

We stroll by the famed Evangeline Oak, which is surveilled by a dour bust of Longfellow, both sitting along the perpetuity of Bayou Teche. One is tempted to take a dip in the bayou, like it's the Cajun Ganges or something, if one didn't have to brave poison ivy and the possibility of water moccasins to do it. A sweet little boardwalk of twenty yards runs from the oak to the visitor's bureau, where we hoped to find a restroom, but no luck. So we made the block to Robert's Lounge, where in the window a neon martini glass blinked futilely against the afternoon sun.

Have you ever seen the loose Bukowski biopic *Barfly*? The scene where the door of the bar opens, the sunlight is blinding, and Booker T.'s "Green Onions" plays? Replace that with Lynyrd Skynyrd on the jukebox and you have our entrance into Robert's. The afternoon patrons inhabited a universe of dark paneling and blinking screens—horse racing on the one near the bar, baseball on the one hanging over the narrow stage, and video poker machines just out of the periphery.

Clarke and I had barely worked through our first beers when a man smiled his way from the video poker machines to the bar with a white ticket. "I'm buying a round for the bar," he said as he slid the ticket across the counter. Clarke and I stared at each other in disbelief—this had never happened to either of us. One day, I thought. *One day I'll be the man who does that.*

As the afternoon shadows lengthened, St. Martinville was seeming a more fortunate destination. We stared at the mirrored bar, at a clock that was flanked by a stuffed squirrel and a mounted trout, as the jukebox cycled through more Lynyrd Skynyrd songs and swamp pop favorites. Then it was 5 o'clock and Mr. Francis opened for the evening.

We make the block to let our beers settle. The Duchamp Opera House sits in congenial splendor on the square by a number of cafés, though the Teche Theatre has long closed its doors. We pass a place by the bridge that splits its merchandise between rap and zydeco CDs and children's clothes. If Trahan's Olde Tyme Barber Shoppe had been open, I might have gotten a shave like I was Sheriff Andy Taylor in Mayberry, so charming is St. Martinville's downtown.

We head past gleaming white City Hall and across some implied tracks where the neighborhood changes its tune from scrubbed Dixie sheen to a scrappy poorer neighborhood. And here the gray rib shack named Mr. Francis lies close to the road. The weathered metal sign swinging over the sidewalk boasts:

MR. FRANCIS
HOME OF THE ORIGINAL
HOT LINKS!
SMOKE HOUSE
BAR-BE-CUE!

I like Mr. Francis's excitement! The service station next door lines up tires at the edge of its parking lot, perhaps because the nightlife on this little corner

is about to pick up. There are three bars in a row directly across the street: Poche's Place, the Candle Light Lounge, and the Rice Pool Hall, as well as another hot links place, but we are at the home of the original, standing at a solitary trailer window waiting for Mr. Francis or anyone.

We realize as we order that there is no place to sit. "They'll let you go in the Candle Light if you buy something," says the woman taking our order. It seems a poetic statement as she pads off into the depths of the trailer to fix our plates.

There is something singular about the experience of waiting outside a narrow window for a Styrofoam plate of barbecue. You are in a weirdly exposed place as a consumer, left to stare around awkwardly with other customers, hoping when they call "rib plate" out through that tiny portal and you grab it, you grab what is actually your plate. I say this as someone who has made the mistake of grabbing someone else's plate at the long-closed Snowflake BBQ in Baton Rouge's The Bottom neighborhood, failing to note my place in the dissipated line of the waiting hungry. Things got sorted out in a gentlemanly-enough way, but it was awkward.

We cross the twilight street to the empty Candle Light with our clamshells of fragrant smoked meat, but the older woman in the immaculately quiet and still Candle Light, in fact the only person in the place, resolutely says we can't bring food in there. We decide the answer will likely be the same at the neighboring establishments, so we wander back the three blocks toward downtown. I consider eating from my open container on the steps of City Hall, but I'm afraid of sullying its bleached white columns with sauce. Eating at Robert's seems equally awkward, so we march with our ribs growing heavy to the little park around the Evangeline Oak to show old Longfellow what we bought.

What to get: I have some doubts that Mr. Francis came up with the original recipe for hot links, but the sandwich is the way to go. It is a fat, juicy, three-quarter loop of pork, the deep reddish brown of an oxblood wingtip. The link sits in a pool of sweet sauce between two pieces of store white bread, as fitting a plinth for presenting supple beauty as the clamshells Botticelli set up for Venus. The truest sign of its quality is the short length of smoke-blackened, sauce-stained butcher's twine tying off the ends of the link. Mr. Francis has a deep sense of presentation.

The sweet sauce offers a tangy counterpoint to the earthy splendor of the sausage, with just enough heat to tickle the back of the throat. I cough a little, getting sauce all over me, as Longfellow looks on bemused.

It was early in the evening, so the ribs, cut into finger-length segments, were not as tender as the lady in the window said they would be as the night wore on, but they were still juicy and fatty. A perfunctory salad and some fries squirted with ketchup made for a delicious mess on the banks of the Teche.

I was really tempted to brave the border foliage and wash my face in the bayou's muddy flow, but a number of high school kids started showing up to take photos. We decided to leave them to their youthful beauty and started to walk back up the block to Robert's for their washroom, their Skynyrd-heavy jukebox, and one more for the road, when we passed a raven-haired woman in a lacy white gown and dark cowboy boots trotting toward the river to have her picture taken. She looked the world like a country fairy in the magic-hour light. I like to think the dusk ends this way all the time in St. Martinville.

THE BEST STOP SUPERMARKET

615 LA 93 N
Scott, LA 70583
(337) 233-5805
beststopinscott.com

The best boudin in the region. Ask anyone.

I was headed to Lafayette when I heard an NPR announcer butcher the word "boudin."

So, okay, maybe "butcher" is a strong word, besides being a bad pun, for she was simply emphasizing the second syllable like anyone trying to give their high-school French a whirl. Boudin, properly pronounced "BOO-dan," is a challenge to expectations.

Scott, Louisiana, a speck of a place just west of Lafayette on I-10, was the reason "boudin" was being mispronounced on *All Things Considered*. The state legislature had just officially proclaimed the little burg the "Boudin Capital of the World." I don't know how the legislature thinks it has such jurisdiction, and even the NPR announcer was bemused that the town of Jennings, just down the road, calls itself the "boudin capital of the universe."

I pull over at the Best Stop in Scott, where the clerks behind the counter are gathered in gossip, Cajun patois dishing out dirt. The butcher in charge of the store's spellbinding meat counter is asking about a customer's camp. I mention the legislature's designation and they feign polite interest. Their world/universe extends to right where they are.

Among the myriad boudin shops, gas stations, and country meat markets that dot the major and minor thoroughfares of south Louisiana, Best Stop

holds a marked level of esteem among the populace. Mention any other boudin place, you get a nod of agreement. Mention Best Stop, and their eyes open wide, as if the boudin conversation just went to the next level.

Part of the reason is that Best Stop is a tidily run place, spotless grocery-store white with a meat counter that operates as the core of the business, as it has in the Scott community for decades. Here you find the small, local butcher shop that scarcely exists anymore. The staff knows their regular customers' orders before they reach the glass.

It speaks to the defiance of time and "progress" that you will find in little Cajun towns. Scott, just an interstate hop from the growing reach of Lafayette's westward sprawl, maintains its identity through little shops like this. I feel something like an interloper, as if I'm inviting myself to Sunday dinner, just ordering links from the place. The woman behind the counter remains indifferent to my musings when it's my turn to order.

What to get: A very modest sum will get you a hot boudin link almost a foot long wrapped in butcher paper and a trio of fried boudin balls in a paper sack, soon to succumb to grease. The Best Stop is considered by many to indeed be the best stop for boudin in the area, no idle boast, for every other billboard around the Scott exit is for either a meat market or a convenience store offering up their take on this capital dish.

At a small picnic table shaded by an awning, my boudin link arcs out like a gas pipeline snaking out of the earth. Lots of green onion takes off the ferric tang one finds increasingly in boudin the farther one gets from the interstate. My link is salty but not overly so, packed enough that I get a satisfying bite through the casing. I like a boudin that snaps when you bend it. The man with the camp walks out with a much more substantial order than I've made, no doubt for a bunch of fishermen looking to drown their lack of a catch in meat and rice. As he hauls bags of ice to his pickup he looks over at me, meat-transfixed, and offers, "Good, huh?" Indeed. Best in the world.

GULFWARDS

SPORTSMAN'S PARADISE

6830 LA 56
Chauvin, LA 70344
(985) 594-2414
Cash and checks only

The freshest seafood anywhere

I love the end of the road, and fortunately, Louisiana's Gulf coast ends a lot of roads. One of those I hadn't been on for twenty years is Little Caillou Road, less romantically known as LA 56. My journey starts on as urban a thing as exists in south Terrebonne Parish, the high-rise bridges that straddle the Intracoastal Waterway where it intersects Bayou Terrebonne. The burgeoning town of Houma—with its strip malls and commercial corrugated-metal industrial buildings—starts to fade around the old airport where blimps were stationed during World War II and where a number of German POWs were kept. The flatness of this part of the state, flatter than even Acadiana's prairies, becomes evident, as does the balance of land and water.

The road is punctuated with bridges that look like steel dinosaurs stretching across Bayou Little Caillou, a poem of a trickling waterway that takes one all the way down to the oil businesses that line a thin industrial belt before the land fully recedes into the Gulf of Mexico.

It is notable that you cannot see the Gulf from Chauvin, but you can see everything that is headed out that way. The charming tangled nets of shrimp boats along the bayou look a little like butterflies whose wings have not quite finished unfolding. Houses become camps perched up on stilts.

Super seafood platter at Sportsman's Paradise, Chauvin

They run the class gamut, from worn trailers that seem to be pushed up by garage hydraulics as if to check a leak, to veritable mansions carefully balanced on sticks.

I notice the water on the west side is a lot closer to the road than it was last time I went out this way, kissing the shoulder at points, a wistful demonstration of the marsh erosion that is sinking this part of the state into the sea. This marked change in the landscape hasn't slowed people down much in Chauvin. There are plenty of people fishing, chartering boats from places like Sportsman's Paradise, just a few miles from the end of the road.

The restaurant for Sportsman's Paradise has been making the best fried seafood in south Louisiana since the 1970s. I know this is a touchy boast, but no place gets their shrimp, oysters, catfish, or the stars of their menu, soft-shell crabs, any fresher. All delicately battered and fried to trap the natural liquors of the seafood. It's pretty peerless.

They actually have other things on their menu. Their seafood gumbo is rich and dark. The Cajuns of south Terrebonne Parish tend to favor Italian sausage over the andouille that gives Acadiana gumbo its smokiness. Here the gumbo has a tang to it, a brightness. Their bread pudding is a rummy mush of French bread and cinnamon, almost a cold soup with the amount of sauce they give you. But while there might be other things on the menu, bring a friend for the main event.

What to get: The super seafood platter (enough to feed three people) is a sculptural as well as culinary masterpiece. Catfish, oysters, butterflied shrimp, and a softshell crab are all fried to perfection and then carefully stacked up with two lemon slices to look like some sort of sea monster, a lost fried crustacean of Atlantis, a Voltron of finger food.

The oysters are contained in a heavier crust than the fish and shrimp, locking in the secrets of the sea transmitted through their smoky splendor. The catfish and shrimp are delicate, holding their character against the batter, but they are but an opening act as far as I'm concerned.

There are not too many foods that seem stranger to eat than a fried softshell crab. The thing is battered and fried whole, conducting a singular alchemy of crunchiness and savoriness. As a kid, I used to delight in getting a fried softshell crab poboy here, crab feet jutting out of the side of the bread like they'd been squashed under a falling cartoon safe, but now I like to confront the creature straight on, maybe dipping it in a little of Sportsman's creamy tartar concoction.

It is a base thing to eat, something ripped from the sea and devoured whole with a minimum of mediation. It's surreal to bite through something your mind says should be a hard shell. It can be disconcerting, and yet it is an upfront and honest way to eat another creature. It's free from any abstraction about what you are eating. The fact that a fried soft-shell crab is singularly delicious helps any psychological quandary one might have. It also seems, perhaps, to be the most appropriate thing to eat way down here at the end of the road.

STARFISH RESTAURANT

3027 LA 1
Grand Isle, LA 70358
(985) 787-2711

A classic beach joint

The trip down to Grand Isle requires traversing the whole diminishing ratio of land to water that is south Louisiana until there is land no more, and on that journey to the terminus of LA 1, one finds society gets leaner and leaner. It could be easily assumed that the main industries in Galliano and Golden Meadow are 24-hour laundromats (lots of fishermen and offshore oil workers wash through here, presumably with filthy clothes) and speeding tickets (the speed limit gets down to 25 at one point right before you reach the bridges).

The giant expressway toll bridge is equally curious. Its span contains two complete 90-degree corner turns and even a T-intersection with another bridge casting its tendril out across the water. I was trailing a boat from Cut Off christened the *Bon Temps* for so long I felt I was at sea.

Grand Isle has been destroyed so many times I'm always surprised there is anything at the end of this journey. Both Kate Chopin's *The Awakening* and the second episode of *Route 66* take place on Grand Isle, but otherwise it is a destination for tarpon fishermen and Cajuns paying down the second mortgages on camps raised on stilts.

Grand Isle is a concentrated microcosm of south Louisiana cultural improbability. You drive through the whole island, longer and more densely populated than you might think after the fifty miles of almost nothing it

takes to get there, to reach the public beaches at the state park on the eastern tip. Compared to Pensacola's crystalline waters just a few hours to the east, the Grand Isle beach looks like the North Sea, the kind of waters only Saxon invaders would brave. Instead, lean tattooed men accompanied a girl in a Rebel flag bikini past us on the boardwalk that took us to the dark, silty water of the Gulf.

There is a palpable sense of exclusion that comes with Grand Isle's relative isolation. On August 11, 2010, the *Los Angeles Times* ran a story headlined, "Oil cleanup comes with tensions in this Louisiana town." The story looked at the surprising number of Confederate flags popping up in the wake of the devastating Deepwater Horizon oil spill, as African American and Latino workers hired by BP to do cleanup arrived on the island. I do not mean to cast the island as whites-only or its residents as inherently racist. The BP oil spill upset not just the ecosystem, but the whole economic system of the Gulf region, forcing people out of careers they had held for generations, and the reverberations of such a catastrophe can cause more damage than any hurricane.

So why go? Because Grand Isle is just about the only point of contact Louisianans can make with the Gulf waters that define the state geographically and economically. The rest of the Louisiana coast is either strictly marshlands (though unfettered development and the withering of barrier islands are making short work of that) or is cordoned off by the oil industry. At least in the toe end of Louisiana's boot, it's the only beach, and it is our biological imperative to go to the beach.

OK, you're on Grand Isle. You are miles from anywhere, exhausted by sundown, and where do you go? If you are looking for drinks without the trappings of polite society, there is Big Daddy's, right across from Daddy's Money and a few other watering holes that may or may not be encumbered with daddy issues. Kickin' Chicken, the one beachside fast-food place besides a dreary Subway, is closed at night. So, unless you are willing to slog all sandy and sunburnt back up LA 1 to Chris Moran's Marina or Barrios Seafood in Golden Meadow, you'll likely end up at the Starfish.

As classic a beach joint as possible, the Starfish glows a neon green right off the main drag at the midpoint of the island. Fear may set in when you mistake the thrum of dance music from the drive-through daiquiri place next door as coming from the Starfish, but rest easy. The Starfish is classic, south Louisiana casual dining. It's packed most weekend nights, with the kitchen suffering from overload, but you can bide your time observing the best example of Cajuns at play.

A large family behind us, likely escaping the close quarters of their camp by crowding together at a restaurant, pull yet another table into their adopted conclave. One of the dads starts rattling off who is and isn't of drinking age and then begins to specify who is a Bud drinker, who is Bud Light, who is Miller. While the craft beer scene is starting to take hold in Louisiana, I still admire the fierce brand loyalty of the region's cheap beer drinkers.

Another table is occupied by a group of teenage girls working through some hand-clap game learned at some variant of cheerleader camp. Yet another table has haggard fishermen digging into poboys. Families of all stripes, many of them sunburned, laugh around the tables.

What to get: This was a lot to think about, but I had plenty of time waiting for my cup of gumbo and mixed seafood platter. The seafood platter is just enough to share, and the seafood, as one might suspect, is fried to perfection. The oysters have a satisfying bready crunch to the batter, as do the shrimp, and the thick planks of catfish almost magically stay moist and flaky in their delicate batter.

Oddly enough, for a restaurant perched on the shore of some of the Gulf's best fishing, the Starfish is well-known for its fried chicken. Thick, crispy, and homestyle, it tastes like the chicken my grandmother would fry up in a skillet shortly after wringing the bird's neck. Why fried chicken? Maybe after a day of looking at your catch looking back at you, fried chicken is exactly what you need.

Regardless of your main course, get the fried jalapeño pepper stuffed with crabmeat. The sharp tang of the seeded peppers brings depth from the crabmeat stuffing. It's an excellent offering after a day at the end of the earth.

ABEAR'S CAFÉ

809 Bayou Black Dr.
Houma, LA 70360
(985) 872-6306

Sometimes a left-hand turn leads you to one of the best Cajun restaurants around.

"You sure this is where it's at?" I asked my mom when we made a left-hand turn down a street where I've always gone right.

I grew up practically around the corner in Houma, Louisiana, but only recently did I venture to the venerable ABear's Café on a short stub of Bayou Black Drive. It's been there for fifty-one years and is one of the best Cajun restaurants around. Who knew?

Not me. But then I've always set my sights on the distance. In my little bedroom in Houma, huddled around the warmth of the stereo I bought with my first donut shop paycheck, I populated my world with tapes from New York City, London, Australia . . . anywhere but here. I had to travel the world's music before, in my late thirties, I really got a taste for southern blues. I mentioned that to my dad, and he asked if I wanted any of his mother's old blues 78s that had been gathering dust in a closet just outside my bedroom door. Therein were Guitar Gable, Jimmy Reed, and Bo Diddley in the original shellac. It's a little like finding out King Tut was buried in your backyard.

This day in particular, I was headed to the end of Grand Caillou Road to take in some local fare in the bayou-strung Dulac, hoping for a culinary dispatch from the end of the earth; but the restaurant I'd planned on was unexpectedly closed, with few other options down there. Mom said, "Well, there's ABear's back in town."

We sat at the light for Barrow Street and Bayou Black Road. I'd taken a right turn there a million times—I went to a church youth group at First United Methodist right there and later would zip off that way to Thibodaux to take advantage of the liberal ID policies of the Colonel's Retreat, a college hangout, in the 1980s. Much of my formative years involved a right turn at this intersection; yet she said to go left, and there it was tucked behind a giant oak tree on a short dead end where the Intracoastal Waterway meets Bayou Black.

Jane Hebert and her husband bought the place that had been the family home of Judge Edward "Jimmy" Gaidry. "I think there were eight or nine kids raised in here," said Hebert. And with a modicum of changes, it remains. A bustling lunch crowd trod the same hardwood floors as have countless hungry Houmans at ABear's for a half a century.

"Fifty-one years, actually," Hebert said. "My husband did all the cooking until about five years back." Hebert is a common-enough name in the area that I wondered about the outsider-friendly spelling. "That's what it sounds like," she flatly replied.

ABear's was resplendent in its homey-ness. Its whitewash walls and beadboard ceiling filled the room with cathedral light as contractors consorted with local businessmen and bridge-club ladies found their tables. I loved the woman seemingly penned in at the old-fashioned cashier's counter, flanked by glass display cases filled with Mardi Gras decorations. She, like the restaurant, carried an air of always having been there.

Wherever I go, I always try the gumbo, and not out of some Louisiana jingoism. I want a gumbo to knock me out, and yet most restaurant gumbos are dishwater thin. The broth in ABear's was smoky, rich, and brown—chunky with shrimp. It bode well for the meal. Even the potato salad that came with it was tangy and substantial.

I got the special: Catfish ABear with a side of red beans. An extended fan of thick catfish filets was delicately blanketed with "ABear Sauce," which lay on the spectrum somewhere between Hollandaise and tartar sauce. Slightly acidic, it elevated the earthiness of the catfish. The generous helping of creole-style red beans tied the whole plate together. I know this sounds like a lot of fancy talk for a catfish plate lunch, but it really was that good.

I generally prefer a brown jambalaya to a red one—a common variant you'll see among Terrebonne Parish Cajuns, where tomatoes are added to the rice, shrimp, and sausage—but the one at ABear's might turn me around to it. Again, it made the fat, juicy shrimp pop in the dish. This was turning out to be one of the best Cajun restaurant meals I'd ever had, and it was making me a little angry.

"Why haven't we ever come here before if it's just around the corner, right here by the church?" I asked my mom. Rhetorical question, of course; we couldn't really afford to eat out much growing up. Hebert told much of the same about her childhood. She grew up in Big Bayou Black, where, two or three times a year, her family would cross the bayou in a little flatboat that her dad made and then catch a ride on the Greyhound bus to get to Houma.

I would take such an arduous journey to get here for the restaurant's all-you-can-eat catfish and live music on Friday nights.

ABear's is pretty famous for its peanut butter pie, and I can see why. Cajuns have a lock on a lot of culinary wonders, but pies are not among them. I sampled the peanut butter and the chocolate pies and was in a swoon of fluffy wonder. Their chocolate pie was a perfect, airy consistency, thicker than French silk, but not so much as pudding. The peanut butter pie was something I imagine Elvis gets in heaven.

Dropping my mom off before heading back to Baton Rouge, I started eyeing the side streets that for decades have been rendered invisible with familiarity. Later, I did the same in my own neighborhood, wondering what undisclosed treasure I'd find if I, just once, turned the other way.

GRIFFIN'S POBOY and GRILLE

1015 W. Tunnel Blvd. #A
Houma, LA 70360
(985) 580-1777
griffinspoboy.com/

The Swamp Boy—an unthinkable marriage of a smoked hamburger, poboy, and Philly cheesesteak

I grew up in Houma, yet I still have no sense of it. There is a transitory nature to the place, despite how dramatically it's grown since I lived there in the 1980s. Big-box stores seem to be taking over every sugarcane pasture we used to cut through on our way to the decaying, outdated mall.

It's not my own distancing at play. Houma has a hard time forming a sense of itself. It is what the down-the-bayou Cajuns, the most distinctive group of people on earth, refer to as "town," where you go for court, Mardi Gras, or Wal-Mart, but it's not where one lives one's curious idiosyncratic life.

Houma has a tunnel cutting under the Intracoastal Waterway, by the way, should you be looking for a sudden, sodium-light-lit break from the town's endless strip malls and fast food joints. It separates the town into two sides indistinguishable from each other. There are a million decent cheap Asian joints due to Houma's burgeoning Vietnamese community, yet I'd be hard-pressed to point out a really good place for a bowl of pho. Small taquerias spring up in old Pizza Huts next to the ever-present competing Houma chicken chains, Danny's and Sunrise. Danny's is good, but my money is on Sunrise, and particularly their fried catfish plate. A not-insignificant portion

Marsh fries at Griffin's Poboy and Grille, Houma

of my teenage yard-mowing money went to a paper basket of catfish from the Sunrise on Barrow Street.

There are seafood places galore, a million poboy shops all trundling along for years, coming and going like the tide. I miss the roast beef poboy at Robbie's II on West Park and the oyster poboy at the Zesto that used to be on the bayou side near the hospital, but they are gone. When I ask around about where I should really go to eat in Houma, I get a smattering of new sushi and pizza places, never what I'm after. It's like being a teenager again.

Then, everyone eventually says, "Or, you could go to Griffin's. Get the Swamp Boy."

Griffin's Poboy lies among a collection of boiled seafood places on Tunnel Boulevard, nondescript in the way most good things in Houma tend to be. No frills, a near affront to curb appeal, adorns one of the best places to eat in Houma. The dining room is fine, service is fine, but not exactly exuding atmosphere. My mom, daughter, and I launch into this event headfirst with an order of marsh fries, a bowl of gumbo, and the fried bacon-wrapped shrimp.

"Marsh" is Griffinese for "with gravy": the fries rest saturated in a bowl of roast beef gravy topped with a lion's share of melted cheese, making the meal a stunt version of the "boo fries" or poutine you might see elsewhere. Fat Gulf shrimp are wrapped in bacon, battered, and deep-fried, an excess.

It's okay. We are here for the Swamp Boy—an unthinkable marriage of a smoked hamburger, poboy, and Philly cheesesteak. Like the aforementioned tunnel, the Swamp Boy is a startling plummet into new territory. Two massive beef patties rest on a forearm-sized section of crispy French bread, topped with a blanket of melted cheese and the ubiquitous gravy. Now, this may just sound like an exercise in culinary excess, but in each bite, a strange Cajun alchemy occurs. The earthiness of the roux in the gravy meets the tanginess of the cheese and the robustness of the burger to create what I can only call "gumboness." It in no way approximates the celebrated gumbos of Louisiana, but it replicates the complex mix of flavor signatures that separates a gumbo from any old stew. I'm almost tempted to ask for a little filé (dried and powdered sassafras used as a thickener in gumbos made without okra), but I am already too deep into the sandwich.

The Swamp Boy is no dainty affair. I've used up all the napkins at the table and need a clean shirt by the time I'm done. I am like the sandwich: a bit of a mess, maybe too much to handle, and a product of the curious push-me-pull-you that is Houma. I pull out on Tunnel Boulevard from Griffin's parking lot to head to my parents' house near the Intracoastal Canal but instead stay the course until I am bathed in those yellow lights of that curious tunnel, thinking this most ordinary place is special after all.

NEW ORLEANS
and NORTHSHORE

MIDDENDORF'S SEAFOOD RESTAURANT

30160 U.S. 51 S
Akers, LA 70421
(985) 386-6666
middendorfsrestaurant.com

Crispy, paper-thin catfish filets—the world's best

Going to Middendorf's feels like going on vacation, even if you live in the area. Chances are you don't live in the Manchac/Akers metropolitan area, since hardly anything is there besides the restaurant. Middendorf's is perched on possibly the only solid piece of earth in the thin strip separating Lake Maurepas from the enormity of Lake Pontchartrain. Aside from a few marinas and bait shops, there isn't room for anything else.

The journey sets the vacation atmosphere. You drive to Middendorf's over one of south Louisiana's seemingly endless expanses of highway elevated over dense, tangled swamps. I wonder if there isn't a more efficient place to put interstates than on concrete stilts, but then I love driving them. Even in the densest traffic, there is something magical about being suspended over such an amphibious landscape. Descending the highway ramp is something like coming in for a landing at this miraculous little outpost of fun.

If you are a Louisiana sportsperson of means, you can arrive by boat and dock at Middendorf's private marina. There is almost always a wait for a table, but I love to walk the marina banks and peer into the luxury cruisers and party barges tied up, watching the sunburned, inebriated boaters disembark for shade and more drinks on Middendorf's covered patio. I don't really want a boat myself, but I want some wealthy friends that have one, primarily so I can pull up to Middendorf's like a true emissary from a faraway place.

I try to take every newcomer to Louisiana here, partly because it puts you in contact with the reality of the state's landscape. Louisiana's water is often more visible than it is accessible to people just visiting, and it is important to get up next to it, to feel the gravity of all of it around you. I live here and yet I feel a little more deeply rooted every time I head out to Akers.

Like I said, Middendorf's feels like vacation. There is a beachlike sandlot next to the patio for the kids to go bananas in as you wait for a patio table. There is an indoor restaurant proper, and I hear it is very nice, but I could not imagine forgoing a spot on the balcony.

Seagulls seemingly levitate on the lake breeze, hoping small children pelt their French fries in the water. You keep your sunglasses handy if you sit by the rail and gaze out past the flags fluttering over the marina, as the Amtrak City of New Orleans blares past, as the time and place dissolve. It's a hell of a place to be.

I expect Louis Middendorf thought so when he wound up there in the Manchac swamp, destitute after the stock market crash in 1929. His wife Josie's people were there, eking out a life of hunting and fishing. But Middendorf had other ideas.

With his World War I veteran's pay and a loan, he opened the first café right on the banks of Pass Manchac, which connects the two lakes. The family has owned the restaurant ever since. It grew by leaps and bounds in the 1970s, when I-10 connected traffic from New Orleans to Baton Rouge, and then again in 1981, when I-55 opened between Ponchatoula and LaPlace. The deck and sandlot were added to the restaurant in 2008.

Middendorf's has endured out in the wilderness despite the odds. While it managed to escape the widespread devastation that much of the area suffered from Hurricane Katrina, Hurricane Ike brought a ten-foot-high storm surge through the area in 2008 that nearly swept the beloved restaurant into the water.

Had the restaurant not come back, this would have been a devastating blow to the area and southern food enthusiasts alike, largely because of one single item that has been on the Middendorf's menu since it opened: the legendary thin-cut fried catfish.

What to get: Josie Middendorf developed a recipe for frying paper-thin filets of catfish, and for more than three-quarters of a century, people have flocked to the restaurant for it. The filets look like someone somehow dipped a wave in cornmeal and fried it. The filets are thin and crispy as a potato chip, almost two-dimensional, yet they retain the essence of fried catfish.

Middendorf's has a full seafood menu, ranging from oysters to frog legs, boiled shrimp, and crabs, but to be quite honest, I cannot imagine going there and not getting the thin-fried catfish. Even the idea of their thick-cut catfish sounds like I'm missing out on one of the culinary world's singular wonders.

Unless, that is, you are there in October, when a German entrée is offered on Wednesday and Thursday nights. Louisiana has a sizable German heritage, but now that Taste of Bavaria in Ponchatoula is gone, one is hard-pressed to find German food in south Louisiana—so I might be convinced to forgo the thin-cut catfish for sauerbraten served with a pretzel.

Or, I'll just get what I want, which is the root of the vacation mindset. Maybe you want something more out of life than eating the world's best catfish with a lake breeze in your hair, sipping a daiquiri, and dreaming about owning a party barge. But it's my vacation, after all.

ROCKY & CARLO'S RESTAURANT & BAR

613 W. St. Bernard Hwy
Chalmette, LA 70043
(504) 279-8323

Homey Italian fare and ladies are invited

One of the first things you might notice about Rocky & Carlo's Restaurant is that ladies are invited. It is painted on the window, emblazoned in neon, written on every T-shirt and plastic cup in the place. I happened to have my favorite lady with me, my daughter, so I was glad I did not have to leave her in the car. We'd had a whirlwind day in New Orleans, shopping and seeing friends and racing all over in pursuit of the specialness the city can offer up, and we were ready for some comfort before the trek home.

Comfort is what Rocky & Carlo's is all about. It is easy to imagine that for many children growing up in Chalmette, Rocky & Carlo's *is* eating out. It has sat on St. Bernard Highway for nearly fifty years practically unchanged by the ravages of taste and time. Katrina dumped four feet of water in the place in 2005, and it was rebuilt in its former image in 2007. In February of 2012, a fire tore through the place, and yet come May that same year, it was back open.

The food at Rocky & Carlo's is homey Italian fare, but they have their own way of doing things. First of all, you line up to move through the restaurant cafeteria-style to order but not pick up your food, then order drinks and pay, including the tip. They are quick to note that any money left on the table is for the bus staff. Then, you are left to find a table in the vast expanse of the room and a waitress just finds you later with your food. It can set the

Veal parmesan and mac & cheese, covered in red gravy, at Rocky & Carlo's, Chalmette

more service-minded diner on edge; how do you control your meal without the push-me-pull-you with the server?

Here you don't and, frankly, it is a bit of a relief. I put 20 percent down as a tip in good faith.

While waiting, we take in the scene. Dads and uncles take a stab at the claw machine. Moms and aunts sneak off to play a little video poker. Folks wander over from the bar to greet families and kiss babies as they all sit, waiting to be found by that waitress and the bounty she brings.

What to get: Rocky & Carlo's has a full-service menu, but the only thing I have ever gotten or seen anyone else get is the veal parmesan with mac & cheese, each slathered in red sauce, with a "wop salad" on the side. To most of south Louisiana, the pejoratively named wop salad refers to the olive mixture that goes on a muffaletta, but here it is mixed greens with a vinegar and olive mix sprinkled with Parmesan cheese. A milder cousin to a Caesar, it is the palate cleanser for the main event.

Their mac & cheese is closer to the soul food tradition of cheesy spaghetti, the kind served as a side at a thousand church fundraiser barbecues, except it is made from long, uncut spaghetti noodles, adding the starchy deliciousness and extra heft. The veal parmesan is lightly breaded, fried just right—belly-full. The entire plate, unless you specify, is slathered with their red gravy, a juicy midpoint between a tangy marinara and the "sweet gravy" many family Italian restaurants serve.

It is the kind of meal that will satisfy the horde of picky kids that have washed into the place for half a century, large enough to justify the expense of taking a family out. It is in many ways the last family restaurant standing. Similar meat-and-three type places across the country have been replaced by the ubiquity of chain restaurants, same at every exit. So why does Rocky and Carlo's matter? Why bring up a veal parmesan joint right outside one of the greatest dining cities in the country?

Mention it to anyone who grew up in the area, and there will be a groan, a release, a glazing over of the eyes. I remember the first time I ate there. I was with a friend who was living back home in Chalmette after college, and during the course of a day of garage sales, he had magically scored an authenticated Roy Lichtenstein print for $20. He even told the people at the sale that this was worth something and they said, "That's why we have $20 on it!" He wanted to celebrate this find in traditional form and we went there, same as he probably did after a good report card or a little league game as a kid.

But it matters to the city as a whole. New Orleans proper tends to snub its suburbs. Chalmette was the default punchline of a thousand jokes growing up there, but really, the working-class outer banks of New Orleans is where its soul can be found. There is no pretense whatsoever to Rocky & Carlo's, and yet it is curious, idiosyncratic, and memorable. I'd never say this is the one place you need to eat in the New Orleans area—that option changes as often as the wind. But I'd say at some point, you gotta get your veal parm and mac covered in red gravy next to your wop salad at Rocky & Carlo's. Without it, the culinary picture of the whole of New Orleans is incomplete. Besides, ladies are invited!

CRABBY JACK'S

428 Jefferson Hwy
New Orleans, LA 70121
(504) 833-2722
crabbyjacksnola.com

A fantasy of New Orleans food camouflaged in a stretch of industrial reality

Evidence points to the world arguably not understanding itself a bit, yet the world has an idea of what New Orleans is about. New Orleans, in the eyes of the world, is greenery spilling off wrought-iron patio railings as the line of sight stumbles down a narrow, puddled street of shuttered doors, each with a low stoop, bohemians living among old people among wealthy people chock-a-block in a contentiously congenial stew of a town. New Orleans is rooms of wide tables in well-lit restaurants, serving a million red beans and several times that number of grains of rice every Monday (washing day, you see), 'cuz that's how we do it in N'awlins, dahlin'.

New Orleans is all-night bars. It is art galleries and street musicians. Cocktail sipping. Dog walking. Joie de vivre. It has this thing called Mardi Gras that strings the years evenly along a streetcar line of congenial relationship, bringing the others of this world into its fat, happy lap.

It is all of those things, mind you. Then there is the contra-New Orleans, where everyone lives a semblance of college bohemia deep into adulthood, where your life is dotted by new and old restaurants, new and old bands, near-ubiquitous tattoos, an abhorrence of tourists, and a sneaking suspicion about anything or anyone that would choose to exist in a non–New Orleans environment.

When my friends from Baton Rouge move to New Orleans, they general fall into that second category. Literally fall in, as if pushed by the life they leave behind. One particular family of friends, who seemed shockingly bohemian by Baton Rouge standards, landed perfectly into a sprawling book-lined house uptown by the river, and their life is an endless bike ride to the community garden or the art studio or the park or the etc. Theirs is a beautiful life, and I too wonder why anyone (me) would choose to live otherwise when I visit.

I like to use their house as a home base when making a day trip to New Orleans, hoping to draw them along on a culinary adventure. They have, by and large, been everywhere, so it's not much of a draw. The youngest (long-time friends with my now teenage daughter) expressed a very New Orleans–style concern that if I was to keep writing about these great little lunch places, people would find out about them and they wouldn't be fun anymore. My daughter assured her, "Don't worry. Nobody reads his articles anyway."

New Orleans is at least one more thing—a large city where a giant part of the populace is not colorful, not brass band musicians, does not have art studios or residential chickens or even tattoos. They are bozos that cram the interstates like everywhere else; they shop at Bed Bath & Beyond and Sam's Club like everyone else. They are as suspicious of New Orleans's seedy and diffident reputation as anyone, maybe more so since it's their city. Pierce the bubble of what truly makes New Orleans a unique place and it is suddenly a very normal place.

My transplanted friends usually take me to a local hangout in a local neighborhood with local everything. So, on a recent visit when they suggested we go to Crabby Jack's, my heart leapt a little.

Crabby Jack's tells a transplant's story as well. The Jack in question is Chef Jacques Leonardi, a New York farm boy who wound up in New Orleans by way of the U.S. Coast Guard. While serving as an officer during the day, he spent nights in Chef Paul Prudhomme's K-Paul's and in 1996 opened Jacques-Imo's Cafe, one of the most celebrated dining establishments in the city, with Crabby Jack's to follow only six years later.

Crabby Jack's is situated on a miraculously uncharming industrial bend of Jefferson Highway (Hwy 90, the pre-interstate east-west artery through the city). The beige building would likely disappear into the utilitarian landscape were it not for a bright orange sign boasting WORLD'S LARGEST PO-BOY! SEE IT! PO-BOY MUSEUM! It's like suddenly being accosted by a carnival barker's cheery roar on a desert trail.

The inside of Crabby Jack's blasts you with bright orange walls and copious folk art paintings, creating a contrast with its surroundings as pronounced as a strobe light in a well. It is bustling with customers in a vaguely defined line—more of a cluster—at the register. More customers are circling, jockeying for spots at the long family tables. We take up a free tail end of a table like we are the last passengers for the life raft.

In an orange flash, we are transported back to the original state of New Orleans, the charm offensive relieving you of your workday normality. I peer cautiously at my neighbor's food; her shrimp poboy looks divine. When I see her pull out her phone to snap a shot, I ask if I can take one too and suddenly her whole party is posing their plates for me. Each speaks to their allegiances. "I always get the brisket here," says the woman across from me. "I feel funny getting it anywhere else." The restaurant is a din of chatter. I know all the gossip of the women next to me by the time our food arrives. I offer a photo-op to my new neighbors, but they politely decline.

What to get: As my new friends said, there is enough here for everyone to have a favorite. Those drawn to the palace of wisdom that lies down the road of excess might be into the "Fleur De Bree," a poboy Frankenstein of the restaurant's signature baked ham, roast beef debris, and gravy. A gilded lily, perhaps, but then you see plenty of regular lilies in your lifetime.

The fried seafood comes highly recommended. My friends order a shrimp, oyster, and catfish combo with a side of fried green tomatoes. The batter has just enough crunch to it without overtaking the seafood, while the fried green tomatoes are delicate enough to occupy that netherworld between solid and soft without being mushy. Their tartness has me thinking I should have gone for the fried green tomato poboy when my actual order arrives and I join the Crabby Jack's echelon in having a favorite.

The slow-roasted duck poboy is one of the best ideas anyone has ever had. A generous portion of dark brown duck, dark as the night when a lone wolf howls to the moon, is slathered over a Leidenheimer's loaf with enough gravy to render this sandwich a logistical disaster. But what a magical disaster!

I recognize duck is not everyone's bag; its liver tones and stringiness can turn the less-adventuresome eater away. But if they ever had it roasted by whatever alchemical wizardry Crabby Jack's employs, it would be their new favorite too. My neighbors are a little unsure about the mess I attempt to lift to my mouth, perhaps rightfully so, as it threatens to come apart.

I have a philosophical block against eating a poboy with a knife and fork, so I wrap it back up in the butcher paper in which it came and slowly tear away at it as one would an overstuffed burrito. It is amazing, with all the pervasive gravy-ness of roast beef debris while being unmistakably richer in flavor.

I glance up from my beloved at the trio of painted windows the way backseat lovers might consider a headlight grazing the windshield. The stylish old-timey fonts declaring "Jambalaya—Potato Salad—Dirty Rice" backwards, superimposed over the crystal clear plainness of the truck lot across the street, seem almost a postmodern representation of this poboy, which is an unmistakable tradition inverted a little, its elements put together differently, creating something special.

This restaurant's place in this dull neighborhood does the same. The tables are populated with those perfectly fine normal people who work in the lackluster industrial buildings. One is tempted to picture their offices, their trucks, their lives, yet here they are in this riotous orange supernova of smoked duck richness with me. There are, for a moment, no lines. Anything is possible! Everything is everything else!

The smoked duck is making me deliriously full, if not simply delirious, halfway through, and I call it a draw with the leftovers. As we exit, one last windowpane that says "Fried Green Tomatoes" backwards over the forced perspective of parked cars strikes me as the best painting, or at least best-framed conjunction of imagery, I've seen in years. Maybe I'm just open to new things more than most. Maybe my critical acumen is softened by a bellyful of the best duck poboy ever. Maybe I just like any place that inspires one to have a new favorite.

DONG PHUONG BAKERY & RESTAURANT

14207 Chef Menteur Hwy
New Orleans, LA 70129
(504) 254-0214
(504) 254-1568
dpbanhmi.com/

Pork buns, the ultimate hand-held food

When I leave the cities in Louisiana I'm confounded why there are roads laid out to the places to which I am going. I suppose the circumstances answer the question—I am not the first person to ever go to New Orleans East, for instance—but are there enough people going there to justify the tangle of concrete flyovers that take me from the urban wonder of New Orleans across the bleak expanse to Dong Phuong Bakery, a bright sparkle on a ribbon of concrete that is Chef Menteur Highway?

It is not entirely alone. I marvel at the concept behind We Never Close Po-Boys, tucking it away in my mind should I find myself out there at 4 a.m. The former Relax Inn sits off the road, freshly painted like a roosting peacock. All signs of possible life. With the abandoned gas stations and anonymous warehouse facilities all around, it would be understandable if you drove right past Dong Phuong Bakery & Restaurant.

Early the morning my daughter and I went, the bakery was abuzz with preparation. First thing you see is a heaving bin of blond yellow poboy loaves, and these are the key to Dong Phuong's greater place in the New Orleans and Louisiana culinary landscape. After years of French occupation,

Vietnamese cooks have taken a number of cues from the ubiquitous Paris boulangerie and run with them.

As their website proclaims, *dong phuong* literally means "east" in Vietnamese, but I suspect for many New Orleanians it means the reason they trek out this way. De and Huong Tran came to the area in 1980. De worked at a grocery store and studied engineering; his wife Huong baked the pastries she had learned from her father's bakery in Vietnam. Within a year, it became evident that this bakery was something needed, at first by the Vietnamese community and gradually, by the culinary mavericks of the New Orleans dining scene. Dong Phuong's poboy bread is a key element in the rethinking of what the poboy is—vanguard outlets in the city like Killer Poboys and Green Goddess use Dong Phuong bread as opposed to the bakeries that have defined our region's sandwich for decades.

What to get: Staff is slicing an orgy of cold cuts for the oncoming *bánh mì* lunch rush, so my daughter and I take to the pastry counter, where things really start to get interesting. Dong Phuong's pastry dough is vaguely sweet and largely rich. Their milk bread rolls make amazing sliders, but my money is on the pork buns. A small, compact ball of delicately seasoned pork rests a little loose inside a crisp hood of dough. Cut it in half and it looks a little like Darth Vader's custom TIE fighter and is equally lethal to one's morning hunger pangs.

One is hesitant to call it perfect because the ethos of a Vietnamese bakery is not preciousness and detail but assembly-line repeatability. The room is lined with mung bean mooncakes and fluffy steamed buns. You feel you cannot go wrong. My daughter opts for an electric green puffy steamed bun stuffed with savory minced pork. It looks like she is eating an alien egg.

The greatness of these pastries is that they are the ultimate hand-held food; the fact that we don't have Vietnamese bakeries on every corner instead of ubiquitous fast-food joints is a failing to understand the true nature of comfort food. Steamed pork buns are as warm and yielding as a Big Mac but are actual food. My daughter and I dig into our steamed buns as Chef Menteur Highway starts to repopulate with businesses, the closer we get to the city.

We get to the Bywater neighborhood sated, ready for a day of hipster commerce. I'm going deep into the stacks at Euclid Records while she explores the neighborhood craft market across the street. The Bywater is in a lot of ways the cultural future of New Orleans—gastropubs and dive bars sitting along the same potholed streets that tie it to the city as a whole.

Thumbing through albums, I start to wonder where we are going to have lunch until I realize I left my debit card at the bakery.

I'm guessing I did this subconsciously, because we arrive in the thick of lunch. The parking lot is full, and the restaurant attached to the bakery is hosting a wedding. Music is blasting; music resembling hiphop-laced Jamaican dancehall with Vietnamese singers takes over all rational thought as it tears through the wall from the restaurant. I locate my errant card and take it to the *bánh mì* counter.

The *bánh mì* is cold cuts on one of those miraculous delicate baguettes combined with an array of spicy pickled vegetables and peppers. The meat and bread are a dead ringer for the *jambon* sandwiches in any French street bistro, but the pickles give it an earthy center, somewhere between sour and bitter and umami on the flavor spectrum. There are numerous combinations of meat with which one can dress up a Dong Phuong *bánh mì*; everything from liver paté to toasted fish patties to French cold cuts.

The woman behind the counter is furiously making *bánh mì* in bulk, wrapping each skinny sandwich halfway in foil so it can be handed out like racing batons and eaten by each person in the receiving line. She is stacking them up in a gleaming pyramid just as a waitress from the wedding next door runs up to tell her they need yet another dozen. Watching her make them is like watching an industrial film demonstrating the curious maneuvers of factory machinery. I'm so spellbound by this and the deafening Viet-reggae from next door that she has to tap on the glass to ask me what I want. I pause for a second to look at the menu and she frowns as if to say, "Great, an amateur," but as soon as I get "French cold cuts" out of my mouth—a *dac biet paté thit nguoi* in Vietnamese—it is already stuffed with pickled carrots and cilantro, wrapped in foil, and handed to me. I try to say thanks but she is deep into making the next pyramid.

I'm checked out, reminded to grab my debit card this time and I'm out the door. This is fast food in the velocity only, for the meats, the bread, everything is produced in house and I feel like I've ripped somone off by getting such a sandwich at such a modest price. Never mind the (second) trek through the gray expanse of New Orleans East; this sandwich is a ray of sunshine with each bite. I regret not having an ice chest handy so I can stock up for the week and eat nothing else but shimmering alien egg pork buns and one of the best sandwiches around.

living relatives, Uncle Robert and Aunt Ellie, she lived in a peace she'd never known. Rose was born seven months after her mother had made a desperate run to be clear of her twisted and wasted husband.

Years later Rose, thirteen years old, returning from school, heard her mother screaming and hid behind the well in the rear yard of their secluded country home. She watched as two men, one a short, fat, dumpy man, the other tall and lean, drug her mother's body from the small frame house, and dumped it as if it were nothing more than a tow sack full of flour into a waiting wagon. Later she recalled how the men stood by the tail gate, rolling cigarettes and smoking them. On sleepless nights she often heard the thick and vulgar laughing of the men as her mother lay dead behind the drop-gate of the wagon. She remembered being afraid they would see her or hear her pounding heart. Nor could she forget how after a very long time spent discussing the disposal of her mother, in voices loud enough to be heard from behind the well, they finally climbed onto the wagon and left. To her, it had felt like a day. In reality the ordeal had lasted no longer than a half an hour.

But there was so much the horrific event had forever seared into her young mind, things she would never relive again—the house hidden away in the woods, the smell of a hot dinner awaiting her when she returned home from school each day, her mother's singing, and the sweet, feathery touch of her mother's lips on her cheeks with her goodnight kiss. With the exception of a daguerreotype found later in the family Bible of her being held by her mother, Uncle Robert and Aunt Ellie standing next to her, she would have been unable to remember even those two she had loved as much as her mother.

But the unforgettable things, those things singed into her mind, haunted her from that dreadful day forward; blood dripping from her mother's hand as it hung over the top of the tail gate, the sound of the slow *drip . . drip . . . drip* of blood splattering on dry, brown oak leaves below the wagon. She remembered picking up an oak leaf, a heart, stained blood-red upon its paper thin surface. Making a reckless dash into the house, she retrieved her mother's Bible, the one which held the picture, and placed the heart-stained oak leaf inside it.

The nights were different. She dreaded the fall of night for along with it came things which she did not want to relive. She dared not close her eyes for when she did, the grisly scenes of the violent murder would play over and over again on the back side of closed eyelids.

Uncle Em, her mother's brother and the last relative she had left on the face of the earth, took her in, claiming to all who inquired that she was the child of a distant relative who had passed away. It was a lie, but a necessary one, a ploy to hide her real identity from her father, Hesper Griffen. Emmett understood there would always be those who were curious about the sudden appearance of the child, but knew his neighbors, out of respect for him, would not question him about the pretty, young girl. As time passed, and when Emmett eventually felt safe to do so, he began to refer to the young girl as his daughter. He prayed the simple solution would fool the neighbors and the two of them were successful in doing so. And he continually warned her to stay away from the crazed man to the north

Rose led a sheltered life, but she so despised the man that caused her being, she felt no guilt, no sorrow or anything when he died. Instead of hatred, she wished for confirmation after being told of his death in the woods north of Swift Creek. It took a long time for her to get over her fear of the woods, but finally she entered them looking for the body she wished to spit upon, but hogs had devoured everything in their path.

***

Upon his death, Hesper's personal papers were searched for an heir, but none was found. Emmett, though, had in his possession the original certificate of his sister's marriage to Griffen which had been given to him for safekeeping—and proof enough of Rose's birthright. With his dying, like it or not, came all of Hesper's earthly possessions and the need for Rose to make a life altering decision.

She wanted nothing to do with anything of her father's. She was neither ashamed nor confused by her decision to walk away from her rightful inheritance. At first, she fought off suggestions that she should lay claim to his estate, The Meadows. Like her husband, she desired no more holdings and wanted no more slaves, and especially anything which had belonged to that evil man who had lived and died north of them. They had all the material possessions they desired. There was no room left in their overcrowded lives for more possessions, more complications.

Regardless, there were the slaves, those poor, lost and childlike people of The Meadows, who were ensnared in a life in which they never made decisions, and therefore, were incapable of doing so after the death of the man they themselves had often wished dead.

But Hesper had been mentally ill and given to strange acts. The birth certificate in Emmett's possession proved that during his sister Abigail's and Hesper's brief marriage, their daughter Rose was conceived. The Meadows, by default, was hers, even though she felt to receive it would acknowledge Griffen as her father and therefore diminish the horrid nature of the man. That she could not and never would allow. He had become something that should be forgotten.

Burdened with a sense of foreboding, Rose spiraled into a grinding darkness. She'd seen so much in her life, violent things women should be spared from seeing, that she feared the insanity within her father could find root and grow within her.

But the slaves of the inherited Meadows had to be taken care of. To do less would have been to be less than the dead man himself. Sam knew his wife's heart was divided and when she recovered, she would see the wrong in walking away from the helpless slaves. She would need time to heal, but those humans held in bondage had little time—only fear. Sam understood why she did not want to claim ownership of the land or the mansion to the north of Swift Creek, but those things were part and parcel of Griffen's dying. So Sam, the husband, the protector of his wife, acted in her behalf.

Henry and his wife Sara took over management of the abandoned mansion. They saw to the needs of the panicked slaves and began to restore the age-worn building into the magnificent dwelling it had once been.

In less than a year, Emmett Detwyler, the man who adopted Rose and sheltered her, died in his sleep. He, too, left everything he owned to her—The Ferns, eight thousand plus acres, three hundred thirty-six slaves and a hollow running through the entirety of her body from which her very soul was sucked. Again, a gut wrenching agony filled her. Sam understood she had gone deep within herself to heal and prayed she would return. He wondered if she could live without that good man, Em, the man she considered her *real* father. He felt her leave and watched her spiral into the dark catacombs of her mind again. There was little he could say or do to guide her back. There was nothing she would hear. He held her tightly for days, never leaving the house, barely leaving her presence. The children remained as quiet as church mice and never came up the stairs to bother their mother. But out of fear and desperation, they hounded their father with their own concerns for their mother whenever he came down to dine with them.

As did the slaves of The Meadows, those of The Ferns also, lived with their personal fears. Unlike those poor souls who had been tortured and killed on a moment's whim by the sick Hesper Griffen, the slaves of The Ferns knew such a good man as "Marse" Emmett would not have abandoned them—not even in death. They knew that because they knew Rose.

***

The morning's sun shining through the bedroom window confused her. From within Rose's dark, gray, and damp catacomb world, a place void of all she had once known and loved, she saw confusing images, each in sharp contrast with the others. Instinctively, she knew the cave-like place meandered aimlessly, so she tore small strips from her dress and dropped them onto the packed dirt. They would help her find her way if and when she decided to return. So real was her netherworld, when at long last she did return, at the foot of the bed a feathering of ragged pieces torn from sheets awaited her.

In the strange dimension existing within her mind, for a brief moment she felt the lightness of floating beyond the bedroom window, her arms stretched forward, begging to be seen and pulled back into the world she barely remembered. In the next moment, Rose saw the hole into which she fell as it glowed and swirled like the maw of a tornado above her. And, too, she saw herself as she lay broken, at the bottom of an uncovered burial crypt. The face she sought, the face she needed—Sam's—hung silhouetted and floating in the gaping hole above her, so clear, so wrecked with anguish, and still out of her reach. But she had to try. She struggled mightily to touch his extended fingers. She heard his pleas for her to come back and she knew she must. To stay in the tomb was to die. Exhausted, confused, and hurting, she rose as a mist from a lake and returned to his arms. Her eyes opened and there he was, holding her, his lips against her temple, as he had been doing all along, and would continue doing until she fell soundly asleep and no longer felt the tug of her despair.

At Sam's request, Isaac and his wife moved into The Ferns. Rose sensed she was relieved of a worry but could not remember the reason for worrying so. No longer able to make decisions, she slept—such was the poor shape of her heart and the clutter of confusion in her mind. The Ferns continued as before, except emptier with Emmett's departure.

Thus within two decades Swift Creek had more than tripled in size. But as said, such wealth came at a high price for the two.

Swift Creek Plantation, The Ferns and The Meadows had merged into one and all were thriving. Sam's family was healthy, and he looked forward to the day he and Rose could enjoy sitting in the wing-back rattan chairs on the front porch, mint juleps in their hands, watching their not-yet-born grandchildren playing in the lawn spread before them

***

The afternoon skies turned gray, the clouds promising relief from the afternoon heat, and hinted of a cooling breeze. The summer of Eighteen and fifty-eight had proved to be what the Farmer's Almanac said it would be—excessively hot and brush-fire dry. Almost every day of the last month, mid-day, Sam instructed the overseer to send the slaves home to rest and cool in the shade of their shanties. With the sweat blackened leather collars laced tightly around the mule's thick necks unbuckled, the harness and traces laid back upon plows and wagons, the mules, glistening with sweat, headed toward the shade of the tin roofs attached to scattered barns without being led by the slave boys. The youngsters filled their emptied water troughs and awaited orders to harness them back to their burdens when the sun fell low in the west, still leaving time to make up that which had been lost.

Sam stood by the far corner of the lawn, not aware he was looking northwest towards Lexington, Virginia, his thoughts drawn by the knowledge that his son, Thaddeus, was there attending the Virginia Military Institute. He thought it unusual how his son who had so strongly resisted attending VMI, the initials for which the institute was better known, had recently expressed his interest in the fine art of Artillery. He smiled, remembering "Tad" had called his Professor, Thomas J. Jackson, the Artillery Instructor, an "odd duck." Sam agreed upon learning of the Professor's appointment as Major General of the Army of Northern Virginia that perhaps the man was a bit unusual, after all. Not often did a Presbyterian Deacon, or any man of the cloth for that matter, forego his church appointment to teach matters of killing. *Very odd indeed*, Sam thought.

Sam considered Tad's teacher a pious man—one given to righting wrongs through witnessing to the sinner. The only way he could imagine a man of the cloth giving up such a revered office in order to teach the ways of war was if Professor Jackson really did believe there was a rend tearing apart the Northern states and those of the Southland, now called Dixie.

Regardless of the reason or reasons, there had been talk of the North and the South severing their ties, dissolving their union, but there had been such talk for a long time. War was coming. He had long ago hoped such a division in the United States of America was unlikely, impossible even. And with his son now at VMI, he wanted more than ever for his people, the South, to stop propagating the need of war. Surely sounder minds would prevail, he prayed.

Still, he felt confident his son would be home before such an unimaginable thing could befall the country. He prayed daily the next three years would pass quickly and Tad would come home from the military school, his chest ablaze with medals, and give up the novelty of his latest passion, artillery.

If only those damn fools up North will stop pushing and pushing us, he prayed.

Chapter Six: Eighteen and fifty-seven. The entitled one.

A gift was given to him. Something new and a marvel to behold and adore. A tiny life named Thaddeus was held in cautious and calloused hands. The father held the gift as if it would break, and the hard man others thought him, teared. He kissed the newborn, yet feared the newness of it—the fragility of it. A bond which would never break rooted deeply into father and son. The newborn gurgled and spit mother's milk. And the father walked the room, hoarding the new thing in his life. For now, the child was his, all his.

That was the meeting of father and son.

The years began to pass—far too fast for the father, far too slow for the boy. The father watched his son grow. He was anxious to teach him, to warn him and protect him from the dangers of life—and of the joys it held. The father knew the ways of the world, his son did not, therefore the father taught him many things, but protected him from far too much.

But a child drenched with worship always expects more. Most parents know when to withhold affections and replace them with a corrected balance of affection. Too, they know when to discipline. Sam knew, but couldn't. It was not in him to be harsh. But he needed to be.

The privileged one—the heir apparent—had just turned seventeen years old. Thaddeus' ten years of schooling in the Carlton

County school was finished and behind him. He was happy to call it quits with the three-room building and the tight-lipped spinster who taught grade one through ten in the white-washed clapboard sided structure.

To prove his refusal to obey his parents insistence that he continue his education after the ten years, he crushed the diploma into a tight wad of paper and threw it into the wastebasket by the door. That was a mistake and he knew it. His parents would ask to see it. Retrieving it, he felt a flush of embarrassment for his irrational, if not childish behavior, and after stretching the creases from it as well as he could, he purposefully stuffed it into his shirt pocket hoping that would account for the wrinkles.

The certificate filled him with mixed emotions. He'd obeyed his parents' continual demands that he finish the ten years of schooling the small school provided, from which he garnered only a simplistic and basic education, but remembered their mention of yet more education to come—college.

By an illogical reasoning, he assumed he knew at least as much as the pinched-faced spinster who wore her hair in a tight bun. Ten years was enough for him.

With his schooling behind him, he believed he should be considered an adult—a full grown man, mature—and entitled to do as he wished.

Only just that morning, Tad had fled the small school in Fort Harwood, anxious to have books, homework, and teachers far behind him. Homeward bound, he detoured by O'Day's Livery to admire his newest possession.

Arriving home, there was no answer when he called for his mother and father. He was relieved by their absence, but the day was far from over. Laying the Certificate of Completion upon his father's desk, he thought the act may prove he was now man enough to face his father.

A collision was building in Swift Creek. Leaving the quiet of the empty house, Tad left for the calm and serenity of the "Red Slater Corner."

The infamous corner, a small spur of lawn extending out and into Swift Creek, was a favored place to hide from the constancy of family. He loved his family immensely but occasionally needed to escape the never-ending girl talk and incessant giggling of his two sisters, Samantha and Izzy.

A week after the first purchase he'd made as the full grown man he now thought himself to be, he lay on a pallet of grass, chin cupped in hands, and awaited the delivery of his first major decision as an adult. He nervously watched the driveway as it wended through the oaks.

The morning sun beat down upon his back, warming him, and groggily, he lay daydreaming about everything—daydreaming about nothing. Forcing himself awake from a sleepy haze, the result of the warmth of the morning sun, he lay still and watched the circular drive from behind a screen of broom straw not yet sheared by the slaves in charge of the lawn. He had no desire to see his father. Not just yet.

His mind wandered to the jut of land he lay upon. He wondered if the stories his father told him when he was a boy were really true or just another way to keep him away from the creek, and a chance drowning. Almost word for word, he recalled how his father said he'd killed a man named Red Slater on the very piece of land on which he now lay and explained to his son how *that* Red fellow had tried to kill him and steal Willie, his slave boy. He'd told Tad also of how "Uncle" Henry had been badly beaten by the same man.

At first Tad, thought the infamous corner perhaps haunted, a place to be avoided. Often he'd hear rumors of lights at night, tales of rising white mists and unknown things floating above the spur of land. He'd never seen any of those things, but his youthfulness kept him from the area, especially when the sun fell away and the dark of night rushed in. When older, he thought it possible that the child-like Willie, inclined to tell fanciful stories, was behind the rumors—trying to scare him. So he learned to ignore the ghost. Eventually, Willie sought the peace and quiet of the spit of land and joined young Tad on the spur, therefore voiding his concerns of ghost and goblins.

He remembered, too, how he'd found his father's unexpected revelations startling, but even so, was greatly impressed by the telling of it. To him, his father was a king, the kind of man by which all other men should be judged. And the fact that Willie himself, middle-aged now, still simple-minded, and as devoted as ever to his "Massa Sam," would never venture alone to the corner, therefore gave credence to what his father had told him. When approached, "Uncle" Henry would not verify nor deny the story when questioned by the lad. Nowadays, he saw little of his uncle, although Henry managed The Meadows, the plantation north of Swift Creek, which his parents had inherited the summer before. With never-seen ghosts rising from the supposedly blood-soaked ground, Tad put the story behind him. Besides, upon the corner, grew the perfect grass upon which to lie or sit, as mosquitoes buzzed and fish ignored his baited hook.

In truth, he lay almost upon the very spot where Red Slater did die, and near the place Red's dimwitted brother Daryl collapsed while clutching his shattered hand. His father had tried to kill him as well, or so the story went. There was also the strange way his father had made him promise to never tell his mother about the Red Slater corner. "Our secret" he'd said. So he never did, and never thought much about the story—except whenever he desired catfish or peace and quiet and freedom from his bothersome sisters.

Behind him, unnoticed, a catfish hooked through its mouth, fought the hook and cane pole stuck in the ground. But Tad had lost interest in fishing. He was waiting and watching for the gathering storm approaching the big house.

Soon the tromp . . . tromp. . . tromp of two horses sounded, one with a rider, reins in hand, leading a magnificent barebacked stud. The windy dervish approached from the lane wending through the maze of old oaks as it snaked toward the front entry of Swift Creek. Tad rolled over onto his stomach and pulled the weeds and grass before him into a blind and watched his mother and father greet the man leading the stallion he'd bought earlier.

The coal-black stallion, beautiful but skittish, well over sixteen hands from the ground to its withers, loomed over the other horse, tossed its head and danced away from his father's approach.

Upon the wind floated the occasional words spoken between the two men, a few of which were, "Your son went plum crazy over him." He strained to overhear the balance of the conversation, but the this way and that way of the shuffling breeze seemed to not care much in which direction it blew.

Now joined by his mother, his father and she scanned the distant edge of the woods bordering the lawn. He knew the game was up and they were looking for him. He'd been expecting it. As the gentle breeze settled, he heard the man on horseback say, "Well, Mr. Biggs, that's 'tween you and that boy ah your'n." He pointed at the stallion and added, "He's bought, paid for, and delivered."

Hearing his name called, Thaddeus pushed himself up into a sitting position. His mother and father locked their eyes upon him and continued talking to each other, while pointing in his direction.

His father waved him forward. "Tad, get down here. Come to the library." His voice edgy, and sharp, carried to the far edge of the front lawn—sharper and edgier than usual, which meant only one thing to the boy . . . *They're mad*. He watched as they turned, climbed the steps and walked inside, neither speaking to the other.

Thaddeus Samuel Biggs, the eldest child and only son of Sam and Rose Biggs, stood and brushed away the loose weeds, leaves, and cockleburs caught in his clothing. He combed his straw-blond hair with spread fingers and headed toward the mansion.

"Well, you done the deed," he mumbled, "face the music."

He waved to the liveryman as he was riding away. Toby, the twelve year old stable boy, led the stud toward the barn. The young slave held the reins away from him as far as his short arms allowed, and readied himself to flee if necessary, while he watched the coal-black stud dancing behind him.

The stud no longer looked as gentle to Tad as it had when corralled behind the livery in Fort Harwood. He'd begun to suspect the wisdom of making such an expensive purchase, and his judgment in doing so without discussing it beforehand with his father, reckless. Indeed it was, but the deal was irreversible.

He shouted for Toby to wait, and approaching the large horse, his confidence failed to return. Earlier, he had ignored the skittish behavior of the stud when corralled, and now it seemed he saw a wildness in the horse's huge, dark eyes. The twitching of the skin beneath the black hair seemed to carry its own warning of an unbridled spirit.

Yet, all he understood was how badly he had wanted the black beauty. His decision, the largest he'd ever made on his own, was a good one . . . *Who could argue that?* he mused, while fortifying himself for the coming war of words with his father. And the horse *was* magnificent, the most impressive horse he'd ever seen, except for maybe Queenie, his father's very old and most prized possession. He knew if anyone knew horseflesh, it was his father, and that he of all people would see the wisdom of his purchase. Even so, he'd suspected the spur of the moment purchase would upset his father, and he was right. Still, he had to have it.

He already owned Racer, the small speckled roan, and could ride it or any horse he chose, for that matter, on Swift Creek Plantation, with the exception of Queenie. She had been turned out to pasture years ago.

A last, but cautious brush against the stud's neck and he turned towards the big house. His pitch, practiced since returning from Fort Harwood, began to seem weak to him. Again, he repeated the argument. "Father . . . this horse . . . there's not another one like "Thunder," he'd decided to name it, "except for maybe Queenie, in all of Carlton County, probably not even in the rest of North Carolina, maybe in all of the States." Yes, that would be the grounds for his case. Surely his father's anger would subside after hearing his sound, mature reasoning and high praise of *both* Queenie and the stud.

He pushed open the custom-made mahogany door which held the stained-glass windows and panels designed by his mother. He thought of his father's often told story of how, very long ago when he was building the house, his mother had shown him her hand-drawn, whimsical sketches of wished-for stained-glass windows and of how he'd commissioned a well-known glass company in New York to make her wish a reality. And, too, of how he'd taken his mother to Fort Harwood, convincing her of some illogical reason to spend a day and perhaps a night, while skilled craftsmen installed the window inserts and side panels. All as a surprise for her.

From the stable he imagined he heard Thunder snorting in derision at him. Toby, too. The image of his father's long ago surprise for his mother evaporated.

The loud, sharp "clack" of his hobnail boots slapping against the pristine oak floor advised him to retrace his steps to the porch and remove his boots. Hobnails would have marred the floor and he did not need his father any madder than he imagined he already was. The white socks he wore were stained grass-green along the soles and yellow at the heels and toes, the result of the hot day and a boot maker's poor choice of tanning solutions.

He sniffed at the boots to see if his feet smelled and decided they most certainly did. Quickly, he headed to an always-filled trough of water. He removed the sweaty socks, stuck them deep into the boots, and rubbed at his feet with a soaked handkerchief.

***

"Yes. Father," Tad said, entering his father's combination office and library. From behind the couch, he bent to kiss his mother's cheek thereby buying motherly support, if necessary—it always worked.

She reached back and ruffled his thick, unruly blond hair. She never did like confrontations but knew one was on the way She wished to be anywhere but here. *Such a handsome boy . . . and so beautiful*, she thought the description effeminate, but that was a mother's prerogative. *He looks so much like his father when he was younger. Hardly ever any trouble*—and after the kiss, thought—*devious though.*

Tad walked around the couch and sat in the chair positioned directly in front of his father and began picking at his nails.

"Where did you get that stud, Thaddeus?" Sam asked, trying to show anger that he'd been defied by his son. He seldom used his son's full name—but always when irritated. "And why?"

Secretly, Sam thought the horse was as grand as his Queenie in her earlier days. He visualized his beloved black mare grazing in the far fields and how she walked slower and slower with each passing day. *Kind of like me*, he mused.

"I bought him from O'Day's Stables. He's something, isn't he, Father?" In thinking his father might be considering rescinding the purchase; he wisely redirected the conversation by adding, "He looks like Queenie, doesn't he?"

Sam's face softened, a sign he was thinking of Queenie. *He does at that . . . just like her.*

"I took some money out of my account in Weldon. Mr. Graystone opened it for me. I told him it'd be alright with you. I paid for him with my own money, Father." As if to make the purchase something more acceptable. "Only five hundred dollars. He'll be good for our stock, don't you think?" he suggested, seeking an edge.

His father's face turned beet red—flushed with anger. "Five . . . hundred . . . dollars? What the hell were you thinking? We could have built at least eight more cabins for five hundred dollars." His example was not intended to suggest he was buying more slaves—he didn't need more, nor did he want anymore, especially not with the slave issue heating up throughout the country. He said it for comparison's sake, so the boy could understand the amount of money it took in the real world to buy such a magnificent animal.

"Just when did you decide you were old enough to make a decision like that? Yesterday? Two months ago? When you got out of school? Was that it? Full grown now, huh? Ready to run the place, are you? Did you consider coming to me about it? And just what do you know of breeding stock, Thaddeus?" he asked.

He paused, waiting for the boy's response. But all he saw was the blush sweep across his son's face.

Trying a different tack, Tad ventured. "Mother, please tell Father I'm too big for Racer," referring to the roan he'd owned since he had been taught to ride. "My feet drag the ground when I'm on her. People laugh at me when they see me coming. I'm grown now, well almost, and I *need* a horse like Thunder. *Swift Creek needs* Thunder." He blushed, knowing he had greatly exaggerated Racer's diminutive size. "How's about if I give Racer to Izzy? She's always begging me to let her ride him." So far, he thought his approach a success.

His mother muffled a laugh with her handkerchief, and Sam smiled, almost prepared to join her in laughter as the two sat visualizing their son's feet dragging on the ground.

Tad then knew the horse was his to keep.

"We'll talk about that horse later. It came as a surprise to us. But for now, your mother and I have something else we need to discuss with you." The sudden change in conversation caught Tad off guard. Seldom did his parents discuss things of importance with him, and they'd never asked his opinions.

Sam reached for the desk drawer and removed a pale blue envelope, bordered in dark blue. He held it up as if it held great secrets. "Son, your Mother and I have some good news for you," and both watched as the young man's eyes locked onto the envelope. "You've been accepted into VMI."

They did not tell him which college or where it would be—they had not known themselves until the recent arrival of the envelope now held before him. Sam had campaigned ardently for his son's admittance into the legendary college in Lexington, Virginia. He read the form twice before he understood his son had been accepted.

Confused, Tad asked. "I've been what and to where?" He looked at his mother hoping for a clarification of the announcement, but she merely continued smiling.

"VMI," responded his father, his smile beginning to narrow.

"VM what?"

"VMI. It's a school, kind of a college like the one over in Raleigh. Except it's not for just everyday learning. It's a military school. VMI, the Virginia Military Institute in Lexington."

"Mother," Thaddeus pleaded, "I don't want to go off to a college and especially not to a soldiering college."

"A soldiering college? So, you have heard of it? Well. Guess what. You're leaving in three weeks," announced his father.

"Oh no, I'm not," said the boy, as he defiantly crossed his arms across his chest. Furrows of determination creased his brow. "I'm done with school."

His father's hand slapped the desk. Tad's eyes flashed from his father's narrowing eyes to his mother's. But she remained quiet.

"Oh . . . yes . . . you . . . are. That decision is not yours to make. It's not a damn horse. You have no say in this. We, your mother and I have made that decision."

Tad stood—angry—ready to argue. The desk slapping was unlike his father and the idea of arguing with him seemed unwise. But he knew he had an ally in his mother. She had always been the one he sought when seeking a counter to his father's decisions.

"You best sit down and pay attention, Tad," said his mother, sternly. "It's already done." And defeated, he fell into his chair.

And then, again, she remained quiet. She felt trapped between father and son—but she was not going to be coerced by a gentle kiss.

She knew the man she married and who fathered her only son had always been unable to discipline the boy in the manner in which a father should. She understood why—and she was there to support the decision she had agreed with.

***

The two, she and Sam, had discussed their son's future many times. Each reassured the other that was what parents do. Sam could upon occasion raise his voice a decibel or two, even glare at their son with a cold hard stare—enough to back down grown men, but the boy was not his adversary—*Tad is his son*, she thought.

She recalled the long talks she and Sam had about her husband's upbringing in Petersburg, the small town just beyond the state line of Virginia. She knew Sam as a boy had been starved for the love of his father—and that of a mother, as well. He'd told her how his own father had often slapped him and his mother around when he came home drunk, and that his father always did come home drunk. She remembered him telling her how, after drinking heavily, his father would hit him hard enough to bloody his nose and how he could still hear the muffle of his father's voice, his tongue thick with alcohol, as he slurred the words and sprayed a foul spittle upon his face, "Clean that mess up when you're through bleeding." She knew the liquor-besotted man never expressed regrets or begged forgiveness from the two people he told others he loved—but when behind closed doors, battered.

She understood the soft and gentle nature of her husband.

He'd also told her there were never any pleasant conversations at their dinner table—none like those which other families shared—only scowls, grunts, and threats. *That's why our family meals seem like celebrations to him*, she thought. Rose and her husband, in so many ways, had shared similar childhoods.

He'd told her how over the span of his first sixteen years he had grown to hate his hard-fisted, drunkard of a father and grown to care little for his indifferent mother. The man's daily diatribe served as conversation in the wrecked family. The slaps, the yelling, the swearing, and the unwritten volumes of the constant belittling of his son and wife had taken their toll. She understood how the drinking—the favored love of the hard-hitting, drunken man—sealed the family's doom.

***

She and her husband had discussed the lack of discipline of the boy, both acknowledging each had been lax. Sam knew he'd been the weaker of the two and admitted as much. It wasn't in him to discipline the boy and on the rare occasion when he did, he would sneak a fatherly hug, his way of apologizing to the boy without saying the words. Rose knew the man she married could never be the hard man his father was. She understood her husband feared his father's uncaring ways had tainted his own blood and that the first harsh words with his son would be the first of many—and he would spiral down a short path to becoming a man much like the father he despised.

The boy was head-strong and opinionated—characteristics Sam both admired and despised. And the cycle had grown—a command, or well-intended criticism directed at the boy often brought a stubborn refusal from his son. At first, it was adorable to see the child cross his arms, stamp his feet and shake his head in defiance. As he grew Thaddeus learned to use those things as weapons. The boy needed discipline, the purchase of the stallion proof enough of that.

There was no nearby college that could provide the discipline which Thaddeus had not received at home. The Virginia Military Institute could and would be hard on the boy, but he needed direction and firmness in order to become the mature young man which he thought he was.

In the library, sitting in front of his father, counting on his mother's support, Tad argued that ten years of reading, writing and doing numbers was enough.

"No thank you," he answered to college.

His mother turned to him, a strained expression on her face. It pained her to say, "Did you not hear your father? He and I are both in agreement."

The young man sagged, defeated. Without his mother, he'd lost.

Her next words were the hardest she'd ever spoken to her son. "I was not sure if I wanted you to go off to school, especially one as far away as Virginia, but after that stunt you pulled," referring to the purchase of the black stud, and that, only one of many recently, "you're going and you are not to argue with us about it."

Chapter Seven: The fall of Eighteen and fifty-seven. The entitled one sees life as it really is.

A boy, the son of privilege, spoiled and arrogant, found himself under the grand entrance of the large building—flanked on the one side by his father and on the other, his mother. The expression on his face was one of determination—as were those of his parents. He'd have no part of this place nor of the dandies, dressed in their pretty dark blue wool uniforms and saluting at anything that moved, and generally acting the fool, he thought. He'd figure a way out, or maybe get expelled by acquiring a long list of demerits. He'd make himself unwelcome somehow. And he didn't care how. Out was out and out meant home. He'd do whatever it took to be expelled from a school he did not even want to attend. Something so crude even his father's wealth and good name could never convince the old codgers who ran the place to allow him re-entry.

Upon arrival in Lexington, his mother and father escorted Thaddeus Samuel Biggs into Professor Thomas J. Jackson's office. The lad jerked his shoulder from beneath his father's firm hand and slouched into the couch before being invited to do so by the stern looking man on the far side of the desk.

The glower on his youthful face was nothing new to the teacher—he'd seen it all—the determined scowl, and that look of *not me, I'm out'ta here*. He'd seen the frayed nerves and the red blush of color on the faces of parents who knew the reason their young sons behaved so. Thaddeus' mother and father, like the others, were embarrassed because of their need for others to do for them what they had been unable to do themselves. And that was to make a man out of the boy.

When spoken to, the young man would not answer, or if at all, he mumbled only basic grunts or indecipherable monosyllabic answers meant to offend.

The professor expected courtesy but received none, nor was he surprised. His age alone entitled him to respect from those younger than he, and especially those entrusted to his charge. A few questions designed to draw the boy into further discussion failed and again he saw the blush rise upon the cheeks of the newest set of parents in front of him. But respect would come and in abundance.

He knew Samuel Biggs and his wife from previous meetings and thought they were good people. But in Sam he saw the odd mixture of a doting father and the beginning of a fierce determination to be a father, a guide to his son. In that, he had Sam down pat. The missus was another issue. She was quiet and said little, but when she spoke, he saw a woman who said enough to let others know she was not to be trifled with either. He thought the two made a good team, husband and wife, but they both seemed equally incapable of being firm with the impudent and scowling young man sitting between them.

He studied the boy. The Social Studies course, one of many he taught, described impudence as generally an act; a carefully planned and exaggerated rudeness and lack of respect to the parents usually. Such had been his experience as a teacher and Thaddeus Samuel Biggs was the reigning king of impudence.

"Young man," he said. "This attitude of yours is going to end right now. You're dismissed."

Sam and Rose looked at Professor Jackson, the man who'd promised them Thaddeus would be allowed to attend the Institute. They doubted their decision to enroll the beloved child in an institute which demanded such harsh discipline from its teachers. The insolent young man sat still, staring at and challenging the professor. The professor stared back.

"Cadet Morgan," shouted the professor. A young man wearing a blue uniform, pants, and blazer trimmed in dark blue stripes stepped through the door. Upon entering the room the Captain at Arms turned to face the Professor, snapped to attention and saluted.

"Sir?"

"Mr. and Mrs. Biggs. You too, boy," he said, snapping his finger at the brooding young man. "Hey. You.' And snapped again. "It starts right now. Cadet Morgan, take this young man from the room. I find his presence disruptive and disrespectful. Throw him in the hole."

Thaddeus' head shot up. A look of surprise shadowed his face. As the startled eyes moved from the professor to the cadet, the teacher watched the boy's reaction. He raised his palms from the table in such a manner as to caution his parents to say nothing.

The cadet stepped behind Tad, ready to guide him from the room.

"On your feet." Thaddeus, at a loss for words and with his decision to be a rebel beginning to fail him, stood.

"March."

Turning to Sam, Professor Jackson asked, "Do you think I was harsh just now?"

"Seems a bit to me," answered the boy's father.

"In your letter just received, did you not say he'd just bought a splendid stud and without your approval?" asked the professor.

"Yes."

"And what was your response?"

"Mad at first, but I could see he had his heart set on that horse. So I gave in to him."

"Did you hear what you just said? Since you won't, I'm going to see to your son. Tell him how life works." Standing to leave he told his first lie, a well intended half-truth. "He'll not be allowed to see you when you leave. Don't ask. It won't happen." He stood to leave, but turned back to the shocked parents before him. "The Virginia Military Institute has harsh requirements. You were told of all of them. I'll be gone for a half hour. You and your wife have time to think. But the first answer I need to hear when I return is why you brought him here. A half hour."

***

"So? Why is Thaddeus here? Is it because of his horse?"

"Partly. That was the last straw, I think. He knew I, we'd, be mad but he did it anyway. Bought that horse knowing it was no where near riding. The stable man said the horse had a wild nature, but its spirit had been broken and it could easily be ridden, but said a full grown man ought to finish the breaking."

"So, you're saying the horse had a youthful spirit. He was wild, rambunctious, in further need of maturing?"

"Yes."

"Mr. Biggs. Mrs. Biggs. I'm not much of a dancer, so let's quit with the dancing. The horse is just that, a horse. It's the boy who has a youthful spirit. He's arrogant and immature. You've let him roam free. It took a wild horse to show you a boy gone wild. That's why he's here. That's why most of these young men are here. They can't be controlled. I'll break his spirit but I won't wreck him. When he leaves he'll exceed your expectations. They always do," and then he finally smiled. "Now Cadet Morgan will take you and the missus to see your son. I ask only that you do not lie to him. I know I said you would not be able to see him before you left. That was for your son's benefit, not yours. He needs to know life was not created for his benefit alone. Do not tell him everything will be alright, even though it will be. For now, and this is important, he must start thinking. When you leave it is important that he feels lost.

"Cadet Morgan."

The two turned as the young Captain at Arms entered the room and briskly snapped to attention.

"Take Mr. and Mrs. Biggs to say goodbye to their son."

***

One week later Tad dropped a letter into the slot next to the provost's office door, and immediately dreaded doing it. It was full of childish rants and, the irony of it, proved he really was where he belonged.

"There's some mail come for you, Missus," said Holt, pointing at the stand by the door. The pale sky-blue envelope, bordered in a dark blue frame, on which were emblazoned the words Virginia Military Institute was handed by Holt to Rose.

Recognizing the letter she said, "Go tell Mr. Biggs Tad has written."

"Yes'm," replied the house servant.

Dear Mother and Father,

It hasn't happened yet. I still do not like it here. And I have resolved myself to not like it at all. Why can't I come back and go to a school closer to home? I still don't understand why you chose a military school as a place for me to get an education.

If you spent one night, not to mention the past month here as I have, knowing you Father, you would have already told those teachers and especially that very strange Professor Jackson where he could hitch his horse.

You said I needed direction. Well Father, I get plenty of that here. Everybody except the Plebes, and that includes the upperclassmen and every single teacher, Professors, or whatever those old men want to be called, spend the day shouting orders and directions at us new fellows. A first year plebe like me can't even walk down the hall without one of the cadets or professors shouting 'To the left . . to the right . . . stand up . . . sit down . . . or their all-time favorite, 'against the wall, Plebe' or some such foolishness. If someone other than another plebe tells me to stop writing, even though the only time I can write is during the morning mess, I got to do it. I'm about ready to take orders from the school's mascot. That old mutt's been here forever. Reckon that makes him my boss, too. You and Mother probably had to scratch his chin when you came up here . . . seems that's all he lives for.

I want to come home, but I promised both of you I'd try . . . that I'd stay the first full term. But, Father, for the record, I made that promise under duress. And as usual, there's no getting around you.

That Professor Jackson you put so much stock in is an odd bird. Did you know that when you gave me, your only son, *the son that loves you, to him? I'll write more about him when I get a chance or can hide from the "Uppers." That's what the upperclassmen are called behind their backs—but we got to call them "Cadets" when we speak to them, which we can't do unless they say we can. How's that for a conundrum? That probably doesn't mean much to folks who've never been exiled to a military prison like me.*

Well, mess is almost over. Here they come, right on schedule, shouting orders, grinning like pigs, and having a gay old time of it, too. If one of us plebes smiles back at them, or says a single word, we get to pull weeds along the drives on Saturdays, or maybe polish cannon until the glare blinds us, or if we're having a really good day, we can whitewash the privies; now, there's grand fun. I had to wash that mutt two days ago. Oh yes Father, this is a fine place.

I'll write more when I get the chance, but that might not be until I graduate into the Cadet ranks. Or maybe, I'll be home by then—kicked out by that strange old man. Sorry about the coffee stain, it's crowded at my table.
Love you Mother. Father you are finally back to Like a lot.

Your son,
Plebe Thaddeus Samuel Biggs
P. S. How's Thunder doing?

***

  As a youth he'd known he could have his way with his father, that he could manipulate him—play him like a fiddle. But his mother, now there had been one hell of a surprise. No way did he expect her to side with his father over such an issue. She'd always been his savior, the one who'd always seen things the right way—his way. If only he could turn back the clock.

  In less than twenty-four hours his world had imploded with a simple act of his father ripping the end from a pale blue envelope.

  The trip from Carlton County to the Institute was no longer an idle threat, or the joke he believed it to be at first. There was no way his mother and father would send him from home to what he considered practically a foreign land. But once inside the hallowed walls, reality had begun to sink in. The first thing he learned was a plebe was nothing, lower that dirt with four years waiting on him.

He, like all the cadets, despised their teachers, and he especially disliked Professor Jackson. But the man was different than the others. He carried a sense of right and wrong with him and one of fairness. The man was quick to publicly correct a wayward act and quicker, yet, to praise a good act.

Once he got to know him, Tad couldn't help but like the Professor. True, the middle-aged man did often act strange in the class room, but he certainly did not deserve to be called "Tom Fool," not behind his back like he'd heard some of the cadets, the reckless ones especially, do a lot of times. He'd never done it himself, thought of doing it once or twice, but that wasn't in him. He never once joined the others as they called him "Tom Fool."

Occasionally, he felt and saw a hardness about the man, somewhat akin to that which a killer might exude. Or a simple act of kindness, consoling a student he'd moments before scolded, or inviting cadets and plebes alike to join he and his wife for Sunday dinners in hopes of easing their homesickness. He saw the man was well liked and much respected by his peers, in spite of his strange tics and mood swings.

In passing conversations, *plebes exaggerating lies and gossip*, he reasoned, Tad learned the professor encouraged and sponsored reading classes for the area's Negro children. As many did, Tad too wondered, what had the man been thinking? How could he not know State law forbade teaching slave children. In general, the town folk accepted the man's strange behavior, but using the whites-only church in which to teach black children was where they drew the line. Others praised his Christian act of love when he sponsored, and paid for with his own funds, the reading classes in the basement of the Negroe's Presbyterian Church at the edge of town.

Even stranger, in addition to Artillery and War Maneuvers, were the other classes Professor Jackson taught at the school—Natural Philosophy, and the new Science of Optics. "What are they?"

the plebes asked, as did many of the cadets. He, the balance of his classmates, and some of the Cadets, if not all of them—were confused by the differing assortment of courses taught by the man. They, along with the school's regents, soon learned the man was woefully unqualified to teach any of those courses, with the exception of Artillery. In that course, he was truly a "Teacher." A painting of him, dressed in a Major's uniform and fighting Mexicans decades before, hung in the entry hall.

Tad was greatly interested in the man's past. He was obviously not a fool. He watched the strange acting professor, and studied him as if he were a lesson to be learned.

***

Tad sat at his desk, and with his crude graphite pencil scratched imaginary battle scenes on lined beige paper. He, along with the other plebes, the "newbies," or "babies" as they were sometimes called, stood at attention when Professor Thomas J. Jackson walked into the room. The man walked past them, his shoulders stooped, with his loaded arms diminishing his stature, and paid scant attention to the new class of plebes. Instead, he eyed the lemons, hawkishly counting them—a day's supply cradled in the crook of his arm. He dropped the books and the day's lessons upon his immaculately clean desktop and carefully pyramided the lemons.

Tad's jaw locked. Lemons affected him that way. He could hardly bear to watch as Professor Jackson cut a lemon into quarters and sucked at the acidic fruit. Tad's mouth puckered, his teeth hurt. With the remaining lemons cut into wedges, and stacked within easy reach, the professor stood and walked to the classroom slate. As the chalk dusted his fingers, the slate screeched "September 15th, 1858 until 1862, or until . . .." And he sucked at a lemon wedge again. Facing the students, he closed his eyes and slightly angled his head, looking as if he were studying the nature of lemons. A look of sublime enjoyment brightened his face. His eyes still closed, he lifted his left arm and bent it at the elbow, pointing his opened hand towards the ceiling. With his right, he crossed his chest and supported the bent elbow. He remained quiet and still, the cadets all thinking him asleep until a small tight smile broke upon his face. The class watched, pondering his strange behavior as his eyes rolled back in ecstasy. Holding the wedge aloft he said, "Ah. That's better. Helps my blood circulate; one of my arms is shorter than the other.

"Some of your friends didn't make it past me last year—others just barely," he stated simply and matter-of-factly. "So tell me, did you slackers figure out what you want to do this year?" His eyes had still not fallen to the level of the seated students. "Most of you are brand new. Newbies, babies. That doesn't make you special, just new," he said to the first-year students as he stood. "Or do you understand the nature of Artillery? They protect. They kill. You want to live or die?" He slapped the desk and the students jumped. "You slack off in this class, I'll dismiss your little baby asses as promptly as I did some of you the first time around. If given a second chance, and that being my decision, no one else's, if you slack off again, you're headed home to mama. While you're dragging you suitcases, I'll kick your scrawny little asses through the arches myself."

His eyes had now found theirs and burned into them. "I don't ever want to see a one of you laying dead on a battlefield, not one of my battlefields, shot through the stomach by Master George over there," he said, pointing at no one, pointing at everyone. "Or blown to hell and back, pieces scattered across the field because one of your mates stuffed too much powder down the barrel. Dead because somebody slacked off. You new boys, you Plebes, ask those second-timers how quick I was to send them home to their mamas. Don't follow my rules—home to mama. Show disrespect for me or the staff, or anyone older than you—even that dog Ralph—even he's older than you, it's back home to mama."

Again he sucked at the wedge. A drip of clear juice fell, glistening, into his beard. Tad's teeth hurt.

"You're mine, now. Newbie's, ha," he snorted, sounding disgusted. "What a bunch of babies. Still got your nanny's soap behind your ears. But you're my babies until you leave this class. Might be four years, might be tomorrow. When . . . depends on you."

Tad had heard the man suffered from the occasional fit of stuttering. He'd never heard the professor stutter, only the exaggerated and mean-spirited 'Ta . . .Ta . . .Tom Fu . . . Fu . . . Fool' of those who dared mock the man behind his back. Secretly, he hoped to never hear it. It seemed to him the man suffered enough maladies and such ridicules were immature and unchristian. He did note that on some days Professor Jackson's pattern of speech seemed overly sharp, crisp and mechanical, as if each word was being worked hard before being uttered.

***

Professor Jackson drug a finger down the list of his student's names, looking, and finally settling on a choice, he stood, walked to the window, and closed the thick curtains. The room became dark. He called out, "Master Thaddeus Biggs? Which one of you little boys is Plebe Thaddeus?"

The harsh command frightened Thaddeus. He stood at attention and cautiously answered, " Sir."

"You hate your mother for giving you that name?"

"Used to, Sir."

"Over it yet?"

"Yes Sir. Mostly."

From the room came youthful tittering ceased as Professor Jackson looked from student to student and then back to Thaddeus.

"Plebe Thaddeus. Are you a trustworthy man?"

"Yes Sir. I am."

"I am leaving the class in your charge. I'll be absent for a few minutes. None of you are allowed to leave your seats. Do not do it. No going to the privy. No water. No nothing. You new fellows are about to receive your first artillery lesson. You slackers might think you know where I'm off to. So no talking, no passing notes. Keep your mouths shut. Much will depend upon what you do in my absence." He turned back to Tad, "Plebe Biggs, I turn the class over to you."

"Sir. Yes Sir," Tad said.

The class already quiet, became quieter than the inside of a closed coffin. Not even the shuffle of a boot on the floor, nor the soft whispery turn of a page was heard. There were no jokes, no "Tom Fools" mumbled. Only a quiet and eerie silence.

A deafening explosion rattled the exterior wall, shook the shutters and danced the curtains. Dust jumped from undusted edges of the wood trims around the window. The plebes collapsed sideways from their desks and, scrambling behind them, sought shelter. The pressure in the room popped eardrums which quickly returned to normal.

With the command to stay seated now destroyed, the plebes hunched in fear, rose onto their knees, and slowly stood erect. Voices began to void the other rule: stay quiet.

"Lightning?" more than one asked.

Others responded, "Ain't no lightning that loud."

They stood their spots, afraid to venture from the room.

Into the room stepped Professor Jackson. "That was the sound of killing and being killed," said Professor Jackson as he stood in the opened doorway. The light from the hall magnified his height and his width, and the fear felt of the man. "You'll learn to love that sound. You hear that sound, it means you're not dead."

Feeling embarrassed, the plebes and those repeating their failed first year pulled at the desks, setting them aright, and gratefully slid onto the attached seats.

The professor began laughing gleefully. "You slackers thought the upperclassmen were going to haul you out'ta here, didn't you? Haze you with their belts like they did last spring, right? Got you again, didn't I?

"Crowd by the windows. You'll see your schooling for the next four years."

Tad and the rest of the plebes, now knowing the secret their professor hid from them, had mixed emotions. Each confident that only lightning striking within feet of the building could have made the noise, stared at the short-barreled mountain Howitzer, its barrel exhaling wispy tendrils of blue-gray smoke, the ground below the yoke gouged deep from the recoil. The big brass gun was surrounded by a sharply dressed Artillery Company of upperclassmen, each standing stone-like and at attention, saluting the flag flying above them.

Tad thought it unnecessary for Professor Jackson to ask, "If I told those men to turn that Howitzer on you, would they?"

Tad alone answered, "Yes Sir. I do believe they would."

Chapter Eight: Eighteen and sixty-one. Into the horn of plenty.

A warrior he was. A warrior of man—a warrior of God. A strange life—that killing he did. A blessed life—the conversion of evil men to God he practiced. Eccentric, yet well thought of. He'd seen Mexican children, after a cannonade, bleed out as they lay spread face down on the red clay yard in front of the family's hacienda and stepped over them as if they were no more than logs ready to be cut up for the coming cold night. And then pick up a kitten, new to life, and put it in his uniform pocket. He sought knowledge of all things. To learn was his life's obligation. He lashed himself when he errantly said a swear word or birthed a vile thought. Yet, on the battlefield he swore vehemently when prayer and heavenly guidance were needed the most. He was a professor and taught war, yet he was a deacon in the Presbyterian church. He was a contradiction. He was an oddity.

Thirty-six years old, the heavily bearded man, his forehead high and slightly slanted, hairline receding, sat on the front porch and stared at the grass in the yard. The small lawn in front of his two-story brick home in Lexington, Virginia was dying, struggling with the final throes of an imminent death from the summer heat. Thomas Jonathan Jackson sat reflecting upon his past—a life filled with conflict and contradiction. In a former time he'd been a warrior during the Mexican War. And in that warrior resided an inconsistency—he was a meek man, one who believed praise was something due others but wished none for himself. He was keenly aware that those often repeated larger-than-life tales of his acts of bravery and of his innate abilities to lead men into battle, had made him a legend from Mexico to the Canadian border.

The man was of two hearts, one for the state of Virginia and one for his God and knew there is no room in the soul of any man for such divisive issues, one at odds with the other. He often wondered if the wars of his past would hinder his entrance into Heaven. He prayed his acts of Godliness would allow it.

His new wife Mary Anna . . . a garden . . . a house filled with children were about the extent of things it took to make him happy. He sought a deaconship in the Presbyterian Church of Lexington, Virginia. And when approved, he prayed it was his God granting him a life with no more of the bloodletting of war.

As rumors raged of coming troubles—the talk of the South's decision to break ties with the Union—he found his heart in a tug of war again. His life had been about the Union and the existence of the United States of America. But of late, it seemed that the Union was testing the entirety of all its people, those north and south of the Mason-Dixon line. He saw an argument growing within both sides—men who wished to preserve the United States intact and men who wished to dissolve it.

He saw men willing to argue, but none willing to compromise. At night he awoke from the flood of Mexican-War nightmares filled with crying, dying men and smells of the rot of death. He spoke of the new war—the one coming—with his wife Mary Anna, and often he could not return to sleep. He believed the South was within its rights to separate itself from the Union, but once separated, he did not think it could last. He prayed if it did come to a war between the South and the North, its outcome would be long-lasting and far superior to whichever new government survived, if indeed either did. In those previous wars in which he had fought, an excess of life was used up and the wealth of the country spent. A new country would demand much of its citizens but afterwards the money and men, both, would be gone. Still, he feared the demise of the Union loomed not far in the distance.

To him, the Constitution was a rock-hard thing—something written in stone, unbreakable, unbending, indestructible. It was to him a thing which could not be altered without the consent of the people. And now, the Constitution he'd lived by was being challenged. As in all struggles, the challenge would either be won or lost. There was no room for a compromise without an agreement of the people, and the Constitution had limited federal power. It did not have full power over that strange but popular institution favored by the Southland—slavery.

He believed the Federal government, without amendment to the existing constitutional law, could not demand slavery be voided, or do so without an expressed approval of all its citizens. That same law had no right to interfere with the desire of those who did favor slavery. A long-lived portion found in that revered document granted to each state, north and south, east and west, the right to govern itself. A conundrum he called it. In order to survive, the states had to cling to their rights and if forced, try to destroy the Union or preserve it. A conundrum, indeed.

Now a teacher, no longer a warrior, he relied on his God. With his fervent Christian upbringing, he had long ago freed the slaves he and his family owned. Many of those freed men elected to stay on the family plantation, but he paid those in the same coinage he paid the white hired-on workers.

His neighbors thought him a man at odds with them—most of whom owned huge plantations and many slaves. Some thought him traitorous to the State of Virginia which allowed the buying and selling of human flesh. But he never counseled them to buy or sell the Negro and his refusal to express his opinions confused them. He avoided miring himself into drawn-out conversations of slavery. He knew voicing his opinion would have confused some and angered others. He believed if the North wanted the enslaved Negro free, that was a choice they either had to live with or act upon. And likewise, if the South was determined to keep their slaves toiling in the fields, that was their decision. Right a wrong or further an evil—a hard decision, that. He feared greatly a war was on its way and it would not be like any other fought on American soil.

As with some of the existing laws, he took issue with many of Virginia's state laws, laws adopted by men. He refused to abide by Virginia's laws against educating Negroes and taught slave children to read in the basement of the Negro Presbyterian Church near the outskirts of Lexington, Virginia—the expenses which were incurred, he covered. Teaching was in his blood.

Although a graduate of West Point, he was offered and accepted a professorship at Virginia Military Institute in the sleepy foothill town of Lexington, located in the Blue Ridge Mountains of western Virginia. His prayer to be shed of war and bloodletting was not long-lived.

***

At the outbreak of hostilities between the North and the newly-established Confederate States of America, Jefferson Davis summoned the thirty-seven year old legend to the Executive Offices located in Montgomery, Alabama. Upon his President's request, the soldier-turned-teacher relinquished his long held position of Professor of Artillery and a series of other lesser classes which he taught at the Virginia Military Institute, and girthed himself with the utilities of war.

Alongside the General, and into what both thought to be little more than a momentary break in their unfinished education, rode the newly appointed Captain Thaddeus Samuel Biggs, the best Artilleryman the professor had ever taught. With the Governor of Virginia's permission, the Brigadier General, an honorary title bestowed upon him after the Mexican War, Thomas J. Jackson was followed into the Shenandoah valley by many of the same young men he had been teaching at the famed institution.

During his four years as a student of Professor Jackson, Thaddeus Samuel Biggs, although young and recently appointed Captain of Artillery, had himself proved to be a leader of men. The teacher felt the young student qualified because of his marksmanship with the massive cannon and his rapport with the young plebes and cadets.

Simply stated, General Jackson wanted the young Captain with him. Therefore, the appointment of Thaddeus Biggs to Captain of Artillery was a precondition of his own acceptance of the proffered commission of General.

General Jackson's mission was not to march into a hotly contested land, its battlefields already filled with fire, smoke, blood, and death. He and his cadets, although few in number, were sent to impress upon the North the Confederate Army's might and their devotion to support the South's cause. To a man, each knew the importance of the valley. It was the South's food basket, a rich land overflowing with the good things of nature. Only if it survived the ravages of the war, could the Confederacy survive and they were intent upon keeping the valley as their own.

After a year of dreadful battles and mounting losses, the blue clad Union began to think of their own needs and sought to rape the Shenandoah Valley of its riches. They reasoned a pillaged land would become too poor to recover, thence of no value to the Confederacy.

The arrival and presence of General Jackson and his command proved consoling to the valley's citizens. He realized the task assigned to him would be difficult. The land was beleaguered. It was beginning to show a different wear and tear of war. It had by now supplied an excess of men—fathers and husbands, young, middle-aged, and all farmers.

***

His mission proved successful but things rapidly changed. In August, eighteen and sixty-one, General Thomas J. Jackson was promoted from his honorary position of Brigadier General to Major General of the Army of the Confederate States of America, and handed a new directive—"Leave immediately for Harpers Ferry."

As the year began to fade a sinister but expected threat began to be rumored from the east. Between the Shenandoah Valley and the white-doomed buildings of Washington, D.C., the nerve center of the North's war machine, lay the peaceful mountainside village of Harpers Ferry. The foothills surrounding the small town gave way to an anomaly of inaccessible and rugged mountains. Harpers Ferry was considered a fortress, built in a strategic point and desired by both the Union and Confederate army.

The spit of land at the base of a hill to the east jutted into the Potomac River proved to be a convenient ferry landing for shallow draft boats and barges heading east and west. The small city was war torn and fractured. Its disarray of buildings, still held desperately to the steep hillside, while others of lesser quality and care of detail fought a constant battle with the pull of gravity.

Bolivar, a stone's throw west of Harpers Ferry, occupied a much higher position and the huge brick buildings upon it served as an artillery base for the Union army.

If ever a town begged to be fortified with men and weapons, it was this coveted little village. But all was not as one thought of the scenic and idyllic town. Within it lay the remains of the U.S. Military Armory. The huge building had been burned to the ground by the Northern Army after word of the South's arrogant act of secession from The United States of America was received. Proof of its existence, the brick foundation lay collapsed and in ruins. The abandoned machinery, the smelters, the forges—the iron and steel alone represented a great value for the South. The railway had been destroyed along with the simple bridges; the village was cut off from points north and east, south and west. The North did not need the armory, but certainly did not want the armory and the damaged machinery, the tons of iron and steel, to be melted down and re-poured into weapons of war to benefit the renegade Confederates.

Recognizing the value of Harpers Ferry, it quickly became a focal point of the Yankees and they raced back to the village they had attempted to burn to the ground with hopes of reclaiming it. But their attempts to halt the Confederacy's approach from the west failed. The rails from the north, the bridges—everything was destroyed by the Union in a vain attempt to keep the rebels from gaining possession of the hillside town and the plateau village of Bolivar nestled above it.

Jefferson Davis and his cabinet depended on Major General Thomas J. Jackson and his soldiers to use an unguarded route from the west to take and hold Bolivar Heights, the small area above Harpers Ferry.

***

While riding an army-issued and war-ravaged horse, the Major General first saw the reddish brown horse which he felt would be a good fit for his wife, the loving and gentle woman he'd married four years earlier. The farmer he bought it from told General Jackson the horse's name was Fancy. Seeing the animal was ill-named, the General decided the horse, any horse, deserved a better name, and that the farmer must have had one hell of a sense of humor.

As he studied the horse, the words "ugly" and "ungainly" crossed the General's mind. Even though others thought the mare an unwise investment, he believed the animal had possibilities. But it was the gentle manner in which the diminutive horse with the inquisitive dark brown eyes stood near him and nuzzled his arm, vying for his attention, which made the General reach for his wallet.

While awaiting an opportunity to deliver Fancy to his wife, the General began to ride it daily in order to break it to the saddle and further its already easy-going nature. But the Commanding Officer, who could have the pick of any horse in his army, found the mare easy to ride and responsive to his reins and softly whispered orders.

Growing tired of hearing the occasional snicker after calling his mount Fancy, he decided to give it a warrior's name, but somehow the steed became known as "Little Sorrel" instead.

Thusly, the horse became a part of him and a big part of his life.

Little Sorrel met his requirements, so guiltily, he reneged on his promise to give the horse to his wife and bought her a replacement—it, too, a gentle animal.

Through the back streets of Sharpsburg, a full days march north of Bolivar, and into the fields filled with corn and wheat, General Lee was entangled in the bloodiest battle he'd ever fought. He desperately needed help. From Sharpsburg came an urgent plea from General Lee. General Jackson left a small contingency of his men in Harpers Ferry to finish the battle, to see to the wounded, both Yankee and Confederate, and corral the balance of the Union prisoners.

Leaving the men he could spare, he ordered them to create havoc—throw everything they had at the enemy that might appear in his absence, and to stash weapons and ammunition throughout the woods alongside the enemy's approaches. "Stall them as long as possible," he said. "Scatter your guns, as many as you can carry, from place to place. Hide them close to the roads they have to come after you on. Kill as many of them as you can. Then catch up with us. You'll find us. There's a stream to the east of Sharpsburg—Antietam, it's called. Come as quickly as you can."

Chapter Nine: Eighteen and sixty-two. Early summer. Seven days fighting. Six nights chasing.

A far away battle is still too near. Generally, infantrymen felt that way. But a leader, a good leader, could make his men look forward to doing battle. General Jackson, anxious to be in the fray disagreed any battle was too far. The men could turn tail and run, casting their arms and their new country aside. He would shout and swear at those who might, thereby ignoring his promise to his wife and himself that he would not offend his Heavenly Savior. But none would flee, he knew that. Instead, such was their faith in him they would set the pace of which he would follow.

As for Little Sorrel, what else could be said? Little Sorrel was an ugly horse.

The long column of the Confederate infantry shimmered and danced in the rising thermals of the early July morning. The distance of those who emerged from the heavy woods of White Oak Swamp reminded the soldiers awaiting the soon arrival of the head of a snake crawling from its den. The butter-nut colored serpent grew greatly in size as General Jackson's men approached, and the slithering body snaked through building clouds of dust. The soldiers were a tired and dirty lot.

As officers rode alongside the column and shouted commands, General Jackson swayed to and fro, neither asleep nor awake, atop Little Sorrel. The mare adjusted her gait, careful to not spill her load. Born to the saddle, "Old Stonewall," as his men called him since Second Manassas, held tightly to the saddle's pommel. The sun was centered overhead—time for what remained of their meager rations of hardtack and salt pork. The great man was unaware of the crossroad they were approaching.

Little Sorrel held her gait carefully. To the infantry, it seemed she knew what to expect of her rider. Her ears were always slanted backward, listening for a soft word, the click of the General's tongue, a light tug of the reins, or the slightest touch of the spur. The mare was not much to look at, and with the exception of the man napping in the saddle, she would have been just another horse and hardly worthy of note. Some called her downright ugly—others said she looked more like a mule than horse. But such things were never said within hearing of Little Sorrel's rider. She stood fourteen hands from the ground to her withers—not very large, and barely meeting the standards required for an officer's mount, especially considering the rank of and the high esteem in which the heroic man upon her back was held. She was ill-proportioned, her chest narrow and weak. Her rump, conversely, was overly wide and heavily muscled. Her rear legs seemed shorter than the front, and made the rider look as if continually leaning forward.

In reality, her size was more in keeping with the smaller horses used by cavalrymen. Those men needed quick and nimble mounts to fight the swift in and out required of swords and close contact, and cavalrymen tended to be small men, thus lighter.

Even after a long night's rest, each new march for Little Sorrel was started with her neck sagging and head hanging low. She never seemed fresh or well rested—never quiet up to her task. From the distance, one would have thought carrying the tall, rail-thin man would have wrecked the animal.

With or without a rider, her gait was a contradiction, that of premeditated and cautious steps, yet her hooves were always well planted. Her thin skull was slightly misshapen and made Little Sorrel's ears appear more of a donkey's than a horse. First impressions, she appeared to be a farm horse, one broken to the plow, and worked from dawn to dusk. A sparsely covered and mottled reddish-brown skin stretching across the body gave it the appearance she was never brushed or curried.

But General Jackson loved the mare. He found her gait never changed, except with the occasional trot. Her cautiousness of foot he needed, since he was often found reading maps and writing orders while in the saddle, and had little time for the road beneath. He trusted Little Sorrel to see to his well being.

***

Thomas J. Jackson awoke with a start. He'd timed his nap well. He cared deeply for the men marching with him and for that he was perhaps the most beloved General in all of the Army of the Confederate States of America.

Orders were given voice and his men fell out and ate the tiresome, monotonous rations.

Stonewall was everything Little Sorrel was not—at first glance, an odd pairing, the two. At six foot three, he was one of the tallest officers in the Confederacy. A year earlier, and not far from the White Oak Swamp to the east of Richmond which they had only now marched out of, many of the men standing before him had fought in the first battle at Manassas to the southwest of Washington.

The Northern Army had been badly defeated during the second battle fought near the creek thereafter to be known as Bull Run by the Northern army. It was on the sloping battlefield that General Jackson earned the moniker of "Stonewall" while sitting on the undersized horse, refusing to give an inch to the killers from the North. General Jackson, promoted to Major General after Second Manassas, did not much take to his new rank and thought such good things should be bestowed upon those who really deserved them.

As the men finished their noon meal, without orders to do so, they began to reform their respective units. There was much that had to be done. Rumors were McClellan and the Army of the Potomac were preparing to attack yet again, and that the Northern General had advanced his infantry towards the direction from which the rebels would approach. Orders were given to report to General Jackson any activity of that nature. To the southeast, atop a hill, cannon were positioned in long lines and waited for battle. This much General Jackson had garnered from men he had ordered forward to find the enemy.

***

The stink of brackish and stagnant water, the ghostly swaying of Spanish moss hanging profusely from cypress trees, the slithering water moccasin's racing across a road more mud than packed dirt were now behind them and White Oak Swamp a thing of the past. Little Sorrel remained jittery, nervous, as the noises of war rumbled from the distance. The occasional boom of guns set her skin to trembling, but not as often as before. She was now a warhorse.

The General pitied his worn-out soldiers and Little Sorrel, but he knew he had his orders—confusing as they were. Worse yet, he was lost. But he dared not confess such a thing to his men. He knew they wanted to overtake the blue-clad "Billy Boys" they had chased from the Swamp. They wanted to prove their mettle to their General, so he would not give them reason to slow their chase. He would allow them to chase a bit longer but eventually they would have to break off from the pursuit and leave for the battle building upon Malvern Hill, *wherever Malvern Hill is*, he wondered, and destroy the remains of the Army of the Potomac, and its commander, the young and cocky General George B. McClellan.

***

The egomaniacal Commander of the Army of the Potomac, General George McClellan, had been given the directive by the Northern War Department to destroy the Confederacy's capitol city, Richmond, Virginia. Brigadier General Thomas J. Jackson, as Lee's field commander, was given orders to save the city.

General Jackson thought McClellan's strategy of fighting and running an unusual one, but that was how the Yankee commander had fought thus far. There was no rhyme or reason for many of the things the prideful man did. In addition, during almost all of the previous battles, General McClellan had fought half-heartedly, as if on guard, expecting to be overrun at any moment by an uncountable mass of Confederate soldiers which he always thought about to rush his position.

General Jackson knew the man, in reality, always held back in reserves more men than he placed upon the battlefield, errantly believing the confusing and often incorrect statistics he received from the Pinkertons, the security agency he used to keep tabs on the size and whereabouts of the Confederate Army. But Jackson was always outnumbered, while McClellan's fear of being vastly out-manned made him hold back men in reserve. Being misinformed, yet again, of the true count of the enemy, McClelland was anxious to flee south to safer, and perhaps for better grounds from which to fight.

And so the week-long battle continued, each army killing, butchering the other. "Yankees" fleeing into the night—Rebels chasing them thru the dark. The past week had been spent in a series of running skirmishes; days filled with war and killing—nights depleted in an almost fruitless, yet bloody chase of fleeing Yankees. Jackson learned the hard fought and deadly series of running skirmishes— large and small, had already earned a name—the Battle of Seven Pines, or was it Seven Days?

The General had heard it called both, but thought Seven Pines more likely the real name since the series of battles started at a small crossroads to the north of Mechanicsville, not from where they now tugged at mud-choked cannon.

Six nights were now a part of history and the seventh day of the running battle began to grow louder and hotter as the cannon fire increased and the sun rose toward its afternoon zenith. The swamp had been a jigsaw puzzle of roads, with none of them heading in any direction shown on his map. The near recovery of three of Captain Biggs' cannon from the murky swamp and glue-like mud had taken a toll. The Yanks taken prisoner were only able to grapple the cannons, but unable to pull them from the mire, they tied them off, still submerged, to bridge pillars and trees standing by the ditch banks.

***

Little Sorrel was exhausted and battle weary, the men worn and dragging. General Jackson dismounted and led the horse behind him. He would let them rest at the farmhouse in the distance, he thought. The farm would provide much needed water for thirsty men and animals, the woods bordering the backyard could provide a respite from the growing glare of the sun.

"Whoa, little lady. Easy girl. Whoa." Major General Thomas J. Jackson spoke calmly, an effort to soothe his horse as they approached the crossroad in front of the farm house. The intersection was not named on his map, nor did that surprise him. The swamp they'd exited, a scratch of graphite pencil-wide, had deceived the army into thinking the swamp merely a creek. But the thin scribbled line had turned into a morass of watery backwash filled with mosquitoes, water-moccasins, and an unnamed maze of sinking roads, and drowning and dead cypress trees.

He wondered if General Lee knew about the poor quality of the maps produced by the topographers. He made note he should speak to the man about it when he next saw him. He turned to his horse and gently brushed her neck while beckoning an infantryman toward him.

"See that farmer over there? The one by the barn? Bring him to me."

The infantryman saluted sharply and returned with an elderly man supporting himself with a cane made from a twisted Muscatine vine.

"Good afternoon, Sir," said General Jackson. "Tell me. Did you hear any cannon firing down this way? And your name, may I ask?"

"Name's Narlz. Narlz Ericksen. Folks come over from Norway, so I been told. Pleasure to meet you," he said, extending a hand turned useless for hard work by arthritis. "I shore 'nough did, Cap'n," answered the man, his answer more mumble than words. All of the southland, Virginia being no exception, spoke with a hard to understand drawl. And the drawls varied from county to county.

The General was not offended that the elderly farmer addressed him as a "Captain." It was merely the man's way of telling him he didn't know the rank his uniform represented. And he knew the elderly man was as likely to call a private "Cap'n" as readily as he would a general. Besides, Cap'n was considered a cordial greeting in most parts of Virginia.

"We heard some, too, now and then, Mr. Ericksen, but not enough for us to get a fix on them. Which way did they come from? Where is the Poindexter's farm?"

"That cannon shootin' was coming mostly from that there way," he answered, pointing the elaborately whittled grapevine cane toward the southeast. "Cap'n, y'all musta been a whoopin' up on dem Yankees' asses real good last night. Place was a boomin' all 'round. Sum'a it sounded shore 'nough like it was close by to that

Poindexter's place you'se askin' 'bout, down that way," and pointing the cane toward the southeast, he said, "Maybe one, two miles if y'all was crows."

"Well, since we're not crows, how far is it if we decide to walk?"

"Walkin'? Bit longer. Two, three miles."

General Jackson and others thought the man entertaining, especially in light of the fact that an occasional and far off boom did vibrate the air around them.

"Which road should we take to get there?"

"Y'all got'ta go that there way fer a spell," he answered, pointing east. "Bout a mile, I reckon. Down near dem there woods. Y'all see dem trees way off yonder? Turn right on that road what's headin' souf'."

Studying the uniformed officer in front of him, the aged man pulled an antique, round eyepiece, scratched from years spent in a pocket with forgotten sand slowly ruining the once perfectly clear lens. An age-darkened leather fob fell across his white beard. "Pardon me fer askin', Cap'n," he said, studying an unfolded, dog-eared piece of print he held before him, "but ain't you that ole' Stonewall feller what were in dem papers dem Yankee fellers was ah throwin' ever which'r way when they come fast-footin' it through here this mornin? They was a gitin' rid of ever'thing they had what would hold dem up. Y'all shore put the scare of God in dem sonsabitches. I moan tell ya."

"Yes Sir." answered General Jackson, and around him he heard the soft ripple of whispers. Some thought it unusual or perhaps below a general's station, and especially a Major General's station, to "Yes Sir" or "No Sir" a lesser man, but that was the way of the General. At VMI, his fellow teachers told him he was polite to a fault. It was true, he was, but choose to consider it a compliment.

"Some folks did start calling me Stonewall after we fought at Manassas last year," he smiled at the aged man. "Heard it pretty often, actually, but I never heard nobody call me old. Compared to a few of my boys," he said, swinging his hand out and pointing at the growing number of soldiers milling around, "I reckon I am a bit long in the tooth." Dust covered faces sprouting a dozen or so dark and coarse hairs—the beginning of whiskers, belonging to boys still in their teens, stared up at him. But most were men in their twenties, and others, were older men—fathers out to earn a few dollars to help support the wives and children back home. "Some of them are young enough to call me old." He smiled at the older man, "But you're old enough to call me son. How about that?" Curious, but not wanting to show it, he asked nonchalantly, "What paper are you talking about, anyway?"

The farmer handed a tattered slip of newspaper to him.

The horse, small of stature, and he, tall and gangly, always left an indelible memory in the minds of those who'd watched the defiant act of bravery by the Major General. Unknown to Jackson, the iconic image of a tall man sitting atop a small horse had been captured on a daguerreotype picture making apparatus had already circulated through the northern and southern newspapers.

He was a celebrity and did not know it, but he'd had no time for papers. They were considered unnecessary luxuries for fighting men. He barely was able to keep up with the constant heavy flow of confusing orders and counter-orders from the Confederate capitol recently re-located in Richmond.

"Right here. Front page, Cap'n," he said, pointing at a picture of a thin, gangly man sitting upon a dark toned horse. "I can't read a lick but my wife said the letters spell out yer name."

"Well, how about that? It does look like me. I reckon that Stonewall thing must'a took. Good likeness of Little Sorrel, too, don't you think?" patting his horse's neck, again. Anxious to get back to the business of killing, he asked, "How long ago did those fellows come through here? Many of them?"

"Started 'bout daylight and they kept at it till 'bout an hour ago. They sure as hell know'd you'uns was after 'em. I weren't a countin' but I'd say 'bout two hun'ert ob' 'em. Runnin' like scairt' rabbits, I moan tell ya. Once't in a while there'd be one or two ob' 'em a huggin' the woods over yonder. They shore as hell is laying low fer now, though."

The elderly farmer studied the mud covered general as the infantry crowded round. He knew he was in the presence of the mightiest army in the entirety of the United States—his wife had read story after story to him of the might and ferociousness of the southern fighting man. So, although older than the man before him, he felt a certain protocol or respect should be shown by him. So he asked, "Cap'n Stonewall, y'all been in that there White Oak Swamp up yonder?"

"Trying to drag three cannon out of that damn mud. Shallow enough to ford, my ass," he said sarcastically, as if speaking to the soldier who'd told him the swamp was not very deep. He blushed, realizing he'd sworn in front of his men—some being the same soldiers who watched him pray each morning and before a battle began.

For a fleeting moment, he was proud that he'd been a Deacon in the Presbyterian church. But that was a different time and seemed long ago and such pride was a sinful thing. He knew some of the men called him "the Deacon" behind his back. It didn't bother him. His had been a better life with his beliefs in God, but that life was before the War Department came and got him.

"Your President wants you," was what he'd been told. But the Good Lord willing, he'd return to his position "when" and "if" he returned home. He never worried about what lay in his future. Whatever came, came. He was prepared for it. It would be the good Lord's decision anyway, not his. With a life spent watching men die while others, like himself, returned home unscathed, he'd learned only the Heavenly Father knew the answer to the when and if parts.

"What's the name of that road we came down and that one across the way?" he asked, thumbing back to the dirt road behind him and then at the macadam road on the far side of a field of tobacco.

"Well, that one y'all come down is White Oak Road. Ain't much of road though, ask me, but I reckon you know that already. Most people make an effort to stay clear ah that there swamp," he answered, and pointed at their muddied clothes and mud splattered horses. "Some people go in and that's the last you hear of 'em. Happens mor'n you might think. That one over yonder," he said pointing east and across the field, "is the Charles City road. And it goes to, well, Charles City."

"All those Yankees come running from that direction?" General Jackson asked, pointing north toward the recently crossed swamp.

"They come a'runnin' down the White Oak Road same as y'all . . . 'cept a helluva lot fas'r. I reckon most ob 'ems still at it. Runnin', I mean. I moan tell ya.

"Yes Sir. All night they come bustin' through here. Sonsabitches wrecked my cornfield and damn near stripped ever' single leaf off'a my tobacky," he said, jabbing the cane in the direction of the trampled tobacco field. "They lickety-split down that there road up yonder, the one what heads souf toward Malvern's Hill," he answered, pointing along the Charles City road. "Y'all need to go 'bout a mile and turn souf' on Old Union road, if y'alls trying to ketch up with 'em. Shoot twenty of 'em for me for stealing my corn and tear'n up my tobacky."

"You said Malvern's Hill?"

"Cap'n, sum'a the folks here 'bout call it Malvern, some say Malvern's Hill. Me, I always know'd it as Malvern's Hill cause dat's all what's there. Just a hill. Ain't even a big hill. Ain't no town. But there's a crossroad down below it."

"Thank you Sir, and your country," referring to the new Confederate States of America, "appreciates your help." General Jackson stuck his boot into the stirrup, preparing to mount Little Sorrel.

"Say, Cap'n. You'se gonna' bring that paper back to me, ain't you? The missus ain't through with it."

"Oh. Sorry," answered the General and shifting in the saddle he handed the paper to the man. "I can't see where that ugly fellow on the horse looks anything like me, but that sure is my Little Sorrel," he said stroking the sorrel's neck.

"Cap'n Stonewall, Sir. Would you pencil yer name on it?" the elderly farmer asked sheepishly, "Fer my wife, you know?"

Stonewall took the extended paper. "Yes Sir. Reluctantly, I will. I fear it is an act of vanity, but you have been of great assistance to me and my men."

"My woman thanks you. I'm moan tell ya," proffered the man. "If'n y'all wants sum', why don't y'all go on out in the cornfield and grab up sum'a that corn. Mind you, the ones on the ground only . . . just dem ears what dem Yankee fellows knocked off last night. They'll go to ruin and rot, what with all the rain we dun' had. Same with the tobacky fields. Grab up dem leaves, too. Just the ones what's on the ground. Don't go breakin' off no new ones. Gib' 'em two, three weeks to dry and y'all have sum' good smokin' tobacky all winter," and added as an afterthought, "That is if'n y'alls still fightin' that long."

"You, Sir, are a fine example of the citizenry of our new country and I thank you," the general said, smiling as he saluted Narlz Erickson.

Turning to the men, General Jackson said, "Go get what you can. You got a half hour. Then we march. On your honor and because of the kindness of your fellow citizen, Mr. Ericksen here," and pointing at the farmer he added "I give you fair warning . . . do not do an ounce of further harm to his crops."

***

He and the man continued their conversation to which the elderly man was able to add greatly to the directions in which the army needed to go. Both turned towards the sound of thumping hooves as a horse raced toward them from the west. General Jackson was pleased, but confused to see his Captain of Artillery arriving.

The young captain slid from his sweat-foamed horse and approached his commanding officer. "General Jackson," he said, and not taking the time to salute, asked. "What happened, Sir?"

Seldom would a man of lesser rank and especially one so young ask such a question of one of superior rank, but these two, the older officer and the young captain had developed a bond similar to that of father and son.

"Thaddeus," he said, instead of addressing the man with his rank, "after everybody got across the bridge, I had those blue bellies we got back there in tow get up on the bridge and set hooks on your cannon. Like fishing in mud, it was. Hard to see, but they finally got them hooked." He stopped and pointed at the farmer.

"Sir. This young man is my Captain of Artillery. Captain Biggs, this is Mr. Ericksen."

"My pleasure Sir," replied Captain Biggs, as he reached down to shake the weathered and calloused hand. "There's a family named Ericksen down my way. Carlton County. Fort Hardwood. You related to anybody down there?"

"Cap'n," he said, in answer to Captain Biggs' query, "most likely, but don't know."

The greeting finished, General Jackson continued. "After pulling them guns out'ta that mess, I was going to run them down to you. But Little Sorrel got tangled up in the hook ropes . . . lost her footing, whatever . . . and went over head first. Almost fell on top of me, she did, and plopped me in the mud on the bridge. And your three cannons are still stuck in the mud."

Thaddeus looked over the head of the general and counted the prisoners held under guard. "Well Sir. Begging your pardon, but those thirteen fellows can't pull those guns out. My horses barely got the rest of those cannon across that bridge. I had my doubts about that bridge, with those rotting logs supporting it, so I sent a man to look for another way across. And there was one, not much better though. It would have set us back two hours to get to it," he said, pointing northeast "and I had to get where you sent me," and then pointed west, in the direction from which he'd just ridden. "General Corning wasn't there. Nobody was. And I wasn't exactly sure where we were, either, Sir. That map I had was all wrong. I only have thirty-seven cannon with me. I could sure use those other three."

"You and your men head down toward that noise," the general said, and explained the route he was told to use. "Send one of the boys to bring up the rest of your men and the guns they have with them, and get them here on the double quick.

"Leave one man here to tell General Corning, when he does show up, but he might not come down this way, where you all got off to and for him to come along posthaste. Don't worry about those cannon back there in the ditch. Those Yank's will do what they're told," said the General. "And there's another hundred of them coming up behind us. They'll lend a hand or lose a hand. Up to them."

"Yes Sir," answered Captain Biggs.

"How many guns does Corning have, do you know?"

"Heard close to fifty. Seven or eight of those little mountain guns, those little Howitzers. That should put us in pretty good shape when we get there."

General Jackson brushed the mud from his uniform and, with a dirtied handkerchief, dabbed at his forehead. "Walk with me," he ordered the captain.

"Permission to speak, Sir," requested Captain Biggs.

"Speak," answered General Jackson.

"The Yankees are bombarding the field off to the south and east of where I was. Sounded like two, three miles from us. One of Captain Fritz's men came looking for me and said they were in a hell of a mess, and needed the cannon I had, but being under your command, I told him no."

"Well, I do need you. As soon as your cannon get here, you head on down. If we can believe this map," he said, shaking his head as if doubting the map already, "there's a hill. Don't know how high it is, and from what I've heard from Mister Ericksen, McClellan has spread all his cannon clear across the crest of that hill," and pointed at the map. "Now look here," and dragging his finger down the sheet of paper, added, "That Ericksen fellow says there's a ravine, pretty wide and deep here," he said, pointing a finger at the northernmost end of a drawn-in hill, "and maybe deep enough and wide to set your cannon in. According to him there's a woods to the back of the wash and a newer growth to the south. Might not be enough cover, but the height and the roll of the hill should serve as a blind for you."

The general put his hand on the young captain's shoulder. "Thaddeus, I do not like where I am sending you, but we all have our orders. Use every precaution to get in there without being detected. Send infantry to the east of their position to distract them and tell them to raise hell with their guns."

From the west the pounding hooves of a horse began to grow louder and dust began to rise into the air.

"That's Corning, there. Isn't it ?" the general asked.

"It is," announced the young Captain.

General Corning had pushed his unit hard, but rest was not to be had. Next to the other two officers, he reined his horse, tugged off his cap, from which sprang a tousled mass of curly red hair, and wiped at the sweat on his forehead with the sleeve of his field coat, more dust and dirt than cloth. "General Jackson, Sir," he said, saluting his superior, "How do we get down there?" he asked pointing south toward the noise, appearing anxious to re-enter the fray.

A brisk snap of his wrist indicated the Major General heard the man. "Captain Biggs told me his maps are wrong. So's mine. You have any problems with yours?"

"Ain't been hardly nothing right on them," replied General Corning.

"Well, let's put that behind us. You seem to understand the urgency of what's happening down that way a couple of miles. Do you?" asked General Jackson.

"May I speak freely, Sir?" General Corning asked of the field commander.

"You may."

"Sir, it is my belief that McClellan's men have already left. He's as close to Hampton Roads as he's been in weeks. My scouts tell me there's dozens of boats waiting down there along the James, to load up McClellan's army. But he's going to try to stall us with those cannon he's got on a hill down that way," pointing southeast. "Them Yanks are a cocky bunch. Between my unit and Captain Biggs' we have almost a hundred cannon. That's enough to get them blue-bellies up on that hill to hitch their mules to those guns and haul 'em out'ta there."

"Ahh . . . General, were it only that cut and dry. They have the hill and we have the land below. There is only one place we might be able to get into. Captain Biggs and I have been discussing it. And please, as a favor for me," he asked General Corning, "will you condescend to Captain Biggs' command for the remainder of the next fight? There's no time to explain my request, Sir, but it's of the utmost importance. The captain will explain it to you on the way down. But first I believe as you and the young captain do, if the Union boys have mounted that hill and drug their big guns up there, we'll not get them to leave as easily as we have for the last few days, but we will get them off. I have been ordered to close on the enemy. However, I am not in agreement with my superiors' decision to place cannon in the swale at the bottom of that hill. I can not imagine that will move the enemy. But it can not be helped. I will send you every cannon I can find and place them due north of the hill our enemy is on. There's a slight rise just north. Perhaps enough of one to give us the advantage, but I believe it will cost us dearly."

Captain Biggs said, "But Sir. You are the field commander. Can you not send us as you see fit?"

"Captain, I would. Unfortunately, I serve at the wish of General Lee, but I'll send all the Infantry I can to support you and General Corning."

General Corning saw the sorrow in General Jackson's eyes. "Sir," and saluting his superior, he added, "I'm at your service."

And again, to Captain Biggs, General Jackson said, "You and General Corning decide how to place your artillery. I'll be along soon with the three cannon stuck in the mud . . . well, as soon as they're brought up. They'll be muddy, but we'll scrub the barrels and clean the vent holes." And dismissing them, he said, "Gentlemen, please by all things Holy, be careful."

Cautiously, the farmer joined them. "Cap'n, Cap'n, Cap'n," interrupted the elderly man as he addressed all three. "Old man Brockstedder has a farm down that way," and thumbed over his shoulder toward the sound of cannon. "He come through here 'bout an hour afore y'all did and said he was ah git'n out'ta that place quick as he could. He tole me they got gunboats squattin' in the James River jus' offshore from the Shirley place. He said them shingles on the big plantation house was a liftin' ever time one of them guns throw'd a chunk'a iron over it to this side of Malvern's Hill. How he got through there is just plain 'mazin'. Stuck to the woods' what he said. His wife's crying so hard she got the hiccups and then the young'uns started carrying on, too. And pardon me, but he said y'alls in fer some Holy hot hell. I think so, too. I'm moan tell ya that."

Chapter Ten: July 1st. Eighteen and sixty-two.

How easy it is to die. How hard it is to live.

"Don't seem like much of a place to fight, does it?" Captain Biggs said to General Corning, pointing at the slight rise before them. "We're here," he said dragging his finger across the government-brown and water-stained topography map. "Place has two names . . . Poindexter's Farm and Malvern Hill."

Both men, binoculars to their eyes, studied the hill to the south. "You see anything, Sir?" asked Captain Biggs.

"Nothing but those boys. What the hell are they doing? He asked, pointing toward a small unit of butternut-clad soldiers who seemed determined to climb the gentle slope and mount the hill with two names.

"Should they be going up that hill just yet?" asked General Corning. "General Jackson said McClellan left his rear guard up there. But I don't see any. You?" Each agreed they saw no evidence of the rear guard of the Army of the Potomac.

And to an aide the young Captain said, "Ride over and tell those fools to come down from that damn field and fall in behind us."

The general added, "For the sake of it, I do not understand why he wants us to place our guns down there," speaking of General Jackson's orders, while pointing to the deep wash time had cut into the bottom of the hill on which they now stood. "I hardly see any reason McClellan would change his way of fighting and running. He always runs after a battle. Probably half way to his boats as we speak and for once, we just plain ought'ta let him be."

Captain Biggs nodded his head, thinking the same thing. The hill before them seemed just another rise among many and he could see no value in either the Confederacy holding it, or for that matter, those "damn Yankees." But *orders are orders*, he thought, and who was he to question General Jackson? He opened the torn and frayed map yet again and studied it closer, looking for secrets he and General Corning must be unaware of.

"What are you thinking, General Corning?"

"Captain Biggs. I do not believe it is wise for us to go down in there—not if there really is Yankee cannon waiting above us out of our sight and I'm not saying there is. But we'd be like ducks tied to a string and surrounded by hunters, if there is. Besides, you really think you can get our cannon down in that cut?"

"Don't want to, but got to. From what General Jackson says, this is the place. Don't like it any more than you, but there's Malvern Hill," he said pointing at the trees drawn onto the map, and then at a swale separating two opposing hills. "Don't see much cover for us while we're setting up, though."

"Well, that is not a fit place to fight from is all I'm saying. It's an already-dug grave, Sir. We go down in there, we might as well lay down and shoot ourselves in the head," the superior officer countered. "I just want that on the record. That gully's going to be the death of both of us and most of our men. Sir. This is nothing but insanity."

A quarter of a mile north of the wash, the captain and the general studied the lay of the land with field glasses, each studying the hill across the shallow valley.

"There they are, but there's no hundred guns up there. All I see is about twenty or thirty," said Thaddeus.

Out of the west woods a rider, slumped in the saddle, his head held low, raced toward them, frantically waving them away. "You all need to get on back. On the other side of that hill them Yankees is holed up. They got cannon all the way across the crest of that hill and more of 'em lined up behind 'em." The man paused, embarrassed that he had just told two officers of the Army of Northern Virginia they should move back. He unfolded his body, stretching himself to his full height . . . he was no coward. He tugged at the reins and set spurs to his mount, "Well, it's your hides." he mumbled, anxious to be on his way. Nether of the officers spoke to him as he rode away, but suddenly, the man pulled hard on the reins to bring his horse to a stop. He turned back to the two officers "Y'all come on, now. Them fellows up on that hill are gonna ruin your day," and then set his spurs again.

"I can see the damn cannon," answered Corning, testily. "But what I can't see is how many are stacked up on the far side. Maybe a hundred more of 'em like he says. But they won't need them. Hell, we get in there, them blue-bellies can roll rocks down on us if they got a mind to. I don't like it. No Sir. I do not like it at all."

Thaddeus turned toward the infantry massing at the woods a half-mile distant. "I have an idea. How many infantry do you have, General?"

"Right at three thousand, five hundred."

"I've got about half that, maybe two thousand, at most," stated Thaddeus. "If we are to take that hill, we've got to lay down a field of fire to keep 'em back behind those cannon we can see." He turned in his saddle, and looked in all directions, visually judging the number of infantry. "What do you think of this? Send our boys up there, except keep them in the woods as long as possible. You send some of your men, two thousand or so, across that way," pointing to the west. "Leave your other fifteen hundred back there in those woods," he added, pointing behind him towards the north.

"Tell your men on the west when they get in the woods to start climbing the hill. When they get to about the middle of the hill, spread them out just inside the tree line and tell them to wait for the order to charge. There's going to be some of those Yankee scouts hiding in those woods, too. Sharpshooters, for sure. Make sure you put your best rifles up front to even things out. And watch the sky. I'll send up a flare to tell you when to send them toward the cannon."

General Corning began to understand the captain's plan.

"As for the fifteen hundred men behind us, we'll use them as a diversion. Tell those fellows to pack and load like they never had to do before. With any luck those cannon up front will waste all their powder trying to destroy what they think is the whole of our army. Worth a try. Maybe.

"I'll send the two thousand I have to the east. Same plan as yours. That'd be two thousand on the east, two thousand on the west, and those behind us," he said, pointing towards the woods again. "Stay low. Stay in the woods. I'll tell my men to watch the sky for a flare and I'll send them in right away. That'll draw fire towards them and away from you. When you see the flare, hold your men off for three minutes or so, and then rush them toward those big guns of McClellan's, shooting with everything they have. McClellan's artillery will turn most of his cannon toward the east and fire on the obvious—my men coming toward them. The rest of his cannon will already be blasting away at the men back there in the woods behind us, but the largest guns I saw up there were twelve pounders. That's plenty big enough to throw the balls over us, but nothing that gets out this far will be as accurate as they hope.

"Timing is critical. Maybe we can catch them in a crossfire. They'll either run off or bring up everything they have out of sight behind them. You see them start pounding away at us down here, double quick your men up that hill. Tell them to load fast and shoot faster. I'll tell mine the same. Our best chance for setting my guns down here is when they turn their cannon to the east to try to run off my infantry. If I am to get my cannon in place like General Jackson said for me to do, I'll need the biggest distraction this war has ever seen."

"I understand, Sir," replied General Corning. "But didn't General Jackson say he was on his way down here?"

"Yes, he did, but those fellows up there," he thumbed toward the crest of Malvern Hill, "will just roll the rest of their big guns forward if they see him coming. And they will see him. They've got the high ground. And the general will be kicking up dust. Our best chance to get out of this alive is if we quit and left now, but that won't happen." The thought lodged in his mind, but to do so would be to challenge General Jackson, and that was something he would have no part of.

The younger officer seemed to have a grasp of war and the maneuvers required of it. He prayed he appeared more confident to the elder man, General Corning, than he felt, but his eyes betrayed him.

"God willing we'll meet up there, dead center, and shake hands. Now, General, if you are in agreement with me, let's get started."

***

With orders given and repeated, Captain Biggs and General Corning left for their prospective duties—the captain to the east, the general to the west.

Late afternoon, as the red ball of the sun neared the treetops to the west, a flare, its payload, a hard-packed ball filled with chemically enhanced gunpowder, exploded high overhead. Streamers of red hot marble-sized pellets screamed out in all directions as the pull of gravity drug them down upon the top of the hill into the trampled wheat. Dry and brown, it burned as if each straw was made of matches.

Captain Biggs, below the rise, watched as plumes of smoke rose from the hill above. The Union cannon roared in retaliation. A hail storm of solid shot, exploding shell, and molten shrapnel rained upon his artillery in the wash. Unknown to him, he and his men had been seen. They were now the target as the Yankees loaded their cannon with exploding shell and solid shot.

Seeing the enemy below, the enemy on the hill rotated many of the outer guns toward the swale and lowered their cannon barrels down the slope toward where Captain Biggs was directing the firing of his cannon.

Slanted steeply the tilted barrels presented a new problem for the North. A flurry of men ran to and fro, collecting anything that could be packed into the barrels in an effort to hold the shot and shell deep inside, tight against the gunpowder. Finding little, they stripped clothing from the dead, and using that as wadding, packed it into the barrels.

With an excess of wasted firing, the firing above soon began to slow.

Captain Biggs saw an advantage. "Roll those cannon as far into that gully as you can. Be quick about it. The infantry is using their ammunition up fast. Hurry men. Kill the recoil. Shovel a hole for each wheel and one for the beam," ordered Captain Biggs. "We're going to be way too busy to go chasing after these guns."

Freshly supplied, the noise above began to increase yet again, as the deep-throated explosions of the enemies' cannon, the rattle of rifles and musketry, coupled with myriads of differing noises tore at the young officer's sense of timing. The once-blue sky, was now a witch's cauldron of dark and light grays. The smells of war's machinery, the rancid and eye-burning gunpowder coupled with a black hail of iron shrapnel, pounded the ground all around. Captain Biggs wondered how long he'd been at placing the big guns into position. Was it the hours he felt it had taken—or the fifteen minutes he'd been taught to do it in? The firing of his cannon began to slow. He checked the guns and his artillerymen. Beside their assigned gun, each man stooped and watched the heavens as the killing iron rained down upon them.

"Keep at it, men" he shouted. "Don't let up. Melt those barrels, if you have to."

General Corning returned and assured the young captain his boys were gaining the hill. "Doing a damn fine job of it, too." As suddenly said, a spray of red, mixed with gray matter, exploded from the rear of the general's head. Startled and reacting to his adrenaline-fed reflexes, Captain Biggs reached out to the already-dead general who remained seated and erect in the saddle. As he grabbed the sleeve of the man's field coat, the body slumped to the side and fell to the ground.

The captain slapped at the side of his head. *Of all things, stung by a bee*, he thought. A trickle of blood fell from his left temple. The smell of burning flesh engulfed him. A smoldering piece of iron protruded from his upper right chest. *And now my blouse is on fire*, as the sliver of iron in his chest sizzled and smoked. His last complete thought was of how to snuff out the fire.

The concept of time suddenly ceased to exist. How else could he account for the things he saw, the things he felt, the things heard in a millisecond. The loud noises, the cannon roaring, muskets rattling, men screaming, faded from his hearing. For the briefest of moments he sought the answer of which he'd heard first—the fuse in the shell above him igniting the gunpowder within, the soft crack of the iron shell splintering into a thousand pieces, or the whistle of shrapnel speeding toward its destination. And which had he felt first, the percussion that pushed him from the saddle, the feathery flutter of the triangular-shaped piece of a wagon wheel's rim as it raced towards his upper right chest, or the impact of his body as he crashed atop the soft dirt rimming the hole which had not been there moments before?

Did he remember the dark skies above turning black with smoke? Or the body laying motionless and quiet upon the crater's rim? Did he know that was his body? He was no longer aware of the wounded laying scattered about, who only a fraction of a second before pleaded desperately to be allowed to abandon their guns and struggle to the rear.

He remembered nothing.

**

"Captain . . . Captain . . . Can you hear me?" asked the man bending over and peering down at him.

Chapter Eleven: Stonewall rides onto the field, searching.

General Stonewall Jackson had led a charmed life. His daring during the Mexican War was the thing of which legends were made. He had never been seriously wounded during the revolution, but witnessed the death of many under his command. At the outbreak of hostilities between the North and the South, he chose Thaddeus Biggs as his Captain of Artillery, never thinking it possible such a man, so well trained, so good at his craft, would ever be wounded. But he was wrong.

The Cannon and rattle of muskets eased and finally ceased. From out of the woods to the north, a man dressed in a general's soiled uniform, riding a tired and worn horse, emerged. The grime and dirt-covered man sat slumped, exhausted. He rode the length of the swale—searching. His eyes danced from body to body as they lay scattered. *"What have I done?,"* he cried, and asked of the Heavens, "Oh. What have I done?"

General Jackson, in one of his previous warrior lives, had seen all manner of wasted and broken forms of men, Mexican and American scattered about the battlefield. He could tell from a glimpse which of the broken men were no longer residing in this world, and which were soon to leave. *Dust to dust*, he thought. Perhaps, out of respect for such brave man, or maybe in search of forgiveness from his Heavenly Father, he closed his eyes, titled his face towards heaven, and offered a silent prayer.

As in all the battles which he had fought, those in Mexico and here in this new country, the Confederate States of America, the men scattered below whispered things only he could hear. The dead, in their stillness, admitted they were gone, finished. And those not yet through with the gift of life pleaded with their eyes, *"General, don't give up on us,"* and returned to their hard fight to hold onto the last spark of life burning within them. But the general, so familiar with death, knew whose spark would fade and whose would not. Killing taught things like that.

Others—mangled and pressed into odd and impossibly misshapen mounds of flesh—jerked, twitched, and struggled to draw into their bleeding lungs their last breath. Vultures flying above glided lower and lower, ravenously eyeing the buffet below.

Hard at work, stretcher bearers stepped from body to body, opening this one's eyes, rolling that one over—checking vital signs—making on-spot decisions, deciding who should be carried off the field, and who could not survive the iron storm of death which had rained upon them. No man should ever be told to go onto a battlefield and play God, they thought.

The ground was thick with the detritus of war. Human and otherwise. Countless shells, many not yet exploded lay scattered—too dangerous to be gathered—each packed with shrapnel—those bits and pieces scrounged from the battlefield and the waste product of the foundries of both sides—furnace-slag, and needing to be avoided at all cost. The killing field so thick with things no longer of value that one could not walk across it without caution, spoke of the ferocity of the cannon fired from the hill above.

For the briefest of moments, General Jackson, tears in his eyes, thought of shouting to the Heavens, *"Lord, why have you forsaken us?"* but he realized it was not within him to mimic Jesus.

Turning to the stretcher bearer below, he called, "Where's your Captain?" he asked. "Where's Caption Biggs?"

The infantryman sat on the ground with a dreadfully wounded, dying man cradled in his arms, turned his head towards the man upon the odd-looking horse. And with a bit of rancor, asked, "Sir. You see what I see?" the question soaked with sarcasm. "Maybe that's him," he pointed to a man laying under a horse, his face slowly being covered with glistening slime-covered entrails oozing from a horse's belly with each beat of its huge heart. "How's about that'un? Or him? Take yourself a pick. Does it matter?" From his throat exploded an agony such as only heard from others dying in the gully. Unashamedly, private William "Gus" Murray began to sob. His reddish beard—now crusted purple with dried blood, his arms red from fresh, looked wild eyed and inhuman. But within his chest beat the heart of a good man—a caring man, a sad man, a man at the verge of collapse.

General Jackson dismounted his horse and stepped to the man. He held the broken man to his chest and he, too, began to cry.

"Good man. They all matter." And the Deacon within the General said, "Let us pray."

From bent knees they stood. General Jackson scribbled a note on sweat-soiled paper and said, "I desperately need to find my Captain of Artillery. It would be an act of kindness if you would help me. When you do, tell him to come to me post haste. He's wearing a dark blue field jacket. The army has been recalled to General Lee's headquarters. Look for anyone wearing a Captain's Artillery jacket, dark blue, trimmed in red. Most likely, down in there," he said pointing to the gully to which the young officer had been sent. And shaking a finger, he repeated, "Down in there. Down in there. Tell him we must leave immediately. Two hours. Will you help me?"

"It's git'n ah mite bit dark, General, but I will find the Captain. An' you afterwards."

As the black of night slithered over the rolling hills and headed for places west, it towed from the east an unsettling quietness. The only noises were those of owls and other creatures of the night as they braved their return to the war-torn woods and fields. From the top of the hill, muffled sounds of men and cannon leaving the high ground, spoke of yet another nighttime flight of the Army of the Potomac. McClellan and the Army of the Potomac were on the move.

And too dark to see, Gus went in search of the 47th.

Chapter Twelve: Eighteen and sixty-two: July 2$^{nd.}$ Stretchers and field hospitals.

A strange thing, patriotism. Loyalty to a cause does not necessarily have to be a learned thing. It can be born of bravado and promises—bravery which has not been tested and promises which cannot be kept. Anyone can brag of their bravery, but eleven dollars a month was something Private William Gus Murray had never seen in his life. If anything happened to their warrior husband and father, the men with the papers he ex'ed his name on, assured him his wife and children would be seen after for his service to his new country. And each of those men knew they were lying.

Dark gray sky toward the east, the smell of coffee brewing and salt pork frying aroused Gus from a fitful night's sleep. Moans and cries floating from the scarred battlefield mingled with the sizzle of salt pork frying in the unit's single frying pan. He thought of the contradictions of the two sounds, one of dying men, the other of men eating to live. He dug in his pocket and found his last piece of hard tack and wondered why everything to do with war had to be painful. The hard tack hurt his fingers as he wrenched it apart into two manageable pieces—and both of those hurt his teeth and gums.

Lying next to him and watching Gus's return from the netherworld of sleep, Jasper said as easily and nonchalantly as if he were saying good morning, "They's gonna shoot you when they find you'se come back. You know that don't you?"

"Tell 'em. I don't give a fried dog turd. Shoot me? That can't be no mor'n a tiny bee sting compared to dem last seven days and nights we dun' spent chasin' dem scairt-ass blue bellies. But if'n I'd a know'd we was gonna' have to run after dem damn Billy Yanks like we did, I don't reckon I'da cum' back nere' soon as I did."

But bitter, Gus had returned. Most of the 47th North Carolina Infantry, Co. A., admired the man's spunk, his sense of honor. Others thought him a fool for returning after so long an absence. "Gone and forgotten," they laughed with others of like opinion. Many of them were convinced he was dead—his skeleton bleached white by the sun, lost on a year old battlefield, and beneath a thick, green growth of weeds fed by his decayed flesh.

"You'd been better off if'n you'd stayed gone, Gus," offered Jasper, as he placed a brotherly hand on his friend's shoulder. But he was glad Gus had gone home and snuck back into camp—and not deserted like some said he had. He wanted, at the right time, to ask how he had run off like he did. He wanted to know his secrets.

"My littlest one, Aluious, died. You 'member me getting that letter? The rest of my young'uns damn nere starved to death, too. I ask General Peterson if I could go home an' see to 'em. 'No.' That's all he said, 'No.' Waved me away with ah fork, like I was ah fly pestering him. Didn't even say he was sorry for nary ah one ah us what needs to go home. That fat motherfucker just sat there cuttin' up ah steak, grease drippin' down in his beard, and lookin' up now and a'gin to see if I was still there. So I lit out. Damn right, I did. Found Sara sick in bed when I got home. My momma, seventy-three years old she is, was doing what she could, taking care of my sick wife and the rest of my young'uns. And not ah damn thing on the place for dem to eat. No rabbits. No nothing. Even the damn squirrels so bony you could'a used their backbones for ah comb. I put some rocks up on Little Al's grave and ah week later, done the same on Sara's." His eyes glistened and he wiped away a tear. He wasn't ashamed of shedding tears—all the 47th had cried. And cried many times.

"So, Home-Guard or no, I put in ah crop, mostly corn, beans, large gardens, mostly. Busted up an acre or two for tobacky . . . onliest thing what's worth trading, now days. That new script ain't worth ah bottle of warm horse piss. Makes ah good ass wipe, though. But that tobacky will get 'em most ah what they needs. Waited for the first hard freeze so I could salt away the hams and stuff the sausage in the washed out guts. What weren't gonna keep, I pickled. I was luckier'n most. Able to get some salt. And that's all gone, now.

"Remember how they bunched us all up on the mustering field down by Samaria? Told us two months fighting, maybe three. That's what they said, ain't it? No mor'n ah hun'ert days. That's what they said. Tole us we was the blessed ones, cause there was fellows waiting in line for ah chance to get at dem blue bellies and that President Davis was gonna give everybody who wanted to, a chance to kill sum'a dem Yankees."

Gus sat motionless for a few minutes, lost in thought. He stirred the red coals of the dying fire with a twisted and gnarled oak branch. A hard stare crossed his face as his jaw muscles flinched. Looking at Jasper he said, "Long as I live, ain't never ah 'nudder man gonna tell me what to do 'bout my youn'uns."

Jasper understood. He worried each night and most of each day. He had been trying to summon the nerve to slip out of the camp at night and run off like Gus and lots of others had. And like the rest of the 47th, that last battle they fought, the one named after the hill, was the closest the unit had been to Carlton County since they'd left North Carolina, and now they were camped in the woods—close enough to hear the wounded moaning and smell the early odors of death.

"Better git all the rest you can," Gus said to Jasper. "We'se been tole we got'ta git up wid the sun and flatfoot it sum'mere's north ah here."

Not me. I've had it. Jasper Thigpen decided. If given the right opportunity, he'd run.

"Here comes one of dem horse sitters," he said to Gus as General Lane rode up. Jasper whispered to Gus, "Be best if you make yourself scarce."

"You. Come here," ordered the general as he pulled back on the reins of his mount. He stared down at a man in his command he'd not seen before. "You lost? What's your name?"

"No Sir, I ain't lost. Private William Gus Murray, Sir," Gus answered, as he sharply saluted the general.

"What's your company?"

"The 47th N. C. Infantry, Company A. Sir."

"Not new?" repeated the general. "If you're not new, how's it I've never seen you before?"

"Went home, Sir. Got back the day before we started in on the Yanks back at Seven Pines. Been chasing 'em all the way down here."

"Went home? For how long did you go home, Private, ah, what was it? Murty? Murphy?"

"Murray, Sir."

"You skip on us, did you Private Murray?"

"Yes Sir. Kind'a."

"Kind'a? Either you did or you didn't."

"Well then, Sir. No. I skipped on General Peterson."

"You were one of Peterson's men?"

"Yes Sir."

"You get permission to leave?"

"No Sir. I asked, begged him. But, no sir, he wouldn't let me go."

"You a coward?

"No Sir. I ain't."

"Come back on your own volition?"

"Don't know, Sir. Ain't never heer'd that word a'fore."

"It means did anybody drag you back and get paid for doing it?" the general asked, his voice rising,

"I come back on my own."

"Why did you leave, soldier?"

"Well, General. Like I dun' tole that General Peterson, my wife wrote and begged me to come home. Tole him my baby boy was dying and the rest of 'em was hungry. So, yes sir, I did ask General Peterson to let me go. But all he done was shake his head and wipe his face in his shirt sleeve, farted, and said 'no'. That man weren't hungry like my wife and children was. He sat there in the shade of his tent, eating ah steak. He throw'd most of that piece of meat to his dog, licked his fingers and dismissed me with a flip of his hand."

"Well, can't argue with that. He was a son of a bitch, but you need to be more respectful about how you speak of your superior officers."

"I am, with dem what I respects, Sir."

"General Peterson's dead," said General Lane

"Choke on a steak, did he?" sneered Gus.

Gus stared at the general on the horse. His eyes and face, if could be heard, said, *"And why would I give a shit?"* But such a reply would have gotten him shot without a court martial.

"Most likely," agreed the General. "I knew that man. He was a Brevet General, a real piece of work, that one. Somebody owed him a favor. Saw to it he got stars put on his collar and gave him command of the 47th. You know I can have you court-martialed for taking off the way you did, and bad-talking the officers like that, don't you? Shoot you if I want to. Understand?"

"Sir," said Gus. "I dun' lost Aluioius, and my wife Sara died soon after I got home. I started up a garden or two. Planted some trading crops. Butchered my hogs. After I made arrangements with my brother for my children to be taken care of if'n I don't come home or if'n their grandma passes, then I come on back. But if'n that's what you wants to do, shoot me. But a'fore you do let me say sumpt'n to my mates. I'll tell dem they all ought'a run off. We was lied to, Sir. I can't respect nobody what lies outright to good men like dem. They fought seven battles, Sir, and a mess of skirmishes. Not nary ah one ob 'em never run back to the rear or off in the woods. They's been at it since we got mustered up and they all been shootin' and killin' and gettin' kilt ah lot longer than they was promised they'd have to. Now if'n you wants me to, I'll stay and fight like I promised I would when we ex'ed in our names back home. And us boys of the 47th don't lie."

"Well, Private Murray, you're back now. And that presents a conundrum. You know what conundrum means, don't you?"

"No Sir. Ain't never heer'd that word, neither."

"Simply put, it means I don't know what to do with you just now. Jackson's got us on the march. I'll ask the fellows about you. If you're a good man, I'll let you live . . . if not, you'll die. For now, you are going to stay here and help with the wounded and burying of the dead. That's the worst of all duties. It'll be part of your punishment. I'll think on the rest later. Can I trust you, Private?"

"Yes Sir. You can. But General Jackson ordered me to find his Artillery Captain for him."

"You need help?"

"Yes Sir."

"Then pick a man to help you with the stretchers."

"Yes Sir. I like that one," pointing at Private Jeb Mosely. "Me and him's neighbors back in Carolina."

The general waved over an aide. "Go get that man out of line. Bring him here."

***

With the rising sun, the few left of the 47th N C Infantry lined up, about faced and marched north. Privates Murray and Mosely stood watching as they left. Between them, on the ground, lay stretchers, most soaked in blood.

Private Jasper Thigpen lay deathly still for an hour—then quietly pushed away broken tree limbs, leaves and dirt. He doubted the roads west would have any Confederate soldiers on it so he would chance his escape. Nor was there a need to fear the blue bellies—they'd fled the night of the battle. McClellan's Army of the Potomac was already boarding gun ships and fleeing for the safety of Washington. But care had to be taken. Upon the bloodied battlefield, stretcher-bearers had begun the early morning loading of the wounded. He felt much as Gus had—those who had talked him into joining the 47th had lied, plain and simple. They'd told him not to worry, they would see to his family. They'd lied and he knew it.

Man-sized forms lay all about. The soldiers were scattered as if by a tornado—no rhyme, no reason as to where they lay. The color of uniforms, some blue, most butternut, meant nothing to Private Murray or Private Mosely. All they saw were men needing to be taken quickly to the nearest field hospital—and many, many more that needed to be buried.

Jasper Thigpen marched deep into the woods, followed the banks of the James River west, and stole a boat with which to cross the mighty James.

Chapter Thirteen: Eighteen and sixty-two: The week after the battle at Malvern Hill.

Shimmering like the wind-blown surface of a spring filled with crystal clear water, a brilliantly white and vaguely human form floated above an arched threshold. Spider-web thin tendrils of vapor seemed to anchor the mist to the form on the ground. The golden threshold separated the darkest of all things dark and the brightest of all things bright, and the translucent figure awaited the command to depart the wrecked body below it—or the command to stay and give it hope.

A voice beyond man's hearing said, "No. Do not leave. Stay with him. Protect him."

Obediently, the form remained.

Full of static and tension, the air trembled above the crumpled and bleeding body. Captain Thaddeus Biggs did not feel the tension nor the static. In the west, zigzagging flashes of red and pink ripped across the skies announcing the approach of a thunderstorm. But he did not see the flashes. A deafening noise, similar to that of a laboring train, barreled down upon the carnage scattered all around. The artillery captain did not hear the roar.

Moments before, the ground had shaken violently. The Union artillery shell, packed with gunpowder and bits and pieces of scrap iron and slag, its singular purpose to destroy everything within its reach, had accomplished its mission. Large and small pieces of shrapnel, all deadly, found their targets. Men and horses collapsed to the ground—most on their way to death—others lifeless and empty as they fell.

Clods of dirt and loose soil rained upon the body as it lay at the edge of the crater left by the Yankee shell. Cool rain began to soak the wounded man's dark blue artillery uniform, quickly turning it shades darker, as the fabric began to streak with mud from the dissolving dirt.

The young captain lay motionless atop the newly formed crater, its razor-thin edge separating life and death.

Heavy cannon collapsed upon the ground, their carriages and wheels disintegrating into a splintered oblivion. Caissons exploded with ground shaking fury as the powder stored within ignited. Blue-gray tendrils of smoke and wispy steam rose sluggishly from the depths of the newly formed crater and floated away from the raging battle. Raindrops hitting the shrapnel of iron and steel sizzled into small haloes of steam and were instantly dispersed by a light breeze.

A curtain of red fell across the man's face. A tear began to form in the corner of his left eye; a trickle of blood fell from his right. It broke across the bridge of his nose and dripped into his rain soaked beard. The form above and the man below remained connected—one to the other.

But then darkness, only darkness.

Slowly, striations of beautiful bright lights and spasms of flashes began to dance in the darkness behind Captain Biggs' closed eyelids. As quickly as they began, they faded.

The quivering mass inside the young captain's fractured skull had regained enough of its nearly spent life to know time was wasting, and that time was of the essence.

"If our vessel dies, we all die," it shouted, realizing the dire straits it and the body were facing. Instinctively, it began sending signals of desperation throughout the body at the edge of the crater and at the edge of death. Convulsions began to contort the body on the ground.

"Stop fighting me," the reasoning part demanded, and the man lay still. Twitches of a bleeding eyelid and a dirt covered cheek, begging to be noticed, spoke of an unknown degree of life yet remaining within the tattered body.

Like loose leaves of a book whose binding had given way to age and the pull of wind, splintered thoughts swirled from the body.

The organ at the center of the man's being knew the thoughts were of great importance. Desperate to gather the fleeting bits of knowledge before they sailed out of reach and were lost forever, it greedily grabbed them and compressed them into confusing images. They could be sorted later, reasoned the orb; perhaps they contained the foundation on which life could be rebuilt.

"Hurry up, hurry up. Get going," it commanded the other organs. Unknown to the motionless soldier, its thinking part fought desperately to halt the death march its owner was on.

The throbbing center of the man grew stronger, yet the combined weight of pain and the constant struggle to restore the vital parts sucked hungrily at the limited strength which remained.

"We have to become one—quickly," the brain shouted. Gambling, it used the last of its strength and sent tingling signals throughout the body to restore itself.

By fractions, the broken body and the swollen gray mass merged, each taking from the other what it needed to survive.

Willed by something unknown—a loud command or an unspoken thought from a deep and hidden place, the eyelids fluttered and suddenly opened wide.

"Yes," cried the brain. It now knew it could survive and that it would survive. The shimmering mass, the protector, once thinking its work on earth was completed, whispered encouragement. "You can do it, but you must want to. The choice is yours, now."

The Captain's senses slowly began to become organized—not much, but a start. He saw blurry gray clouds floating high above. He had the sense that a crystal mist was falling upon him, seeking to enter every pore of his body. He smelled the acrid smoke of burned gunpowder and the coppery smell of blood. He heard not a sound except the intense roar growing deep within his head. And the last sense to restore itself was that of pain. How very badly he hurt!

He lay still, not knowing if he could move or if he should try. He didn't know if he wanted to move. Alive or dead made little sense to him. He had not gotten that far yet, but alive seemed right. Dark thoughts—more vision than thought—continued to race before his *unfocused eyes. He heard booming noises from a hill that he could only see in his mind. He felt the crinkling pull in his beard—blood drying and clotting on his sun-heated cheek. He felt the sticky warm flesh of something—or someone—sliding down his exposed neck. Such visions were strange. They confused him. They made him fearful.*

As the body and brain began to merge, the body grew tired and became complacent. It was the shell, the vessel, the protector of everything and it was failing its job. Thankfully, a growing awareness of guilt began to build, the result of the manipulations of the brain forcing it to face the realities of life or death.

"Don't you dare quit on us," demanded the struggling orb, sending the message coursing through the man.

He now understood the mist had always been a part of him and the choice to live or die was his. Embarrassed to think he had considered giving up, he willed his eyes toward dark forms and shadowy movements above him. Frightened, the eyelids closed as they rolled back, retreating toward a remote, dark and becalmed place. But sensing the importance of their presence, they returned to the shapes hovering above them.

"Captain . . . Captain . . . Can you hear me?" asked the soldier standing over him.

Gus stuck the handles of the litter into the still freshly turned mound of dirt and balanced himself on his knees. The slight rise behind him was littered with both shallow and deep holes, and countless wounded and dying—each the result of Yankee shells raining down upon the Confederates during the hot and waning hours of July first, eighteen and sixty-two. The high ground, Malvern Hill, had been strategically fortified by the union with upward of thirty five cannon with rumors that hundreds more were held in reserve beyond the crest.

At the base of the hill, and spread the length of the gully, out of view of the Yankees above, the Confederate army had amassed their countering cannon and confident Artillerymen. Within a few brief and hard fought hours, the Army of the Potomac had decisively won the last of the six battles it had fought during the last week. Of the other five, none could claim bragging rights, neither the North or the South. But at night, around cook fires, the events of the day were exaggerated and slanted in favor of the teller of the stories. The Billy Yanks claimed victory at Oak Grove, as did the Johnny Rebs. The same with Mechanicsville—each side claiming victory. Gaines Mills, Garnett's and Golding's Farm were not mentioned often but when spoken of, both sides bragged about how hard it had been to drive the enemy away. As the days wore on, the Federal Supply Depot at Savage's Station served as the backdrop for still another battle of which to lie or tell the truth.

***

Only a few short hours before, Gus and Jeb had been doing their share of killing. Now, their rolls were reversed. They were working on the saving part of war—the gathering of the wounded and dying. In a manner, they had become gods—deciding who lived, who died.

Gus reached into the pit and carefully wiped away the molasses-thick grime of blood, sweat, and grit from the face of the young officer lying in the crater. Turning to Private Mosley, his stretcher-mate, he said, "Hey Jeb. This here's that Captain fellow I been telling you about. You know, Stonewall's Artillery Captain. He's from down our way, Carlton County. He shore looks kind'a young to be ah officer, don't he?"

"How come you think this here fellow's his artillery captain?" asked Jeb.

"Onliest person here 'bouts what's wearing ah dark blue jacket trimmed in red. That's ah artillery captain's coat he's got on, fer shore."

"If'n you ack's me, it looks like he's done seen all'a his days," responded Jeb

Reaching inside his blouse Gus pulled out a pad and pencil. "What's this place called. You know? We's got'ta give it some kind'a' name."

Jeb answered, "Heard sum'r the boys call it Poindexter's Farm and udders call it Malvern Hill. Write down the one you like. Unless you know how to spell that Poindexter fellow's name. I don't. I'd call it Malvern Hill, if'n it were me. 'Cause if it weren't for that damn hill," he said, pointing south, "me and you wouldn't be toting these here fellers right now. Malvern Hill. Jus' call it Malvern Hill and be dun' wid it"

And brushing aside more dirt from the forehead of the mangled and bleeding officer, Gus said, "Can't say he look's none too good, but let's get him up out'ta there and loaded up."

Whether the man had "mustered up" from the same county as he and Gus carried little weight with Jebidiah Mosley. He paid scant attention to what Gus seemed to be implying.

"I don't give a squirrel's ass-hole what county he cum' frum. If'n he was a captain, colonel or a general, he ain't gonna' be one fer long. He can't last much longer. Look at him. Leave him be, Gus."

They had seen hundreds of badly wounded men today—all bleeding—all "torn to hell and back." *Torn to hell and back* being another way of saying "this 'uns dun' fer." He and Gus had carried at least that many shot up and dying men to field hospitals which were already filled to overflowing before they could return with a new man. Jeb thought the officer in the hole did not look much different than any other bleeding and torn up man—the dark blue jacket, trimmed in red, aside. But, he too, fell to his knees and sank into the loose soil rimming the depression.

"Well, let's git him out'ta there, anyways. I'll get his shoulders. You grab his legs. Be careful. He might come apart on us," said Gus, his face inches away from the wounded officer's.

The body below was eerily twisted into impossible positions. The right shoulder, bent harshly inward and toward the sternum, while the arm and hand, with extended dirt-covered fingers, held tightly to the round of the opposing shoulder. From under the curled-over shoulder, a large and red blotch, its sheen an indication of a recent wound, spread across the front of the officer's uniform—a warning to the stretcher bearers that the collar bone was broken and cutting into internal organs. A triangular piece of a iron, arrowhead-shaped, likely from a caisson or wagon wheel rim, stuck through the blouse of the officer's uniform and quivered with each beat of the heart beneath it. A crust of blood had formed over his left temple, it too spurting minuscule red drops with each surge of blood being forced through a swollen artery. Only the quick flash of the dirt-splattered eyelids and the fading heartbeat kept the two men above him.

"I don't know if we ought'a do that just yet," said Jeb. "We get started in yanking on him, I don't think he'll make it. Maybe we ought'a go on to the next one. Check back on him later."

Gus ignored him and leaned back over the form below. "Captain. Captain Biggs. Can you hear me?"

"Gol-dammit Jeb," Gus said. "I knows we'se friends but we dun' got our orders. Them what's still breathing gets toted off the field first—that's what that General tole us to do—this'uns still breathing. Maybe not much but his wind's strong enough to blow dem blood bubbles up on his lips. And something else. Look here," and lifting the flap of the field jacket, he exposed the heavily soiled blue of an artilleryman's uniform. "This here's General Jackson's Artillery Captain. Give me a chunk'a that paper." Pencil in hand he scratched a brief note of the man's condition and from a note tucked in the jacket pocket, he found confirmation of the captain's name. "See? That there's his name."

Jeb watched as Gus wrote. He wished he could write pretty like his friend.

"All I'm saying is this 'uns' good as dead," answered Jeb, falling back on the seat of his pants. He hung his head, too tired to hold it upright, and added, "He just don't know it yet, Gus. Leave him be."

"This ain't no time to git in ah piss'n match. Neither one'a us got rank on the udder'n, but if'n you don't get down here and hep' me, I'm gonna clobber the shit out'ta you. You ain't God and I ain't gonna' try to be one. I seen enough dying for one day. This man ain't gonna' die off on us if'n I can hep' it. Let one ah them sawbones up yonder at the barn make that call. I sure as hell ain't gonna' do it and you ain't need'r. Now hand me that stretcher and git your skinny ass down here."

Defeated once in battle the day before, each decided there had been enough of dying. As gently as they knew how, they loaded the young Captain onto a heavily used and blood-stained stretcher. Gus jumped in alarm as the officer's eyes flashed open and struggled to focus on the forms above. A deep, guttural sound—more death-gurgle than moan—rattled the fresh droplets of blood anchored upon chalky white lips. And as suddenly as the eyes opened, a trickle of blood from the gruesome bruise on his left temple seeped into the man's eye. Both eyes closed and rolled back into the calm darkness they favored, preferring the unknown to the dreadful shelling they'd been watching for a week now.

"Don't you go to sleep on me, Jeb," demanded Gus. "I got'ta run this over to that Stonewall fellow."

With that, Gus left in search of General Jackson. In his hand he carried information the general would not like.

Upon his return, he and Jeb pulled the weighted litter from the crater and searched for their hospital flag. There were too many flags flying, most of them field hospitals, and all the flags were similar. From the distance they could not identify the tent they'd left not long before. Finally, they spotted their flag with the three bold patterns of red, white and blue identifying the tent as belonging to General Jackson's command, and hurried towards the dark green tree line before which the flag stood.

As Gus and Jeb entered the tent they were abruptly halted. An orderly, his apron tinted red with blood, growled "This 'uns' a captain. Let's see," he said running a finger along the jacket's trim.

"Captain of Artillery, I'd say. Y'all tote him to that new hospital what's just been set up for officers. We're plum full-up in here. And them what's laying out there in the sun's got first dibs, anyhow. Go down that wagon trail," the man said, pointing south at the thick woods and the dark throat of a tree-sheltered road. "There's 'spose to be an abandoned cabin and a big barn back in yonder. Some of the overflow's being sent there. You can't miss it."

The aide outranked Gus but not knowing the degree in which he did, Gus pleaded with, "Sir, he won't make it that far."

"Well, that be his problem, don't it, soldier?" he said pointing at the stripes on the bloody sleeve of the uniform. "Most likely General Jackson's artillery man, that young feller' he's so proud of. Heard tell old Stonewall moved this lad's artillery up before the rest of our boys was ready. Now that was about as dumb as stepping in hog shit and scrapping it off with your nose. Besides, done tole you we'se full up. That new hospital can take him . . maybe," said the aide. "Git him over to that cabin," he said, pointing at a wagon path that led into the woods. "I don't think he'll hold on that long, though."

The orderly saw the worry in Gus' eyes and said apologetically, "Look. We ain't got one lick of medicine. No rags, no beds. Look around. Every inch done got a body flopped on it. And General Jackson'd have our asses if we don't do our best by that fellow there but we ain't got no best left. We ain't got nothing left." He dismissed Gus and Jeb with a final flip of the hand. "And tell the General that if y'all see him."

The soft sucking noises of the surgeons' and their aides' boots being pulled out of the blood-soaked mire on the dirt floor below the surgeon's tables assailed their senses as they left the tent. The moans, screams and crying of the wounded, remained imbedded in their ears and replayed constantly. The wounded and dying, their numbers climbing by the minute, lay everywhere, beneath the shade of the oaks, in the dark shadows cast by the barn, while others lay ignored in the heat of the sun. Their water blisters leaked a clear fluid as gun shots and bayonet stabs seeped a smelly, yellow pus. Lost blood, congealing and slippery, covered the walkway leading into the tent, suggested blood-red bricks had been laid by skilled masons as a welcome to the field hospital. Bluish-black blow flies hovered by the thousands near the tent flap, awaiting someone to enter or leave. Maggots, hatched from the flies' eggs deposited into the growing heap of amputated arms and legs, slithered and dug their way into the pile and gave the impression the mound of dead appendages was alive.

And each, Jeb and Gus, were thinking the same, *What a blessing death will be for many of these poor fellows, so near death they know they are dying.* The sight of men drinking desperately from dippers of water, unaware the same water flowed freely out of countless holes left by shrapnel and bullets, led them both to whisper similar prayers. "God. Please take those who can no longer bear the pain."

Gingerly, they stepped over and around the men scattered haphazardly like sticks of firewood upon the ground and trudged toward the direction of the wagon path. Inside the leafy tunnel the rot of the wetness of the ground assaulted their senses. Spanish moss hanging from the oaks' limbs added an ethereal feeling to the dark woods. The nerves of steel they had abundantly possessed during the late afternoon battle, and lost in the night's troubled sleep, had been replaced with a fear of the unknown of the darkness of the pathway. Dying men, or worse yet, dead men might be lying within feet of them. They could not see them, but each felt them.

Near the end, the path began to fill with smoke and the smell of roasting meat, obviously burnt, made their mouths water and their stomachs growl.

Walking from the woods, they saw the dark-gray corner of a log-cabin. Upon each log jutting out from the corners hung a wide array of things needed for war—discarded shirts, trousers in need of both washing and patching, ragged kepis, their visors bent or missing, rolled blankets and "possibles" tote-sacks, cartridge pouches filled with unused powder and shot, and canteens void of water—thus void of value, with a wide range of muskets and pistols of all calibers laying alongside the wall of the cabin. Knapsacks lay where they were dropped. Ants, lured by the smell of hardtack and salt pork gone bad, carried the rancid food to their queen.

Two haggard orderlies accompanied by an oddly colored, but very beautiful woman, stepped from the cabin and onto the porch as Gus and Jeb approached. With a wiggle of his fingers, an orderly beckoned the stretcher–bearers inside.

Once inside, they were directed to a cot by the far wall. A clean sheet was spread upon it. Testing the cornhusk mattress, they felt the residual warmth from the previous occupant. Gus and Jeb struggled to remove the young captain from the stretcher, but every fiber in their being was aching, their strength gone. Another orderly, he too wearing a soiled white apron, shouted as they tried to lift the young captain. "You damn idiots are going to tear his arm off if you keep tugging and pulling at him like that."

Instantly, Gus stood to confront the ill-mannered man. The young captain's arm fell hard to the floor and lay at a grotesque angle. Angrily, Gus spun toward the orderly. He'd had enough. The arteries in his neck grew in size, his eyes burned with anger. "Yesterday me and this here fellow," pointing at Jeb, "was soldiering, shooting and killing other men. Killed hundreds of 'em, you son of a bitch. Afore our muskets cooled off and the stink of gunpowder was off the field . . . 'fore we could sit down and tear up the rest of our teeth with hardtack, we was told to start toting these men. You think that fuckin' apron gives you the right to talk to us like that?" His anger so complete he was shaking. "Officer or not, you speak to me or him," pointing at Jeb, "like that again, I'll kick your ass so fuckin' hard you'll have to throw up so's you can eat your next meal. Now get the fuck out'ta our way, you ignorant, stupid bastard."

The man wearing the apron sat the wash basin he was holding on a stand next to the wall and fled the room. Gus sheepishly looked around the room, ashamed of his loss of temper. Slowly his humanity returned. He saw curiosity in the eyes of all those who had witnessed his rage—and fear in the caramel-colored woman's eyes.

An older man of about sixty entered the room and looked about, searching for the source of the yelling.

"If'n you'se the doctor what's in charge," Gus said, "I done been told to tell you this here fellow's with General Jackson and the general he'self tole to me to ask you to take good care of him. Said to tell you he'd consider it a kindness." With that, he turned and left the room to join Jeb on the porch.

The surgeon followed him.

"Well, I am in charge' said the elderly surgeon. "You can't talk to one of my men like that," he said, his voice loud and clear for the benefit of the other officers in the room. "What's your name?"

"Name of John Becker, Sir," Gus lied.

"His?" the surgeon asked, pointing at Jeb.

"He be Charlie Wright," another lie.

"Which unit you two with?"

And with a third, Gus answered, "South Carolina, 33rd Infantry, Company F."

The surgeon turned to an aide standing nearby.

"Get their names and write them up."

The aide did as he was told and shooed Gus and Jeb from the porch.

"We got two names, does we? asked Jeb.

"Do 'til we git clear of this place," Gus grinned.

Gus, free of the room and the self important officers, sat on the porch floor and cupped his head in his hands, trying to hide his shame. He had gone too far and it had scared him to learn he was capable of such anger. He thought it odd how he had pointed his musket at men and pulled the trigger and killed them. He'd never been mad at them, not even once—angry, yes but not to the degree he'd just learned he was capable of. He owed everyone in the room an apology, especially the woman. She had caused none of this and he was sick to his stomach.

"Ma'am. I'm so sorry. Me and him," pointing at his friend still tending to the man they'd just laid upon the floor, "been at the killing and the toting for almost two full days. Nothing to eat, hardly a mouth full of water and these idiots, these sonabitches, sorry ma'am" pointing at the man who had offended him, and who'd foolishly returned to retrieve the basin, "they got to where they think we'se mules or sump'n. Each one of 'em shouting different orders at us. And not a damn one of 'em got no rank higher than me and Jeb. Does you?" he shouted at the orderly.

Ironically, his outburst of anger suddenly spent, he seemed calmer. But the orderly doubted it. He dropped the basin, and sought a more accommodating place in which he could continue his grisly work.

The woman understood anger. She, who'd never lived a day without anger near her, answered calmly enough so Gus knew he had been forgiven, "Heard worse."

A tear dripped from Jeb's cheek. "Gus. I can't do it no more."

"Jeb. We gotta. There's a whole mess of 'em out there. Rest ah bit. I'll go and help clean up that captain."

Another tear. "It ain't that I'm worn out. I am. But I can't wrap my mind around nothin' no more. I can't look at no more dead bodies, everything's gone blood-red in my head. When I was talking to the doctor and that pretty woman, all I seen is burnt faces and blood runnin' down 'em. I can't go back, Gus. I jus' cain't. "

"Here, lay down next to that fellow over there. Take my field jacket for a pillow," he said, unbuttoning and folding it. "I'll stretch out our leaving for a bit. Get some rest if you can."

***

From the well in the rear yard, the beautiful woman, neither black nor white—her skin an unnamed color of caramel, or that of a ripened peach covered with a heavy dusting of ash, her hair walnut-black with streaks of brown—labored, carrying fresh buckets of water into the cabin. She'd heard the names "high yellow" and "mulatto" whispered from man to man. Many said she was a house servant, one deserted by her master. Others said no. Perhaps she was a slave, perhaps not, and she no longer knew which. Regardless, she found the terms insulting. In reality, she was a "Quadroon"—a person more white than Negro, and worth nine hundred and eighty-four dollars. *Call me as you will*, she thought.

She ignored the comments and her efforts of tending to the men earned her a great deal of respect from the wounded.

When asked by the surgeon whose home they were using as a makeshift field hospital, she answered, "It be Massa Strickland's."

The surgeon, a Brevet Colonel, designated himself in charge. "Miss," he asked, now knowing she was a slave, "Where is Mister Strickland?"

She would not and did not look the colonel in the eye, but pointed towards the woods on the far side of the yard. "He dun' run off'n dem woods when all dat noise got going out yonder," pointing towards Malvern Hill. And back to the well she headed for more water. She returned to the porch and handed a dipper of water, first to Gus, then to the much-improved Jeb.

"If'n y'alls hungry, we ain't got much, but follow me." And she led the way into the back yard. "Take what's left of the bean soup. It's been watered down so much it's a lie to call it soup. Got a bit of pork and some collards. Take as much as you can. We'se gonna make some more soon as they bring more hogs up here and cut 'em up."

***

The muffled noises of wagons rumbling along the path through the woods, and entering the yard, proved to be a major attraction to the soldiers lying about. The long-awaited ambulances had finally started to arrive. Careful of the men on the ground, they pulled up below the oak in the yard.

"Who's in charge here?" asked one of the teamsters.

A soldier, his arm hanging in a bloodied sling, pointed at the gray-haired man standing in the doorway of the overcrowded cabin. The Brevet Colonel wiped blood from his hand onto the apron he wore and handed a blood-encrusted bone saw to an aide. "Clean this off. Soak it in hot water if you can find any. Just get it back to me quick. There's arms and legs waiting."

Only then did he acknowledge the private in the lead ambulance.

"You in the ambulance . . . come here," he said, in a voice, used to giving orders meant to be obeyed. The driver hustled down. He knew from his tone the man, although merely a citizen appointed to his high station as a favor owed him by someone of military position and power, was used to being obeyed.

"Sir. Private Wilson, Herbert, 47th North Carolina, Company A. Old Stonewall, sorry Sir, General Jackson sent us. Told us to load up as many men what ain't near dying as we can and head off to that big hospital over in Richmond with 'em. Chicamo, he called it." Turning to Jeb and Gus, he hello'ed them with, "Hey Jeb. Hey Gus. Y'all look 'bout done used up."

"It's Chimborazo, not Chicamo," the surgeon said.

"What is?" asked the private.

"The name of the hospital," the surgeon replied, testily. "Well. Go on man. Hurry with it. Can't you see we're busy? How many more wagons y'all got coming?" asked the haggard surgeon. "Never mind, just tell them sum'bitchin' generals to keep 'em coming."

"Sir. General Jackson sent you these orders. They's here in this envelope. He told me to tell you to read this stuff for further instructions. First off, we'se suppose to start taking them what can make it to Richmond in these wagons. Since you'se the surgeon, he said for you to do the picking and choosing. And wants the first of 'em loaded up today and on their way. All we needs to know is who goes this load and we'll get 'em. And I'm supposed to tell him how many is here. How many you think?"

"Thank you, Lord. Thank you Jesus," said the exhausted surgeon. "Take the ones with a piece of this pinned on them," and handed a striped shirt to the poorly mannered orderly. "Put a strip on the ones who can make it. You all start loading those, but you best be careful with them. Put the worse off ones in the canvas slings and put those you can on the floorboards. As far as the count goes, they come and go all day . . . not the bad hurt ones, they ain't ready for a wagon ride, not yet."

"The General wants to know if you have a Captain Biggs here."

"Can't say. I'm not on first names with any of 'em. I just cut off legs and arms and sew up what's left—don't have time for names. That man over yonder. Him. That scrawny pain-in-the-ass over there, the one ripping up that striped shirt, he keeps account of the names of the coming and leaving. Maybe he'll know."

The surgeon turned to go back inside, but paused. "We just got a new one in. Ask them two fellows over there. They called him by name, but I didn't hear it."

The surgeon turned to get back to his cutting and sewing. As a second thought, he turned and said to the ambulance driver, "Private Wilson, was it? When you get back, tell General Jackson we need more provisions."

"What kind?" came the logical query.

"Everything. Damn it! And while you're standing there with your thumb up your ass, get one of your drivers tearing up a shirt, too. We're going to need a lot of strips. I'll get that orderly," he said, pointing at the man Gus had just had a word with, "started on the list right away. That'll bring him down from his high horse a bit," he added, knowing the teamster had no idea of what he meant. "He'll write down the names of the ones who are leaving and your man can pin a name and a piece of shirt on each of them. They'll be the ones who's leaving. I'll tell the orderly to give me a copy and one to you. You give yours to whoever's in charge of this goddamn mess." He shook his head in despair, "If anybody is."

The surgeon shouted, "Delmar. Get off your ass and get over here. Show this man the one's who can make it to that Richmond

Hospital. You and that soldier pin a rag on their shirts or pants, while you're at it."

The orderly seemed despondent—and at the verge of tears. He'd had a rough day—busted from head orderly to shirt ripper, all in one fell swoop.

"And you, Private. All the men are near dying . . . every damn one of 'em's more dead than alive. Now, I've done all I can do for these fellows. So don't you go killing them off running the mules faster than you got to. Jackson says anything about you holding up the line, tell him to come see me. On your way back find out how many more ambulances are coming down here. Make sure they know where we are. Draw them a goddamn map if they don't have enough sense to listen close."

***

Thus began days of decisions . . . who left, who remained. The ambulances continued coming, loading, leaving, but not fast enough for the surgeon, and God-awful slow for the men waiting in the shade of the large oaks in the yard. Those too weak or those bleeding out from the surgeon's saw, began choosing sides—figuring a way to heal or how to talk the Good Lord into taking them home with him.

"Ma'am, with your permission, me and Jeb's gonna' hang around fer a few days. That surgeon fellow seems kind'a anxious to close up shop and I don't think the captain's no where's near ready to go wagon bouncing. So we kind'a wanna stick around long enough to see he gits a fair chance at living."

Chapter Fourteen: Eighteen and sixty-four. Spring. Adair's treachery.

"Been that way . . that way . . . that way. Been in every direction there is from here," Bucyrus "Buck" Vance mumbled as he turned full circle in the middle of the road, arm extended, fingers pointing. Sometimes he thought himself lost, but never was, merely in a place he'd forgotten. The foothills of the Blue Ridges, the Outer Banks floating in the Atlantic, south to Charleston in the state of South Carolina, and even to the country's capitol, Washington—he'd been to them all. In the decade during the long walk, he'd seen more of life than most men would in a lifetime.

Walk. That's what he did. The past no longer called him, urging him home, and was nearly forgotten. Home had become unimportant to him. It was the road he needed, the carefree life of it.

He walked in order to distance himself from that previous life in which he perceived he had been a dismal failure. No, he wasn't lost. More like meandering aimlessly. But he had to admit it surprised him considerably when he saw the sign on the road post pointing toward Weldon. He had reached the age where it was important to seek the meaning of a thing and the sign was one of those things he felt he should consider.

"How did that get there?" he asked, talking to himself. He'd been doing more and more of that as the miles passed by and he walked his solitary walk. Sometimes he laughed aloud after telling himself a joke—or a made up story in order to give something new a worthwhile reason to be remembered. Perhaps he invented newer meanings to make things more to his liking than the truth was.

But that Weldon sign. He knew he was dangerously close to a place he did not want to be. He understood it wasn't Weldon as much as it was the backwoods town being far too close to people and things he did not want to be near. In the morning, he'd backtrack and head *off in another direction. He wasn't sure where he'd go, but the one thing he did know, it wasn't toward the plantation owned by Samuel Biggs. Although he would like to see Sam again, he'd rather walk through the gates of hell than walk through the gates of Swift Creek Plantation. Too many memories there.*

He was hungry and searched the shoddy pockets of his overcoat for the remaining half of a late fall head of cabbage, but it had avoided its destiny by falling through a frayed and bottomless pocket. An odd thing he'd learned on the road—if he had an apple in his pocket, figs in a handkerchief, or a head of cabbage in a tote sack, the thought of food was held at bay for hours on end. Sometimes one meal a day was enough. But when those edibles where no longer there, ready for his pleasure and at a time of his choosing, his immediate hunger would be ravenous. Maybe, he reasoned, it was the emptiness of the road and not the total lack of food, that drove the hunger to the point of obsession.

His foot hurt but not enough to stop and rest. But soon he began to favor it. The difficulty the pain brought with it sucked the remaining energy from him. Recognizing the sticky slide of raw skin slipping in fresh blood across leather worn smooth by miles and time, he collapsed upon the bank of the deeply worn dirt road. He dug a pea-sized piece of gravel from within the far reach of the shoe and searched for the gravel's entry point. A finger, damp with blood was pulled from the worn out shoe, so he knew in which direction he would travel—he needed food and another pair of shoes. He could find both in Weldon. He never ceased to be surprised at what people would throw away.

He looked again at the sign. "Weldon, it is."

Exhausted, he crawled into the cover of the woods and slept. And the dreams returned. Those vivid dreams.

In his dreams, he reached to straighten the nonexistent copper-clad star as he had done a thousand times before, and checked for the reason of the lightness of his hip upon which he'd once worn the huge and cumbersome Colt Dragoon. He dreamed of how fitting it had been to throw the worthless sheriff's badge he'd ripped from his shirt into freshly deposited cow flop in the street in front of the jail he'd just slammed the door shut on. His days of fighting both corruption and those angry at him for fighting it were almost finished. One last job remained and that great burden had been lifted from him when he dropped the killing mass of Mister Colt's iron and steel down into the Fort Harwood Central-Park well—the townsfolks' only source of drinking water. At first, he thought the gun rusting away thirty feet below at the bottom of the well was the ideal way to feed the misery of the weapon back to the very people who had demanded so much of it.

"Maybe you dumb ass bastards will choke on it," he laughed as he heard it splash below. "Or at least it might rust your brains." *A good joke, that gun dropping, a good pay back*, he thought, until he remembered the town's water had always tasted of rust and smelled of sulpher. Rust from ore in the ground and the stink of sulpher, for the town had always been a living hell. So nothing was gained and nothing lost of his wished-for retaliation.

There were times afterwards when he wished he had the weapon again, or something similar, a slant-back Sharps would do, or maybe a long and sturdy belt knife, a Sheffield Bowie, but a blacksmith-made D square knife would suit him fine.

***

He'd willingly given up the job as Sheriff of Fort Harwood. Try as he might he could not rid the small town of the disease eating away at its citizens. He could easily picture them as those African cannibals he'd read about—they lived to eat away at each other.

He felt his long tenure as the sheriff of Carlton County had been basic, at best mediocre, and at times self-serving. He'd finally grown a conscience and wanted—needed—to be a better man. But such things could not exist in the hell-hole of Fort Harwood. He'd promised himself he would find a place where he could become what he sought, even if it took forever. And then he took to his walking and searching.

"Bad times on dusty roads," he often said, warbling the words from an old song no longer heard much. The first part of the verse was all he could remember and he sang it often. During his first three years after leaving Fort Harwood, he had been on all of those back roads of which the song complained—thinking, as he trudged along, how someone had complained of the same roads and put the misery of them to tune. He seldom had a direction or ending in mind, and preferred the back roads, those not well traveled. He had seen the sailing ships coming and leaving Wilmington, climbed the rugged trail to the peak of the highest point east of the Mississippi River, as Mount Mitchell lorded it over the lesser mountains of the Blue Ridges. From one extreme of the state to the other he'd marched, one foot after the next. Within a few years, he'd seen all of North Carolina and then reversed his voyage. But in all of his aimless drifting he'd steered clear of Fort Harwood, Weldon, and Swift Creek.

    He was older now—no longer trustful of others—always on his guard, keenly attuned to dangers. Life on the road had become different, harder. The rumblings of war had changed everything—people's generosity, their trust in their fellow man. Some feared him because he walked, others because he refrained from conversation. He learned to stay clear of any town big enough to brag of their "Home Guard," a mob of old men, and hairless faced boys too young to join the Confederacy. Generally, the boys and the elderly play-soldiers were a mockery to the Confederacy and traitors to those they'd sworn to protect. Instead, the guns bought and paid for out of the town's treasury provided them with a twisted sense of power, allowing them to rob and kill as they saw fit. Many times he'd been chased relentlessly by such Home Guard with its old men and young boys anxious to steal from him even though they could see all he owned, he wore. Or at least they could march him through the town, and use him as proof they could protect their neighbors from worn out drifters if the need arose. And, too, there was the right to carry pistols and muskets.

    He understood the exuberance of the young and their joy of carrying a gun—that's exactly what sheriffing had done to him—except he'd been paid a pittance. Like the make-believe soldiers, his chest had puffed out, and his conscience had clouded with the right and the wrong of things. Not so well did he understand the older men, those too old to enjoy much of anything. Maybe some thought they were a necessity for their neighbors and reveled in the praise heaped upon them, but he believed it was mostly the fact that the young men made them feel vibrant and useful again.

Whenever stopped, he was questioned about his loyalty and to which side. He thought that a stupid question to ask of a stranger. Who *would* admit to being a Northerner while walking through the very heart of Dixie? He found it odd that as many people who spoke eagerly of the war, others prayed for the salvation of the Union. The war had been raging for over a year and Buck saw little hope of it ending soon. He could not count the times he'd heard "damn niggers this" or "damn niggers that." The wealthy white men had to blame someone for the troubles encroaching upon their lives. But in such conversations it was not smart for a stranger to voice an opinion.

His journey may have helped him. He didn't know. But he now felt the wiser for his walking. Sometimes he questioned his own sanity, the reason for his existence, even the walking part. Reluctantly, he admitted to himself he'd wasted those years. He no longer felt cynical of his fellow man, and refused to judge them of their actions. Nor did he still feel the sting of blood which in his former life had stained his hands. In truth, he mostly felt empty and lost. It was time for his road to end.

In returning to Carlton County he'd considered people might still recognize him, but thought it unlikely. He no longer resembled the robust man he'd once been, but more a vagabond—a creature worn down by the road, weary and dirty, and much in need of a shave, haircut, bath, and new clothing, not to mentioned the sixty pounds of muscle and fat the roads had stolen from him. If he could accomplish those things it might give him the confidence to face his past again.

But he was so tired. He knew he would never return to Fort Harwood, but how he wished he could emerge from his hiding place at the inner edge of the heavy woods along Swift Creek and call out to the dear friends he'd watched from a safe distance. Seldom did a day pass that he did not think of Sam and Rose, Henry and Isaac.

***

"How time flies," Adair Graystone said to the empty office. Lost in thought, he sat behind his leather-topped desk and leaned backwards into the heavy chair. An expensive Carolina Gold clamped between tobacco-stained teeth, its embers dying, slowly burned into a finger of gray ash. An overfilled glass of bourbon sloshed in his right hand. Sam Biggs was on his mind. Thinking of Sam always made him nervous. And his nerves required alcohol.

Two decades before, and fresh from Virginia, a well-dressed man walked through the front doors of Adair Graystone's struggling business, that of managing the financial matters of those needing managing and too busy to see to it themselves.

A tall and muscular man wearing the aura of one who felt he owned the whole of Weldon, filled the doorway to his office. Without formal introduction, Samuel Elywn Biggs handed Adair Graystone a Carolina Gold, a rare and expensive cigar. And now, years later, Graystone remembered taking the cigar from the man while he sat and waited for the newcomer to speak. How he wished he'd not taken the cigar, a luxury he then could not afford and one he could not now live without. How he wished Samuel Biggs had never walked through his office door.

Struggling with the new business, the financial advisor was therefore miserly. He removed the gold-gilded band, worth so little that the entirety of the gilt brushed upon it was hardly worth more than a few grains of salt, and stored it in his desk's drawer. Next, he snipped the end, struck a match, and began to suck on the cigar as if it would be the last Carolina Gold he'd ever smoke. He put the snipped-off end, a nail-sized clipping of the cigar, into his pocket and thinking the man before him would think that odd, blushed and quickly explained, "I'll save this bit for my pipe."

As he exhaled, the thick smoke added to the closeness of the office.

Without being asked, the stranger settled into the leather covered chair across from Adair's desk, and pointed his own cigar at him. Even now, Adair could remember his first thoughts of the man—*who the hell does this cocky son of a bitch think he is?*

"Name's Samuel Elwyn Biggs," came the answer. "Yours is Graystone, right? Adair Graystone?" With the simplistic greeting completed, Samuel Biggs exploded into a litany of financial talk. He asked the right questions of Mr. Graystone and received the correct answers. Agreements were quickly made, names inked in as needed, and, with the meeting completed, Samuel Biggs stood to leave, but then turned and said, "Remember this, Adair, and we'll do fine."

Adair recoiled when the stranger, so cock-sure of himself, dared to call him by his first name.

"I didn't just walk in off the street. I know who you are and how you run your business. I have many friends, people you know who have vouched for you. The 'who' is not important right now and I hope I never have to get upset with those friends, so in fair warning I will say I'm not a man to be trifled with." He tipped his hat, and added, "Don't let me down. Good day, Sir." Their first meeting, from being handed the rare and expensive custom-made cigar to the veiled threat, had lasted fourteen minutes and forty-two seconds.

Too, Adair remembered how embarrassed he'd felt that he'd practically bowed to the stranger, and the vague feeling that he was now somehow subordinate to a man he did not know. But he *had* decided he was fond of Carolina Gold cigars.

Sam stood in the doorway and put his hat on. As he did, Adair answered, "Oh. No Sir. I assure you Mr. Biggs, you have nothing to worry about."

***

Most men would have taken the comment as a warning, or have been insulted with the harshness and surprise of it. Some would have demanded such a rude person leave their office, but Adair would have let this Mr. Biggs fellow call him a foul-breathed buzzard, a piddling piss-ant—anything—for the kind of money he was about to reap from an association with the man who gave away the prized and expensive cigars wrapped with gold-gilded bands. Therefore, he gave little thought to the veiled warning—and that was the first mistake of many he would make while dealing with Samuel Biggs.

All in all, it had been a good day for Adair—the best in a year thus far filled with failures. He'd landed the largest account he'd ever had the good luck to service. How pleased he was his inevitable flight from Weldon had been forestalled. Perhaps he could save his struggling business after all.

But there was something about the man that unsettled him. Maybe it was the way the stranger, without saying a word, demanded respect, or perhaps the threatening size of the man. Soon enough he would learn that first meeting with Samuel Biggs and the promise of wealth that came with it, was one he should have avoided.

***

Since that day, he had prospered, and like Weldon, Adair had changed. True, he'd made a lot of friends when he and his wife moved from Vermont to the warmer climes of North Carolina. She was sickly, but held on desperately to the lonely life she lived. Old friends died off, some moved away, and others simply disappeared. Years passed. Adair grew quiet and withdrawn and never sought new friends to replace those lost.

Weldon had grown considerably since that long ago time. Townsfolk still smiled at one another and exchanged pleasantries—most well meaning, others hollow and vacant.

Adair's world dwindled to two places, his home and his office. Now-a-days, he spent more and more of his time standing—hiding, actually, behind the dark curtains of his office watching Weldon's townsfolk ramble past. He had his reasons to hide. He'd done some things he should not have done. He had not followed Sam's advice. He had trifled with Samuel Biggs.

His acts of friendship were a front. Many of his clients soon realized his excitement over the faith they had put in him was merely an act, a way to soothe them as monies drained from their accounts—others stayed with him out a thwarted sense of loyalty.

Seldom did he invite a client into his home. And when he did, to the occasional visitor the missus appeared healthy, but even those occasions dwindled, and her husband gradually became her caretaker and began to wish she'd get on with her dying.

He envied those walking past—those carefree citizens who never seemed in a hurry. He dreaded his daily strolls down the town's planked sidewalks, the coming to work and the going home. He often had to fight a spontaneous impulse to walk to the end of the street, turn north, and head back to Vermont—minus the problems he'd created and the wife he felt had drug the life from his soul.

His had been a solitary life. He nursed his wife as well as he could when at home, but found the need, the desire to be gone, growing. She had long ago found if she clung to him, needy and child-like, he would see to her needs, but eventually she overplayed her hand. He was tired of his work, tired of his wife, tired of Weldon.

Now, when Adair spoke, it was as if he was angry. His mannerisms became suspect. Nervous tics developed. He sought not the company of others—found them troublesome, for in their presence he needed to remain sober. He preferred the sound of a cork being pulled from the bottle in front of him to that of their constant droning on and on about their small, insignificant lives—things of which he did not give a damn. His days were confined to the limits of his business and his home, his nights controlled by a sickly wife and a ever-growing need for alcohol. Therefore, his firm remained small and Sam Biggs remained his wealthiest customer.

His office of late was more and more off-limits to customers, old or new, and generally, the door between his office and his employees remained locked during office hours, even as he sat inside and behind his cluttered desk. The employees stayed clear of their boss when his door shut—and even more so when he occasionally ventured from his sanctuary. They busied themselves hoping their efforts to look overwhelmed by their workload would keep him at a distance. They found him distracted, to the point of being unapproachable. Few ever tried to approach him unless matters of extreme importance pressed them to knock upon the heavy oak door separating their meager work stations from his opulent office. Mr. Wiggins, the assistant manager, was much easier to approach and not nearly as likely to snap at or belittle those who sought needed answers. Each employee knew there would be hell to pay for a reckless violation of Adair Graystone's privacy.

Soon, the always-locked door gave birth to inevitable rumors.

Their jobs were not at risk. Adair's employees and their insignificant lives and unimportant problems were of no concern to him—bigger troubles vexed him. And he believed those vexations would be the death of him.

Now, he stole. That was his new job, his new purpose in life. He was a thief. There was *real* money to be made stealing. Not the pennies-on-the-dollar commissions he made, but real money. A lot of money. Ignoring the purpose of his business, he seldom advised his customers and those he ignored soon sought advice from his competitors.

***

Today an old partner was coming, one also well-versed in Adair's secondary trade. Because of the impending arrival, Adair felt the scratch of a hemp rope around his neck. Indeed it was a bad day—the kind of day he could get killed. No way could the cotton merchant and Sam Biggs be in the same town. No, of all days, not this day. But that was what Adair feared. Samuel Elwyn Biggs was the last person on earth he wanted to see today.

To the emptied room he said, "I can't wait to be shed of this toilet of a town for good."

Hands shaking, he reached to the shelf above the file cabinet for the bottle of Old Hebrew, his favorite bourbon. "Two fingers ought'a do it," he mumbled, and poured four. A new oddity had developed—mumbling, but he was unaware of it. Slowly his nerves settled. So he poured himself yet another glass of the fine bourbon, seeking the bottle's version of tranquility. He had no problem with being drunk if that was what it took. He watched as the amber liquid sloshed onto his fingers, and then licked at the precious liquid.

But something was askew; the day did not ring true—different, somehow. He felt the static of building tension. Paranoia? He imagined people were staring at him. He was sure he heard his name whispered by the passerby's on the street. *Is it all catching up with me?* he wondered. *Am I found out? Does Sam know? Does my wife know?*

And he heard whispers from deep within his head. *Look where your greed's got you*, they teased, hoping to drive the point home. He tried to tally how much money he had earned over the years working for Sam—and how much he'd stolen. But the knots in his stomach demanded more whiskey.

"A lot, and I deserved every red copper of it," he mumbled, staring at the glass of honey colored liquid slowly salving his guilty conscience and fortifying his corrupt reasoning. "A hard man to work for, that Sam. Everybody knows that—me more than most, what with him always coming at me with 'Adair, do this. Adair, do that.' Like he owns me or . . . like I'm one of his damn precious slaves."

Realizing he was speaking aloud, he feared sharp ears pressed against the outer door would hear him. He felt an urge to snatch the door open and throttle those who stood beyond eavesdropping.

Again the thoughts. *Yes. It is a lot of money, no doubt of that. He'll kill me. He'll kill me for sure.*

"Well," and again speaking to the man in the wall mounted mirror before him, he said, "There you have it, Mr. Adair Graystone. It's all out in the open. Big as life. You threw in with hogs," speaking of the soon arrival of the cotton buyer, "and you and him wallowed good, and here you are complaining about being dirty. Now, ain't that a hoot."

He did not care for the way his conscience could turn on him. One minute—his savior, praising his clever thievery—the next, an enemy condemning him to the depths of Hell.

He'd always eased his guilt by telling himself what he'd done for years wasn't really stealing—*no, that's not at all what I was doing. Stealing is what it's called when folks take things which do not belong to them. I only took what I was entitled to.*

Adair had long worn two hats—one sized for an advisor, the other for a thief. He knew the trick to wearing two hats and both fit him well. He'd stolen only what he felt he was entitled to, such as when small bonuses were not forthcoming. He listened carefully, seeking inlets into the funds of clients who did not understand finances. He'd been Sam Biggs' advisor for two decades and early in their long relationship, he'd started his thief-hat wearing—a small bonus here, a bit larger there, especially whenever he felt Sam owed him and probably would have given it to him, anyway, as a reward for his hard work and his diligence. He'd practiced his lines well. "I took a small advance against my commissions. I didn't think you'd mind that much, Sam. You don't, do you?"

Each year as their relationship grew, he bequeathed upon himself a renewed and stronger sense of security—and with that, a growing conviction of his entitlements.

He'd grown comfortable with what he thought was the rightness of his actions. He'd made a lot of money as Sam's advisor and more by stealing from him. He considered himself the thinker of the two—the superior. He thought Sam a dullard. "But Sam is wealthier than I. And from *my* doings, not his. Shit," he complained to unhearing walls, "that man would screw up a game of solitaire if left to his own devices. He needs me . . . and he damn well knows it."

The dark part of his conscience interrupted his musings. *Maybe I should'a took more.* Guilt and tension always eased whenever he heard *that* approving voice in his head.

Not sure whether he was speaking aloud or mumbling, he again counseled himself to be quiet. He felt *their* ears pressed against the door. He stood and placed a glass against the paneled wall and listened but heard only the rumble of guilt already within himself

One thing he was sure of: as long as he lived in Weldon, and kept running Sam's empire, Sam Biggs would never know how much he had actually been sharing with his "most trusted" advisor and he would never find out, either. Besides, if he did, it'd be too late for that dimwit to do anything—he and the missus would be long gone.

He reasoned that by not stealing from Sam on a steady basis he was not like other thieves. "It's not like I did those things every year. No," his mumbling resumed, "I didn't start taking stuff until the middle of the eighteen forties or so, the year that man from the cotton mills in Vermont sailed up the Albemarle looking for cotton to buy. Yeah . . . forty-four, forty-five, could'a been earlier . . . right around then, though. No, it was a bit earlier . . . that first time. Forty-three." He recalled how frightened he had been that he was going to die if Sam found out about the deal he'd struck with the cotton buyer—how he'd started shaving money off the top of everything of Sam's he sold to the merchant as willing to steal as he.

There were times he wished he'd never heard of Gleason McDermott, or those damn Gordon Cotton Mills in Vermont, for that matter.

***

A light *tap . . . tap . . . tap* on his door ended the galloping thoughts racing through his mind, and as he opened the heavy door, he extended his hand toward a leather chair, and said to his secretary,

"Pour us a drink. The expensive bourbon." Drinks handed to each, Adair said, "That will be all, James. See no one bothers us."

"Gleason," he said. "Sit. Sit." A younger version of Gleason McDermott followed the older man and stood next to the cotton merchant. Adair did not acknowledge the stranger. He shut the door to his office, then closed the wooden blinds he had installed years ago in order to spy on the "spies" in the outer office and led the cotton merchant to a maroon-colored leather chair.

His and McDermott's long relationship had always been contentious affairs—one thinking himself superior to the other and each trying to enforce his will upon the other. Neither much enjoyed the union they shared but found their mutual interest in stealing had advantages.

Instantly Adair's rage built, his face flushed red and his temper flared. "Who's that?" he demanded, pointing threateningly at the stranger standing next to Gleason McDermott. "We had an agreement. No new people. Ever."

"What? 'No well hello Gleason?' No 'how are you doing?'" the cotton broker asked, "This is Nathaniel Bolton. Been an associate of mine for years. Thought it was time he got to know you, Adair. Nathan, meet Mr. Graystone. Adair, Nathaniel."

The veins in Adair's neck were pencil thick. "Meet me? Why the hell does he need to meet me? What's he doing here?" Ignoring the bewildered Nathan, Adair grabbed McDermott's arm and pulled him towards the rear door of his office. "Come. Have a word with me."

He snapped at the younger man, "Bolton, Brighton, or whatever, you finish that fucking drink. Put the glass on the counter. Do not pour another one. Do not sit down. And do not leave this office. Understand?"

The younger man looked at his father, his eyes pleading for an explanation.

***

Adair and McDermott stepped onto the porch attached to the rear of the office. Beneath the decking, a drifter who in a former life had been a sheriff, lay quietly, hoping not to be discovered. He desperately needed the protection of the tight quarters below the porch.

His bones had warned him the coming night was going to be a cold one and full of rain—he knew weather from being on the road for so many years. Sand, dirt, and debris filtered through the cracks of the planks above and upon his exposed face. Very carefully and very quietly, Bucyrus "Buck" Vance, the former Sheriff of Carlton County and the small town of Fort Harwood, fifteen miles to the south, pulled a dirty handkerchief from an equally soiled vest pocket and spread it over his grime-covered and bearded face, while choking back a stifling sneeze.

As chance would have it, he'd found the crawl space and settled into it only moments before the two men above stomped from within the building and proceeded to kick dust and dirt upon him. He willed them to go back inside. Instead, they ignored him, preferring to argue and shout at one another.

The drunker of the two, Adair, yelled, "I asked you, motherfucker, who that youngster in there is and I don't mean his goddamn name. Now, you already told me his name is Nathaniel Bolton or some-such bullshit. Do not tell me his name again. Tell me why he is with you. Who is he to you? I want to know why he's in my office, and it better be good," Adair shouted, not realizing or caring that he was spraying spittle onto McDermott's face.

The second voice from above was gravelly, raspy, sounding as if the owner was a heavy smoker. "Screw you, Adair," interjected Gleason. "Who the hell gave you the right, or for that matter, the balls to talk to me like that? You want me to bust your nose, right here, right now? I'd be happy to oblige you, you dumb-ass redneck peckerwood. You look like you're about to bust a gut. Neck arteries popping out like ropes. Calm down, you scrawny asshole," said the man. "How long me and you been at it? If I say you can trust him, you can trust him. He knows what's at stake," and explained their relationship—not the father and son part, but that of one thief teaching another.

And McDermott never said a word about this trip being his last ever. He was rich now, as rich as a thief could be. He and Adair had been at their stealing for a long time. All he desired for the remainder of his life was to live in safety back in Vermont. That, and to get drunk, and stay drunk, in front of a roaring fire in an oversized fireplace.

"Well, Gleason," said Adair. "He better goddamn well know what he's getting into. If Biggs hears one out-of-the-way word, a careless comment, a whisper, hell, even if a fart don't sound right to him, he'll kill us both and that boy inside."

To the man below the porch the word "kill" sounded like a bell's first ring—always the loudest. Instantly everything else became unimportant, the cold—the hard ground, the acrid odor of men using the rear porch as a urinal whenever urgently needed.

Adair's temples pounded from anger and with a sneer of sarcasm spreading from one side of his face to the other, he continued, "Did you tell that youngster drinking my bourbon in there he might could get himself killed for what we're doing? No? I bet you didn't." He paused and pushed the door open enough to look at the young man inside. "Is he even old enough to drink?" he asked.

"Older than he looks," answered McDermott.

"As I was saying. Did you forget about when Biggs killed them two fellows, those slavers up by his place? Done it cold as a chunk of ice. I'll bet you didn't tell him that neither, did you? And ain't it strange how they found that crazy loon, Griffen, deader than a rock no mor'n a half mile from Biggs' house? What the hell do you think he'll do if he finds out how much cotton and tobacco me and you skimmed off'a him and shipped up north while he's home sleeping like a baby?"

"What I told him, I think, is my concern, not yours." answered Gleason. "You dare come at me with blood in your eyes, calling me a motherfucker, when there's things you said you were going to do before I got back. Well, I'm back now, so I want to know who you're going to use to get the cotton out of Brantley's warehouses this time?"

"Same as always. Ezekiel and Bear."

"And that's my point. Them darkies are Biggs' darkies."

"Everything these parts is Biggs', you damn fool."

"Well, they been balking the last few times. You know what they say about loose lips. Them two get to talking, especially to their women, the games up," warned Gleason. "And you promised you'd get rid of 'em."

"Yeah, I did say that. And I will. But couldn't see the need for it, not just yet. They ain't gonna' talk."

"What makes you so damn sure of that, Adair? 'Cause Griffen's gone? Seems to me that'd be enough for them to get a little bit of backbone back in them."

"Got'ta use your thinker," Graystone said, tapping his temple. "There's ways to get your point across. And, yes, I did try to find some other darkies, but ain't too many of them allowed out'ta the fields nowadays, not with that fighting starting up in Virginia. And don't forget I told you right up front there ain't nobody gonna hire out their field workers with that mess going on.

"Besides, don' worry about it. I took care of it. Got to running through my mind Ezekiel and Bear could go to that new fellow what runs Griffen's old place, that Henry something fellow, and 'fess up to what they been doing the last few years. You know how those darkies are about getting in Heaven and staying out of Hell—dress up of a Sunday morning, get to church and start in with their whooping and moaning to the Lord. They get that spirit jumpin' on 'em, they's liable to get to confessing their sins. So I sent a message for the two of them to come down to the docks and I had me a long talk with them. Let's say I kind'a reminded them it would be best if they stayed quiet about things. Stuck my knife out and pulled a finger 'cross my neck and reminded Zeke and Bear they have them women and their babies waiting on 'em over at Johnson's plantation north of them. Old Zeke took to shaking like the devil was after him, me saying that to him. But Bear . . . when we're done, I'm going to have to kill him. Zeke too, most likely.

"Got the feeling they was about ready to revolt. So when that Beckham fellow, the overseer from the Johnson Place come into town, I had me a talk with him. Gave him two hundred dollars, and when he asked me what for, I told him to snip the ears of Zeke and Bear's women a half inch or so so they'd for sure stay quiet." With a twinkle in his eyes and a grin upon his face, he pinched his own ear. "You know the soft hangy-down part. Well, he done it, and them two darkies know it."

"Ain't it amazing what two hundred dollars'll do?" laughed Gleason McDermott.

"So, like I been saying, Ezekiel and Bear's in this mess for the long haul. They understand that, now. They know if they start running off at the mouth, they'll get strung up. And I told them I'd make a point of their women and their children being at their hanging, even if I had to buy them myself and haul their asses out there to watch the two of them dancing on a rope. And I would, too. No. Them two ain't gonna say nothing to nobody. No Siree. But just in case, got me a back-up plan."

"And that would be?"

"Broke me a hole through the floor down by the docks. We can always chain 'em up and dump 'em into the river."

"I like that, but wait a fucking minute. That overseer, Beckman? You fool. What makes you think you can trust a man you just gave two hundred dollars to? How soon will he be back to hold us up for more?"

"I ain't worried none about it. He won't."

"Sound awful sure of yourself."

"Well, let's just say I already tested that hole. And if I was you, I wouldn't eat no fish out'ta that river for a long time Old Beckman was struggling something fierce trying to swim with all them chains wrapped around him."

"Hmmm'" answered McDermott, nodding his approval.

"What about that sorry-ass piece of shit Brantley? He still playing by our rules?"

"Gleason, you know something? You're about rat-ass stupid. You in his shoes, wouldn't you? You think after we caught him a huffin' and puffin' over that little boy he done spread out on that bale of cotton, he'd tell anybody anything? Sure as hell won't never say a bad word about us, not even as bad as we are. Not to Sam. Not to nobody. We could'a moved twice as much cotton, hell three times as much, down to the Sound and he wouldn't never said nary one word. He knows the town would hang his withered up nasty ass for what he done to that boy—and them others, too. He still trembles when he sees me. Probably mess his pants when the two of us walk in tomorrow and tell him to get gone for a while."

"Me and you are getting out of this line of work," stated Gleason. "It's time."

Adair stared at Gleason, but said nothing.

"What with the war up and starting, you know as well as I do, there's no way I'm going to get them barges up here to Weldon ever again. It's over after this. The North's blockading the Carolina sounds and inlets already, and you can be sure the mouth of the Pamlico won't be open much longer. My guess, another two months not even an eel soaked in axle grease could get past them gunboats they're going to send up the Neuse River."

***

Over a decade earlier, Bucyrus Vance had thrown his sheriff's badge in the cow flop in front of his office in Fort Harwood, the seat of Carlton County. After the troubles he, Sam, and their old friend Emmett had seen and shared, and the violent things he'd done, he'd had enough of being an ineffectual lawman. He'd decided to leave Fort Harwood and look for a new start. Now, years later, he lay under a porch in Weldon, North Carolina. And Weldon was closer to Fort Harwood than he ever thought he'd be again.

Life was full of oddities. He'd worked at the occasional gypsy circus during his roaming. Seen some things. Cows born with two heads, both chewing their cud. A dog with five legs. Two babies born sharing one body, both dead and floating in alcohol, and a girl with lobster claws for hands. And the things he'd heard—stories of rocks and fish raining out of the sky, horse riders without heads, and ghosts. Who could understand such things?

And what was the chance that on this very day, this very minute, he'd be laying under a porch, and hearing the things he'd just heard. How was it he'd walked into Weldon when he did? Was it a sign? Was his time used up? He wondered if fate had finally caught up with him.

At first, he thought the two men above were drunks having an argument—one mad with the other. But the name, *Sam Biggs* startled him. There was no mistaking *that* name. He and Sam had been friends for many years. *Might still be*, he thought. And to hear people standing above him talking of how they were stealing from his friend shook his very being. But *that* name—Hesper Griffen, he'd thought he would never hear it again, rang in his ear like a Sunday morning church bell. Alarmed, he jumped, hitting his forehead against a porch joist. The two above continued arguing, thankfully as loudly as when they'd started.

There were only four people in the world who knew what had happened up in those woods above Sam's mansion, and he was one of those four.

He realized even if their long ago friendship might have been destroyed, he had to go to Sam's plantation and warn him of what he'd heard. His stomach knotted, but he had no other choice.

Too many strange things were happening. He didn't know if he could face Sam's wife, Rose. She, of all people, he feared seeing the most. He'd killed her father and figured Sam would have told her by now . . . or maybe not. It would have been a hard thing for any man to do—tell his wife a thing like that, but still, he couldn't be sure. Obviously, she suspected he'd been involved with the man's death by the way she'd avoided him. *Will she still steer clear of me now?* he wondered. *Maybe she won't even be there. Gone somewhere. Off visiting friends.*

Finally, the two men above, both considerably drunk, had worn out or resolved their differences. Buck didn't care which—he only wanted to hear the two of them go back inside and the door close. From within the room, he heard the muffled conversation continue, but heard nothing clearly.

***

"So, what you pansy-asses like to drink up there in the land of bloomer wearers?" Adair asked condescendingly, a twinkle in his eyes.

McDermott glared at Adair. "Best not to say things like that. Vermont's your home and if you haven't forgot, it's the one you want to go back to."

"True. Just trying to get a rise."

As always, Gleason seemed to have a need to show himself Adair's superior. "Have you any Beefeaters? Best gin in the world. Or has our import from England caught on down here in the land of the dullards yet?" smirked McDermott, himself not ready to forgive and forget.

Nathaniel snickered at his father's clever sarcasm.

Slowly, with a bit of alcohol doing its work, the banter between the Vermont thief and the financial advisor eased. The meaningless chatter had long ago grown tiresome to Adair, but in the spirit of business, especially their business, the game had to be played for a while. It was their way of doing business, first the insulting, then the appeasing, and always the drinking.

The alcohol's calming effect was useful—it took the edge off of things. And stealing was something one needed to be loose for, free of the snagging edges of hurt feelings, and the fear that came with their line of work.

Tonight was the end of their association. The meaningless banner served as a necessary coffin lid for their nearly dead business. And the reference to dullards did not go unnoticed by Adair Graystone. He knew Gleason's way was to try and piss him off, make him mad, draw first blood, and establish dominance over what most likely would be a contentious meeting. Generally, whoever gained the best footing dictated the terms. But neither the banter, nor the push and pull of their game ever seemed to alter the end results. Gleason would buy and Adair would sell—the way it'd always been and the way it would end.

He knew Gleason, as well as himself, were thieves trained, self-taught to gain the upper hand by whatever means possible—a sarcastic word here, a cutting, grinding comment there. But he understood the need to gain control of their meeting and the importance of alcohol.

He turned to the cabinet and pulled the opened bottle of gin from the top shelf. He hated the taste of gin—the smell of it gagged him. Vile piss only a man like McDermott would drink, he thought. To him, it tasted of an odd mixture of things gone rotten, and that it smelled of the same. But an opened bottle, a specially ordered bottle from Richmond, now partially emptied—*some of it purposefully poured out in the alley*—would give the impression that he himself might have a weakness for the foul-smelling beverage remaining inside. And that, too, would mislead Gleason.

Returning to the business at hand, "Excellent taste you have," Adair said. "It's hard to come by, and I might add a bit expensive for us dullards, but worth every copper it cost. What about you?" he asked Gleason and then the same of the young man. "Same thing? I've a fine rum from the West Indies, or perhaps something a bit different. Maybe some of that "Wicked Willie" some of the folks around here make. But beware, that stuff comes with a warning. Might be better to stay with the gin if you fellows are not used to a man's drink."

As a matter of manly pride, the older of the two visitors, Gleason, said, "No. Wait. Let me try some of that . . . what did you call it . . . Wicked what?"

"Close enough," chuckled Adair. "Close enough."

Seldom could even the biggest drinkers in Weldon handle more than a third of a glass of one-eighty proof Wicked Willie. Adair handed each a glass three-quarters full.

"What took you so long to get up here from Washington? You have trouble coming up the Pamlico?" referring to the sound that flowed inland from the outer banks.

"The Captain got the tides wrong. Damn fool. Drunk. We missed our passage and had to make new arrangements."

"Well, you're here now. Let's get down to it. How much you want this time?"

The final game had begun.

"That's going to depend on how much you have and how much you expect for it, Adair."

"I've got three hundred fifty-plus bales stored over at old man Brantley's warehouse. Fifty more coming in. Your boat hold that much?"

"We got enough boats," responded McDermott.

"Alright, then. I want the same price for it the mills in New Hampshire will give me. That's one-hundred sixty-five dollars per bale, if you take it all. More if you don't and I'm not of a mind to split it up," answered Adair. "You pay the storage and loading. Like always, I get an extra twenty percent, upfront. That's another thirteen thousand two hundred. No records, either. I'll make out a bill of sale for the four hundred bales, one hundred, sixty-five dollars each or however many you want, but the price per bale goes up if you buy less," the argument always similar, always effective. "You get the receipt when your voucher is deposited in Biggs' account. Then I'm through with it. The deposit, good or not's your problem, not mine. Make it out the same name as always—Sam Biggs. Nothing's changed."

"Look here, every damn time you raise the price on us. Too much. You got to lower it. If you do I'll take it all."

Adair stood. He reached out for the unfinished glasses of the home-made whiskey. "Then our business is completed, Gentlemen." The two men pulled their hands back, knowing if he took the unfinished drinks, the deal was closed and shut.

"Now why would I cut the price when there's buyers over at the Weldon," referring to the only hotel in the town of the same name, "right now waiting for my answer? You want it or not? Simple as that."

"They know how to get it down to the deep water?"

"That'd be their problem, not yours. Cotton is cotton here, but it's gold in the northeast."

"You got the same deal with them you got with me?"

"No, I don't. But you for one, ought'a know what a handful of money passed the right way'll do. What with the war shutting off every road 'tween here and there and now the Pamlico, you'll easily double your money, even at the new price."

McDermott knew it was true. "Bolton, write out a voucher for the sixty-six thousand dollars. Four hundred bales. Samuel E. Biggs. Get a receipt for it. Give Adair his thirteen thousand two-hundred in cash. But like he said, no record for that."

Adair nodded his head towards the door of his office, indicating he wanted the younger man out of the office.

The young man, puzzled, looked at the older man, McDermott. Mc Dermott shrugged his shoulders and nodded his head. "Go."

"You trust that youngster to stay quiet about this?" Adair asked, concern creasing his brow.

"Don't worry about it, Adair. Like you said, we're through." answered Gleason McDermott. "He gets paid well enough to know a good deal when it hits him in the face. You got your end covered, right? When we going to get started on this haul?"

"Ain't much of a hurry. You and that youngster get on down to the Weldon and lay low. Might be another week, maybe longer 'fore we get our first frost and then a week or so for the picking and baling. Could be a month. Probably less. And don't worry about me! I got a sight more to lose than you. The morning you're gone, headed towards the Sound, I'll still be here worrying."

***

Buck lay still, and struggled for sleep, but it shied away from him. But he was warm and dry and finally his eyes grew gritty and heavy.

In the chill of the morning, still wet with a mist from the fading rain, he poked again through the worn shoes, searching for gravel. His search for shoes would have to wait. He ripped a strip from his tote sack and doubled it once, then again, and stuffed it into the shoe. He sniffed the air of the close quarters he lay in and smelled dog piss. Looking at his pant leg, he knew a dog had paid him a visit during the night. He looked like and smelled like a drifter and not the sheriff he once had been.

Buck's quarters were cramped and so was he from the cold night. When ready to leave he drew the attention of hungry, scavenging dogs, which promptly raised a ruckus. The hinges of the door above him complained as Adair slammed it open, and threw an empty bottle at them.

At first light Buck fled the crawl space and once out of sight, shook out his travel-worn coat. He brushed at his hair and picked at the sand burs, twigs, and leaves caught in his beard. He began his long walk towards Sam's plantation.

He had no idea of how much his life was about to change.

As he rounded the corner he heard the rear door slam outward against the porch siding again.

"Now, I said git," yelled Adair at the pack of dogs as he let fly with a load of double x buck shot from his two-barrel shotgun.

Chapter Fifteen:, Eighteen and sixty two: August. Your son is alive.

The Twenty-third day of July, Eighteen and sixty-two.

My dearest friends, Samuel and Misses Biggs.
 Thaddeus is alive. Of this I am sure. Although alive, he is badly wounded. This letter must be brief, so quickly provided within are the most basic of facts. Tad is in the private home of a man named Tink Strickland. He is the only wounded man remaining there and thus he receives an abundance of care from the two women nursing him. Your beloved son and my officer has been receiving the best of care regardless of the remoteness of the Strickland farm.
 Enclosed is a map to direct you to your son. Be wary. There are those still trying to profit from the battle. I have been advised, as of yesterday, it is the opinion of those men I sent to find him, he is weak and in need of much bed rest. However, provisions, both medical, and

that of food, have dwindled and in most cases, are non-existent. I fear the members and servants of the Strickland family are near starvation themselves.

Please make haste to gather your son. There should be no one who would interfere with your plans. If such does happen, use this letter as a pass to anyone hindering your passage. Take provisions of both necessities, food and medicines, and as much as is possible for both your son and that family which has given their all.

I shall expect Thaddeus' return only when you and the Missus so determine he is fit to do so. I will anxiously await correspondence from you of his recovery to renewed health.

May our beloved Heavenly Father grant aid, assistance and his blessing upon us all.

Faithfully yours, and with this closing, I send the deep love of Mary Anna.

Major General Thomas J. Jackson
Major of Artillery
Army of the Confederate States of America

The joy of receiving the letter immediately dissolved the heavy gloom suffocating the Biggs family. The new letter, it too, brief and concise, merely indicated the soldier was healing but not yet recovered. It spoke of emergencies and encouraged swift actions. Attached was a map of Tink Strickland's farm on which was penciled that the map should be memorized and then disposed of, and the same with the brown envelope in which the letter and map had arrived.

The pressing weight of not knowing lifted, and for the first time since the arrival of the government issued letter a month before, the family felt the warmth of sun upon their faces. Sam immediately put his plans formed weeks earlier into action. He was the father—and his son was alive. Holt was told to saddle a horse and go for Henry and Isaac.

Isaac, his wagon loaded, met Sam in front of the Biggs' mansion. All precautions stated and restated, Rose and the two daughters, Samantha and Izzy, hugged their father and husband. With a click of the tongue, the two wagons lunged forward. Henry's third wagon joined that of Sam's and Isaac's and the caravan headed north.

***

The fledgling town of Hopewell lay eight miles to the northeast of Petersburg. With easy access to Richmond, the small town found itself the newest harbor in Virginia. It lay convenient to the great James River flowing past and northward to the new capitol of the Confederate States of America. Daily, a constant stream of war machinery, foodstuffs for the soldiers, and fodder for the Confederate's beasts of burden were loaded on the barges that awaited such freight to be transported northward to Richmond or, if needed, across the mighty James to points northeast.

Founded in Sixteen hundred and thirteen, the small town had grown minimally compared to its neighbor, Petersburg, to the west. Few knew Hopewell's founding predated that of the larger village of Petersburg and the founding of Richmond as well. Yet its growth had been stunted and slow, while its two neighbors grew rapidly.

Sixteen miles to the northwest, workers dumped dirty ashes and spent slag from the big furnaces of the Tredegar Iron Works, Richmond's largest industry, into the once clear waters of the James River. Now the James, with Tredegar's poisonous waste still being dumped into the river flowing alongside the massive iron works, had long-since killed off all fish and wildlife dependant upon the wide river. Most called the wide and deep river "the Big Black" as it flowed—void of life—slowly past Hopewell.

Sam, Isaac, and Henry, with bits held in hand, led their wagons onto the barge they were directed toward. The Big Black seemed more ocean than river today. A summer squall rocked the open-sided freight hauler and the three men felt their stomachs roil. Storms were a common occurrence, but few were ever this strong and most never long-lasting. The barge rose and fell as the river grew turbulent. White caps of wind-driven waves broke across the three-foot-high bow and soaked freight, beast, and man. Sam and Henry stood by the mules and held onto their bridles in a vain attempt to calm the animals. Isaac raced from wagon to wagon to secure their loads. The incoming tide, assisted by the first gale of the early summer, shoved the barge toward a dock in the distance.

"So where y'all off to, Neighbor," asked the man leaning out the window of the wheel house. "Captain Tom, they calls me." He stuck his arm through the opening and shook Sam's hand. Without waiting for an answer he took a pencil from his ear, licked the graphite tip and asked a second question. "That's three wagons and three men. Right? Y'all off to the hill?"

"If you mean where the battle was fought, yes. Do you know the quickest road to it?"

"Shore do. Today that's it up yonder." He answered, and pointed north, as the boat turned in the tide and headed up river away from a roadway which lay directly across the James and appeared to lead east through a thick stand of timber and to Malvern Hill.

Before Sam could ask why they were heading out of the way, Captain Tom saw Sam studying the road across the James and pointed toward the dark clouds rolling in from the Atlantic.

"Can't fight a hard wind and ever come out the winner. Got'ta go where it takes us. That other road's up yonder a bit," he said, pointing toward a bend in the James River. "So where you say you'uns is from?"

"Didn't. I own a place down below Weldon. The three of us do, that is."

"One of them big plantation places, huh?"

"Swift Creek's fairly big," Sam answered.

"I been to Weldon, once. Once was enough. I like big towns. A man can make money in a big town," Captain Tom said and smiled.

"If it has a river and you have the only way to get across it. Yeah. My guess is the size of the town's not as important as the need to get across the river," answered Sam.

"I see you have a good head for business," laughed Captain Tom.

The crew of the open barge fought the storm's destructive effort as well as they could. Wagons and their cargo were secured to the shabby railings with aged and water-soaked ropes. The ropes and railings moaned loudly and sang strange songs only Captain Tom and his crew understood as the twisted strands of hemp fought to secure their loads.

The lead wagon, Sam's, was a simple farm wagon, painted green, striped with yellow, and equipped with a spring mounted-bench seat, the bed behind the seat filled with food and medical supplies of all manner. The second, it too a farm wagon, was simple in style and although once painted a matching green, it was now a weathered gray. The bed was shaded with an oiled canvas hung from a center support. From a distance, the wagon turned ambulance looked more of a tent on wheels. Under the tent, a maze of rope, woven together, suspended from rail to rail, served as a hammock with two corn husk mattresses spread upon it. And last to board was a third wagon, it also packed high with foodstuffs and other needs for a trip of an indeterminate length, all of which were likewise covered with oiled cotton and canvas tarps.

"Sam," said Henry, pointing as the dock they just floated away from drifted toward the east, "I think we're heading off course."

"Yeah," Sam answered, "But I reckon," pointing at the boat's captain, "this is not his first crossing in such weather." To emphasize his agreement with Henry, he pointed the whip he held in his hand toward the north. "Hope there's a dock up that way. Sure as hell won't get over to that one," he said, pointing across the river and the dock on the far side they were slowly drifting beyond.

Around the bend, the captain and crew probed the depths of the water and poled the barge into a narrow slot in the landing. Pushed by a rogue wave, the clumsy boat slammed home into the pocket of the large timbers of a weather-beaten dock. The ten minutes spent securing the unruly freight hauler to its mooring seemed to Sam an eternity. He was close to Malvern Hill and anxious to get under way.

Finally, the captain raised the gate and waved the wagons and teams forward. "Sorry 'bout the ride. Damn wind messes up my schedule," he said, apologetically.

"Can't say as it's your fault. Given the circumstances, I thought you did a fine job. Thank you," offered Sam.

"Kind of you, Mister," answered the barge's captain. Pointing toward a maze of ruts and holes, he added, "That road'll take you to that Malvern Hill place you asked about. But it takes a round-about way to get there. Maybe a blessing of sorts we got blow'd off course. That road down yonder straight across from the dock was the one y'all would'a had to use if the wind hadn't come up like it did. It's in real bad shape. Plum worn out by dem damn Yankee cowards running over one another to get down to them boats what was waiting to take 'em home. But this road is shot all to hell in places, too, especially where some of dem same gunboats tore it up with dem exploding cannon shells. That rain three days ago didn't help none, neither. Washed out even more parts of it. But farm wagons coming from that way," he said indicating the area where the battle must have been fought, "is waiting every morning, so I reckon y'all git through. They did. Good luck to you, Sir."

Sam touched the brim of his hat, ready to bid the captain goodbye.

"May I be so bold," interjected the captain, "as to ask if y'all know . . . I mean really understand what it is y'all is gonna ride into? Wagons fixed up like that one with the sling in it ain't rigged that way 'cept for one reason. You come to git your boy and take him home, ain't you?"

"Well Sir. No. I don't know what to expect, but think it will be mostly bad. What I do know is the last battle my son fought in was in a place called Malvern Hill and there's rumors he's in a field hospital up there somewhere."

The captain looked saddened. "No sir," he said, "dem fellers was there . . . but I'm sorry to tell you they ain't there no more. Dem boys done been cleared out, hauled off. All dem what could make it—the lucky ones—was sent to Chimborazo Hospital up in Richmond."

"I am aware of that, friend, but I was told by good authority some of our boys are still being seen to by families scattered about."

"I heer'd tell of that, too. Been told there's a young officer, half alive, half dead on the Strickland Place."

Sam's heart leaped. Proof at last that his son was, or had been, nearby. "How do I get there?" he asked the man.

"Over that way," he answered, pointing to a far away rise of thick oaks. "You'd think they'd see to the officers first, unless they's real bad hurt. Stay on this road. It's a bit swoopy—twists and turns this way and that," and as he described the turns he snaked his opened hand back and forth, "but it'll get you there. Don't try no shortcuts. Y'all try taking a shortcut through dem there woods you'll drown dead, for sure. Dem swamps and backwaters rise and fall with the tide and this one today's the wors'est I ever seen. But dem woods over there ain't a fit place for man or beast, even when it's bone dry. And watch out for that Strickland fellow. He's a very unpleasant man."

The barge's captain removed his hat and with misty eyes, said, "May the good Lord guide you to your son and give him back to you strong and healthy. My boy was at Manassas, that second time. He's buried sum'mer's up there. Me and the missus is gonna' go fetch his body once we get enough money put up. His mates sent a drawing to us showing where they laid him to rest. They wrote us a fine letter about our son, too. Well-liked, our boy was," and his voice caught.

Sam merely nodded to the boat captain. He saw himself in the man and felt an obligation to acknowledge the loss, but feared a comment would turn into a catch in *his* throat. Again, he touched the brim of his hat, a gesture of goodbye, and said, "Isaac. Henry. Ready?" And slapped the reins down on the mule's rump.

***

The James River, now crossed, was the southern border shown on the sketch General Jackson provided, so Sam knew the battlefield was near. As each hoof sucked and pulled through the soaked and muddied road, the distance to their final destination shortened. The fear of the unknown—was his son alive or dead, was tearing at him. He prayed constantly for the welfare of Tad, and thought of little else.

The passing scenery vouched for the richness of the black swamp land. Near the outset of the meandering road, fields rich with the promise of corn, tobacco and cotton lay destroyed by soldiers in search of things edible, and that which remained had begun a slow rot. The fields were generally small—the thick growth of impenetrable woods explained their tight boundaries. The condition of the road exceeded the boat captain's assessment of the extent of damage.

The three wagons entered a darkly shadowed land of death beneath a tangle of thick trees filled with green foliage. It was a sinister place to ride through and the three of them, all of a Christian inclination, felt the presence of lost souls and tormented spirits.

A pervasive odor unlike any the men had ever smelled before floated with the gentle breeze as it found its way over the fouled and stinking, brackish swamp waters and through the trees. Wadding, stolen from blankets intended to provide comfort to Thaddeus, was robbed of bits of cotton and rolled into cotton balls, soaked in camphor, inserted into nostrils, making the passage bearable. But as of yet, not a dead body had been seen. *Something has been at them*, they each imagined without voicing the thoughts. *Varmints, hogs gone feral?*

Asked Henry, "If this ain't Hell, how could Hell be something worse?" Neither Isaac or Sam answered. They were too busy with their own thoughts of the evil men could do to one another. Each man rode along near tears.

Twice Sam led the three wagons onto the high cut of the dirt road and each time, dilapidated farm wagons creaked and moaned westward toward the barges waiting for new loads to ferry back across to Hopewell. On the bench seat of the first sat a man and a woman, both in the high end of middle age, and on their faces, drawn tight in sorrow, lay the roadmaps of their personal journey into Hell. Behind them in the wagon-bed, lay a form tightly wrapped in a heavy covering—maybe an oiled tarp, or a rug from their home. The second to pass carried a man of indeterminate age and a boy of about thirteen. Two slaves, walked behind, shouldering dirt-caked shovels. A tattered canvas hung from the opened tailgate, exposing a boot minus the leather sole, revealing the white of the bones inside. The tarps did only a fair job of containing the odor of the soldiers inside. The lesser odor of decaying flowers following the farm wagons doing duty as a hearse, reminded Sam of vases of flowers kept too long with the water they stood in gone dark and sour.

Sam could not help but feel a deep sadness welling up inside his chest. Understanding the meaning of the forms in the back of the wagons, Sam, Henry, and Isaac removed their hats and held them to their chests as the wagons creaked and moaned past. Out of respect for the cargo of wasted life, few words were exchanged. Indeed, what could be said?

Further along and closer to the battlefield, most of the homestead cabins and outbuildings sat void of owners, slave, or animals. Unknown to Sam, the families, almost in unison, had abandoned their homes and material possessions as the crescendo of cannon fire rolled toward them from the north, growing louder and closer. Sam had never been near a battle before; the farmers had. They had been listening as the cannon roared and the muskets rattled for the last few days and knew it would soon be at their door. So they fled to safer places, praying safer places existed.

Continuing the journey, the ride remained oppressive. The wild flowers and young saplings seemed dead, their branches dipping. New sights and stronger odors assaulted their senses. A sticky and sweetish humidity hazed the air with a new odor. Entering a break in the swamp, bodies began to be seen—some without a distinctly human form, an indication they had died soon after the battle and had suffered the indignities of decay and animals. Others, still recognizable as human, had died more recently. Nature had begun its work of cleaning the forest, of all things of death, with the exception of bleached and scattered bones.

And here, too, the fields had been vandalized, not for want, but out of a rank meanness. The tobacco was too young to cure for smoke or chew. Cotton bolls were still green, their pear-shaped pods sealed tightly and filled with white and tightly compressed fibers, had yet to open. Corn, with kernels not yet rowed on cobs, lay trampled and without value.

Nearing a curve, leading into yet more swampland, Sam fought to rein the mules to the far side of the passage. The mules suddenly turned skittish, refusing to continue. They snorted and neighed, and with enlarged dark eyes sought other directions in which to flee. They tried to back up the wagons with wheels locked by levers. Their frenzied efforts to turn half-circle were defied by the long wagon tongues, the tightened brakes, and narrow roadway.

The dirt road had grown muddy and slimy from the storm waters ponding on it. Sam dreaded climbing down to deal with the stubborn animals. But as he did, an odor even more rank than any he'd ever smelled before robbed him of his breath. Immediately, Isaac and Henry crushed handkerchiefs to their noses and dribbled drops of camphor into the white cloth. Nothing had ever prepared them for the odd sweetness which filled the air. On their plantations, all had chanced upon the dead and rotting bodies of livestock and wild hogs while working the timber or hunting. They knew those smells, but this was something they could not put a name to—something different—something very different.

Approaching the mules, Sam reached for the bits in their mouths and looked ahead to check for the best passage beyond the curve. The inside and lower cut of the road, soaked through and through, looked and felt spongy. The outer curve held deep rain-washed gullies. Brackish water threatened to overflow the road. High tide, Sam remembered.

He'd hoped he would not find the source of the horrendous stench, positive something which smelled so foul would be a horrible sight to see—and he was right. His stomach roiled, deciding to reject its contents, and Sam fought the need to let it. He gagged when he saw the gelatinous round form resting atop the spongy dirt by the lower edge of the road. Attached to it, something trailed into the brackish, tea-colored swamp water. His mind refused to acknowledge what he believed it to be, and tried to convince him it was something altogether different. He'd seen similar things while boating across the

Chesapeake Bay south of Hampton, Virginia. Jellyfish they'd been called. But this was larger, more of the size of the elusive Portuguese Man-of-War. Against hope, he prayed a high tide and the push of westward winds had blown the translucent creature into the swamp. The round globe appeared water-logged and milky-white. The flesh and the color of the thing suggested it had been in the water for a long time. He prayed the blob would only be a dead jellyfish or its larger cousin, a Man-of-War, but upon closer inspection his prayers failed him. The strands of blond hair destroyed his hopes.

One of the first to die in the battle, Sam knew, recognizing the human shape of the form after reluctantly approaching it. He imagined a young soldier struggling through the swampy waters, eager to run toward the fighting or eager to steer clear of it. The going or the leaving mattered nothing to Sam. He could not judge others of things which he did not know.

But he knew and dreaded what he had to do. Common decency required he examine the shapeless form of translucent flesh, to confirm that which he suspected. Whoever it had been deserved at least a symbolism of respect—and the kindness of a stranger bidding him farewell. A prayer, too, he decided. And something else he needed to know—something that would take every ounce of his very being to accomplish. The odds were long that it might be his son, yet it was within the realm of possibility. The unrelenting *what ifs* of the future far outweighed the not knowing of the present. He understood the condition of the form would deny him proof of who it might have been, but still he could not leave without trying. He had to be sure. He turned the head with a limb stripped from a tree. Gone were the features of the man the form had once been. The remaining strands of hair, turning swamp-green from algae, and bits of the flesh that once filled out a soldier's face were still sloughing off. The unseeing milky eyes stared at him, begging an unknown something of Sam. The churning bile in his stomach built into a final rage and fought Sam's determination to not allow its release. And Sam knew he would lose.

He saw the dark blue of what was left of Union-blue trousers. Relieved, he had found the answer he sought. Guiltily, he was ashamed at the relief he felt. A part of the decency he'd strived for his entire life, was chiseled away and he felt as if his soul had shriveled because of it.

Reeling away from the worst sight he'd ever seen in his life, he gave in to his stomach's need. Hanging his head, he asked of no one if things could get worse.

Isaac and Henry, although witnessing the scene from afar, paled at the horror.

Standing, Sam threw his loose blankets over the mules' heads and motioned for Henry and Isaac to do the same. His lungs pleaded for a full breath of fresh air, but each needed breath became a struggle. He began to turn pale and staggered. Again he felt he was going to throw up, but his efforts resulted only in dry heaves. His heart pounded in his chest with no set rhythm, racing one moment and slowing to a near stop the next. He fell face first into the mud of the road.

In seconds, Henry and Isaac were by him, turning him over, wiping mud from his face. Isaac pulled the cork from a vest bottle of whiskey and dribbled it into Sam's mouth. His gasping for breath eased and his color began to return, but not by much. They laid him upon the mattresses intended for his son. Henry pulled his wagon into the lead and Isaac brought up the rear. The driverless wagon, once the mules had settled, followed not knowing the reins were merely loosely wrapped around the brake lever.

An hour later, Sam, still pale, pulled himself into a sitting position and called out to Henry. "What happened?"

"Don't know, Sam. One minute you were tugging at the mules, the next, your face was in the mud," answered Henry.

Isaac added, "You look like that hired man from down my way when he was plowing. 'Cept he died. Bad heart was what Doc Yardley said. You seen Doc about this thing you got, Sam?"

Sam had been feeling bad and for some time, too. He'd said nothing to no one about it. Not even Rose. But Rose had asked him what was wrong a dozen times. Even then, he'd not been straight forward with her—giving her an answer, but never the truth. And now he had to lie to his best friends or his mission would be cancelled.

Seeing their reactions, logical and expected as they were, Sam knew he'd done a great wrong to the two best friends he'd ever have.

Ashamed of himself and his selfishness, he was embarrassed that he, without thought of Isaac's and Henry's concerns for their own sons—Isaac's two and Henry's one, who were out there somewhere, and they, themselves, in harm's way. How could he have done such a thing? How could he have become so indifferent to others? To apologize would have been answered by them with the sincerest of truth. Henry and Isaac would have demanded to go with him and if refused, he knew they would have followed at a discreet distance.

He realized he would have done the same for either of them and prayed, for their sake, it would never come to that. The soul-salving thought helped, but did not eliminate his guilt. A stricken conscience suggested he send them on their way, but they would not go and he knew that, as well.

Within a couple of hours he felt his strength returning. He knew it would happen again, but did not know when. It had been happening more and more as the days wore on.

"Can you continue, Sam?" asked both Henry and Isaac.

"I feel fine. Good as new," he lied. "We're here. Let's get it done."

***

Emerging from the dark of the thick woods, the waste of war was overwhelming. Before them lay the remains of battle—scores of bloated horses and mules, broken wagons, muskets with burst barrels, battered canteens, bent and broken swords, cannon with their exploded barrels flowered outward. All manner of clothing—butternut and blue—lay scattered about, their colors or odors frightened the mules and created an uneasy passage.

An occasional stranger cautiously stepped from the woods and eyed the approaching wagons. Convinced the wagons were sent to recover the dead buried about and not the Confederate Army with orders to collect anything of value, the men returned to scavenging the battlefield. Shrapnel and iron was stuffed into shabbily built hand trucks and wheelbarrows. The Tredegar Iron Works in Richmond was buying scrap and iron. From where the hallowed bits of metal came—freshly mined ore or from bloodied fields—the buyers no longer cared. To them, and the scavengers, iron was the new currency of the Confederacy.

Once it was determined the trash-pickers meant them no harm, they holstered their revolvers and leaned the shotguns against the wagon seat.

The road improved by bits and pieces. A gentle slope gradually rising from the edge of the swamp contradicted the term "hill" when used with Malvern. So often had Sam heard of Malvern Hill, he expected something more prominent, higher than the fifteen feet or so it stood at its summit—a contradiction upon which he did not dwell.

Clear of the swamp the road offered two choices. One was to climb the hill, the other, to follow a branched-off road skirting the swamp's edge. Heavy war machinery had gouged deep slashes across the battlefield and destroyed the road ascending the hill, making reaching the top difficult. The map he'd locked away in his mind said the lower road skirting the hill and hugging the woods would lead to the Strickland Farm.

Off the trail, an occasional wagon path broke free from the dirt road and snaked into the deep woods, quickly disappearing into twists and turns shadowed by dark tunnels of black-green leaves. And each new passageway had to be searched. Thaddeus could be waiting down that road, or the next.

Henry and Isaac took turns walking far enough along each to judge if it was a roadway to a cabin or merely a shortcut into the fields. Sam offered but was denied his turn to check the pathways.

Most proved to be no more than paths leading off into fields, and others were clogged by broken wagons and debris. Logic said inhabitants beyond the choked section, would have to clear the paths out of necessity, but thus far, each exploration had ended in a judgment call.

Around the bend and fluttering in the last remnants of the earlier squall, a red and white striped flag flew atop a pine stripped bare of limbs.

The previous days of summer winds had ripped the banner nearly to shreds and all but blown it away. Torn sections snapped and popped in the breeze, as streamers of unraveling threads fought for freedom, appearing to have an unspoken desire of their own to be done with the battlefield. For a second, the frayed streamers of the letter "H" stitched in blue, realigned and became recognizable. The embroidered symbol indicated the possibility of a hospital down the farm road.

"Let's give that one a try," said Sam

Chapter Sixteen: Eighteen and sixty-two: Late spring edging towards summer.

Life is a gamble. Who has never heard that? It begins and ends with a gamble. A newborn, its tiny heart pumping an odd fusion of differing bloods, finds soon enough the meaning of the word "gamble." It is Celine's heart pumping that blood. More French than Negro, she no longer resembles her distant ancestors who slaved in the fields. Her rare beauty, her features small and French, and skin the color of caramel, can open doors for her. She has to take the gamble.

As she walked from the barn to the chicken coop, the woman unconsciously watched the edge of the woods and tugged the hammer of the Colt to half cock. The very thought of the thing in the woods ever touching her again angered her and filled her with hate.

Her skin, the color of caramel—not burnt, but light— suggested she was a mulatto and of about thirty years of age. At birth, she had been named Celine Boudreaux Chauvin. The two surnames, both French were heavy anchors, always choking her. They served as constant reminders of the two different masters she'd belonged to during her short and troubled life.

For many consecutive generations Celine's ancestors had been owned by Frenchmen who had grown wealthy growing sugar cane on their palatial plantations in Louisiana. Her mother and grandmother were also light skinned, and evidently considered desirable by *their* lecherous French owners, but Celine's skin tone was shades lighter than that of her immediate ancestors. The progression of the lighter and lighter skin color, spoke of long-standing and abusive sexual relations forced upon those who came before her by previous plantation owners, as well as other unnamed Frenchmen. By the time of her birth, her tainted bloodline was almost of pure French heritage.

"Mulatto" or "Quadroon" as such people of mixed blood were sometimes called, were destined to live a lifetime of confusion—too white to pass as a dark-skinned person, and not dark enough to be considered a Negro. Skin color could be a blessing and garner special attentions—or serve as a reason for unrelenting disdain, born of jealousy by fellow slaves. The unwanted attention of the white master for his light-colored slave was always that of a sexual nature, while her darker skinned brethren daily chided her as being the master's whore.

Celine had learned long ago, the lighter the skin, the more desirable the Negro female seemed to be to the white man. Conversely, the darker the skin of the Negro male . . . the more the white master feared him, and the quicker the fearsome dark slave was delivered to the auction blocks.

Never did Celine or her mother toil in the fields. Such was an unasked for benefit to such women, as well as a reason for further scorn from those of a darker skin color. So like her mother and grandmother, she saw to the varying needs of their white owners and their palatial mansions. Such needs could be those which required a hot fire for boiling wash water or of things best hidden in the dark of night.

A handed-down history proved the three women, Celine, her mother, and her grandmother, all light skinned, one lighter than the next, were from a long line of other mulatto slave women. Celine correctly understood the curse of mixed blood had started long before her grandmother and then her mother were overpowered and used for carnal pleasure in the Louisiana sugar cane fields owned by their master, a drunken French-Canadian named Boudreaux. But records were never kept of such liaisons. No records meant no need of denials of accusations against wayward men for the wrongs they'd done.

And with Boudreaux's genes fouling her own, Celine was of the lightest color thus far. Boudreaux's illegitimate daughter had inherited the hazel eyes of her absent father, his thin face and straight nose. Her ears, small and tight to the head, reminded others of those of the master's, as well.

Her blood evolved into something more French than that of her long forgotten ancestors from Africa. Boudreaux never admitted he'd fathered a light skinned daughter and she never knew him as her father. She'd been told many times by other slaves that she could pass as white, and even as a French woman, and they had urged her to do so, but the lack of a birth certificate denied her the chance to try.

Shamed by rumors spreading about him, Boudreaux sold his caramel-skinned daughter—the proof of his betrayal of his wife—to yet another Louisianan named Jacque Chauvin. Fearing financial ruin from the rumors which continued, and in order to put them to rest, Boudreaux sent Celine's mother to Fredericksburg to be sold at the weekly slave auction. Rid of a child he didn't want, and a mother who could still tell secrets, Boudreaux thought himself clever.

Chauvin, born a French-Canadian, had fled a dubious past. Although the child, Celine, was merely a toddler, a sick lust deep within him began to grow. The desire he had for the young child frightened him, made him nervous, but not enough to fight it. His decadent mind became clouded with visions of a naked child—teasing, luring, with arms extended, begging him to come to her. Desirous to keep the lovely creature near him, he placed the newly acquired child in the charge of the head Negress with instructions to teach his newest possession the ways of the household duties.

As the years passed, Celine's beauty grew, as did her master's debased desires. She developed into a well-endowed young woman and eventually found herself Chauvin's new house servant. Before long her duties became something more than just seeing to the needs of the house.

Chauvin, enamored of the beguiling creature, overpowered the teenaged girl and in his own wife's bed had his way with her. Caught in the act, his wife demanded he rid the house and his heart of the threat, as she railed against the one female her husband wanted more than the woman he'd married.

"Put her on the block in Fredericksburg," ordered the wife. Thus Celine was free of the debased Chavin.

***

The auction house in Fredericksburg was faltering, business fluctuated from heavy to hardly worth pounding the gavel. The easy money to be made with the slave auction would never again be as lucrative as it once had been. In the past, before issues of morality as they pertained to slavery became the fodder for all conversation, the do's and don'ts of preachers, and the confusion of war, the unspoken desire of all men of wealth was to own slaves—and more than they needed—black-skinned status symbols.

In the decade before the war began, the topic once used as a way to brag of one's wealth had become muted and discussed only in private. Politically, the buying and selling of Negroes had become something best left unsaid and deals were consummated behind closed and locked doors. Self-serving interpretations of well chosen Biblical scriptures regarding slavery separated the God-fearing men and women of the North from their counterparts of the Southland. The country was fracturing over slavery.

The fields remained as productive as ever, but the number of slaves had reached its zenith. Rumors that the Federal Government was intent upon freeing the slaves had taken root.

Seldom used, the sandstone auction block on the corner of Williams and Charleston Street in Fredericksburg suffered only the wear and tear of children standing atop it, slashing the air with wooden swords. With the exception of an occasional auction, the beige-pink block slowly became a silent sentinel to the past.

***

Tink Strickland swayed, drunk and sweating in the heat of the noonday sun. The pavement burned through the soles of his boots, and the heat from sun-baked bricks radiating from the surrounding buildings scorched like a second sun, turning his already rose-red liquored face a darker shade of red.

He'd counted the money in his pocket many times over. He scanned the crowd to see who his competitors might be. He worried who he might approach for a loan if he won his bid but came up short of funds. He fretted if the small bank in Hopewell would really loan him the money he'd asked for. They said they would, but he'd heard they were almost bankrupt themselves.

Fredericksburg sweltered in the mid-summer's heat and the hot, muggy wetness of an Atlantic breeze wafted through the town as if God, in His infinite wisdom, was punishing the small village and its inhabitants for becoming one of the largest slave auction centers in all of Virginia. Over a door behind the sandstone block at the edge of the street hung a rough-sawn pine plank. Painted upon it in loud carnival colors were the words: SLAVE AUCTION EVERY SATURDAY NOON. NEGROES FOR SALE. From a barred and shuttered storage room below the sign, muffled cries and moans from the slaves inside ruptured from the throat of the door each time it was unbolted and pulled open. A sand-and-litter-filled dust devil danced around the auction block, and gaining strength, broke free. Leaves, sand, and paper followed the invisible curse from God as it twirled and danced up the street. Some saw the dust-dervish as a warning from above and departed the auction before it started. But not Tink. He held his footing and drank from an almost-empty bottle.

***

Delbert McBride stood soaking wet as sweat cascaded from his hairline. His heavy jowls and the folds of a fleshy neck sagged over the sweat-stained collar of the shirt and tie he must have bought when he was fifty pounds lighter. He stared longingly at the brown jug of rye whiskey sitting in a basin of cool water on a three legged stool behind him. Bending forward from his auction stand, he nearly lost his balance. Regaining his stance, he took the handwritten note extended to him by the owner of an aged and worn black man standing at the base of the auction block.

"Genl'men. Any ah y'all what's got any interest in git'n yer'sef ah darkie today, step on up." Delbert waited for the crowd to respond. Two of the six remaining prospective buyers, either disinterested in the lot of Negroes on display or beaten down by the heat, turned and left. The old black man did not interest the crowd of bidders and his owner helped the elderly man dismount the block.

Four bidders remained and Tink was one of those four. Without further ado, Delbert ordered the next slave to be brought forward, but again, no bid was offered, nor was any interest shown in the muscular middle-aged black man. McBride neither cared nor cajoled the prospective buyers. His face indicated he could care less if the auction continued or not and instead of one at a time, he beckoned the next lot of two slaves forward, one male, one female.

Turning away from the prospective buyers, Delbert toweled the sweat from his face. He ordered the previously unsold slaves back into the sweltering holding cell and promised them he would tell their masters, drinking and carousing at Dingle's, to come and get them. As he told them the lie, he checked the level of rye in the brown bottle again—in another half hour, it, too, would be empty. And to Delbert McBride that meant the deadline for the auction to end had to be moved forward. Due to the excessive heat of the noonday sun, Dingle's Inn at the far corner beyond Williams and Stevens Street was already enjoying an impressive amount of customers and on a day like this, they would be drinking heavily. To Delbert's way of thinking, they were drinking *his* beer and *his* whiskey.

The lot Tink had waited for stepped onto the block. Only he and another gentleman in a white summer suit now stood in front of the auctioneer. The white-suited man had been glancing at Dingle's doors, also. He appeared to be as interested in the female as Tink but his chalky face shouted "heat stroke."

As Delbert called for "The Viewing," the last of the two slaves stepped forward—a young and light-skinned colored woman and a tar black and mean looking young male. The woman lifted her cotton dress and stepped upon the block. Tink watched as the age-yellowed skirt opened, exposing her calf, her knee and a portion of her caramel-colored thigh. His pulse increased as he gasped at the vision before him. The loose-fitting trousers he wore began to bulge and his hands began to perspire.

His competition no longer able to tolerate the thought that there was cold beer waiting for him at the corner tavern, stood and trudged through the heat to Dingle's Inn.

Another wasted day, thought Delbert. He wanted desperately to be finished with the failure of a sale.

"Mister," called Delbert as he looked in all directions. "Let's put an end to this bullshit. Make me an offer on this fine looking creature. Too fancy, too delicate to work in the field, but she'd make a fine house servant. How much you gimme for her?"

Tink knew to the penny how much he had in his pocket—one thousand three hundred forty-two dollars and thirteen cents.

"You want me to make you look good to your boss. That it?" Tink asked.

"Well, you know how it is. Wouldn't hurt none to get rid of some of these darkies. Don't want the day to be a wash."

"Well, let's talk," responded Tink, who for the first time in a long time, felt in control of something and intended to make the best of it. "I help you, you help me. My wife's mad as hell about me being here. Make me look good to her and I'll help you shine for your boss. I got me five hundred forty-two dollars and, let's see," as he dug into his pocket and grabbed the loose change, "and four cents. That's your'n if you'll sell me both that high yellow and that buck over yonder," pointing at a young, hard-muscled black man of about twenty years of age, and quickly thought his terms dangerous. "I kind'a think that one's a mean nigger, though. He always stares at you with hate eyes, does he?"

Already in his hand, Delbert held a pencil and receipt book. "What be your name, good Sir?"

***

From generations of frenzied in-breeding and the continued infusion of dominant genes, Celine's caramel color was set fast and unyielding. How many times had she'd been told that with all of her features, her color, her eyes, the thin cut of her nose, silkiness of her hair, she could have run away and lived the life of a white woman, or a fine French lady? But such an escape was impossible and she knew it.

Tink's first child by Celine was named Malcomb and the boy was cursed with *his* father's genetics. His skin was lighter than all of his kin born before him.

Despite the continuation of the blood curse, Celine loved the boy and found the world a better place with him in it. Tink's drinking soon became his second favorite pass time. With God's grace—or curse—Celine again became pregnant. Jacob arrived nine months later and on Christmas eve. Foolishly Celine threatened to take her son and run. The threat garnered her a backhand across her face. She fell backwards into the corner, landing on the butter churn. When she rose she held the handle of the churn, and wielding it like an axe she swung it with a force intended to kill, but her aim was poor. With one hand Tink caught the handle in mid air, and with the other he grabbed her tiny wrist and twisted her to her knees.

"So. Let's see how it feels," he snarled. With his threat came a cruel beating.

As she lay crumpled on the floor, Tink drug out the bill of sale and sneered at her, his clothing rancid with days old and soured sweat, his breath foul with the smell of cheap whiskey, he said as he pointed his bony finger at her, "You best be remembering who you is. You're a nigger, my nigger," and read aloud the words " . . . says here 'a mulatto Negro, female,' and I'm glad as hell there ain't no mention of the total waste of the five hun'ert dollars I spent to buy you."

***

In order to impress his wife with his business prowess, he'd lied to her and told her he'd paid only a hundred dollars for the female, and four hundred and forty-two dollars for the buck. To her, the spent one hundred dollars did seem a good deal, but the four hundred forty-two for the male seemed a waste and proved to be such. The brawny Negro with the mean eyes, ran away within a fortnight.

***

Exhausted, Celine paused halfway between the smokehouse and the cabin. In doing so, she placed herself in harm's way. Lillie Beth called out to her, warning her not to turn her back to the woods.

The past few weeks had been but a whirlwind of events which she would never be able to forget, no matter how long she was cursed to live. Exhausted from the demands of the previous days, Celine did three things she had never done before—she'd turned her back to the woods—defying—daring, even, the creature within to come out and approach her. And the second, she held the Colt revolver she'd taken from the dead soldier laying on the battlefield, cocked and covered beneath the folds of her dress. Then she started sobbing.

The entirety of her life was spent merely enduring each new day. Her every concern was for her master's two children, Lillie Beth the elder and Billie, now eleven years of age. And like the two of them, he had abandoned her and his newest son Jacob, also. The four of them were all the innocent victims of a deranged man. And now that Malcomb was gone, she forced herself not to think of her firstborn.

For a long time Tink was a binge drinker, drinking only when the need pulled at him. But as of late, he was drunk more than sober and when drunk, he was violent or incoherent—usually both. His irrational mind required he blame others for his many failures. During such an alcoholic haze he had exploded into a drunken frenzy like none other, and bashed his illegitimate son Malcomb against a tree. As alcohol seeped from his every pore, he mumbled repeatedly of how a woman in the creek demanded the boy for her own.

Celine fled the horrid scene with her son's body in one arm and her newborn in the other. She buried the only thing that had ever loved her not far from where, just a few years earlier, she'd watched from dark shadows as Tink Strickland split his wife Jacqueline's head with a hatchet.

With the Colt tucked into her apron pocket, a mallet in one hand, a froe in the other, and a knife pilfered from the kitchen stuck in her ragged belt, with no place to go and no one to turn to, she returned to the barn.

Tink had disappeared and not been seen since the day the cannon began to roar from atop the nearby hill and the resulting shockwaves began to fill the woods and yard of Tink Strickland's farm.

Celine understood how the killer of her son thought the roar of the cannon was God's angry voice condemning him for what he'd done. She prayed the evil man was dead and being well attended to in the special hell he'd made for himself.

Eventually, her fright of the shabbily constructed barn led her to seek shelter in the farm house. For an unknown reason, she did not think he would enter the very cabin which he had built. She reasoned as long as she stayed near Lillie Beth and Billy, she and Jacob would be safe. But inside, three people lived a life of fear, and the baby cooed and suckled his mother's breast.

But the thing in the woods desire for her had not diminished. She often felt his eyes, hidden behind the dark-green curtain of foliage, as they burned into her, undressing her.

If she had been frightened of him that gruesome night when he'd killed his son, their son, she was not prepared for what walked from the woods towards her. The man she hoped dead wore the same clothing, shredded by the thorns of briars and brambles and the rot of the humid swamp, that he had worn the night he'd killed her son. His hair and beard were matted with the detritus of decaying matter found within the woods. The flesh below his eyes, purple from drinking and lack of sleep, accented the vacant stare of his eyes, and he smelled as badly as he looked. The thing, once human—now void of humanity, mumbled incoherently as he walked towards her. As the door slammed open, it extended both hands, blackened and wet from the mud of the swamp, she awoke and shuddered.

Badly frightened, she understood the sign to be a warning delivered by dream. Part of her wanted to flee with the children, but flee to where And how? All she could do was watch the woods and keep her weapons within reach.

She lived in desperate fear of the violent man. Any mother would, she knew, if they had watched him kill their firstborn son as if he were of no more value than a flea-bitten barnyard dog.

How she hated the withered little man. Like most small men he roared like a lion, thinking his vulgar shouts and angry demands would enhance his stature and standing with his neighbors. His ravings were always those of a man who sought to impress others, but the roar of cannon fire from the hill beyond the farm had sent the cowardly bastard fleeing.

Now, she awaited his return. She'd made a decision. Although he'd banished himself to the dark hiding places of the woods, he would emerge someday and when he did . . ..

Life had not much improved for her and the children, but now gone were the wounded soldiers, save one that she and Lillie were caring for. Food had been abundant while the men dressed in butternut were there. But now even things discarded by the army were gone, used up, and the garden ruined.

No longer did the lecherous man, in his self-imposed and wooded kingdom stand and undress her with his eyes while she cooked, cleaned house, and washed the ever growing mound of clothing. She had made a decision and crossed her heart, thereby declaring it irreversible. Yes, she would kill him for what he had done to her and their firstborn son. She would reload the Colt and kill him a second time for what he'd done to his wife. And then a third time for the sake of his motherless children.

And Tink Strickland knew she would kill him.

***

The battle had flooded the hill beyond the woods with blood and death. A month later the hill still bore gouges and fierce odors.

As in all wars, hospitals filled to overflowing and other buildings were sought just as quickly for those still needing to be cared for. Tink's cabin and outbuildings were confiscated as a field hospital. For the first week after the battle, Celine, Lillie Beth, and Billy labored hard as stand-in nurses. Afterwards, on a daily basis, the wounded who remained were removed by ambulance to the Chimborazo Hospital in Richmond.

The cabin had lost much of its lure. Too many memories. Too many blood stains—the red of blood turned rust brown on pine floors. The cabin was no longer a home, merely a temporary place to breathe. But the remaining soldier needed the security offered by the cabin walls and they needed a place to sleep.

On the back porch, daring Tink to come to her, she sat lost in grief for herself, the children, and the soldier—an officer, too wrecked to heal, too weak to be moved, so the cabin remained a jail. The stink of decay of bodies scattered randomly in the fields saturated the air and overpowered the sweet smells of the Virginia countryside—the sweetness of fresh grass, budding flowers and the breeze from the Atlantic. But the thought of inhaling the essence of another's soul tormented her.

Beyond the smokehouse and at the edge of the woods, a too shallow trench had been dug and filled with amputated arms and legs. Through the foot-thick cover of dirt seeped the same odors, the same gasses. Such brutal undertakings—amputations. Each demanded the quick back and forth thrust of a surgeon's saw, without the aid of chloroform or morphine, which promised less pain and only a slight chance of recovery.

She thought of the irony of how something as simple as applying linen to deadly wounds could bolster a gravely mangled man's determination to live. And for some it did. Others tried to see the promise in the bandages, but for them, the wrappings served only as a harbinger of the end.

A few minutes passed before she gathered herself and the still empty basket. The bastard would not take her up on her dare, and the children were hungry. She desperately needed to find something to feed them.

***

The wagon path meandered deeper into the woods and varied its course only when needed to skirt trees grown too large to cut and remove. The center hump, grown thick with grass, briars, and weeds indicated a lack of use to Sam and his two friends. At the far end a prism of sunlight dared to enter the throat of the tunnel-like road.

The grind of iron-rimmed wheels crunching gravel sounded from the three wagons as they exited the path and found themselves in the front yard of a small cabin. Varying shades of gray suggested the cabin had grown considerably. Bedrooms had been added, the kitchen enlarged, even the dogtrot had been closed off front and back, perhaps for a large pantry or another needed bedroom.

The weathered rocking chair on the front porch, with back slats missing and the rear of one rocker cracked, but held together with rusted nails and a twist of wire, was more a pile of firewood than a place to sit and watch the day's end approach.

The chain holding the porch swing had rusted through, dumping one end upon the cypress planks of the porch, while the other end died a slow death of choking, hanging from its rusted chain. In general, the cabin looked empty.

Beyond the rear corner of the cabin Celine watched as the wagons pulled to a halt by a large oak. The woman reached into the deep pocket of her apron and wrapped her tiny fist around the Colt revolver—the second time of the day. She was tired and still in the frame of mind that she was ready to kill if necessary, and thought herself ready to die for the same reason. But that would leave the man's daughter, his son Billy, and her Jacob destitute and alone. She would have to forgo the dying part, but held firm to her willingness to kill.

And why not kill, she questioned. That was all she'd seen for the last month. Death was nothing new and now it seemed the basic reason for living. There was no fear of dying remaining within her.

No food, the seep at the bottom of the well more mud than water, and the new shoots of the summer garden eaten away by marauding rabbits, reminded her of the one time she'd ventured onto the battlefield a half mile distant on the far side of the woods in search of anything edible. Hardtack, the scourge of soldering, would have been a dessert to the children, she thought. But nothing edible was found. She'd pried the Colt, its barrel still factory blue and the hammer a rainbow of heat-treated colors, from fingers gone stiff. The officer would never shoot it again, she reasoned, so she robbed the officer of it along with the orphaned pouch of lead shot, percussion caps, and a flask full of powder. She now wished she'd taken the shotgun at his feet—rabbit stew would have been a king's treat today.

Chapter Seventeen: Eighteen sixty-two: Late July, to mid August. Life changing decisions must be made.

Being born a slave, especially female, meant entering life without much and no hope of ever having much, with the exception of a life of toil and a lot of unpleasantness to look forward to. For a girl child, those few years spent growing large enough to be of service to the "Master" seldom allowed for days spent playing and being a child. Old enough to walk was old enough to be of some service, if only something minor or seemingly insignificant. And that thing was called "Training." There was always things needing to be done for the family into which the child had been born, if it was only drying dishes, helping their mother boil water for washing clothes, or fetching a piece of firewood for the fireplace. Most young girls by the age of puberty already had an inkling of what lay ahead and by whose hands those things would be done. Boys might have reached their coming of age a year or so later, but when it did arrive they reacted with reckless abandon. From servitude for the family, to servitude in the fields, and to boys having their way—life was not much of a life, girls tended to think.

Celine was born the child of a slave, but she was born nearly white, her skin even whiter than that of her mother. And white-skinned Negroes had specific problems—invariably they became playthings of the Master. Because of her "gift," as others called her color, it appeared to many of the darker-skinned slaves she received special privileges. But they did not know what was forced upon her in the dark of night. If they had known, they would have understood the hate she held inside for the color of her skin. Her distrust of all men had grown as she grew older.

From her hiding place beyond the rear corner of the cabin stepped a woman pointing a revolver at the man dismounting the lead wagon.

"State your business and be quick doing it. Then be on your way," she ordered. The loud click of the revolver's hammer locking into full cock put meaning to her command. "Y'all done picked this place clean. Took everything what weren't tied down." She held the Colt in her right hand and made no attempt to hide or threaten with it as she shielded her eyes from the sun.

Sam heard the grind of the sash against the window jamb as it was being raised. A thin white arm, that of a young female of an indeterminate age, held a well-aimed musket leveled at the big man's chest.

"Miss Ceely done told y'all to go back up on the hill," said a girl's voice from inside as she pointed the long barrel of the musket in the direction from which the men had arrived.

"Good morning, ladies," said the man in the front wagon. He dropped the reins and held both hands chest level as did the other two men in the wagons behind his.

"Ma'am," he said, "If you think we're some of those trash pickers, we're not. We're looking for my son. I heard there's a place near by that might be taking care of him." With the further explanation of why they were there, he expected an answer, but she held her silence and continued to stare at him.

From the shelter of the corner of interlaced logs, Celine watched the men climb from the wagons—each too old to be soldiers, each too old to be a threat. But men were men and she trusted not one of such creatures. Approaching her, they each removed their hats, a not often-seen act of respect for women of color. She reasoned it might be a ploy to deceive her, to get her to think they were gentlemen. *That's the way of men,* she thought.

The dirt of the long journey clinging to them attested to the honesty of Sam's answer. These men were not the trash pickers who had been scavenging the countryside since the battle. Although dusty and grimy, their manner of dress suggested they were men of wealth.

Over the years, she had grown adept at reading men's faces, especially their eyes and lips. She'd learned to never take a man at his word or to trust his smile. Some seemed pleasant and turned out to be just that—pleasant and cordial men hoping to spend a brief conversation with a pretty woman. Others could smile until their lips cracked, but she dared not let such men, their faces lecherous, their eyes cloudy with lies yet to be told, close the distance between she and they. Years before she'd lumped all living two legged males into three categories—that of gentlemen, that of illiterate trash, and the dead ones as a gift from God. She had never found any reason to alter her opinion of men.

She instinctively understood men found her attractive—but for her that was not necessarily a good thing. Her hazel eyes were a complimentary match for the color of her skin, as was her thick, wavy, and glossy dark hair which fell to her shoulders. They always brought to her more attention than she sought—and far more than she wanted. Those looks of theirs, some lecherous, others furtive, all shifty, had never changed since the first time a man looked at her. A polite turn of her lips was now all she offered as a greeting. The weight of the revolver fortified her long-standing decision to be shed of men in general. A careful scrutiny of each man provided no reason for her to fear them as they approached. A finger coiled around the trigger supported the confidence of her determination.

She was approximately thirty years old, still young, but the years had taught her things. Her hazel eyes, those of an older woman filled with suspicions, grew hard and dark and revealed little except a fierce resolve in seeing that her order was obeyed. Her examination—overly long and overly cautious of the men as they approached, gathered needed information. But an almost unseen tremble of the long barrel of the Colt advised Sam to be patient. He held his arms away from his body while telling Henry and Isaac to stand back. He held his tongue, allowing her time to voice her stipulations, knowing she would voice them only when and if she felt safe.

She continued to stare at the strangers, her eyes jumping from one to the other and from wagon to wagon. She saw nothing to fear in their eyes or in the wagons, and thought the tented wagon resembled an ambulance, something she'd grown familiar with. Finally, the revolver's barrel slowly fell toward the ground.

"There's a flag by the end of the road, or what's left of one," Sam said, pointing back toward the dark maw of the passage they had just exited, "that said there is a field hospital back in here."

She turned to look deep into the woods that edged the yard beyond her and scanned full circle the green woods surrounding them.

"Don't know nut'n 'bout no flag. Look for yourself. Was one here, but that hospital you'uns asking 'bout's long gone. It and de wounded got loaded up and hauled off somewhere," she answered, believing only desperate men and women would have come into such a God-forsaken place. Plenty of mothers, fathers, wives, and men hired for an unpleasant job, had already come looking and asked the same question of her many times before. "But dare's a graveyard down by dem pines. Sum' ob 'em's got planks wid names scratched on 'em."

Sam stared at the ground, crestfallen.

She saw the desperation in the man's eyes. "But dare still be sum' folks what's got soldiers still stayin' wid 'em . . . laid up in their houses," she added.

Sam looked up, his hope returning. "You know where any of these people live?"

"Course I do. What you'uns got to do with 'ennie ah that, 'ennie how? Them ain't no army wagons. That one in the back looks like an ambulance, but it ain't no army wagon. You Home Guard whats turned bounty hunters? Luck turn on you? Things dun' got so bad y'all gone to grabbing bad-hurt boys out'ta their sick beds and haulin' 'em back where they ain't fit to go? Y'all needs to get on out'ta here."

"No Ma'am," answered Sam, thumbing over his shoulder at Isaac and Henry. "We're from down below Weldon past the Carolina line. Been told my son was here while the fighting was going on and I have reason to believe he may still be in these parts."

"Been hopin' is what you ought'a said," Celine answered. "Lots ah dem fellers was here. I seen myself a lifetime of shot up men in the last month. Lot of 'em gonna stay here for good. But I reckon y'all done seen some of that, too."

"We have, Ma'am. And a worse sight I've never seen. We mean you no harm. I just want to fetch my son and get him home. Can you tell us where some of those neighbors you mentioned live?"

"You think what you dun' seen was bad, duz you? Well then, you'uns should'a been here when de ground was shakin' and bleedin'. It'll go to my grave with me. But I duz ramble on. What your boy look lac, ennie how?" she asked, intently staring at Sam.

Her eyes betrayed her and gave Sam hope. They held the look of someone comparing features—faces, perhaps voices. Her color distracted him and he reasoned she could be a free woman, perhaps one of French ancestry. He felt a need to be cautious and not to hurry the woman. He was not sure if the woman was a farmer's wife or a farmer's slave. To label someone as something they may not be could end the conversation. Regardless of her station, she had been polite and courteous to him. He felt obligated to treat her the same.

"Ma'am, my son's twenty-three years old. Very tall. Six feet. Blond hair the color of straw. Last time I saw him it was cut short. He has blue eyes, like mine. Told he's got my nose, my mouth and chin. He's big across the chest and has powerful arms. Last I saw of him, he had a new beard growing, the color of straw, too. Probably dark now like mine used to be," he said thinking the comparison worthless, but her face softened.

"Ain't sayin' he's your'n, mind you, but maybe you ought to come in and take a look at that feller we'se been seein' after."

"We" meant others were about. "Is your man with you?" Sam asked. She did not answer him and pointed toward the porch steps.

"Ain't no man 'bout these parts. None up and walkin' and I don't welcome none, neither. But if you was sent by God to find your boy, I'll make an exception this one time."

Sam's heart pounded. Could his son possibly be on the far side of the door?

Stepping into the cabin, he followed her through a jumble of rooms and into a rear room. The woman stepped aside and pointed at the form on the mattress by the window in the far wall.

"You needs' a candle, duz you? We try to keep it dark in here. He always be a tryin' to git up when the sun starts to climbin'." As she walked to the corner cabinet, she stopped and leaning into the window, peered intently in both directions.

 A young girl, more grown than child, still holding the long rifle in the bend of her elbow stepped from behind the opened door.

***

"That be your son?" asked the girl.

Sam did not acknowledge her question. His throat had locked and words could not be spoken. Below him, on a mattress filled with corn husks, lay an older version of his son, a man appearing to be thirty or more years old—a haggard and thin version of his twenty-three year old son. Unspoken words, one knotted against the other, refused to be pushed from his congested throat. A single, raspy sob rumbled from his mouth. He fell to his knees and touched the face he would have known in the dark. "It's me, Tad. Tad, I'm here."

He waited for a response but heard nothing. He turned towards the light-skinned woman and his eyes begged of her the reason for his son's silence. Before she spoke, she pointed at the young man on the tick mattress.

"Look."

Sam felt the tug of eyes pulling at him and he returned his son's gaze. Slowly, Tad's eyes focused upon his and as slowly as they focused, they began to disappear behind dark and weary eyelids. A small almost unperceivable curl of the lip returned to a straight and pressed line.

"Well, looks to me like you dun found your son. That boy be your son, don't he? I can tell. He knows me and Lillie Beth sum'," said Celine, pointing to a young lady of about twenty years of age, standing at the head of the bed. "Not always. Sum'times he opens his eyes when me or her talks to him. Udder times, he don't, lac he don't even knows we'se here. He says a word or two now and then, but then he might not say nuff'n for a day or so, sum'times longer. When he first come here, along with all dem broken bones and cuts, he had a knot on the side of his head 'bout the size of my fist," and she raised a tiny but firm fist to show him how large the knot had been. " Me and her," pointing at Lillie, "had to bleed it with a flip-razor, or his skin would'a busted open. Den sum' days he might as well be one'a dem preacher mens what gits to jumpin' and talkin' in tongues, if you believe in that stuff. Me, no Suh, I don't hold with that foolishness. If'n the good Lord wanted one'ah dem jibber-jabber talkers to act the fool, I do believe that man ought'a do it on his own. But lac I said, I duz go on.

"Oncet' a while he talks gibberish, all back'erds, frun'erds, ever which'r way there is. But don't let that bother you none too much. Hardly ever duz it no more. Other times he'll talk lac he's tired of being quiet and goes on for a spell 'til he goes back to sleep. And there we is git'n all ready for a long talk wid him and he's off in Chine'r or sum' place else. Strange thing, our thinkers," Celine said tapping her temple, as she once again returned to the window to scan the yard.

"Is he going to live?" Sam asked Celine, his eyes pleading for the only answer *he* could live with.

"When he got toted in here, I didn't much think so. He kind'a laid there like a washed out bed sheet. Didn't move. Couldn't tell if he were ah breathin' or not. Me? I thought he was dun for when dem stretcher-toters left. Seemed like he was that close to Glory, to me. But then he moaned, so me and Lillie started in takin' care of him." She paused and wiped away the perspiration on the soldier's forehead.

"If'n he ever says he dun seen de Lord, I'd believe him, if'n I was you. That's how close to dying me and Miss Lillie be thinkin' he were."

Sam nodded his head, acknowledging her comment. He thought it too much for her to talk about and too much for him to hear.

"Tad. It's me. Son, I've come to take you home."

With the eighteen years spent with his son he had catalogued a library of the boy's reaction to all things. A flicker of an eyelash served as proof enough, at least for now, that his son knew his father was there, just as Sam knew his son was inside the battered, struggling body. To comfort his son, he said, "Everything will be alright now, Tad. Your mother and I, and your sisters need you. I'm going to take you home. Henry and Isaac are with me."

He knew his son was desperately wounded and began thinking of how to get him home, but he needed more information from the two women.

He stood and faced the woman with the strangely colored skin. "I am eternally in your debt. May I ask of your name?"

"When I was born in Louisiana . . . Baton Rouge be my startin' place, my mammy named me Celine, but seems like everybody wants to call me Miss Ceely. So I answers to both," she said.

And turning toward the young lady, the one almost a woman, Celine added, "She be the reason your son be alive. Come here, Elizabeth. That be her given name, but we calls her Lillie Beth."

Setting the musket aside, now that she knew who the man was, the young woman approached Sam.

"What's his name?" she asked, as her eyes jumped from the father to the son.

Chapter Eighteen: Mid-August, Eighteen and sixty-two.

In that world gone mad in which he has arrived, Sam finds his warrior son and the tattered remnants of a broken family. His search for his boy evolves into a greater challenge. Not only must he save the wounded young man, but he must save the family abandoned by their father, as well. He knows they will die by nightfall on the day he leaves with his son, if he does not rescue them. Is what he decides right or wrong? But, right or wrong is no longer an issue.

In answer to the young lady's question, Sam answered, "His mother and I named him Thaddeus Samuel Biggs." And to the womenfolk, he added, "but, like your names, his didn't take, either. Somehow it got shortened to Tad."

"Tad," Lillie said. Her voice whimsical, as if she'd found a secret and wished to repeat it—and secure it in her memory.

"Why is he all tied up like that?" asked Sam.

"He gets to flippin' an ah floppin' 'round sometimes. This one's," Lillie answered, pointing at the left arm pulled across his chest and secured from side to side with twisted strips torn from bed sheets, " 'cause he's got a bad broke collarbone. The break is still knitting. And see that cut?" pointing at a still seeping and ragged slit, a quarter-inch wide, three inches long, "it opens up and he gets to bleeding like a stuck pig every time. Deep, too. He don't need to be jumping 'round like he does. Me and her," with a quick nod towards Celine "is trying to keep him from killing himself."

"That wrapping around his chest?" Sam asked about the crisp and recently washed bandage torn from a bed sheet. "What's that for?"

Once again, before Lillie could explain, Celine stepped to the edge of the window facing the rear yard and looked in all directions, and stared deeper yet into the woods surrounding the cabin. The older woman glanced at Lillie and shook her head, answering an unasked question. Only then did Lillie continue, "Looks like one of dem Yankees tried to stick him. But dem two soldiers what toted him down here said that it weren't no bayonet—cuts too wide, but it's clear down to the collarbone." She reached across to the table by the window and grabbed a piece of rusty and pitted iron and handed it to the man standing above her. "They said it was a piece of a wagon wheel what got blow'd up near 'em. If your son makes it, you might want to give it to him. Comes with a story he can tell his children someday."

"Do you think he can travel the way he is, Miss Lillie?" his words offering both gratitude and respect.

Lillie's face indicated how little she understood of living and dying. She looked to Celine for the answer.

"Yes Sir. He can travel," said Celine. "Go with y'all clean back to wherever it was you'uns said y'all was from. But he might not live to tell about it. He needs more time. Another week or two would help. Longer would be better," she added. "But that girl there," pointing at Lillie Beth, "is what he needs most. She got him this far, and she can get him further. But Mister Biggs, if'n y'all can get him home wid' out hurtin' him none, I believe y'all ought'a do it. It ain't safe 'round these parts."

That he knew. He'd seen the wasted bodies, the wagons filled with the scraps of war, the ragged men digging in the dirt for iron, copper and any metal the Tredegar Iron works would buy. He'd seen the fighting among the trash pickers. No, this small hidden-away farm would soon be found and when it was, a new wave of inhumanity would be close behind.

Before Sam could ask if that was what she meant, a light skinned boy entered the room and tugged at his mother's skirt.

***

"Mama, I'se hungry," Jacob said.

"Now hush. We'se got company."

"But Ma . . ."

"I said hush. You see me talkin' to this here man? I know's you'se hungry. We all is." And again, she stepped over to the window and peered outside. "Besides there ain't nary one bite of nuff'n in this house and that smoke house out yonder," and pointing in the direction of the backyard, she continued, "ain't got that much in it."

Sam heard the embarrassment in her voice and saw the shame in her eyes. For the first time since arriving, he saw the frail thin bodies of the children, the thin arms and spindly legs, the loose hanging clothing, the sickly gray skin of faces, the skin below the eyes reddish-purple and the tell-tale slowness of movements when required. He'd thought such lethargy was the result of the summer heat, but now knew he was wrong. He felt ashamed of himself for not recognizing the signs of starvation.

His heart had been so filled with joy at finding his son he had failed to see Tad, too, was also badly malnourished. *To hell with this war, and all those who just had to have it,*" he thought.

"Is that true Miss Celine? Are you out of food?" Sam asked.

"Yes Suh. We has been for two days. Dun' dug up the 'tater patch twice looking for sump'n for these young'uns. Tain't nary a thing no where's."

A far away stare glazed her eyes as she thought of how compassionate the men in butternut had been to the wounded, Southern or Union, and indeed to herself and the children. And of how they shared their abundant rations. She remembered how she had stood guard over the two remaining smoked hams the same men tried to pilfer when they left. She'd watched as an officer lashed the face of one of the men. She thought, too, of how the two remaining hams were stolen in the dark of the night a week before by the thing in the woods.

Sam was torn. He wanted—needed to ask more of his son, but he owed these women so very much. He could help, but the help would be minimal at best.

"Miss Lillie. Miss Celine, you sit there with those little ones. Gather 'em up. We're going to fix you up a feast."

Turning to Henry and Isaac, he said. "Get everything we have out of the wagons. We'll re-supply tomorrow. Give these folks some of those apples. That will hold them over for a bit."

"Thank you for your kindness, Suh," answered Celine, "but it be best if'n I be ah sit'n next to the window," and walked back to it with her revolver in hand.

"Can we pull the wagons around back and start a cook fire?"

Celine looked frightened, but answered, "You can, but you ought not. That backyard ain't safe," and gave no further explanation. "Be best if y'all set camp right where you dun' put dem wagons. And Suh," speaking to Sam, "It'd be smart if'n you tell one of your friends to do the cookin' and the udder'n to watch the woods."

Puzzled by the strange comment, he asked, "What is it you keep watching the woods for?"

"Same thing I duz all day long and every night. Massa Tink."

"Do you mean your owner?"

"Yas Suh. Massa Tink. He last name be Strickland."

Sam relayed the strange conversation to Henry and Isaac and told them to put on their gun belts. He put his on, twirled the cylinder, pressed the percussion caps into place, and slid it into its holster. "We're leaving first light. They're coming with us." Neither Henry or Isaac offered any comment. They merely nodded their heads in agreement. They'd been quicker to see things that Sam, in his exhilaration of finding Tad, had not seen.

The meal prepared, Sam said, "You all, come and get it." After the meal had been devoured, the little ones fell asleep. Candles had been scattered about to afford enough light for conversation.

As Lillie cooled Tad's face with a soaked cloth, Sam asked of Celine. "Why can't he talk?"

"That contract doctor," Celine answered, "you know . . one of dem doctors what gits hired by the guv'ment to see to the needs of the wounded, stopped here for all of two long minutes," she answered, sarcasm thick in her throat, "said 'cause his head got busted open." She pointed at the reddish-purple scar running across his temple, from the lobe of the ear to the edge of the eye socket. The wound was healing and the catgut stitches had begun to fall away.

"He said your boy might or might not never talk. That's what he said. But he was so lit-up from drinking, that drunk fool didn't know dirt from squirrels." The caramel-colored woman saw the fear and sadness in Sam's eyes, and added, "But the Good Lord's gonna' see to your boy—I just knows it. I see things, you know?"

"Everybody, listen to me. We're leaving early in the morning. Nobody's staying," Sam said.

And to Celine and Lillie Beth, he added, "God bless you both for what the two of you have done. His mother and I will eternally be grateful."

***

Sam pulled up a chair and sat by his son. He placed his large hand alongside Tad's bearded face. He had no way of knowing if his son could feel his presence or not, but held it there in hopes that he could. Tad drifted in and out of consciousness, but occasionally his eyes remained opened long enough to take in new things. Thus far, he'd said nothing, but moaned a few times and sank back into the peace and calm his mind and body seemed to prefer.

***

Old memories, all happy, flooded through the boy's father. His chest caught when he thought of how happy his dear sweet Rose would be when she saw her son for the first time in two long years. And the happy vision made his eyes water.

Tad coughed and winced. Lillie Beth rushed to his side and whispered soothingly to him. Slowly, and with effort, Tad's eyes opened, hardly more than mere slits—but open, and Sam watched as his son stared at Lillie. Like Celine, he knew things. From the library of things known about his son, he knew the boy recognized the young lady at his side. Things will be fine, he assured himself—more hope than promise.

***

"Miss Celine," Sam asked, "May I be so bold as to ask a question of you?"

"Yes Suh."

"Where is your Mister Strickland?"

"You mean ole Whiskey Man?" she hummmphed.

"If that's what you call him, yes."

"Ole Whisky Man be off in de woods, drunk. He be back in there ah sleepin' in ah burned-out whiskey barrel. He been gone ah week now. He be comin' back soon. He comes and goes. Might stay sober dis time for nigh on ah month, maybe longer, den he'll git drunk all obber a'gin. You'uns'll see him soon enough. But my Massa? No Suh. Dat he ain't. Just 'cause he bought and paid for me, that don't make him no massa ah mine. No Sirree. He don't remember buying me and I ain't reminded him, need'r. Dat's what confuses me de most. When he be drunk he don't knows nobody and when he's sobered up, sum'times he do and sum'times he don't. Two different men live inside ah him an de one doan know de udder'n. An' I ain't none too fond of need'r ob 'em."

"Does he do anything to help you and the children?" asked Sam, already knowing the answer.

"You see a table 'bout ready to cave in 'cause of all the food what's piled up on it? No? You see a man come in here and hug his chil'en? Dem young'uns ah his didn't neither. Sumabitch stole the last two hams we had out'ta the smokehouse while dem young'uns was dreaming 'bout food when they's sleepin'.

"Nah Suh. He only be's ah seein' to his needs. But Mister Biggs, if'n he comes into dis here yard and stands still long enough, I'se gonna' shoot that smelly-ass sumabitch right in the gut and put red hot coals in the hole that gun leaves. Then to make sure he doan never git up, I'se gonna drive a fence post clean through him an' I doan give a goodly goddamn if'n I hang for doin' it, neither. At least that way, maybe the white folks would come and get dem young'uns and my Jacob and see to 'em."

"Why'd he run off into the woods? That's where he lives now?"

"Cause he knows dem folks 'round 'bout dese here parts are gonna' hang him when they finds him. They pretty much all believe he killed his wife—'cause he did."

"If, as you said, you are one of his slaves, then where is the mother of that boy and girl, and what of that son of yours?"

"That young girl tendin' your son and the oldest boy is his young'uns with Miss Jacqueline. God rest her soul," she said, crossing her heart as if in prayer. "The littlest one, the one what's my color, 'cept lighter, is his boy by me. He up and killed Miss Jacqueline, 'cause of me. I seen him do it. Said all she did was complain 'bout him always ah slipin' away of a night to come bed me. Can't blame her none for git'n mad, I reckon. But he bashed my first son 'ginst ah tree like he weren't no more than a ham hanging in the smoke house what'd gone bad. And dared me to say nary one word 'bout it. Fore I know'd it, I was fat with that light-colored boy yonder. My Jacob."

"And the food? He took the food? Took it away from you and his children?"

"Takes whatever he wants when he wants it. That's why I carry this here gun. I'se gonna' even it up some for him killin' my Malcomb and Miss Jacqueline."

"How often does he come around?" asked Sam.

"He be out there now. Can't see him but he be there."

"And there's no one, no neighbors who'll help out?"

"No Suh, tain't no body come by aff'r he turn mean, " she said shaking her head. Thinking it over, she thought the man truly did not understand what had been going on. Sarcastically and greatly exaggerated, she cupped her hand to her ear. "But look'ee. Here dey cum's. Must be a hun'ert wagons full ah folks what gives a damn. Hummmph." And calmer, she said, "Dey stayed clear ah here 'fore that fighting over cross the woods got going and aint ah one ob 'em been here to see after him and his young'uns since. But you reaps what you sow, my mama tole me. Dat be true, dare gonna be sum' Godly reapin' goin' on 'round dese here parts."

Something solid and swung hard, slammed against the cabin wall along the outside corner from where Sam and Celine were talking. Cups and china fell to the planked floor from the corner cabinet and shattered. Sam jumped, startled, as Celine stared at the wall. The children sat up on their pallets and stared at Sam.

Sam walked to the door and motioned Henry, already armed, to walk to the far end of the porch as he walked around the cabin and edged along the back wall. On the ground lay a tree limb about five feet long. There was nothing else to be seen.

"You see anything?"

"Nah. Nothing. But I heard somebody running off that way." answered Henry as he pointed to the dark woods.

"Load those woods with lead. Let the Lord of the Manor know he's not welcome in his own house. Who knows? Might get lucky and hit him."

Chapter Nineteen:
Eighteen and sixty-two: Mid-August. Hot and sultry. Preparations are completed to get Tad home, along with the family who has befriended his son.

Experienced with mentally ill men who nourish their illness with alcohol, Sam understands the two combined can only lead to violence. Time is of the essence—the man will return. And when he does, there will be severe consequences. And blood will flow. He knows by the things he has been told that he can wait no longer—he must do something illegal.

"Pardon me, Miss Ceely, Miss Lillie," said Sam, as he removed his hat while entering the cabin. "Ladies, may I speak with you for a moment?" And the three stepped into an adjacent room.

The cabin remained hot and sticky. But the new day promised it would be an ideal one in which to flee. Sam had made a decision and his face was one of fierce determination. Celine and Lillie stood quietly, expecting to hear of his plans to leave with his son.

"We're all leaving after the sun rises a bit more. You and the children, too. And yes, I know it would be best to let my son rest here for as long as possible, but the truth is, and nothing unkind meant by this, he's no better off here than in the wagon heading home." Knowing the comment sounded as if he was ungrateful for all she and Lillie had done, he hurriedly added, "and I, as well as those two men outside," pointing toward the front yard where Henry and Isaac stood, "think it would be best for you and the children to come with us."

The two women looked tired, exhausted. Both had received little rest during the previous days, and knowing they and the children could no longer stay in the place they knew as home stressed them even more. Although staying was dangerous, they seemed reluctant to leave.

"Ladies. You can't stay here. There's no food. No water, except that swampy run off in the creek, and there's no telling how polluted it is," referring to the dead bodies bound to be floating in it. "It's not enough you have to fetch it yourself and boil it, but each time you go to the creek you put yourself in danger . . . and, those children in there," he said, pointing toward the room just vacated. "It's the same reason why you can't go into the woods to shoot a wild hog or deer to feed yourselves. He's in there. He'll kill you and then come in here after the little ones. You don't have a choice, Celine, Lillie." Finally, he had decided this was not the time to get caught up in formalities "You go into the woods, he comes in the house. You stay in the house with the doors and windows boarded up, you and the children starve. There's only one way you and the children will get out of here alive. And that is, if you come with us. And yes, I agree, this is your home. But now it's nothing but a coffin made out of logs."

"Mr. Sam," Celine's head sagging, "I run off with you and the children, he be coming after me."

"Did you not tell me the other slave ran off?"

"Yes Suh, I did."

"Did Strickland go after him?"

"No Sir. But that be different. He ain't got no chile with him."

"Celine, he killed your first boy and you still think you should stay. Why? For Jacob? Did he show you any respect for being your dead son's mother?"

"Mr. Sam," she said, tears pooling in her eyes. "I wants to go. Lord knows I duz. You don't got no idea how bad I want's to be shed of this place and that sorry-ass dog, but there's laws against us slaves running off. If'n he ketches me he will hang me. An' dare won't be no beatin' first. Nah Suh, you got's slaves. You knows good as I do, I'se dead if'n I stay—dead if'n I go."

"Are you listening to yourself, Celine?" he asked. "Do you hear what you are saying? You're guaranteeing you and your boy are going to be killed by that man. He's already done it, twice. And I will under no circumstance leave you and that boy here. Consider yourself kidnapped."

Lillie stood quietly by the door. She'd overheard the conversation and she was frightened by the fear lining Celine's face. She rushed to comfort the older woman who had seen to her every need since her real mother had *supposedly* drowned.

With the sudden and irrefutable realization that they must leave everything behind in order to continue living, Celine and Lillie hugged each other tight. Sam turned away, affording the two women a chance to console each other.

The first to respond was Lillie. "Don't cry, Celine. Aunt Cora will take us in. You and Jacob, too. And Hopewell's only a couple hours away."

Celine brushed away a tear and said to the girl barely half her age, "Chile, you tried that three, four years ago. Weren't no mor'n two months later that man come looking for you and Billy. 'Member that? You 'member him telling your Aunt Cora to stay out of his business and that he'd kill her, his own sister, if'n she stole you young'uns again. You 'member that, too? Duz you? You think he's found God now and won't dare go lookin' for you first chance he gits?"

"Pardon me, Lillie," Sam said after the two had calmed a bit. "Did you just say Hopewell?"

"Yes Sir. My Aunt Cora lives there," and looked for approval from Celine and the man standing before her.

"Lillie, you need to listen to Miss Celine," using a more formal title to help what Celine said carry more weight, "Hopewell's too close. Only a boat ride across the James. Your father would head there first thing, as quick as he finds out you all are gone. Give me a minute to talk to Henry and Isaac. I've got an idea and all of us will benefit. I'll be right back." As he left, Lillie again hugged Celine and whispered softly to calm her. For a short time their roles had been reversed.

Soon, Sam returned. "Lillie, would you be willing to go with me to my place down below Weldon and see after my son? He's going to need a lot of attention and you've already proven you can provide it. I'll make your help well worth the trouble."

Lillie looked and felt as if her small world was collapsing in on her. "Mister Biggs, if I go with you, I don't want no money, but what about Billy? Can he come with me, too?"

"We'll all go. All of us." And turning back to the mulatto woman, he said, "You and Jacob, too, Celine. You can stay at my place as long as you want and leave when you're ready. You can go whenever you wish. Give this war time to end. It can't last much longer. It's the only thing we can do. You all can get away from here to safety and Thaddeus can finish healing with you seeing to him. What do you say?" he asked, looking at both of them.

"But . . . " said Celine. "Mr. Sam, Massa Strickland . . ." her voice trailed off. She knew there was no other choice.

Sam had expected her to remind him of the man and her circumstances, again. "Four things, Celine. Number one. That Tink fellow," spitting the words as if they were vulgar, "deserted you and ran off into the woods. Number two. He abandoned his children, yours and those by his wife. Three. Did he ever chase after the slave boy who ran away? And the fourth thing . . . he will kill you. It may not be in a week after we're gone, maybe not a year. But he will come after you, use you, then kill you. I have seen men like him. I've seen them rot with meanness and not know what was happening. Nor did they care. That's the world Tink lives in now."

"But what if . . ." she continued—the fear of not understanding the eventualities, but strongly suspecting what was likely to happen, had altered her ability to see the logic in what Sam was saying. She, of all people, had the right to be concerned. She'd known of slaves who'd run off from their masters when she lived on one of the Louisiana plantations. They were caught and tortured in ungodly ways. Tied to the trunk of a convenient tree, their backs sliced with knotted skin-cutting whips. Such things and such sights can only give birth to the kind of fear she felt.

She realized her skin color was light, but its dusty, peach color did nothing to convince her she was of more value for being inside it or that it would stave off the overseer's whip. She'd seen enough to be of two minds. If she stayed there was a chance she might be allowed to live, but each time she gave thought to that, she remembered Malcomb. This big man, this white man was offering her a new life and she wanted to grab it, to seize it, to squeeze her existence into it. Instead, she reeled with indecision.

Sam understood her reluctance to leave. But he could not and would not leave her and the boy Jacob there alone.

"Miss Celine, by law, you are no longer a slave. By reason of your two sons, you are more of a common-law wife to this Tink fellow than a slave, but be that as it may, I don't think even that will hold in court. So, if it will help you, I will lay claim to you and Jacob as my property. In order to do so, I'll have to find someone willing to draw up a receipt of sale. One that show's I bought you from Strickland. And it's got to be good. That way you'll belong to me—but only on paper. It's just a safe guard, Celine. You can work in the house with Lillie if you wish. Jacob can roam freely around the plantation. That way, he'll be close to you.

"I have more slaves than most. I don't need anymore, nor do I want more, but if it will keep you, your son, Lillie and Billy together, I will do it. And one more thing. I do not think the South's going to win this war. I might be wrong. So far we've won just about every battle. Those Union fellows don't seem to have the will to fight like our boys do, but there's millions of them. The South's already running out of money and war burns through money like it was needles in a stand of dried-out pines. When we're done with the fighting and killing, I believe you and all the rest of the slaves will be set free. Lincoln hasn't said so, not yet, but I think he will. Regardless of what happens, you can go or you can stay on my place. That much I promise you.

"I will not ask much of you, but this you owe to yourself, to Jacob, and your dead son and that son of a bitch's children by his first wife. It's a chance to live. When we go through Hopewell . . . and mind you both, do not say the words North Carolina to anyone. That barge Captain might have forgotten where I told him we were from so I'll tell him a different place—tell him we're from down in South Carolina. Close to the Georgia line. That should throw anybody who might get the idea to come after us off our trail. We'll simply vanish.

Now, the two of you find something, a piece of paper, a book, anything that he has written his name on."

Celine and Lillie remained locked in an embrace, each afraid the other would disappear.

Lillie asked, "When do we go?" and hugged Celine to her.

"We're loading now."

***

"Everybody ready?" asked Sam, as Celine unlatched the cabin door. And one by one the inhabitants of the cabin came out to the porch.

"I think it's still a bit too early for anyone to be up and sneaking about the cabin," said Sam. "Now, as quietly and quickly as you can, let's finish loading. I'll lead with the green wagon. Miss Celine, I want you and the two boys with me. Put everything that you can not get by without in the middle wagon. Henry will drive that one. Load it good and sash everything down tight. Henry's got the rope. Isaac will bring up the rear. Lillie, I want you on Isaac's wagon with Thaddeus. We got the rope meshed across from side to side and from front to back. Bring out the corn husk mattresses first. Get them up on top of the rope sling. And blankets. Don't forget the blankets. Grab them all. Now Lillie, since you know how Thaddeus reacts to things, you watch him. If he needs to stop for anything, a rest, water, his private moments, tell Henry and Isaac. They'll pass it along. Henry, you got anything to add?"

"What you can do without stays here," Henry said. "Anything can be replaced so don't fret. We're making a run for it now. And getting out of here is more important than taking along useless items. Keep as quiet as you can. No stirring up trouble we don't need. Isaac?"

"Just that there's not much room under Tad's rope sling. And nobody but Tad gets to use the blankets. Now, we expect everybody to whisper as much as you can or figure out some kind of hand communicating if you need it. And the last thing, when it comes to Thaddeus, Lillie's the last word. What she says goes. Lillie says slow down, we slow down. She says stop, we stop."

And of Celine, Sam asked, "When Tink goes back into the woods, which woods does he go into the most often? Is it the woods back of the house or those out front?"

"Always the back'uns."

Sam called Henry and Isaac over to him for a last minute decision. There were two docks for barges to take farm products and travelers across the James River—the north landing where they had crossed on their way in, and the southern landing, which the tide and high wind had pushed them beyond on their crossing of the James. Therefore, there were two roads to leave by.

Relieved to find out the man did not hide out in the lower woods, Sam did not want to see what he, Henry and Isaac had seen and most certainly did not want the two women and the children to see the thing which was easier for Sam to think of as a dead creature of the sea washed inland.

"We'll take the one that crosses and puts us a bit east of Hopewell. If we try the road we came in on he might hear us and if he does, he'll come running to try to put a stop to what we're doing. And, yes, the same thing could happen on the other road but at least we have better odds of getting off this farm on the lower road."

Henry and Isaac loaded Thaddeus carefully, while Lillie gathered the meager medicines still left. By the wagon, she pleaded with Henry and Isaac to be careful of causing further damage to the wounded man. She slid the supplies underneath the rope-mesh and wrapped them in a sheet to keep them from scattering.

Sam climbed the wagon wheel, took his seat and awaited Henry and Isaac. Next to him and leaning against the wagon seat stood his loaded rifle.

Lillie had left the house in time to hear Sam tell Celine, "We are going to go straight through Hopewell. No stopping until we're in Petersburg. Should make it by late afternoon. We'll be hungry but when we get there we'll get everything we need."

Saddened and dejected by his refusal to stop, Lillie asked, "But Mister Biggs. What about Aunt Cora? Can't we at least stop by so me and Billy can say goodbye?"

"No, Lillie, it's too risky." She saw a fierce determination on his face and accepted the final decision.

"Can Billy manage the team if you're there with him to help?" Sam asked the young lady.

"Yes, Sir, he can handle a team. But I thought Mr. Isaac . . . but why?" she asked.

"I've decided to leave Isaac at the landing once we cross over to the Hopewell side. I'll get him a horse to catch up with us. We've got to make sure your father doesn't follow us. Now, I told Isaac not to provoke him and not to shoot him if your father does show up. I don't need that hanging over our heads. Just told him to make sure he didn't get off the barge but if he did, for him to throw your father in the James and then get the hell out of there."

***

The Hopewell wharves were filled with all manner of contraband. Illegal things flowed to and from each bank. If history had proven wars were counterproductive to living, it had certainly given birth to thievery and counterfeiting, as well.

Sam reached into his vest pocket, removed his wallet and waved it toward Captain Tom. The rope in the Captain's hand fell to the planked floor of the barge and it, in turn, slowly drifted with the tide. Two fingers jabbed in the Captain's mouth produced a shrill and piercing whistle bringing another deckhand running to catch the rope as it snaked over the edge of the barge and into the Big Black.

Sam removed a handful of paper money from his wallet.

"You like greenbacks or Confederate? Got both."

"Prefer greenbacks," came the answer.

"I need . . . let's say something out of the usual. The right piece of paper would be worth a hundred to me."

"I can get unusual things," the next answer, spoken hurriedly.

"You ever seen me before?"

"Why shore. Two, three days ago."

The hundred dollar bill quickly disappeared in Sam's hand. He looked sternly at the captain and asked again, "You sure you've ever seen me before?"

"Can't say as I ever have, Mister. Should I?"

"You ever see that boy and that girl, those white children?"

Captain Tom rubbed his thumb and first two fingers together for Sam to see. "Another one of dem," he said pointing at the wadded bill in Sam's hand, "and I been blind since I was born."

"I need a piece of paper, a receipt, notarized by someone who's willing to be as blind as you."

"What's on it?" asked the Captain.

"Does it matter, Captain Tom?" his voice edgy, challenging.

"Not to me. No Sir. Just need to find the right man."

"I assure you," Sam continued, his voice razor sharp. "you do need the best man you can find. Lets leave it as a special kind of paper work."

"Yes Sir."

"And a horse. I need a horse."

"Ain't got but one. 'Cept it ain't no horse. It's a mule. An old plug mule at that. 'Bout worn out. Was going to eat it, but it's yours for another hundred dollars."

"All I have left is Confederate script. Take a hundred dollars in script?"

"Script would be a hell of a discount, but there ain't much meat left on her ribs. I'll take it. Be down at Vector's embalming tent in an hour. Ask for Moses. Man'll make any paper you want."

"Captain Tom. You ever see me before?"

"Cross my heart. I ain't never once ever seen none ah y'all."

Sam climbed up and onto the wagon seat and stared down at the barge's captain. He shook his head in disbelief. "Eat a mule? Damn."

***

Sam motioned for Isaac to join him. "Isaac. I got a favor to ask of you."

"Sure. Sam. Anything."

"I need you to stay down here by the dock and keep an eye out for that Tink fellow in case he comes after us."

"But Sam, you already paid that captain to cover for us."

"Yes. You're correct. But Isaac, you're a better man than me. You got more trust in your fellow man than I do. I hope he'll keep his end of the bargain and stay quiet, but my heart says that captain will lie to anybody that gives him money, greenbacks or script, and that includes Tink Strickland."

"Yeah. I reckon he would."

"Henry's walking a mule for you over to that street," he said pointing to a street already filled with wagons. "Lay low and keep an eye out for that bastard. Lillie can handle the team for a day or so. You see him, haul ass after us and tell me."

"Okay, Sam."

Chapter Twenty: Eighteen and sixty-two: Mid August, the heat, and the voyage home.

Fleeing toward the safety of Swift Creek, the need to hurry is hindered by the need of comfort for his son. There are many unknown answers to his multitude of questions. Are they being pursued by Tink Strickland? Or perhaps the law? He understands he will have to lie to anyone who might question him of his multi-faceted cargo. Will he be believed? Can Tad survive the tortuous trip home? He tries to hide yet another problem—he, himself, is ill. Can he make it all the way home? The only thing he knows for sure is that he has no choice but to try.

Through with ghastly sights, the James River crossed, and all things of death behind him, Sam prayed distance would ease the pressure and tightness growing deep within. A sharp pain traveled from his left elbow, up his arm, and burned its way under his armpit, and across his upper chest. Bile surged in his throat and he felt deathly ill. He labored to breathe and began to perspire. He'd always quickly recovered from the strange illness, but this time it took longer. A quick return to normal should have been the case, and would have been, except the horrors continued as they walked their wagons from the barge. Alongside Riverfront Street, farm wagons loaded with freshly disinterred remains of the loved ones of grieving families were lined in front of temporary and strategically located tents and rough-sawn plank-sided shacks.

Crudely painted signs spelled out the reasons for the congregating wagons. A white tent long since turned the color of the dust blowing across the street read: MOSES VECTOR'S EMBALMING EMPORIUM . . . DISCOUNTS FOR EMBALMING, while lesser tents bore such wordage as: INCENSE AND OILS. Others used imaginative phrases, also, with OUR POWDERS, BASED UPON THOSE OF ANCIENT EGYPTIAN SECRETS, WILL GUARANTEE THE FRESHNESS OF YOUR LOVED ONE UNTIL YOU RETURN HOME, being the general theme. Bottles promising salves, ointments, and a wide range of odor killing treatments, weighted down sagging shelves. Leaning against the outside wall stood poorly made but expensive coffins, each with hinged lids opened and folded back, exposing the colorful, but shoddy linings available. Placards hanging across them read, TIN-LINED COFFINS SOLDERED SHUT FOR FREE.

On the far side of the road, Sam tugged back on the reins. He backed the wagon into one of the few spaces left. He walked through the maze of wagons and into the tent with MOSES VECTOR'S EMBALMING EMPORIUM painted above the tent flap.

"Tell Moses there's a man waiting on him."

"Worse than goddamn gypsies," he said to Henry. "Men who'll stoop that low must be void of any humanity. Anyone who could profit from war should be flailed at a stake—or forced to face death straight on."

He and Henry hurried past wagons filled with their ghastly freight, each surrounded by the familiar odors of Malvern Hill, and each with a driver anxious to have Riverfront Street and the vendors behind them. Ironically, as he folded and pocketed the fake bill of sale Moses Vector had just handed him, he thought of the wrong of it, but reasoned at least good might come from it.

He had never professed to be a religious man, but in passing the shacks and the vulgar men hawking wares to desperate people, he hoped the much sought after Heavenly Father did exist and if he did, he would judge harshly such men who were willing to benefit from the white-washed bones of dead sons, brothers, or husbands, and the broken hearts of devastated families.

Yet the lingering thought remained unanswered. If circumstances had been different, and he was in a wagon filled with such heartbreak—what would he have done? What trickery would he have paid for?

A few days earlier, Sam, Henry, and Isaac, riding through the small city on the banks of the James, paid scant attention to the coming and going of its citizens. Hopewell held no interest for them. They dwelt only upon the thought that with a simple barge ride across the James River, they'd be close to Malvern Hill—and hopefully, nearer Tad. They had needed no reason to stop at the area's dry goods stores. Everything they needed was in the back of the three wagons they hurriedly maneuvered through the narrow streets as they headed toward the docks.

Passing through Hopewell, it had only been the three of them, but now the three were eight. The wagons followed a slow procession of other wagons heading south. Left behind was practically everything five of the new travelers had ever owned. And Thaddeus only had a whisper of life left to his name. His uniform, of no further value, bloody and torn beyond repair, had long since been burned with the discarded clothing of countless other men less fortunate than he. Of what was not burned, they had probably already been picked through by the trash pickers who had flooded onto the battlefield, Sam imagined.

Finding a dry goods store, Sam said, "Henry, you go and get enough provisions for tonight. I'll see to the need of the horses. Thirty minutes . . . and let's be on our way," he handed Henry a combination of United States currency and that of the newly minted Confederate scrip. "One or the other should take care of it."

He turned and looked at all the wagons as the riders aboard each curiously stared at them. He cautioned those with him, "Don't speak to anyone."

"Lillie," he called. "Tad need anything? How's he doing?"

"He's tired. There's enough Laudanum for another day or so," she answered, "But he's alright for now. How far is it to Petersburg? He'll need fresh dressings once we get there. And some salves and other fixin's."

Henry returned with a bag of beans, and tied in a rag, a cut of salt pork. Fresh ground coffee was knotted inside yet another piece of cloth, and hidden in his pocket was another filled with rock candy. Billy handed the reins to Henry and slid to the side as Henry climbed the wheel and took the seat beside him. He gave a piece of the hard candy to Billy, one to Jacob, and one each to everyone else. Slapping the reins across the mule's rump he pulled out onto the street behind Sam's and Lillie's wagons and the group plowed through the streets of Hopewell.

A mile from town, Sam raised his hand. "We'll camp in there tonight,' he said, pointing at a clearing large enough for the wagons, mules, and eight people. "Let Tad get some rest from all that banging and bouncing. We can make it into Petersburg in the morning. Once there, we'll buy everything we need to get us the rest of the way home. Lillie, you and Celine make a list of things we need and that includes new clothing all around. We are a fine looking mess, aren't we? What was it you called us, Celine? Trash pickers?" He laughed, hoping he had not insulted the women. An odor reeking from the group suggested he add to the list. "Get us a big cake of that lavender scented lye-soap too, alright?"

***

Petersburg soon lay off in the distance and to the north. The wagons' occupants wore their new clothing over freshly washed bodies, compliments of the scented soap and the clean water of a tributary dumping its water into the Appomattox River, a stone's throw north. Piled high upon Henry's wagon were the needs for three more days of travel.

Long before, when Sam had spent his troubled youth in Petersburg, the railroad tracks they now crossed did not exist, but the Weldon-Petersburg Road did and it still ran south and north—south toward Weldon and Swift Creek Plantation, and north toward even more battles being fought beyond Richmond.

Sam hoped he would be able to buy passage from Petersburg to Weldon in order to make the balance of the trip home quicker and easier for Tad. He could easily sell the wagons and goods, but that was not to be. The dry goods store clerk told him the only direction the trains ran nowadays was mostly north toward the new battlefields.

The Confederate States of America had confiscated all of the South's rail system as their own—the Weldon-Petersburg run being one of the busiest.

Soldiers dressed in gray, numbering in the thousands, rushed along on flatbed rail cars too numerous to count, toward the newest conflicts in the far reaches of northern Virginia. They cheered loudly and waved their slouch hats and unit banners, anxious to see for themselves the "elephant," the term adopted for the horrible, huge, killing beast of war. Behind the flatbeds, enclosed boxcars packed with cannon, rifle and musket, and ammunition, raced towards "glory" while butternut and gray-clad men held desperately to the slatted sides. Cattle cars filled with grunting hogs and bellowing cows brought up the rear.

Thaddeus, captain that he was, could have been granted passage, but Sam could not find any record of a southbound train or when such a train might come along. Nor could he be assured his son would be attended to. And without Lillie, he was unwilling to send his son ahead unattended.

After a few minutes spent with Lillie, the two agreed it was best for the group to stay together and slow down when necessary, speed up when possible.

From the distance, Petersburg's steeples and buildings stood tall. A flood of memories rushed through Sam. The Excelsior, which in another life had been his home for many years, stood ten stories high—then the tallest—but it could no longer brag of it. Other buildings reached higher into the skies, but his memories were limited to the Excelsior. *Things change*, he mused.

From the distance, he heard a faint hello. A dust powdered man carrying a horse's bridle in one hand approached. It was Isaac.

"Where's the mule?" Sam asked.

"Plum gave out. This side of Hopewell . . . two, three miles back. Farted twice and fell over dead." He handed the bridle to his friend and Sam hooked it over the wagon's brake handle.

"Old Gray was a good old mule," said Isaac.

"Cost a hundred dollars," responded Sam.

"A hundred dollars for a broke-down, sway-back plug? Damn." Asked Isaac." Awful lot of money for that thing,"

"She did the job. It was a hundred in script, though." said Sam.

"Well, that's different," said Isaac.

They both laughed trying to figure out who'd made the worse deal, the barge owner with the decrepit mule, or Sam with a bridle he did not need.

"Any sign of that Strickland fellow?"

"Nothing. He could still be coming, though."

"We'll deal with it if he does."

Extending his hand to Isaac, he said, "Climb in. That's the rest of us on the far side of the tracks. We were hoping you'd join us before we headed down to Weldon. And that girl, Lillie, handled that team of your'n damn good. Amazing young lady, she is."

"How's Tad?" Isaac asked.

"About the same. Color seems better. Lillie says he spoke to her."

"What did he say?"

"She said her name."

"Well, Sam, seems to me he's a bit better than about the same," said Isaac, smiling.

"Does, don't it?" acknowledged Sam. And he smiled.

The deep ruts of the worn road required they slow down. The same road he and Henry had taken nearly three decades before was still just that—the same ruts, the same potholes. The traffic eased as they rode south, and finally, the ruts not as many, and pot holes not as deep, the ride eased for Tad. Many miles had been traveled, and the ride had been hard on him. Lillie cautioned Sam that his son had begun to look the worse for wear. The tent over the rope sling was hot and Lillie feared a turn for the worse. Upon examination, he saw his son had paled to a chalky white. A raspy pant had replaced the soft breathing of before.

"Henry," said Sam. "Tad's not doing so well. Will you please ride down to Weldon and fetch Doc Yardley? Unhitch the best mule we have and run him into the ground if you have to. Tell Doc Tad's bad off."

Within moments Henry disappeared toward Weldon, six miles south.

Sam's first inclination was to continue and close the distance between where they now were and Weldon, but realizing the distance gained would be minimal, ordered a new camp erected. A quick arrival back to Swift Creek was of little importance compared to his son's health. Celine began an early meal while Sam and Lillie began to see to Tad's comfort.

Henry tugged the reins hard and fought the buggy pulled by two horses to a standstill. Doc Yardley, the Biggs' family physician for years, slapped the dust from his hat and stepped from the carriage. From behind the spring equipped, leather covered bench seat he removed his medicine bag.

"For heaven's sake, Sam, get out of the way," he said, elbowing aside the man between himself and the patient. He pulled back Tad's eyelids and said, "Hmmm." Next, with a funnel shaped instrument he peered into the patient's ears. "Hmmm." Taking a flat round disc-shaped object with two tubes attached, and with a tube in each of his ears, the doctor slid the shiny disc over Tad's chest. Another "Hmmm." A depressor held the tongue in place as he peered inside the mouth. Turning to Sam he said, "He's just plum worn down to a frazzle. Way to hot. Sweating like a plow mule. Somebody get him some water. My guess is," and pointing at the ragged scar running across Tad's temple, he said, "that there's the problem," and carefully probing the red scar, added, "your boy's got himself a concussion."

"We tried to give him water, but he wouldn't take it. What did you say he's got," Sam asked.

"In laymen's terms, he got his noggin busted open. Like a mule done kicked him."

Away from the others Sam asked the doctor, "Is my son going to live?"

"Sam, is that fair? I'm not God. But, I'll be as truthful as I can be. He might die . . . he might live. There. Nobody knows the way these things turn out. A concussion is like an egg with the shell nothing but cracks. Sometimes what's inside leaks out. Sometimes it don't. Keeping it simple, if his brain leaks out, he will die—they stay in, he might live. So far his egg ain't leaked none. Sure as hell don't know why it didn't. Not with that foolhardy trip you took."

"So you've seen the likes of this before?" Sam asked, hoping the man would offer better news.

"Plenty of times. Can't even tell you how many folks I done looked at what got mule-kicked. On their noggins, too. Some of 'em."

"How'd those turn out?"

"Some of 'em dead when they was brought to me. Some, I thought wouldn't last another hour. Others, I'd keep an eye on 'em an hour or so, for their mama's sake, and then send 'em on home. What in the hell possessed you to load that boy up in that wagon and haul him off down that road?"

Admonished, Sam felt a tinge of guilt. "It's a long story. I, we," pointing at the others by Tad's wagon, "had to leave."

"Well, make it a short story."

Sam gave the shortened version.

"Reckon all things considered, you done the right thing," answered Doc Yardley.

"What should I do?" asked Tad's father.

"Not much. Rest . . . let him rest. Lay up here another day or so. When you get into Weldon, bring him by the office. I'll give him a good going over."

Walking back to the wagons, Doc Yardley said, "If half what that girl and that slave woman with her says is true, and I ain't doubting it nary a bit, Tad's lucky to be alive. That girl wants a job, its hers. Tell her that for me. See you in town."

The intended afternoon rest was extended two more days.

***

Traffic heading south was practically nonexistent and when faster wagons did pass, so did trailing odors—most of decay, some of roses and other flowers, rich and thick. Others smelled of harsh chemicals. *Embalming fluids*, Sam thought. Northbound wagons passed without a word being spoken, the riders crushed of life, preoccupied and haggard. Sam knew where they were heading. Husband

and wife—or mother and father, perhaps one and the same, and often with a teenage boy or two standing behind them, nodded hellos and continued on their way. And, too, passed the occasional father, alone on the seat, his face one of desperation, with slaves leaning against the bench seat holding tightly to shovels and picks.

He knew those in open-bedded wagons were heading toward a job no man should do and no mother should witness.

A pair of mules approaching from the south, their brown coats dark and shiny from sweat, and streaked with the gray of age, halted on the near side of the shallow ford of the creek. An elderly man, dressed in the bib overalls of a farmer, tied the reins to the brake lever and stared ahead. The mules' chests bellowed as they sucked greedily for each new breath. Raspy and thick moans matched the rhythm of their rising and falling rib cages. From their thick, dark lips dripped foamy, white spittle.

The elderly man nodded a hello to Sam and turned his face back toward his mules. A calloused and age spotted hand reached across and gently covered an old woman's hand. A soft whisper, that of a husband consoling his wife, said, "Mama, we'll let 'em blow fer a spell 'fore they gits to drinking. They cool down some, maybe they won't bust a gut with that water. When they's finished, we can get gone." The woman sat motionless and did not reply. She stared straight ahead.

Sam understood the plow mules. He understood poverty and he understood the glassy, empty stare on the woman's face. Not wishing to intrude into the couple's private nightmare, he waited for an approach, if such was the desire of the elderly man.

The couple sat patiently waiting for the mules to catch their breath. The wagon lurched forward, but quickly stopped again midstream. The mules bent to the water. Again, the husband placed a loving hand over his wife's. "I'll go ask these folks. I'll be right back, Mama. You hear me?" he asked. With his face etched with concern for his wife, he stepped into the shallow creek and walked towards Sam.

Such a loving gentleness displayed by the old man, Sam thought. He thought of his Rose and her pleas for him to hurry as he left to find Thaddeus.

He had been informed his son was alive—while the spade and the pine box in the rear of the wagon in the middle of the creek, confirmed what he suspected—the aged couple had been told their son was dead.

The gray-haired woman remained seated and motionless and continued to stare into the distance.

The farmer spat a wad of tobacco across the road and onto the far edge. He wiped the dribbled tobacco juice from his mouth on a shirt sleeve stained brown. Reaching into the wagon he gathered the few tools he brought with him and re-tied the shovels and picks into a tightly bound bundle. His work done, he walked around to his wife and said, while patting her hands lovingly, "We'll be on our way soon."

Without acknowledging the presence of her husband or the campers, the gray-haired woman continued to stare at something only she saw.

"Good morning, Mister," the farmer said, directing the greeting toward Sam. "Name's George Sheffield from down near Stanhope." Pointing at the wagon, he added, "That's my wife Hildi. You wouldn't know the way to Hopewell, would you?"

"Pleasure, Mr. Sheffield. Mine's Sam." And he extended his hand. "I've been to Stanhope. Nice little town. And yes, you're headed the right direction. Another day's ride that way," he said, pointing north, "you'll see Petersburg off in front of you. There's a sign pointing east, towards Hopewell. Turn east at that sign and go on about twelve miles or so. You'll come to Hopewell . . . . about a two day ride, all told. Was for us anyway, but we're moseying along kind'a slow." His eyes shifted to the tent covered wagon, and back to the old man.

"You know if there's a boat what can get me and the missus," asked Mr. Sheffield, thumbing over his shoulder toward his wife, "and our mules and wagon across that big river to the other side?"

"Yes Sir. There is. We just came back from the north bank of the James River." He saw no good in saying the name of the battlefield they had left two days prior. His gut told him the elderly couple in the beat-up farm wagon knew where they were heading.

"Thank you kindly, Mister," said the man as he turned to acknowledge the others in the camp. His eyes averted to the tented wagon and he saw the man laying inside. "That fellow alright?" he asked.

"My son. Hurt pretty bad," answered Sam.

Mr. Sheffield stepped forward, and bending to get a better view, said nothing as he studied the young soldier.

"Infantry?" he asked. "Our son was . . . me and his mother there," he added, pointing at the back of his wife.

"No Sir. Captain of Artillery," volunteered Sam, pride registering in his voice, "under General Jackson's command."

"Then he was at that Malvern Hill place?"

"Yes Sir. He was."

Sam saw a sudden burn in the old man's eyes.

After a long moment George Sheffield turned back to Sam, his face now hard and etched with pain. As he headed toward the wagon and his thin, frail wife, the man said, "Good luck to you and your'n."

The farmer climbed the wagon wheel and sat next to his wife. For a long moment, head bent, he stared at the floorboards. He did not say anything, but sat quietly sharing an unknown communion with his wife. He turned back again and stared at the young officer laying on the mattresses. He raised the reins to slap the mules on their rumps, but letting the leather straps fall, leaned in close to his wife and whispered. She answered him, her few words, angry, sharp and unclear to anyone but her husband. Her head cocked a quarter turn toward Sam's wagon. She looked into the tented wagon and then locked her rheumy eyes onto Sam's. Slowly, the old man backed the wagon out of the creek and next to where Sam stood watching. As George Sheffield set the foot brake, his wife turned toward Sam. A burning glare full of hate had transformed her distant, glassy stare, and her weathered face into that of something Sam did not understand—an odd mixture of raw hate, unspeakable grief, and a hint of jealousy.

He had seen such faces on those who had suffered greatly and were near the edge of a nervous breakdown.

"Mister. Our boy was infantry," she finally said, her voice gritty and strained. "Papers say them ones what was in command was fools. Said they put our boys up front as shields to protect their own worf'less asses. I hope that cap'n son ah your'n rots in hell." Her hard eyes bored into Sam's for a long moment, and then she spit brown tobacco juice in his face.

As the wagon crossed the creek, a pressure such as Sam had never felt, crushed his chest and he fell to his knees. Henry and Isaac rushed to catch him and eased him against a wagon wheel.

"Sam. She's hurt'n, just hurt'n. That's all," apologizing for the worn and heartbroken, gray-haired old woman.

Chapter Twenty-one: Eighteen and sixty-two. The last week of August.

The son lies on the bed, his face chalky white. The doctor's prognosis is not good, but the doctor is a good man and he will not lie. He is old, thinking of retiring. His office is no longer as busy as it was during his younger years, but still, he feels obligated to tend those who come to him.
   There is no nurse to help him see to those he cares for, and care and rest is what Tad needs. He has advised Sam to continue the trip home, six more miles, but to use an excess of care with Thaddeus. Before Tad can leave, the doctor turns to Sam, and says, "Unbutton your shirt, Sam. You don't look so good."

   Doc Yardley rinsed his hands and turned toward Sam. As he'd promised, Tad had received a thorough examination and now lay sleeping.
   "His reflexes are consistent with an alert mind. His legs and arms jump when I tap them here," he said, pointing below the kneecap, "and here," pointing at the elbow. "He feels the needle in all the right places. His eyes focus with the light. That's good. Your boy's in

there somewhere, lollygagging, taking his own sweet time. When he's ready to say hello, he will."

"When will he start talking again?"

"Who knows? Had two young fellows, both of 'em 'bout his age. Got kicked in the head by mules. One come around right here in my office. The other one took near on two months. They're both fine now. Your boy'll be alright. All you need to remember is to tell Miss Rose the same thing. He might come out of this fog he's lost in tomorrow morning," he added, as he looked at the floor. "No. Don't tell her that. Women got a way of taking things their husbands say as fact. Tell her I said for her and that girl out there in the office to sit and talk to him. Read him things. That's the best thing for now. Even if he's sleeping. Get his mind working. The tiniest little thing might clear his head. Seen it happen a hundred times. But tell them to give him quiet time, too. He'll tire out easy. He's fighting real hard right now. He'll come around. These things take time. Sam, tell her that, too."

"Then I can take him on home?"

"Well, I don't see why not. You made it this far, but with three provisions. Get him another mattress, that'd make three, all told. And a softer pillow. Two more would be better."

"And number three?" Sam asked.

"Keep that girl Lillie close to him. Somehow, and I don't understand such things, but he knows when she's near. His pulse is a bit faster, right now, than it will be after she's with him for a few minutes. Let her keep taking care of him." He smiled and added, "You know she's taken with that boy of your'n, don't you? And, believe it or not, he's taken with her. You can't see it, but he is. When she's near him, his heart gets to pounding and as soon as she starts soft talking him, he calms down. Watch. You'll see. There ain't no kind'a' medicine that good."

"We've seen that. He sleeps like a baby if she tucks his pillow under his head," acknowledge Sam,

"I'll give her a little more advice on what to do for him."

And of Sam, he asked, "What's this about you fainting? Yes. Henry and Isaac told me."

"Getting a load of tobacco juice spit in your face would make you faint, Doc."

"Henry told me about that, also. I reckon it would'a pissed me off some, as well. But fainting means something a hell of a lot worser than just falling down. Let me listen to your heart for a minute," and he picked up the stethoscope. "Open your shirt."

Sliding the instrument around Sam's chest, he told him when to breath, when to exhale. Using fingers he tapped Sam's back, listening for indications of weak lungs.

"Truth is, it's not the first time you've felt bad, is it?"

"Describe bad."

"Cut the shit, Sam. How's your breathing? Short? Hard to catch sometimes?"

"Sometimes."

"Got any pain running from here to here?" he asked, dragging his finger across Sam's chest.

"Once in a while. Hell, don't you? Everybody gets those stings running across there."

"Your arm, your left one, ever start aching even if you haven't done a lick all day?"

"Sometimes. Not bad, though."

"Anybody in your family die young? Anybody die from a heart attack?"

"Don't know."

"What the hell does that mean, Sam? You don't know?"

"Means I don't know. I haven't had a family, since I started one of my own."

"What about your mother and father?"

"To hell with 'em. That's what about 'em."

"Ok." Reaching into his coat pocket, Doc Yardley held a folded paper out to Sam.

"I want you to take a pinch of this each time you feel tightening in your chest or any of that arm pain. Put it under your tongue. If the pain gets less or goes away, I want to know. If it don't, I want to know that, too."

"What is it?"

"If I told you that, you won't take it."

"Would you?"

"I do. And you will too, if you want to see Thaddeus ever make general."

"Ok. So, what is it?"

"Ever see that white powder that grows on sticks of dynamite what's gone old?"

"So are you saying you eat dynamite?"

"Kind of. This stuff's called Nitrate. Coal miners up in the foothills with problems like yours said they felt better when they was handling dynamite. Said their hearts quit hurting, arms, too. And their breathing got easier. Some said this stuff even gives them a little more of that drive what makes their wives smile. "

"Well, alright then," answered Sam, as he extended his hand.

"Put a pinch under your tongue. Pretend you're dipping snuff. Stuff'll give you a headache right off. Last about three, four minutes."

"Alright."

"Now go tell that young lady to come in here for a few minutes."

"Yes Sir?" Lillie asked timidly, while Doc Yardley directed her to a chair.

"Well, Miss Lillie. How you doing this fine day?"

"I'm fine, Sir."

"You're doing a right good job seeing to young Thaddeus."

"He don't ask for much," she said. "But thank you."

"Well, that's gonna change. He'll get better. But it'll be slow going at first. Seen it take a year or two, after a knock on the head like his."

"Mr. Biggs asked me to see to him."

"Yes, I know. Seems like he did the right thing doing it, too. Only thing I can tell you is be careful. Seen men get hit in the head, good men, and go bad afterwards. Things changed for them."

"Well, I'm not afraid of him. He's mostly quiet. Sometimes he gets to fussing, but mostly when he's sleeping. I figure he's dreaming, so I just talk to him. Usually he calms down and goes back to sleep. He sleeps a lot."

"That's good. Rest. But try to get him up walking as soon as you can so his brain don't go sour. I"ve known that boy all his life. He can be a mite bit stubborn, so if he wants to go outside, it'd be best to take him out . . . let him get some fresh air. He'll wobble like a drunk duck at first, until his head starts sorting things out. He wants to walk, let him do the walking. Don't be a crutch for him. Just be close by, in case. He needs to get his strength back. Talk to him a lot. Different things. Make him start thinking. Ask him questions. Get his brain churning again. That's what he needs."

"Yes Sir. You've known him his whole life?" she asked.

"Was there when he was born. Actually a few minutes late for that. One of the old Negro women from down in the quarters brought our patient into the world. Couldn't wait for me. Always in a rush, that boy. So I just checked him out and saw to his mama."

"Does he have a lady friend?"

"If you mean a girlfriend? None I know of. But he's been gone a long time. That soldiering school up in Lexington and then off traipsing around Virginia with that General Jackson fellow the papers call Stonewall didn't leave him much time for affairs of the heart. You know what I mean?' he asked, knowing she did.

"Well, Doctor Yardley. Thank you for the suggestions. I'll take good care of him," and with that said, she turned to leave. And from behind, Doc Yardley could not see the gleam in her eyes.

***

Henry and Isaac, using a stretcher, loaded Thaddeus back into the wagon already equipped with a new mattress and two more pillows. The three wagons, Sam's in front, headed down Weldon's main street. Nearing the office of his financial advisor, Sam's mind was elsewhere. A quick movement in the doorway of Adair Graystone's office filled the opening with a man in a business suit and as quickly as the man appeared, he stepped back into the office and hastily closed the door.

A block further, Sam's mind was dwelling upon what he thought he'd seen. He climbed from the wagon and walked back to Henry.

"Did you see anything back there when we passed Adair's place?"

"Yeah. Saw Adair open the door and start walking through it. But he stopped—real quick like—then went back inside," answered Henry, "and he patted his clothes, way too many times if you ask me, like he forgot something."

"He say anything to you?"

"Not a word. But he did stand by the curtain over the front window and watch you ride by. Waved at me and Isaac. He looked scared to me."

"Strange," said Sam.

***

The woods had changed from the tall spindly pines of Virginia into the thick old-growth oaks Sam cherished. The wagons turned from the road and entered the meandering drive wending toward his beloved family and Swift Creek Plantation.

Willie ran alongside the lead wagon, darting closer and closer to greet Sam. Fearing the overly exited man would fall under the wheel, Sam pulled hard on the reins.

"Whoa. Damn it, Willie. Every time I come home you've got to climb up in the wagon or try to get in the damn carriage. You trying to get run over? You damn fool. Get back and stay back."

"Yes Suh," Willie answered, but grinning, he remained hanging onto the armrest of the bench seat.

"Massa Sam?" the slow-minded, middle-aged slave asked, as he hid behind his master and peeked at Celine. "Who dat?"

"This fine lady is going to be staying with us for a while. The boy behind me is her son Jacob. The older boy is Billy. Jacob, you and Billy come here. Miss Celine, this is Willie. Willie's my best friend, aren't you, Willie?" Sam said, as he rubbed Willie's tightly knotted tangle of black and graying hair.

Willie smiled a toothy grin and proudly answered, "Yes 'um, I is."

Celine nodded a hello at the man of about forty years of age and extended her hand. Instead of shaking it, Willie began examining it. Turning it over, he ran a finger along the caramel-colored skin. He inched forward and examined her face and hair, and with a puzzled expression on his face, quietly slid back to the far side of Sam.

"What be her color?" he whispered. Sam ignored the question and left the inquiry unanswered. He understood how Willie thought, so a non-answer was good enough for the slave—more child than man.

As quickly forgotten, Willie asked yet another question. Sam bent and listened as Willie whispered, "Duz she be's one'a dem gol'n angels like what's they got's in de Bible? He be the baby Jesus?" he asked, pointing at the boy with the same color skin.

Sam pushed him away and turned to Celine. "He thinks you're an angel and Jacob is Jesus. Quite impressed with you."

Celine's caramel face tinted red.

"Massa, duz you got Tad wid you? Where he be? Huh, huh?" asked Willie, yammering away in his childlike manner.

Sam pointed, as way of introduction to his passengers. "Do not be impolite. First, say a proper hello to Miss Celine, her son, Jacob, and our new friend, Billy." And to the new passenger who had finally climbed into the wagon and sat near Sam, he said, "That young lady back there with Isaac is Billy's sister, Lillie." Turning back to Celine, he added, "Willie helps around the house and in the stables. Fishes a lot, too, don't you Willie?"

Willie smiled and in a sing-song manner sang, "Willie, Billy, Lillie. Willie, Billy, Lillie," and laughed. "I likes to fish. Duz you lac' eat'n eels, Miss Ceely?" he asked Celine. "I'll git you sum'."

Celine thought the manner of Mister Biggs' conversation with his slave, a man he'd bought and now owned, gentle and certainly something she'd never seen before.

"He's sleeping, Willie. Don't bother him. Listen to me. I need you to go and find Mister Struthers and tell him to come up to the big house. You can do that, can't you, Willie? You can see Tad up at the house with everybody else. After we get him settled in, I'll take you in to see him."

He explained to Celine how Tad, when he lived at home, could hardly go anywhere without Willie shadowing him.

And looking toward the mansion, still out of view, Sam asked Willie, "Miss Rose know we're back?"

"Yas Suh. Ebber'body be waitin', but Miss Rose, she be cryin'."

Sam knew Willie's childlike mind was limited to things only he could understand, and that he did not know the strange emotions of women. He bent and affectionately rubbed the man-child's hair again.

"That's what women do sometimes, Willie. Cry when they're happy. Sounds backwards, but it's true. Run along and tell Mr. Struthers to come on up to the house."

Willie headed toward the fields, lumbering along with the slowed gait of a man past his prime, in search of the plantation's overseer.

As the road snaked along through the thick stand of trees, the caravan neared a large mansion hidden away in the oaks. A glimpse through the cover of leaves exposed the white siding, the roof, and the chimney on the near side. From the circular drive of the plantation manor, by far the largest building Lillie or Celine had ever seen, loomed before them. Each thinking not even those big houses they'd seen in Hopewell and Petersburg were as large.

On the porch and beginning to descend the steps were a great many friends of the Biggs family. Some were concerned neighbors, but most were slaves, some holding hoes, others wringing their hands dry in the large aprons they wore while cooking or doing laundry, and others stood at a discreet distance.

Clustered, hand in hand, at the top of the steps stood Tad's mother, Samantha and Izzy.

Overjoyed to see his wife and his two daughters, a dread arose in Sam's chest. He hadn't given much thought to the reality of the arrival and doubts began to tear at him. He should have sent someone ahead to tell her of what to expect. What if she saw Tad asleep, his arms bound tightly across his chest, his temple bruised and red? What would she think? Would she think him dead or alive? Should he rush to her and tell her to not be alarmed in spite of what she saw, and assure her their son was recovering? His biggest fear was of her response to those who did look into the wagon. How would they react? Would their faces reflect happiness or pity? He prayed they would be quiet and respectful. But even subdued faces and whispered appraisals could cause harm. He locked his eyes upon his wife, willing her to return his stare—see his smile, and his extended hands beckoning her to come to him. Yet, on the porch she remained, alone and wary.

He needed, most of all, for her to look at him, to ask him questions with her eyes. "Look at me, Rose, please look," he whispered.

And she did, with pleading eyes. He smiled and held his arms out to her and mouthed the silent words, "Come to me."

As she ran to him, he climbed from the wagon. The two merged into one—each embracing the other with the same intensity they shared on their wedding day.

"Is he . . ." and knowing the question, Sam held a finger to her lips.

"Our son's hurt, but he's alive and improving each day. Already been seen to by Doc Yardley. Come, let's go see our son," he said, and led her through those crowding around the tent covered wagon.

"Everybody back," ordered Sam. "We've got to get our boy in his bed."

Hadley Struthers plowed through the throng, his walk and manner that of a man comfortable with giving orders. "Mr. Biggs, Miss Biggs," he said, removing his sweat-soaked hat. "Willie said you wanted to see me. And that you brought young Tad with you. Thank the Lord for that. How is the lad?"

"Yes, he's here. Henry and Isaac have taken him into the house, Mr. Struthers. He's going to be alright. It'll take a while, but Doc feels good about his full recovery. Thank you for asking. I need to speak to you in a bit," and dismissed the man.

Turning to the gathering crowd, Sam said, "Miss Biggs and I are honored with your concern for our son. I would like to introduce you to two women who, without their care, our son would not be here today." He beckoned Celine and Lillie to his side.

Curious of the new arrivals—the young white lady, the young boy by her side, and especially of the caramel-colored lady holding a younger boy, the same color as she—they stood and gawked.

To the gathering crowd, Sam said, "I want each of you to make these fine ladies feel at home. Tad owes his life to these two women. Therefore, we owe our deepest appreciation to them. Each has now lost their home. Miss Celine will live among those of you who live in the quarters. Miss Lillie and her brother," he said, pointing at the younger lady, "will live in my home. Miss Lillie and Miss Celine will care for Tad as they have been doing. Each of you have work waiting on you, so go on and get to it."

"Mr. Struthers," and returning to the overseer, he said, "Miss Celine is a free woman. If she wishes to do anything around the place, that will be her privilege. She has offered to continue helping Miss Lillie, but that will be her decision, as well. I expect you to find an empty cabin near the big house. If there is not one readily available, and close by, do not remove a family for her. Build a new cabin. And once done, offer it first to the family who could have been evicted. If they wish to move into the new one, give it to them and the vacated one to Miss Celine. If not, furnish it for Miss Celine and her son. There will be those who think she is receiving undue attention so in this way there should be no display of preference. Lastly, see to her needs as well as her safety—there have been threats. She and her son are in great danger. Until such time as proper lodging is ready, Miss Celine and Jacob can share one of the spare bedrooms in the big house."

And turning back to his wife, he said, "Missus Biggs and I need to see to our son."

Chapter Twenty-two: Eighteen and sixty-four: Spring has arrived. And with it, a long-lost friend.

On an errand for his master, Willie walks into the darkened barn. Before him and on a bale of hay sits a man he has seen in his past. The man turns to face in the direction from which Willie has approached. Already afraid of the darkness, the long gray beard and bushy dry hair springing out in all directions, and the blood shot eyes above the sunburned flesh below each, frightened him. Afraid of anything which borders on the unknown, Willie races up to the house and tells his master there is a stranger in the barn.

Willie walked ahead of Sam and cautiously circled around to the left of the man sitting on the hay bale. Arm extended, pointing his finger at a figure, more scarecrow than man, his voice shaking, he said "I knows you," as he stepped back behind the safety of his master.

The scarecrow sat and watched as Sam studied him.

"Buck? Is that you, Buck?" Sam asked, incredulously.

"It's been a long time, Sam. It's really me," the scarecrow man answered. "Or what's left of the me I used to be," his answer more broken grunts than understandable words as he jabbed a stick at a mangy and smelly blue tick hound which seemed intent on biting him.

"Git, dog," shouted Sam as he kicked at the offensive animal.

"Dog? More like a shriveled up pissed off bear," said Buck. With the danger gone, he stuck the stick into the bale of straw next to him.

"What happened to you? Where did you go?" Sam asked. A million questions could be asked of the reappearance of his old friend, Bucyrus "Buck" Vance, but these two seemed adequate for a start. A third, seemed appropriate, as well, judging from the rail-thin body of the man once so strong and full of life.

"You hungry?"

"Been hungry the last ten years," came the answer.

"Willie, go to the kitchen and tell Annie to make up a plate for our guest and you get back here quick with it. While she's getting it ready, bring us some glasses and lemonade. And Willie," he continued, his voice becoming hard, "do not say a word to anybody about our quest, nobody except Annie. And tell her I said for her to be quiet about it, too."

Willie left, seemingly in a hurry to be shed of the barn and the creature in the dark and foul smelling overcoat.

"Where've you been, Buck?" asked Sam.

Buck smiled as if life had played a trick on him. "Be easier to tell you where I ain't been. I've seen some things I needed to see. Saw things I *didn't* need to see. Ten years I spent searching. Walked thousands of miles."

There was a weariness about the man—a bone-breaking exhaustion. Sam could see it in his eyes—that willingness to let go and call it quits with life.

"Did you find what you were looking for, Buck?"

"Sometimes thought I did, but no—I never did, not really."

"Can you tell me what it was you were hoping to find?"

"Yeah. A fresh start. Some happy place . . .," his voice trailing off, ending in a whispered, "Does she know, Sam?"

"She?"

"Miss Rose. Does Miss Rose know I killed her father?"

"No. She doesn't know any such thing, but she knows Henry, Isaac, me and Emmett were there, too, not just you, so if you've been dragging that bag full of guilt around with you all these years, you were wrong doing it. We all killed that sorry bastard. There's more than one way to kill a man. Hell, Buck, way I see it, he even had a hand in his own killing. We just made sure he got on with it." He added as an afterthought, "Did you know Emmett died? Not long after that mess up in the woods."

"No. But, I'm sorry to hear it. He was a good man. Probably the best of us. We all died some that day, Sam," and then he stared at the floor, lost in thought.

When he looked at Sam again, he asked, "Reckon she would talk to me?"

"She talks to the rest of us. Yes, I believe so. Do you want to see her?"

With the simple comment about Rose, Buck had found a semblance of peace. "Not just yet. Not like this," he answered, pulling at the ragged shirt and trousers. "Maybe later."

"So, you planning to stick around for a while?"

"Long enough to see to a problem, but planning? No. I haven't made a plan in ten years."

Willie returned with a plate piled high with food and a pitcher of fresh and tangy lemonade.

Sam drug over a chair long since assigned barn duty, brushed the dust and straw from it, and placed it as a table before the man. As Buck leaned into the food, Sam turned to Willie, pointed at another chair suffering exile in the barn, and said "Bring me that one."

Sam poured himself a glass of lemonade and sat quietly as Buck devoured his dinner.

Buck said, "Sam, I've got something to tell you. It's the problem I just mentioned," and almost choked in his effort to both talk and eat.

The man was famished. "It can wait a bit." said Sam. "Finish your food first. Then we're going to get you cleaned up." Buck, exhausted and in need of sleep, nodded his head, and returned to devouring the meal. He drank heavily of the cold, tangy-sweet lemonade, leaned the chair against the post behind him and fell into a hard sleep.

Willie had returned from other errands Sam had made up to keep him out of the barn. Willie, with his child-like attitudes, could be a distraction.

"Go clean that tub, Willie," he ordered, pointing at the soldered tub. "Build a fire and get some water heating. Much as you can. Be quiet doing it. Let him sleep a bit longer. And when you're through with that, go tell Annie to put some of Tad's clothes, a pair of trousers, a shirt, socks, shoes, and drawers together. And grab some towels and lye soap. Tell Annie if Miss Rose asks her what she's doing, to tell her she's airing them out. Get a mirror from out of my office . . . and a pair of scissors . . . a good brush, too. Now repeat what I just told you to do."

***

Buck stood before the mirror newly hooked on a barn post nail, and wearing only a pair of Tad's drawers, snipped at the tangle of freshly washed, thick beard. He saw Sam watching him as he looked into the mirror.

Buck, once a well-built man, tall, muscular and quick on his feet, was now hardly more than a study of ribs and bones. His face above the thick beard was burned leathery and creased from too much sunlight, while pale skin on his bare chest, torso, arms, and legs bore proof that a traveling man had to wear his meager collection of clothing all at once, layer upon layer, or leave some behind.

The road had eaten the fat from his body and the remaining nodules of muscle here and there on thin arms and thin legs, reminded Sam of the gnarled lumps on the limbs of pine trees.

Buck brushed at the mirror as if a clean surface would improve his usage of the scissors. Mostly, they snapped emptily at his beard, his eyes and mind unable to reverse the need to cut the opposite of what he saw in the mirror.

"Buck, you better let me do that. You're going to cut your damn nose off," said Sam, laughing as he took the scissors in his hand. "I had Willie burn those clothes you had on. Had too. Worn out. You can keep those clothes of Tad's. They fit you pretty good, and he's not using them right now."

"Tad's here? Heard he was with that Jackson fellow, the one they call Stonewall. He's here?"

Sam related the recent turn of events, but worn from the constant worry, he kept the story brief.

"And what's with that smell of dog piss. Did you get in a fight with a dog and it got the best of you?"

"Something like that. It's the end of the story I came to tell you. Ready?"

"Hold on a minute," Sam laughed. "You're starting to look like you been whacking your beard and hair with a cane blade," he said, reaching for the scissors. "Give me those things. You're going to cut your damn ears off. Let me do that."

"Where'd you get all that gray hair?" Sam grinned, running spread fingers through what was left of his own. "Let's finish with that scrub brush you call a beard and that briar patch you call hair."

"Same place as yours, I reckon," answered Buck as the joking and friendly manner the two men once shared, returned. Freshly shaved, he stared in the mirror and traced the wrinkles on his cheeks, "Got those the same place, too, I guess."

"At least you're starting to look like the old Buck," and handing the long lost friend a towel, he said, "Okay, that'll have to do. But you'd look better in the dark," Sam laughed. "So tell me the story."

***

"Day before yesterday, I seen a sign next to the road. Fuck if it didn't say WELDON on it. I thought I was a hundred miles from that town. Hungry as hell, the sky turned black, and it took to raining. Then I was glad I weren't no hundred miles away from Weldon. Figured I could find a place to lay up for the night and stay dry and warm," Buck said, rubbing the smooth skin of his cheeks again. "You got any idea how long it's been since I had a good shave?"

"My guess is ten years. So? You found a place to hold up?"

"Nah. Never tried to get too attached to no place in particular."

"I meant in Weldon."

"Under a porch."

And Sam laid a hand on Buck's shoulder. "Try this place for a while."

"Might give it a try. You know a man named Graystone?"

"Yes. He works for me."

"What about one named McDermott?"

"Can't say as I've ever heard of him."
"McDermott knows you, and you've got a problem."
"What's his problem with me?"
"Them two *is* your problem."

Buck recounted the conversation he'd overheard, almost word for word, an ability common with most law officers, even those no longer in the business of righting wrongs. Sam listened carefully as the story grew into an improbable nightmare he knew nothing of. And as he listened, he thought of two things, an urgent need to confront Adair, and a need to seek revenge.

Three things he knew. The first, he'd never had any reason to doubt Adair's integrity—at least none he knew of. Their association had always been prosperous—but according to who? Adair? The second, he'd been lax about checking his business records, preferring the running of the plantation to pencils, paper, and numbers, but that was his choice—one based on an errant gut feeling of Adair after only one meeting with the man. And the third, Adair was sure as hell going to tell him *his* version of Buck's story.

"And," added Buck, "when that door slammed shut, I drug myself from under that porch like my ass was on fire. Then that son of a bitching dog jumped on my leg and went to humping on me like I'd asked it to marry me or something. I kicked that dog as hard as I ever kicked anything in my life. Must'a made it mad, though. It pissed on me."

Envisioning the moment, Sam laughed and Buck joined him.

Laughing finished, Sam sat quietly, his eyes drilling holes in the hard packed dirt of the stable floor. His face said he'd kicked himself out of the barn, across the huge lawn, up and down the road, and then tried to drown himself in the creek for being so trustful—so stupid. Finally, he stood and put both hands upon his hips, and paced the length of the barn.

From the distance Buck heard a hard fist smack the gate of a stall and heard Sam mutter "Son of a bitch."

Sam walked past Buck and shouted, "Willie. Come here," the command unusually loud and harsh.

"Yas Suh," Willie asked. He didn't like to be near his master when the man was mad.

"Go get Struthers." Willie fled to the far end of the plantation, happy to be free of the barn, and soon returned with the overseer.

"Mr. Struthers. I need for you to ride up to Henry's. Tell him we've got a situation brewing. And, also, tell him an old friend suggests for him to bring along two of his slaves, the one named Ezekiel, or Zeke, and that big buck, the one they call Bear. Then go down to Isaac's. Tell him I need him, too. Tell both of them to drop what they're doing and come right away."

Chapter Twenty-three:
Eighteen and forty up to the late fall of Eighteen and sixty-four: The long relationship between Samuel Biggs and Adair Graystone.

Sam's problem was he was too trustful of people. He preferred to see the good in a man, and overlook the bad. But Adair Graystone had finally taught him a lesson. The man was a snake and Sam had never seen a snake, with the exception of king snakes, "ratters" as they were called, not worth killing. At least Ratters served a purpose—they ate rats.

"Sam, Isaac. What's going on?" and turning to the rear of the wagon, Henry added, "Ezekiel. Take the wagon out back and you and Bear wait for me."

"Yas Suh," answered Zeke. Bear and Zeke looked forlorn as if each was carrying the weight of the world on their shoulders. Like everyone in the area, they had heard of Sam Biggs and were in fear of what they'd heard about the man. The two stared at each other, both thinking the worst—knowing they had done the worst.

"It'll be a bit. We'll send some water out to you. Stay there 'til one of us calls for you," continued Henry.

"Hey, Henry. Isaac. Thanks for coming. Tie your horses over there," Sam said pointing at a stall post. His face wore the added look of a man who was very angry.

Isaac and Henry looked confused. On the way to Sam's they worried about Tad, and prayed he was not getting worse after so much improvement had been made.

"Is Tad okay?" they both asked in unison.

"He's improving," Sam replied. It'd been a long time since Henry and Isaac had chanced by Sam's. He felt an obligation to bring his two closest friends up to date about Tad's recovery. "Thanks for asking. He's doing better. He can sit up without too much help. Still wobbly from that concussion thing Doc Yardley says he's got. Feeds himself . . . well, almost . . with Lillie's help. He recognizes his mother and me, but hasn't really said much to either of us. He talks a little, mostly to Lillie, but Doc says he'll be fine in a few more months. That girl gets him out on the porch to soak up a bit of sun every day. She and one of the slaves are helping with his walking. He uses crutches most times. Bought him two carved vine canes, just in case. And he knows you two were with me when we went to get him. Lillie said he told her that. That's something, ain't it? *He* told her that. We'll go up see him in a little while."

Henry and Isaac smiled, happy to hear of Tad's recovery, even if it was slow, and because they were proud of the part they had played in getting Tad home.

Confused by the answer, Henry asked, "Well, is something else the matter?

"Yes. We have a problem, and there's somebody you both need to see."

"Okay. So who is it?" Henry responded.

"Come on out," said Sam, as he opened the door to the tack room he'd delegated for Buck's privacy.

"Say hello to Buck, fellows."

Buck stepped from the dark of the tack room. A rich smell of leather followed him.

Henry and Isaac were astonished. They'd never imagined they would ever see Buck alive again. Rumors had grown considerably after their friend had disappeared—ten years—a long time, but obviously none were true. The man was alive, and except for the dark and shrunken eyes he looked fit, and definitely not dead. He'd lost a lot of weight and his hair now seemed thinner. He wore that look about him—that weary, nearly destroyed look.

As quickly as they saw the aging of their friend each thought of how old and different they must look to him. "Buck? Is that you,

Buck?" asked Isaac. Together they stepped toward one another and embraced.

Buck nodded and grasping each of his old friends' hands, said, "Yep, it's me. Or what's left of me."

"Where the hell you been?" asked Henry, as he and Isaac hugged their long lost friend.

"Got tired of the man I had become. After that thing up in the woods I decided I'd run away from myself. Did, too. Every morning I'd get my things together and head down the road, 'cept . . . every night, I'd catch up with me and crawl back inside my skin while I was sleeping."

Obviously, Buck had not lost his sense of humor and Henry's had never improved.

"What were you doing," Henry asked.

"Studying things."

"Got 'em figured out yet?" asked Henry.

"Some of 'em" Buck answered.

Both Henry and Isaac were confused. With his simplistic answers, they thought Buck was really telling them nothing had changed. They stared at Sam. Sam shrugged his shoulders.

Sam smiled as his friends renewed their acquaintance, but soon his face grew strained. Buck was here on bad business, and he was anxious for Henry and Isaac to hear the reason he'd summoned them. And that bit of unpleasantness was going to be discussed, but first, they all wanted to hear what Buck had been had been up to for ten long years.

"So what's all the suspense, Sam? Is it Buck who you said wanted to see us? What's this got to do with Zeke and Bear?"

"Buck, tell them what you just told me."

***

"Where's your overseer? That Beckman fellow?" Sam asked Henry. "I thought he'd come with you."

Henry answered, "There's been some strange things going on. A week or so ago he said he needed to take Ezekiel and Bear with him and repair a bridge back up in the woods behind the big house. Something about cutting down some trees and patching it up. Took a saw and some axes. When they got back they got off around by the far side of the barn and I could hear Beckman chewing Zeke and Bear's asses out about something. Didn't think much about it. Doing his job, I figured. Later that night he left again and I ain't seen him since.

"I wanted to know what he went at Zeke and Bear about, so I asked them what Beckman was mad at, and they said something about how he said they weren't setting a good example in the fields and the rest of the slaves were slacking off. Neither one of 'em would look at me, you know, straight on in my eyes. Just 'tween you and me, I think they was lying . . . or at least hiding something."

"And you haven't seen Beckman since then?"

"Not so much as a shadow. Why? What's up?"

"Hold up a second. I want to ask those boys about Beckman." Sam turned and called for Zeke and Bear.

"Which one of you is Ezekiel?" asked Sam.

Ezekiel removed his sweat-soaked hat with one hand and raised the other. "Dat be me, Suh," he answered.

"Then you're Bear?"

"Yas Suh. I is," and the large black man removed his own ragged hat and stood waiting.

"Ezekiel. Don't you lie to me. Not about this. Bear. You hear me?" Zeke and Bear stared in fright at Sam. They hadn't lied yet and hoped the next question would not require them to start.

Nodding their heads, each said, "Nah Suh, we tell you de truf.'"

"Where did Henry's field boss, that Beckman fellow, take you that morning? Don't tell me it was to fix a bridge. You tell me that and Henry and I will go to check it out. If we don't find one just fixed, there'll be hell to pay. So where did he take you?"

One looked at the other, each hoping for support. "Mister Sam. If'n we tell's you dat, Mista' Graystone will kill our woman folk dead."

"Who did you say?" Sam asked, startled.

"Tell him what he asked you and be quick about it," Henry said, his voice growing firm. "Don't you lie to him like you lied to me. Now, where did Beckman take you?"

"Mr. Henry. We had to lie, Suh. He take us up in de woods where dat Mister Graystone be standin' in de road," answered Zeke as Bear's head nodded, seconding Zeke's words. "And den, dey take us up to dat Mister Johnson's place where our womans be."

"What did he want with you?"

"He say he gonna kill our wifes."

Instantly, Sam eyes shot toward Buck. He'd never thought Adair was capable of the sort of violence Buck had spoken of, but if Zeke and Bear were so afraid of the man they were willing to hedge their answers and lie to Henry, he reasoned what he'd heard from Buck had to be true and not merely a jumble of odd thoughts collected from years of wandering back roads.

"Are you telling me he threatened to kill your wives?"

"Yas Suh, he did, an' us'uns, too. An' den our little ones. Said he'd kill all'a us dead if'n we got's to tellin' peebles what he was doin'," they both answered, nodding their heads for emphasis.

As large as he was, Bear was about ready to pass out from fright. He understood that the man questioning them was a big man in the community and he had heard things were done his way.

Few people, especially the neighbors, had any idea that Sam and his wife Rose owned the plantations which Henry and Isaac managed for them. For all they knew, The Meadows belonged to Henry, The Ferns to Issac.

"What happened then?" Henry asked. "Tell him."

"Suh. Lac I dun' said, dat man take us up to de Johnson's place norf of Massa Henry's and fetch'd bofe our womans out'ta de fields. Den he cut dere ears clean up to here with a flip-razor," he said, pointing at the fatty part of his own ear. "Right in front of us. Dey and our chil'uns be crying like Lord A'mighty. If'n dat was not enuf', he took his pocket knife and stuck it in dere lips, right 'chere," and pointed at his lower lip. "An' dare weren't nuff'n in de world me and Bear could do 'bout it." Zeke started sobbing, reliving the memory, and the unbearable shame that he could only watch as the knife sliced and drew blood from the woman he loved.

Bear stood to the side and trembled in anger. "Dat sum' bitch cut our wifes' ears wid dat flip-razor an' tell dem dey best not nebber say nuff'n cause if'n me an' Zeke doan do 'xactly what we'se told to do he come back an' cut dere heads clean off."

"He what?" Sam asked, startled, yet again.

"He say he kill our wifes and chil'uns," Bear said angrily, but quickly remembered such an outburst, shouting at a white man, could have dire consequences.

Sam forgave the man his outburst.

"What did he tell you to do?" Sam asked Zeke.

"He say for us to git ready to go down to dat warehouse what's in Weldon. It be sum'time dis cumin' week. He always cums one night 'fore he needs us an' tells us where to be de next night. It always be de same place, doe."

"Do you know where Beckman got off to?"

"Nah Suh. Reckon he went to see dat Graystone man. But he de one what comes an' duz the fetching."

Sam, for the first time, understood the horror the two slaves had been living under—they had been forced to do things against their will. He realized they did those things for the sake of their wives and their children. He could not fault them for that. He placed a hand on both of their shoulders and said. "We won't let him or anyone harm you or your women folk and none of the children, neither. It won't happen. I promise. You two go back out to the wagon."

Turning to Henry he said, "Just to be sure, does that Johnson fellow own Zeke's and Bear's wives?"

"Yes. He does."

"You have room for their families at your place?"

"I'll make room. What do you have in mind, Sam?"

"Let's just say for now, we're going to make Johnson an offer he can't refuse."

***

They had questions of Buck, not sure they'd heard everything in the rush of the first telling. But the story, told again, was the same as before. Nothing less, nothing more.

Henry shook his head in disbelief, and said "No disrespect intended, Buck, but that's kind'a a lot to try to wrap our heads around."

"Yeah? Well, try wrapping your head around it with a dog humping your leg. Damn dog fell in love with me." Buck looked at

Sam and they both burst out laughing again. Henry and Isaac looked at each other, wondering why the strange comment about a dog caused sudden laughter.

And then of Sam, Henry asked, "How long you and Adair been in business? Twenty-five, thirty years? Did you ever suspect anything was going on?"

"Never. Not really. Looking back, I realize I should have been more involved, but damn, up 'til now I didn't have any idea of something like this. We've all been doing good."

"That's why you told me to bring Ezekiel and Bear?"

"Yes. They're the proof of what Adair is going to deny." Sam opened the door and called for the two slaves.

"Come on back in," he said and waved the two inside. "Go sit over there," pointing at a hay bale. The two Negroes, their hearts pounding, brows shiny with sweat, waited for their eyes to adjust to the shade of the barn. The looks on their faces said they expected to be hung for lying by the four white men. They'd both been told greatly exaggerated rumors of how the big white man, Mr. Biggs, enjoyed hanging Negroes in the barn. They looked toward the beams above for ropes hanging from them, but saw none. Each removed their hats and rolled them in trembling hands.

"How long the two of you worked for Mister Atwell?" Sam asked, pretending he did not know.

"All the years he be de massa. I don't know's 'xactly how long dat be, Suh," answered Zeke. "We was dare 'fore Massa Griffen dun' git 'et up by dem hogs down in de woods."

"I'm going to ask you a question. I'll ask it only once. I already know the answer and whatever you say better sure as hell match what I already know. You understand?" Sam's voice was hard, his temper had begun to rise. It was unfair of him to be mad at the two slaves. True, they were guilty of wrongdoing but he understood they had been forced to do those things.

Ezekiel and Bear had aged considerably since their arrival two hours earlier. Their faces wore a mixture of desperation, hope, and resignation. There was no doubt they knew where Sam was headed with his questions—it'd never been far from their own minds. And now, the worst nightmare in their lives was coming to a head.

"Have you ever stolen anything from me?"

Ezekiel and Bear stared at each other, relieved—the question was not the one expected. "Nah Suh. Nebber."

"Did you ever steal from Mister Atwell?"

And again, the same answer. "Nah Suh. We lacs him."

"Mister O'Reilly?"

"Nah Suh." They began to understand a pattern was developing.

"Well, then, you been helping Graystone steal?" As suddenly as the unexpected question was asked so did the expressions on Zeke and Bear's faces change. The very word Graystone frightened them.

"Suh. I doan think so. He say everything be his'un."

Sam detected the changes in countenance on their faces and asked, "What did you do for this Graystone fellow?"

"We loaded sum'r his cotton for him."

"Mr. Graystone's cotton?"

"Yas Suh."

"Anything else?"

"Yas Suh. Sum'r his tobacky too."

"Graystone's tobacco?"

"He say it be his'un."

"How often did you load up *his* cotton and tobacco?"

"Ebber year, nere 'bout."

"Where did you load it from?"

"Dat Mista' Brantley's warehouse down by de ribber norf' of town."

"Did he come out and get you?"

"Nah Suh."

"Well, who told you when it was time to go down to the docks?"

"Dare be a man come up de road and he be lookin' for de field boss, Mista' Beckman, Suh."

"Mister Beckman?"

"Yas Suh."

"Did you know that fellow?"

"Yas Suh. He dat Mista' Johnson's field boss, de man what owns de place norf' ah Mista' Henry's. De same place where me and

Bear's womans and our chil'uns lib," and with an exaggerated movement he pointed north.

Sam turned to Henry. Henry shrugged and gestured he knew nothing of it.

"What did they talk about? Did you ever hear them talking?"

"Nah Suh. Dat Mista' Johnson's field boss cum tell Mista Beckman to tell me and Bear to git ready."

"How'd you get into town? Beckman take you? Did he tell you what to do or just drop you off at the warehouse?"

"He jus' drop us off down close to de warehouse and den he leeb's ebbertime. Dat Mister Graystone an ah nudder man tole us what to put on dem boats."

"How much cotton did you load up each time?"

"Mos'r de time dem big flat boats was lined up ten, maybe fifteen long. Dey pull under the overhang and we drop forty, fifty bales ob cotton on each one ob 'em."

"How long did it take to load that much?"

"It depen' on how many niggers they got doin' it. Bout six, sebben hours, I reckon."

"They tell you to be quiet about what you were doing? Not to say anything to anybody? Did they threaten you?"

Bear looked miserable and wiped at his nose. He and Ezekiel knew they had been helping steal cotton—they couldn't deny it. But once Bear began to talk he gushered. "Sho nuff, dey did. Bofe ah dem dun' say dey was gonna kill us if'n we told nary one person. An' dey said dey was gonna hang us and make our womans and chil'uns watch us git our necks roped up."

"That's just words. Did you believe him?"

A pronounced "Yas Suh," verified they believed they would be killed if they did not do as told. "Sum'body be cutting on your woman make you belief 'most ennie-thing."

"Alright. Go on back to the wagon. I'll have some supper brought down for you."

***

The discussion had taken an unexpected turn. Sam felt there had to be a reason, or lack thereof, for Henry's overseer's name being mentioned.

"Henry. Who is this Beckman?"

"He's a new man. Adair recommended him. Seemed a good sort. Answered all my questions the right way, so I hired him on about four months ago."

"You ever see them two, Beckman and that overseer of Johnson's together?"

"Can't say as I ever did meet that Johnson's man, but my guess is Beckman's hauled ass. Probably Johnson's man, too. Things getting a bit too hot would be my guess. Both of 'em scared of old man Adair and McDermott as much as Zeke and Bear are."

"So Beckman's not around either?"

"He's gone. No telling where he's at . . . or if he's even alive. That's wild hog country up there and the nights get plenty dark," a simple explanation of how many men disappeared in the deep woods.

"Okay. So we got a problem. How do we fix it?" asked Sam. "Buck? You're on the outside looking in, what do you think?"

"First thing is Adair and that McDermott fellow must have been stealing from you longer than you think. I don't see where how much they stole comes into play. Stealing is stealing. So the question is, how upset does it make you? What do you want to do about it?" responded Buck.

"Well, Adair and whoever in the name of hell that piece of shit McDermott is—they got'ta pay for what they've done. And it wasn't just stealing from me, Buck. It was from Henry and Isaac, too. We always put everything we grew in the same pile."

Sam explained the unique relationship which existed between Henry, Isaac, and he and Rose. Buck knew most of the history of Swift Creek, and that Sam, along with Henry's help, had built a deserted and forgotten piece of land into Swift Creek Plantation. He'd been there visiting many times himself, back during those days. But he'd left, looking for something he never found, before that plantation grew into the largest plantation in all of North Carolina. If given a chance, he would have guessed Rose had inherited the plantation south of where they now sat from Emmett Detwyler, and he would have been right. The old man had loved Rose more than life itself.

In not knowing differently, it had taken Buck a long time to come to terms with and finally accept the man he'd shot so long ago, that old bastard Hesper Griffen, had really and truly been Rose's father. And that his plantation had been inherited by Rose, also. The timely death of his old friend Emmett and the much deserved death of the evil named Hesper, had made managers of the two inherited plantations out of Sam's closest friends, Henry and Isaac.

A lot of things had changed while he was off walking and looking. What were the chances, he wondered, as he sat pondering the improbable chain of events, which turned Swift Creek into such an unimaginably large plantation.

"And we shared the proceeds," continued Sam. "I turned the everyday details over to Adair. He must have worked up a deal with Brantley to hide away some of our cotton and tobacco in those big warehouses by the river. So, see Buck? It wasn't just me. Graystone screwed us all."

Isaac added, "Then Brantley must have been involved somehow."

"We'll look him up and have a talk with him," said Sam. "If this has been going on for as long as Zeke and Bear says it has, there's no way in hell Brantley's not involved."

Sam stood, his back to the rest, and mulled over the predicament they now found themselves in. He turned back toward the men and said. "Look fellows. I don't believe Zeke and Bear have a mean bone in their bodies. They got caught up in a hard place. I say we use them as traps to net Adair and that McDermott fellow."

It sounded logical to the other three men that Graystone, the man referred to as McDermott, the missing Beckman, Johnson's overseer, and Johnson had worked together, and obviously for a very long time, so a confrontation was over due.

As the initial anger subsided, plans needed to be made. Retaliations for wrongs had to be seen to. And if Zeke and Bear's understanding was they would be sent for in a few days was correct, those plans had to be made now.

"Willie," Sam called. And the man-child came running.

"Yas Suh. Here I is."

"Go up to the big house and tell Miss Rose I'll be here in the barn for a while and that I said for her to not come down here. Tell her Henry and Isaac will be with me."

Acting in concert, the four men, all friends, began to formulate their plans.

***

Later, Henry and Isaac returned to their plantations, keenly aware they could be summoned within a moment's notice. If their agreed to plan worked, there would be no blood shed—but if common sense did not prevail, there would be far too much bloodletting.

Sam and Buck continued their conversation.

"What are your plans, Buck?" Sam asked.

"Don't really have any."

"You know you can stay here. I'll fix the tack room up for you. You belong here, Buck. You've always belonged here."

"Well, I'm not too sure about that, Sam. Things change . . . I changed. Some things stayed the same. You and Rose, Henry and Isaac. That's about all I've seen which didn't change much. Life's fickle. You know that, don't you, Sam?

"What do you mean?"

"Well, we don't lead life, it leads us. Puts a bit in our mouths and yanks us from one curve to the next like we're jackasses. Fickle as a picnic day. Pack your eats and your family, ride out to your favorite eating place and then sure as hell, the rain comes down in buckets. Ever happen to you?"

Sam chuckled, "That it has."

"What do you suppose the chances were of me walking around a curve and seeing that Weldon sign? Shit, Sam. I didn't have the foggiest idea of where I was. If'n I'da guessed, I woulda' thought I was near Roanoke Rapids or maybe further up in Virginia." As an afterthought, he added. "And that's a bad place to be with all that fighting going on. And just what was it that took me to the very porch I crawled under to stay out of the weather? How surprised do you think I was to hear your name, Sam, *your* name, as I lay under that porch? That's a bucket full of strange timing I tell you."

Sam sat still, his chair facing Buck sitting on a hay bale. He figured Buck had more things to say, so he waited.

"One thing I learned walking was what I *thought* might be around the curve up ahead of me, never was on the far side of the curve. Not once. Just more road that went on and on. After awhile I got to expecting less and started fetching a bunch of *that*. Then I'd drag my worn-out ass around the next curve and I'd think I'd found paradise. Valleys, deep and green, surrounded by hills too high to climb—Heaven's clouds hanging in their tops like God was washing them. Such beauty—God's creation . . .but then, up from the valleys came men riding down on me, and the same came from the hills above me. My opinion, Sam, is God's biggest mistake was creating man. What a mess we went and made out of ourselves. So you see? Life tugs us along and all we do is follow. And now that damn war," and with that . . ." Buck's voice trailed off.

"Buck, you seem the same to me. Maybe a bit more laid back. Definitely older. But shit, all of us got older. Maybe the wrong word, that "old" part. *Resigned*. That's better. Willing to take whatever comes at us. Maybe what you need is to quit trying to find something to look for. Maybe it's here, Buck," Sam said as he chewed on a wheat straw and pointed his hand in all directions.

"Remember how I wanted you to stay? Offered you a sheriffing job. Told you if you would be our lawman I'd apply with Raleigh for Emmett's and my places to be a county. Big enough. Got bigger since then. Between Henry's, Isaac's and this place we could still be a county. One all our own. Some of the neighbors said they'd throw in with us if we ever did. But that dream left when you left. We all wanted you to stay. You were one of us." He stared at Buck to see if he could detect any visible reaction to what he was saying. All he saw was the same resignation he'd seen years before.

"Would you reconsider it now Buck? Things have changed."

"Bad men don't change, Sam. Look what we been talking about. You know I couldn't stay. Not with Miss Rose. Not with me killing her father."

"Buck. Quit that. That was ten years ago. And you are so wrong about Rose. She never said a bad word one about you. I'll go so far as to say she never had so much as a bad thought about you. And, Buck, your name was never once mentioned in connection to Griffen. None of ours was. That's because all of us killed that man,

Buck. The four of us. Yes, she knows you were there. She knows all of us were there. But that's about all she knows. If I were to use your reasoning, I'd have to believe she despised me as much as you think she despises you. You are wrong, Buck. Wrong."

Sam stood to return to the big house.

"I'll send Willie down with a cot and bedding. When Annie's done with the cooking, he'll bring that down for you, too Or if you like, you can come have dinner with us tonight"

"No. I don't reckon I'm ready for that," he answered, pulling at the loose and sagging clothing he wore. Knowing he sounded ungrateful for Sam's generous gift of Tad's clothing, he added, "But I'm grateful for the these things of Tad's. Besides, you sure as hell ain't no barber. You made a mess out'ta my hair and beard," he laughed. "If you don't mind, I would like to hole up here for a spell. Maybe help you get through this mess. Could be I might stop looking for something that maybe ain't out there," he said, as he looked toward the drive meandering past the barn. "I'm not sure I'm quite ready to give up the road. Not just yet. But I'll think on it."

"Here," said Sam, as he handed Buck a fistful of money. "This is not a gift, it's an advance on your wages in case you decide to stay put for a while. So don't go and get an attitude about it. I want you to work for me as long as you're willing. Stay a week, stay until everything's finished with Adair and McDermott. Stay forever. No pressures. Just keep your eyes open for now. I feel there's evil about. At least stay long enough so we can put some meat on those bones. Do anything you want. Walk the whole place. There's a good fishing hole up near the bridge, that-a-way," Sam said, pointing west. "Will you do that?"

"I'll accept your offer for now. I need clothes and can't go back to Weldon and can't go down to Fort Harwood. How far is it to Rocky Mount?"

"Right at ten miles. Two, two and a half hour ride, depending. When I send Willie down with the cot and blankets, tell him if you need anything. He'll get it. Go over to that corral and pick out a horse. Just don't take that big black stud. That one's Tad's and it's gone back wild."

"No. I'll walk. But Tad? How's he?" Buck instantly saw the harm in his question.

"Not in the best shape he's ever been in. It's been over two years now, but Doc Yardly said he'll pull through." And with that, Sam felt he'd said enough.

Buck saw he should not ask further of Tad. Sam would tell him when he felt he needed to know more.

"Got any women around?" Buck asked, and then grinned. "Had you going for a minute, didn't I?"

"A bit, I reckon," replied Sam and smiled at his old friend.

"That's one thing I never did look for when I was doing my walking. Life's been too messed up for me to bring a woman into it and let her have a go at killing me off, too." And again, Buck laughed.

Chapter Twenty-four: Winter of sixty-four and sixty-five.

Stealing never does pay. It might pay well for a while, but it always comes to an unpleasant end. Adair's thievery could have lasted longer—made him wealthier—that's the nature of stealing when it's well-planned and well-executed. But money always goes to the head. Makes the thief believe he is something he is not. Makes his mouth run, too. Adair enjoyed his wealth and lived to regret how his mouth ran on.

"Pardon me. This the Johnson place?" Sam asked of the dour looking man standing on the front porch of the mansion due north of Henry's place. "My name is . . ."

He was cut short by the plantation's owner, Mr. Johnson. "I know who you are. What do you want?" the man snarled, crossing his arms. "How'd you fellows get past the front gate?"

"Came up through your neighbor's woods, Mr. Atwell, here," Sam said, pointing at Henry. "You know Henry, don't you? That other fellow's Isaac. Say hello to Mr. Johnson, boys."

"Sure as hell explains the trespassing. Yeah. I know all three of you. Seen you here and there." And pointing at Isaac, Elwood Johnson smirked, "You the O'Reilly's boy, ain't you? How're your folks doing?" and not waiting for Isaac's answer, he looked back at Sam.

"They've been dead going on ten years," answered Isaac, the answer returned with a tinge of sarcasm in his own voice.

With the barest of emotion of Isaac's loss, Elwood Johnson said to Isaac, "Whatever." And turning to Sam, added, "What is it you want?" the glare on the man's face becoming more pronounced.

"Well, let's start again. First of all, we might have trespassed, maybe a half mile or so. Henry said we could use his land. Shook hands on it. No trespassing. Came with us, he did. But there were no signs posted on your land, so how were we to know we weren't welcome?" Sam smirked. "Regardless, I'd like to do a deal with you."

"Not interested," responded Johnson, as he flicked his wrist, indicating they were to leave.

"Well, you might be more interested than you think. It's going to be a good deal. But whether we make a deal or not, it'd be in your best interest to listen to what it is I'm looking for."

"So. Get on with it." Johnson answered, making no effort to hide the fact he did not much care for Sam or the two men accompanying him.

"I want to buy two of your Negroes from you. The women called Flora and Cloe . . . and their children, too."

"And I said I'm not interested," came the answer, hard and sharp.

"I assure you, you'll want us to take them with us when we leave," said Sam as he crossed his arms to match the folded arms of Mr. Johnson's.

Johnson's eyes burned into Sam's and then Henry's. He held up his hand as if to stop any further conversation. "This man do your talking for you?" he asked Henry.

"He is a good friend," Henry answered calmly.

"Well, then. Hold on a minute, I'll be right back," said Mister Johnson, as he turned and walked through the front door of his mansion.

Before the door closed, Sam was already dismounting from his saddle and stepping across to the porch, motioned for Henry and Isaac to stay in their saddles.

Behind the porch column, Sam pulled his revolver from his waistband and held it up for Henry and Isaac to see, while forming his hand into a grip and pointing at their belt guns. With a whisper so quiet it could only be understood if one was reading his lips, Sam said, "Get ready. He'll have a gun in his hand when he comes back out."

Boots slapping on hardwood floors echoed through the doorway. Elwood kicked the door open and it crashed against the side wall. As the door swung back toward him, the surprise of one man gone missing and two guns aimed at him spread across his face. He'd pushed the point and all that was left was for him to continue the suicidal confrontation or give it up.

"Where's that big talking son of a bitch?"

"Don't so much as even let the wind blow your hair. Put that two barrel on the floor," Sam said, as he pressed his Colt against the man's thick neck.

"That's good. Now kick it away. Give it a good kick."

As the double-barreled shotgun skidded across the porch, Sam released the Colt's hammer, easing it to rest, and put the revolver back in his belt.

Henry and Isaac holstered their weapons.

"Mr. Johnson. Thank you for not making what could have been a bad situation unfixable. I'd prefer we handle this like the gentlemen we are. Can we at least agree to do that?"

Elwood nodded.

"Here's my deal. I have it on good authority, ah . . . how do they say it . . . oh, yeah, from the horse's mouth, that you and Adair Graystone and a man named McDermott's been sleeping in the same bed and been doing some bad things. And damn if I'm not the one getting the bad things done to him. Let's start out with me letting you know my feelings are hurt," his voice heavy and thick with sarcasm.

Elwood stared at Sam, hatred building upon his face, "What the fuck are you talking about? And who the hell is this Adair fellow? Like I was saying . . . get the hell off my land."

"No . . . no . . . no. Let's try again," Sam said, his voice sounding as if he was talking to an errant child, "we need to be calm about this. I'm not here to fight and don't want to have to kill you. Believe it or not, we," Sam said, pointing to Henry and Isaac, "are here to help you. And don't play me as a fool—you do know Adair Graystone."

"Look, you son of a bitch. You come sneaking through those woods, throw down on me, and go on about how I'm in bed with two more fellows and we're doing something to you? What the fuck are you talking about?" asked Elwood Johnson, a look of manufactured confusion painted across his face.

A simple twitch of his eyes told Sam the man knew what he was getting at.

After spitting tobacco juice onto the lawn, Johnson continued, "And you're here to help me? Well, shit, this I got to hear."

"You've had dealings with Adair Graystone and that other fellow . . . that McDermott. Trust me, I know," answered Sam.

Elwood's face flushed the vivid red of someone both embarrassed—and caught in a lie. "So what is this mean thing I, or the three of us been doing to you?"

Not missing a beat, Sam continued, " . . . and your teaming up with Graystone and McDermott's part of the deal I want to make."

And as quickly as his face had flushed the color of a late evening sun, Elwood seemed to deflate in size and turn chalky white.

"See? You do know why I'm here, don't you? That's what I call a good start. A real good start."

Not asking for permission, Sam said to Henry and Isaac, "Pull some chairs over here. We gonna get us an understanding."

Elwood Johnson turned toward the open door and searched the long hall behind him and quickly said to Sam. "Not here. Down by the barn."

***

Elwood's head swiveled in all directions before latching the barn door. Not seeing anyone, he rushed his visitors into the structure.

"Right up front, Mr. Johnson, I need for you to understand something. We're not here to cause you and your family problems. I tend to believe you've got enough of them already. So, let's keep everything inside the barn. I'll, by God, guarantee you it will be best if all of it does stay in here, but that'll be up to you. First off, I'm thinking about killing Graystone." There—he'd made the threat, knowing it was idle, but realized even an idle threat could be used as a tool against him if anything ever happened to his financial advisor. It was his first real threat, the first real scare he pulled from his bag of tricks, and it'd worked. He knew Henry and Isaac would never use the threat against him—and after their meeting, Elwood Johnson wouldn't either. So the threat, the first to be used, became a non-issue.

Johnson's face turned pale once again. So many things had already been said—things that scared him.

"Last I heard there's no sin in knowing somebody," he said feebly, in an effort to buy time to think.

"Depends if you know that person and you start doing wrong things with him."

"What is this bullshit you keep going on about? I never done a damn thing with that Graystone or that McDermott fellow, neither. McDermott's nothing but an uppity-acting Yankee . . . acts like he's better than any of us. A goddamn fool, to boot. Down here in Carolina what with the war not more than a hundred miles north of us."

"I hope it's true that you're not involved with those two, but I'm leaning towards thinking you are. Let me get some answers from you before I decide," Sam said, as Henry and Isaac slowly circled to eliminate any possibility of Johnson's flight through the latched door. "You see, I already know everything. You try to put yourself up on an altar and act like something you're not, I'll know that, too. So let me ask again. "How much do you want for those women, Flo and Cloe? With their children thrown in."

"Like I said. They ain't for sale."

"Okay. Next question. I hear tell you put a flip-razor to those women. That true?"

Elwood's eyes admitted he knew all too well of the cut earlobes and pricked lips, but he quickly countered, "Hell no. That's bullshit. That was that money-grubbing son of a bitch Graystone's doings. You ain't putting that on me. Fuck you."

"Alright. Another question." Sam said, stepping toward the man. "You saying he did it or had it done?"

"He paid my overseer to cut 'em up. I run him off after I heard about it. You'll need to talk to Graystone about that."

"Why'd he do it?" Sam edged closer. "Cut 'em up like that?"

"I told you to go to Weldon. Go see Graystone. Ask him." Elwood answered, hoping he could change the direction of the conversation.

"Already told you I got somewhat of a desire to kill him. Got the same desire to kill anybody who helped him steal from me. Be best to try to resolve things without him knowing I'm on to him. So one more time, why did he cut those women up?"

Elwood Johnson felt the barn walls closing in on him. He was sure anything he might have done, any association he might have had with Adair Graystone was hardly worth dying for, so logic suggested Graystone should be the man who should pay for whatever he'd done to Sam.

"Trying to keep them quiet about something, maybe."

Sam ignored the simplistic answer. "You mean Ezekiel and Bear?"

"I reckon," came the answer.

"How much for the Negroes?" asked Sam.

"Well, I'm thinking maybe two thousand dollars will buy the lot of 'em," Johnson finally proposed. "But just so you know, them little ones are still crawling in the dirt and messing their diapers. They won't be of no more use to you than they are to me. Hell, two thousand dollars. And I'll be glad to be rid of 'em."

"Well, it is steep. But it's a deal if you give me your word about something. Got the money on me right now," said Sam, patting his jacket pocket "and if you'll make me the loan of a wagon for a day or two."

"What you want me to promise you?"

"That you will not say a word to Graystone or anyone else about those slaves and their young ones coming with us. Don't drag yourself any deeper than you are in this mess."

"Well, regardless of what you think you know, I have had no doings with those two men. I extend my courtesies to them, offer them a glass of tea if they want it. Something stronger if they want that. Every time they came up here it was to see my overseer."

"So you and they are friends?" Sam asked.

"Done told you no," answered Elwood, knowing he'd already said too much.

"Didn't offer us no tea." Sam said, a smirk creasing his face.

"Well, can't much say I see you much as friends, neither."

"I got me somebody that says you're their friend. And that man does not know how to lie. I don't know how involved you are with those two—but I'll find out. Here's another deal I'd like to make," said Sam.

"Hold up." Elwood's voice had begun to rise. "You keep saying you got something pretty bad on me, but you still want to keep making deals with me. You're full of shit. Take your friends and your brand new niggers with you and get the hell off my land," the man spat.

Sam ignored Johnson's threatening tone. "If your overseer comes back, I want to know. I don't suspect he will. Might be drunk and holed up in Weldon. My bet is he's dead. Now listen to me, you stupid son of a bitch. You're involved in something that's way over your head. It is something that can get you killed, either by the law or from somebody behind a tree." Sam stopped and stared at the man, giving the veiled threat time to sink into his brain. "It will be best for you when Graystone or your overseer does show up, either one of them, that you act like nothing in the world has happened up here. Nothing about Flo. Nothing about Cloe. And nothing about their young'uns, either. And you never saw any of us. It would be smart of you to play dumb as a mash eating hog if anybody asks you about those women and those little ones . . . like where are they? Instead you need to get your ass down to Henry's when anybody comes looking for Zeke and Bear, and tell him about it," said Sam, running out of patience.

"Now look at me," his eyes burning with contempt, "'cause if you tell either one of them we were here, I'll make you this promise, you will be my new Adair Graystone—and like Adair, you will be dead."

"Okay. Okay. You made your fucking point. I don't need that kind of problem. I'll loan you the wagon. Keep it as long as you need it," his blood beginning to chill after the cold words of Sam Biggs sank in.

"Well, then. Load 'em up." said Sam.

Chapter Twenty-five: Eighteen and sixty-two: July. Tad's long recovery begins.

Tad had been home for almost a month. The sewing room, convenient to all charged with his care had been converted into a recovery room. Lillie, her brother Billy, Celine, and Celine's son Jacob shared Thaddeus' vacated bedroom as workmen hurried to finish the cabin for Celine and Jacob.

Mid-construction, Lillie and Celine mutually decided they should all live together, the four of them agreeing they belonged together as the family they had always been.

Sam remembered their dependency upon one another and thought it best the cabin should be altered to fit their needs. Therefore, due to the need to increase the cabin in size, he rescinded his order for the overseer to offer it to anyone else. Wisely, Hadley Struthers had never mentioned the offer to anyone.

Lillie was diligent in her care of Tad. There were days when everyone thought him well on the road to recovery and days in which their growing excitement plunged to new lows. Days when Lillie would gleefully announce to his mother and father that she thought he was trying to speak, but after rushing into the room, he would utter not another sound.

Doc Yardley had come and gone a few times, and each time told the family to be patient, reminding them the young man was on the mend. He could merely offer suggestions to Lillie on how to see to Tad's comfort. He saw Tad far less often than the family and Lillie did. They saw him each day, and could not register the slow and barely discernable improvements Tad was making. Doc Yardley, on the other hand, saw him seldom, sometimes weeks would pass before he stopped by, but upon those occasional visits he saw there had been marked improvements. Before leaving, he would always console those attending Tad with the same words of encouragement he'd offered during the previous visit, "These things take time."

Throughout Tad's healing process the family had been alarmed at the sudden and seemingly uncontrolled jerking of his tightly bound right arm whenever Tad tried to reach across his chest and pull at it with his left. When asked about the strange jerking and erratic behavior, Doc Yardley explained there were possibly two reasons and that both were to be expected.

"It's common for the body to struggle, even when we think the person is sound asleep. Heard tell static electricity can do that—cause that jumping around like he does, and then there's the fact he's tired of it all. Seems maybe that he's trying to free the hand he uses the most. I wouldn't worry none too much. Seen it hundreds of times and every time things always worked out just fine."

For the first week after being brought home, Tad lay deathly still, his breathing shallow, his color pale and pasty. Always by his side sat Lillie, attendant to his needs. As days passed into a second week, she still spent most of her time devoted to him. Her hands upon his cheek soothed the broken man and her soft voice stilled the confusion within the damaged brain.

Sometimes she fell asleep in the chair by the bed but was easily awakened by the slightest of sounds. During that week she felt he was improving. Guttural sounds—not really moans—not really groans, but new sounds, indicated he was willing to speak if he could only sort out the vowels needed. He was physically more active. Doc Yardley told Lillie to allow him more and more freedom of movement but to not let him flay about the bed any more than necessary. He needed to start regaining muscle tone and control of his limbs. His right arm was still purposefully bound tightly to his side even when he was awake. An arm flung wildly could set his recovery back weeks.

Each day he struggled more and more to open his eyes. Sometimes they locked onto objects in the room—studying them as if he did not know what they were. Other times they opened and struggled to focus and rolled around as aimlessly as those of a drunk. But each day he would see Lillie from the cloud he floated in, and when he found her, his eyes would follow her about the room. At the closing of the second week, they found her again and he smiled at her.

The first day of the following week Tad announced his presence. As his eyes locked onto Lillie, he smiled and asked, "Lillie?"

She jumped to his bedside and reached for his hand as he continued to gaze at her. She longed to touch his cheeks with open palms, thinking it would help him remain alert and calm. At least, that was what she told herself, afraid to admit she wanted to touch him for her own reasons, but she controlled her desire. And little did she know Tad wanted her to touch his face. Jealous of the moment, wishing to keep it to herself, she knew the family needed to be summoned and as she gently lay his hand by his side, said "I'll go get your mother and father."

Lillie burst into the kitchen and excitedly announced, "He's awake. He spoke. Come quick. Come quick."

Chairs screeched as they were pushed away from the huge family table while a clatter of plates, forks added to the noise.

Rose, the first to arise, asked, "What did he say?" And before Lillie could respond, she turned and said to Samantha. "Go find your father."

Sheepishly, yet filled with pride, Lillie answered, "He called me Lillie," but thought it wise to add, "and then he asked for you and Mr. Biggs."

As his family entered the sewing room, he repeated, "Mother, Sam," his shortened version of Samantha, and then "Iz," his abbreviation for Izzy's already shortened nickname, and asked "Where's Father?"

Sam rushed down the hallway and into the crowded room, but, too late—his son had slipped into the clouds again. He asked over and over what his son had said and then listened intently as the event was retold.

***

The sewing room proved too small for the patient, his nurse Lillie, and often a second person helping her. Tad was moved back to his upstairs bedroom and the new house guests shared the emptied sewing room until their quarters were finished.

Lillie lay sleeping as the first light of a new day filled the window. Legs bent beneath her, feet tucked into the softness of the cushion of the heavily stuffed chair by the window, she slept, dreaming of favored fairylands and happier days to come. The oversized chair, Rose's favorite, had been hauled with great effort from the downstairs sewing room, up the curving stairway, and into Tad's bedroom so Lillie could remain near her charge.

By the beginning of the fourth week, the cabin had been finished and furnished. Celine and the boys were quickly turning it into a home. Lillie would join them at a later date.

A gentle breeze noiselessly billowed the chiffon curtains of Tad's bedroom and teased Lillie's face in a vain attempt to awaken her. She was tired and the shrill songs of mockingbirds and whippoorwills overwhelmed the efforts of the feathery-soft, face-tickling material. The previous night had been a long night for her, and a difficult one for Thaddeus. The few short hours rest she had found after Thaddeus had finally calmed and fallen into his own much-needed rest were adequate to renew her strength.

She awoke and rubbed the sleep from her eyes and stepped to the edge of the bed. He looked at peace. She brushed away the loose hair falling across his eyes. She felt a strange urge to touch his cheeks but cautioned herself against doing it. That could be a dangerous road to go down and she knew it. But she had begun to have strong feelings for the young man sleeping in the bed.

She was jealous of her duty to be his sole nurse and never complained of her decision to see to his needs. She could feed him, and bathe him within reason, of course, and shave his beard. Male house servants could help him with his private needs. She felt a bond between the two—her the caregiver, and he, the one in need of care. She could not erase the memory of the first time he had opened his eyes, back inside the cabin on Turkey Creek Farm, and stared at her. She had then seen something in the deep blue eyes which others could not see. She felt she understood there was something of value inside his broken body—wondering, looking, and confused. She believed he understood she was there to help him.

She could see bits of the man emerge from the protection of the coma he'd slipped into. His struggle to be free of the thick and heavy fog reminded her of chicks pecking away at the safe confines of their shells. For the first time since being brought home, he lay awake for the better part of the day.

Tad had escaped his shell.

The balance of the fourth week was spent helping him relearn things lost. Doc Yardley suggested Lillie and Rose read him books of all kinds, explaining that a simple, short sentence or the meaning of a word could open a floodgate of memories for him. This they did. He began to inquire of those around him of things he needed to know. They taught him how to sit erect in the bed, how to hold a fork and how to exercise his emaciated arm. They were determined he regain his forgotten abilities, to not just talk, but to walk and feed himself.

His progress came in starts and stops, and none provided rhyme or reason with which they could judge his recovery. And so the hours merged into days, the days into weeks, the weeks into months.

He had lost weight he could barely afford to lose. In order to heal he needed to replace the strength which was lost, but there was little solid food he would take from her with the exception of Annie's red-eye gravy, a tangy concoction of grease left over from fried bacon with a few tablespoons of black coffee mixed in. That and Annie's Dutch-oven biscuits quickly became his favored daily staple. And slowly he began to regain lost weight.

He quickly regained the control of his unfettered arm and hand. His calm demeanor faded as his impatience grew. And with the change he sought his independence.

Too early, Lillie thought the impossible could be done and urged him to feed himself with his one free arm and hand. One out of every four forkfuls made it to his mouth, resulting in frustration for him and a growing amount of cleaning and changing of the bed sheets for Lillie and the servants.

Little did she know Tad's ability to understand things had started to bubble up from the dark recesses of his brain—things he'd forgotten. His erratic mood swings added to his frustrations and that in turn fed his anger.

A sudden and expected outburst from Tad brought with it the desire for him to be the Thaddeus Elwyn Biggs he vaguely remembered. Lillie, patient as always, assisted him to feed himself and help guide his hand to his mouth, something he evidently found childlike and humiliating. As she held the fork filled with the biscuits and gravy he loved, he made yet another effort to free his right arm from the bandages used to hold his arm in place. In anger at not being able to do such a simple task, the fork flew from his fingers, frightened the girl, and another nightshirt was ruined. Out of her embarrassment for him, the extra work involved in cleaning the bed clothing, not to mention the distraught patient, she decide he must forgo his favored choice of breakfast.

She saw an anger building within him as he continued to try, but in vain, to free his arm.

"I am not left-handed," he spat, angrily. "Get me out of this contraption."

Such a display from Tad was something never seen or heard by Lillie. She asked Sam if Doc Yardley could come and bring something, perhaps an unknown elixir, anything, that might help calm the young man.

***

"Heard tell you challenged Lillie with arm wrestling," said Doc Yardley. "Now, if you understand me and do as I say, Thaddeus, say so, and I'll cut those bandages off and free up your arm." And turning to Lillie, he asked, "How long's it been held in place like that?"

"Almost two months," the girl-turned nurse answered.

"Then it's time. Either that collarbone's knitted or it ain't. You feel this?" he asked Tad, as he tapped the prominent bulge between his lower neck and the armpit.

"Some," answered Tad.

"Does it hurt?"

"No Sir," the answer clarified with, "Well some, not much."

"You might not be able to move your arm at first. The muscles have probably shrunk. But they'll come back. Regardless, for the first week when you want to move it, you tell Lillie. Let her do the lifting.

You agree? 'Cause if you don't, I won't take a chance of you causing more damage. I'll rewrap it right now. We got a deal?"

"Yes Sir," the young man answered.

"Well then, give me those scissors, young lady," the Doctor said.

"I'm giving Lillie some suggestions for exercise. Willie's going to help her. You follow her instructions. They can help with the arm, but it's about time for you to get up on your feet, too."

With Willie walking close and slightly to the rear of his best friend, Lillie to his right, a morning ritual began. Willie's bare feet slapping against the oak flooring of the hall, the shuffle of Tad's sock-covered feet, and the light tapping of Lillie's sandals echoed down to the far reach of the hall and then back, only to be repeated with each turn around. An occasional complaint was heard, announcing Tad's refusal to co-operate. But complaints or no complaints, Lillie refused to give in to his behavior.

From the first day, Lillie saw a change in the man she was beginning to fall in love with. His first day spent complaining was never repeated. She sensed he knew something of great value was being accomplished.

***

A week later, in the early morning—the time when the dark of night was losing its hold, Lillie's shouting startled the occupants of Swift Creek Mansion as she ran down the stairs "Tad's gone. Tad's gone."

Chapter Twenty-six: Eighteen and sixty-three: late fall.

News of any kind was scarce. Since the mid-summer battle of Gettysburg, reports of the war came in bits and pieces and most of that had been discouraging to the Southern reader. The storm of war, so much approved of in the beginning was now killing the Southland. The small towns near Swift Creek Plantation, Fort Harwood, Weldon, Rocky Mount and a handful of others, suffered greatly from a lack of commerce. Crossroad settlements, such as Ringwood and Arcola, once places to gather and meet friends, had dried up and when mentioned at all, were merely spoken of as a part of history.

The spurts of recovery by Tad became the news his family waited for. But that too, was slow and not always of the best kind. Weeks went by slowly and for the most part, life had fallen into a indifferent kind of existence. The not knowing of Tad's recovery tore at his family and especially the young lady, Lillie. She was in love with a young man who was incapable of expressing his feelings for her.

Hearing the distant neighing of a horse and the pounding of its hooves on the ground, Tad awoke in the predawn hours of the early morning. The language horses spoke reminded him of a purchase he'd made many years ago. But he had spent the last week with a tangle of differing visions and sounds swirling inside his head. He wondered if that was what bees sounded like in a hive, but oddly, he could not remember what a bee looked like. He wondered if maybe the neighing and trotting he heard were merely a part of what was to be his new life. But, too, he recalled how a purchase of a black horse had upset his parents and that in turn, renewed visions of being taken, fighting every moment of the way, to Virginia's Military Institute in Lexington. He recalled being locked away in a room and being guarded by a boy younger than he, and that the sprout of a boy had a rifle. Too, he thought of how his parents sat upstairs with his new enemy to be, a grouch of a man named Professor Thomas J. Jackson. A rush of thoughts, mostly of things he did not want to deal with, such as the roar of cannon, came with the memory of VMI.

His mind was on the mend, but he was at the baby-step part of recovery. New flashes, scenes of his past—all strange and confusing—kept coming from within the clouds he felt clogging his head. He felt as if he would drown from the torrent of things he saw. Little did he understand his mind had slowly retrieved and already catalogued so many long lost things of his past—the roar of cannon, the rattle of musket, men screaming. He had been trained in matters of war and killing. It was only logical that those were the thoughts which fought to be remembered—and the same ones his mind fought to stave off. A profusion of gentler thoughts, his growing up on a large and beautiful plantation, his father, his sisters, and his mother, and other things he loved came and went, cushioning the hard and painful ones. A giant of a horse was one of those images he saw. Slowly he understood the vision was that of Thunder, a huge, coal black stallion. Tad needed to see if he was right about the memory of a black horse.

He climbed from his bed and grabbed the crutches leaning against the wall. He pushed himself upright and slowly dressed. Limited to his left hand, the effort was arduous. His right arm, thin and lethargic, could merely be used to brace his body against the wall. He inched toward the door and with a fierce determination headed towards his newest challenge—how to get down the stairs.

He sat upon the top landing and held the crutches under his left arm. After a short rest he stood on the marble tiles of the grand entry. His thin buttocks provided scant cushioning as they ached from bouncing from one carpeted step to the next of the curved stairway. Another pause, and then he headed towards the stables. The balance of his journey proved easier.

Soon, he stood next to the corral. On each side a crutch stood propped against the upper rail. With his left hand he raised his right arm, grabbed the top rail of the corral and steadied himself. He offered the magnificent horse standing before him an apple pilfered from the night stand, with his left. The stud reared, pawing the air, and charged the man who had bought him nearly five years earlier. No longer was the stud the trusting animal it had once been when purchased. Throwing its head from side to side, it broke to its right and raced away from its owner. From across the corral, large black eyes stared at the man hanging onto the top rail of the enclosure. He snorted loudly and pawed at the ground again.

Tad, with his hand aching from the firm grasp on the fence, continued talking to the horse, soft and soothingly. He was tiring but thought he might be winning his battle to renew old acquaintances, and spread his legs apart to balance his weakened body. He thought Thunder recognized him, if only as a distant and nearly lost memory.

From the near side, the black coat of hair, caught in the morning's sunrise, shined as never before. The skin twitched, a vain effort to ward off insects and Three Cornered deer flies. The horse turned away from the man, ignoring the apple, and in doing so, it reminded Tad of the actions of a child who had decided to retaliate against a parent or a loved one. It reminded him of himself.

Thunder arched his neck to watch the man who had disappeared from his life long ago. The arched neck and the locked-on stare of coal black eyes confirmed the stallion knew who the man across the corral was.

The name "O'Day" shot through Tad's brain. It made not much of an impression on his cluttered mind, and as suddenly as the name came, it streaked away, leaving bits and pieces behind, and a new word flared in his head. "Stables" didn't seem important either, but the two when said together told him he'd bought the black beauty at O'Day's Stables and that, in turn, led to the name of the town in which O'Day's Stables was located—Fort Harwood.

His head began to swim faster with a torrent of new thoughts, some clear, others vague. It seemed the world was rushing in upon him. He felt there was an urgency to remember things. And he understood something new was happening to him, an awakening of sorts, and that he needed to hold tightly to every new thing.

"You remember what you named that horse?" Sam asked as he walked up behind his son.

"Thunder?" Tad asked, more of a question than an answer.

"Yes, Thunder. Good name, too. He caused an uproar. Remember that?"

"There are things I remember, Father. Some things seem fresh as if they'd happened minutes ago. Others . . . blurry, and not very nice. I don't want to bring those back, but feel like I need to. What happened, Father?"

With that, Tad lost his grip and fell to the side. Sam caught him and lowered him into a sitting position. "You're too weak to be out here. You look like you're about ready to fall over. You rest for a while and then we'll talk. With any luck," he paused, "what you need to remember will come to you and hopefully the bad things will fade as the years go by. But for now, let's get you back in the house."

Looking back towards the house, Sam saw the others coming down to the barn—Lillie in the lead, Willie close behind, and they, followed by Rose, Samantha, and Izzy. Sam shouted to Willie, "Go back to the house and get that chair Doc Yardley dropped off for Tad," and spread his palms, thumb to thumb, index finger to index finger, and created a circle. "The chair with the wheels, Willie."

Not long after Willie left, a noise of gravel grinding under iron rims turned everyone's attention toward the house.

"Get out'ta that damn chair, Willie."

***

Two days later, Lillie knocked gently at Sam's office-library door. "He's awake now, Mr. Biggs," she said. "You said come and get you when he woke up."

"Yes, thanks, Lillie. Now find his mother and tell her to meet me in his room."

"How are you feeling, Son?" asked the boy's father as his mother sat in a chair next to the bed. In her tiny hands, his mother held her son's right hand. "You took a nasty turn out by the barn. Remember that?" she asked, as she smiled at the young man.

"I remember seeing Thunder. That is my horse, isn't it?" his mind still clogged with a wide array of varying thoughts.

"Yes, that's Thunder, alright. Name's more fitting now than before you left. You were the only person he'd let on his back."

"If you let me get out of this bed, I'll break him to the saddle again."

"Well, that'll be a while. You were in pretty bad shape when we brought you back to your bed."

"How long have I been here?" the young man asked as he looked about the room.

"You've been home a long time. Willie's gone to fetch Doc Yardley. He'll have a look at you and give us an idea how much longer Lillie's got to keep an eye on you."

"Lillie," asked Tad, his face blushing, his eyes darting towards the door. "Where is she? She's still here, isn't she?"

Rose understood the flush of color crossing her son's face, and smiled. "Don't fret. She's here. Downstairs. Waiting for us to come get her."

Knowing she was still there seemed to calm the young man.

"Father, do you know what happened?"

"Pretty much. But let's start with what you remember."

"I'm not sure what's true or what's not. Everything comes and stays long enough to get me confused. Was I an officer for General Jackson?"

His father nodded, "You were," and waited in fear of his son asking about the general he fought under—himself now dead—killed by his own men in a dreadful accident.

"Tad," said Rose. "You lay still and rest. What in God's name made you go down to the stable like you did anyway? You're nowhere near ready to get out of that bed."

"I needed to," he responded, hoping he would not have to explain his need to escape the confines of the room—and his crippled life.

"Hush, now," his mother replied. "You need to rest."

"I have dreams. I get a lot of headaches." and with his finger he rubbed the long red welt on the side of his temple,

"What happened?"

"For starters, there's that cut you rubbed just now. Doc Yardley says you had a fracture to your skull, by the side of your temple. He called it a 'concussion'," and provided the same analogy Doc Yardley had used—the fractured egg—to help his son understand what had happened. "Says that's why you might not remember much for a while."

Sam reached over to the stand at the end of the bed and held a piece of metal for him to see. "Feel that knot?" he asked his son, as he touched the protrusion to the side of his shoulder. "This came out of your collar bone. It cut clean through it just like an axe blade and it knitted back together a bit off center. One end of the break overlapped the other, like this," he said, and with his hands extended in front of him he laid one finger on top of another. "It's shorter than before and it'll take some getting used to. So listen to your mother and me," pointing at his mother and himself, "and Lillie, too. You can't be wandering off any more like you did. Not 'til Doc says so. And forget about that stallion for now. He knows you're home and your mother and I think he'll let you ride him when you're good and healed and when he's good and ready."

"Yes Sir," answered the young man.

"Then you remember being in the war?" asked his father. "You know how you got hurt?"

"Some. There were a lot of cannon backed up behind me and I was setting them up in a wash at the base of a hill. If my dream's true, we were blasting away at the people on top of the hill and they were tearing away at us, raining those balls down on us like hail. Now and then, a cannon ball would come rolling down the hill, as if their cannon were angled down so steep they'd rolled out of the barrel." Tad lay staring at the ceiling, his eyes jumping from spot to spot as if he was watching the scene he was speaking of. "That part of the dream always ends with noise roaring around me—then sudden-like, there was just nothing, no noise, no pain. Sky's bright as it can be one moment—darker than night the next. And sometimes, when I wake up from what happened, there's two men reaching down to pick me up.

And they're covered with blood, too. 'Cept it's mostly dried blood. And a *lot* of it. I reckon I must have seen enough blood 'cause I always blacked out when those two start pulling at me."

"You were at a place called Malvern Hill and with orders to place your cannon in the gulch. I walked the battlefield. Saw the gulch. There's busted cannon still down in it. Their barrels missing. Place was picked clean by the trash pickers looking for iron. Must be a lot of money in iron, nowadays." He paused for a moment, thinking, "That was a bad place to be. That gulch. Anything else?"

"I don't know how I ended up there, but next time I opened my eyes, there was a log wall in front of me and an angel sitting in a chair washing my face. And a young boy about twelve years old staring down at me. Sometimes when I woke up, I'd be all alone and sometimes she'd be sitting in a rocking chair reading a book. I reckon, keeping an eye on me. Was that Lillie?"

"Yes. Lillie is your angel. The boy is her brother, Billy. I believe she was sent to you. She's anxious to see you. When Doc Yardley gets here, your mother and I . . . we'll all come up and we'll bring Lillie with us."

"You get some rest first," said Rose.

Chapter Twenty-seven: Eighteen and sixty-four: Late summer.

Buck finds the tack room confining, especially since his walls for the last ten years have been trees bordering country roads. He is tired of the road but has been considering returning to that life he'd led for the last decade. But Annie's cooking and the soft mattress on his cot outweigh any immediate need to leave. He would rest for a while, gather his thoughts, sort things out, decide later. Maybe then he'd be back at the walking. But one thing he knew for sure—'til then he'd stay away from the big house.

The walls of the tack room began to close in on Buck. A desire to be gone—a need to be elsewhere, and the *where* didn't matter, tugged at him. Maybe he thought it was the pull of the unknown, the surprises waiting beyond the next curve—or perhaps the strangers, each different from the one before. Not everyone, actually only a few did he ever meet, who were of the same low caliber as the citizens of Fort Harwood and Carlton County that he'd been hired years before to protect, one from the other. Hard and cynical, that was what that previous life had made of him, and in the end he'd tried to run away from it. For the last ten years he found the nature of the strangers he'd met vastly superior from the lowlifes of the County and that hick-ass town, Fort Harwood. But, truth be told, he missed those who he had become his friends in that long ago past: Sam and Rose, Henry, Isaac, the O'Reilly's and many of the people who still lived north of the stink hole named Fort Harwood.

It had been a long time since he had spent most of his days, and nights for that matter, within the four walls of the Fort Harwood jail. It had been his job to watch over the town's drunkards and hell-raisers behind the locked cells of the jail. And unless they were there for anything short of murder, one night was the extent of their welcome. Nightly, he gathered up the miscreants and violators of common decency and herded them into an eight-by-eight enclosure. The rank odor of liquor-soured men and an unbelievable litany of body noises always guaranteed an early release with the coming of the morning's first light.

The dreadful quiet of the barn allowed his mind to wander and in the dark of night he heard the lonesome call of the road he'd grown used to during his ten years spent wandering. He felt closed in—cooped up, and with each passing day the confines of the tack room grew smaller and smaller. He thought it possible even the horses in the corral, with their neighing, snorting, and the occasional kick against planked sidewalls, had grouped together and devised their own plan to be rid of the stranger within the tack room. He lay on the cot and in his mind's eye he envisioned the wild black stallion horse-talking to the others with ways to be rid of the intruder inside.

Sam called the stud Thunder. Buck thought the horse poorly named—"Satan" would have been more appropriate.

***

He'd read the Weldon and Fort Harwood weeklies, the only papers still being printed, from cover to cover many times over. Sam sent magazines he thought he'd be interested in, and in some he was, while others were delegated to out-house service. He studied the sales pages of the Rocky Mount daily, looking for things he'd forgotten even existed during the last few years. Occasionally, he would see the name of a town or place he had passed through during his travels and would feel the desire to revisit them. But his yen to go visiting was diminished by the absence of corns and bunions on his battered feet, and leg muscles often too sore for the walking. After a few days spent resting, his body began to repair itself. He felt the renewal of lost vigor, the strength stolen by the road and hard walking. It was a good feeling, that feeling of younger days. But he knew he needed a break from the career he'd made out of looking for something hidden from him. His bruises, cuts, and infirmities had benefited from the brief stay and besides, he had promised his old friend Sam he would stay long enough to see his oldest friend's newest problem through.

Three days after his trip to Rocky Mount, he still wore the passed-along clothes of Tad's—clothing of a quality he'd never been able to afford on a sheriff's wage. He stored the new clothing he'd purchased, on a shelf above a cubby hole which held an oversized black saddle. By his reasoning, Tad's handed down pair of trousers and the well made shirt would last a great deal longer than the thrown away items he'd scrounged for on the road. The boots he'd bought sat in the corner, shined to a mirror finish from a third polishing. After spending much of his time in ragged clothing and cast away shoes, he thought it wise to save his new wardrobe if he decided to return to the back roads.

He'd bought other things in the small rail-center town—things he'd longed for but had seldom seen during his journey. He drank an ale at the town's tavern and wondered if he really wanted it after the first swallow. A bag of rock candy filled with sweets of all colors and all manner of stripes and swirls lay unopened on the barrel serving as a side table next to his cot. They were things he'd hankered for which had reminded him of his childhood, but his teeth were in disrepair and he feared the candy would complete the destruction the passing years had done to them.

And he purchased other things because he thought he had been deprived of the simple luxuries of life while he spent ten years penniless and broke as broke could be. The smell of rum-flavored bricks of cured chewing tobacco drifted from the doorway of Rocky Mount's one tobacco shop and the acrid burn of snuff dusting the air stung his nostrils and both proved to be poor purchases. But, he had to admit, the tobacco, rolled in fresh store-bought papers, tasted better to him than the used-up nubs he'd chanced upon during his travels. Smoking merely filled a void created by boredom and loneliness.

The bottle of rum he'd bought was such a purchase. It turned out to be a bootlegged bottle of tea-color Wicked Willie instead of the fine bourbon he'd been told it contained. A gut-burning drink renewed his memory of why he'd never drank in the first place. It had been a hard and expensive lesson re-learned. In hindsight, perhaps he should have offered the barkeep a first tug from the bottle. Then he would have known of the bottle's vile contents.

Gums, red from canker sores, the burn of chewing tobacco, and nostrils raw from the acidic dust of the canned snuff, advised him to throw away the ill-tasting rum-flavored chew—one try was enough. The snuff soon followed. Another hard-learned lesson.

He'd never liked the double-smell of sweat soaked saddles—the padded bottoms drenched and soured by horses, the curved and padded seats, by the rider. He saw a blue, feathery dusting of mold on the rolled edges of the seat and guessed the stallion had been without a rider for many years. But the rest of the tack, the reins, saddle bags, and leggings had been recently cleaned with leather soap and wiped down with lilac oil, and he understood what Sam meant when he'd told him years ago how much he enjoyed the earthy smell of tack rooms.

He could only surmise a saddle as wide and long as the one in the cubbyhole could belong on the back of the big black stud which seemed to find joy in charging him whenever he ventured close to the corral attached to the back of the barn. The hardly used saddle was in the first stage of turning brittle and checkered with cracks. He thought the saddle, and especially one of such fine quality, should be better taken care of.

But, he felt there might be bad memories attached to it which would account for it being abandoned and stored away. Tad, according to Sam, remained in a here-sometimes, there-sometimes world, and he wondered if the young man even remembered the large and beautiful saddle. As an act of deep respect for Sam and his son, he turned the bedside barrel onto its side and lowered the saddle to it. Soon, the leather softened as he rubbed saddle oil into it. Finished, it smelled of saddle soap and lilac oil. For a comparison of luster, he sat the shining boots next to it and offered a prayer that Tad would someday sit in it again.

An itch for the road began to burn his legs. The occasional desire to see all the same things he'd already seen began to grow in his mind and started sending signals to his feet. But something about three meals a day being brought to him from the big house outweighed dried beans boiled in a trash-find of a pot.

He hadn't noticed the bamboo fishing pool hanging across two pegs set in the upper part of a wall. Standing on a plow leaning against a stall, he removed the straight and strong cane pole. A diversion, he told himself, checking the line, bobber, and hook to see if they could manage palm sized sunfish or, with any luck, the small bass Sam said he caught in his favorite fishing hole. Each seemed fresh, if not new. Night crawlers were easy to find by the end of the corral where the runoff of animal waste and spilled water soaked the rich, black soil. Armed with the pole and a pail of slimy worms, he set out in search of the fishing hole Sam had bragged about.

Swift Creek ran through the center of the plantation, dividing it into a northern section and a southern. It also served as the northern boundary of the most beautiful lawn Buck had seen during all of his rambling. He stepped down from the bridge spanning the slow moving creek and headed west along the south bank, careful of the meticulous and tasteful landscaping.

The massive trees along the side of the creek were old-growth oaks, never cut, their limbs grown too heavy to fight the pull of gravity, and hanging low to the ground, hindered his passage. He stepped around the end of the furthermost extended branch and stopped dead in his tracks.

Rose sat upon the wrought iron lawn chair she and Sam had installed years before on the spit of land known as the Red Slater Corner and stared in his direction.

His heart raced and for the briefest of moments, thoughts of fleeing filled him, but she had seen him. He removed his wide brimmed hat and rolling the brim into a tight curl with both hands he said, quietly, "Miss Rose."

"Buck? Is it really you?" she asked of the man wearing her son's clothing. "Sam said you were here. You're so thin."

"Yes ma'am. It's me. What's left of me. I'll leave. Sorry to intrude."

"No, Buck. Please come and sit with me" and she waved him to a close by chair. "He said he asked you to come to dinner the other night, but you declined his offer."

"Yes ma'am," Buck answered, his voice almost a whisper. Before him and beckoning him to join her was the one person he dreaded seeing more than all others. But she was smiling. How confused he was. She should have been shouting and screaming for help, throwing rocks, shooing him away—anything but smiling.

"No ma'am. Best if I go back."

"Why, Buck?" she asked. "What would be the *best* in not visiting with an old friend?" Her smile grew and he thought it sincere. "Don't go. I see Sam said he told you this jut of land was his favorite fishing hole, didn't he? He comes down here most every evening. Smokes his cigars and watches the water—or whatever it is you men folk do when you wish to be alone. And Buck, I've been here most days waiting for you," and pointing at the cane pole, she added, "He said he left you a pole in the barn. Looks like you found it."

Buck stood quietly, his head bowed. Never before had he wanted so much to be somewhere else—to be someone else. But he was neither. "There's things what ate at me, Miss Rose. I reckon Sam told you some of it. You know I didn't come here 'cause I wanted to. I just couldn't, you know, drop in so to speak, for a howdy. Truth be known, I thought of you and Sam nere' 'bout ever day. You all were—are, good people. I couldn't face you, not with you knowing what I'd done. I just had to go." He hoped that would do and he was through with the whole of it, and free to leave.

"Buck," said Rose in a tone both soothing and forgiving.

The one soft word, and the feeling with which it was said washed over him. The weight of ten years began lifting. He could handle the conversation to come, but the telling of that day would be hard. Instead, he stalled, "Sam told me 'bout Tad getting hurt. Every day I been asking the good Lord to help your boy make it through. Don't know if he listens to sinners of my standing, though. How's your son doing, Miss Rose?"

"Thank you for your prayers. And they have helped, Buck. He is getting better. For the most part he can carry on a conversation. One clear as a bell. But then there's times when he's quiet, withdrawn and won't respond much to anybody or anything. Could be he's still back with General Jackson . . . back to fighting the war all over again."

Buck nodded his agreement. "Reckon that *is* where he goes off to."

"Sam tells me you feel responsible for killing Hesper Griffen, and that you were unaware of what that sorry piece of work was to me. He told me you quit your job as sheriff down in Fort Harwood when you found out who he was—that he was my father. Said you had a hard time dealing with it. Did he tell you that I didn't even know, then, that he was my father? Uncle 'Em kept the sorry things that man did to my mother from me. Did Sam tell you how much I hated him?"

"Some of it. Not all."

"Sam said you think you alone killed him. And that he tried to tell you that you were wrong. But for some reason known only to you, you didn't listen to him."

"All of them there saw me shoot him."

"Buck, the way I heard it Uncle 'em had already filled him up with buckshot," again, the voice soft and soothing, "But that evil man would not stay down. Wasn't he ready to shoot my Uncle 'Em? Given a choice I would have told you, whispered in your ear if I could have been there, to shoot that ungodly creature. All these years you'd thought you had done me an injustice, when what you did saved the man I loved as much as my husband—Uncle Emmett *was* my father, only him, Buck. He was the one who protected me when I needed someone. He raised me and protected me from that inhuman thing you say you shot."

"Miss Rose?" Buck asked, astounded at what she said. What a fool he felt like—for running away and staying gone for ten years. He walked over to the bench and sat beside her. Neither said a word for a long time. The chirping of birds flying above and the barking of squirrels as they fought over the early acorn fall scattered about in the woods soothed them both. Neither had the desire to forward the conversation. Anything and everything needing to be said had been said. The past was finished.

"Will you come to dinner tonight?" Rose asked.

Buck had been staring at the creek and the far bank of it. Turning to answer her, his eyes were moist. So were Rose's.

"Yes ma'am. I'd like that."

They stood and hugged. Enough damage had been done—enough damage had been repaired.

Chapter Twenty-eight: Eighteen and sixty-five: January. Graystone is found to be a traitor.

The things Buck has overheard has determined Adair Graystone's future. An elaborate trap must be set. Sam is tired of all the killing around him. He has developed a well-thought-out plan for the thieving financial manager and his friend, the man named McDermott, to be brought to justice and not just any justice. They will be dealt with by the Confederate government.

A gentle knock resounded from the front door of the mansion, interrupting the family's evening meal. Sam laid his fork onto his napkin and glanced at Buck. Each knew the moment had arrived.

"See who it is, Holt," said Sam, careful not to let Rose see the concern on his face. "Tell them I'll be right out."

Holt sat the decanter of wine upon the sideboard, and entering the foyer, opened the massive mahogany door. On the porch stood Henry and the Negro slave, Ezekiel.

"Yes, Suh, Mr. Henry?" asked Holt of the manager of the plantation to the north of Swift Creek.

"Holt. Is Mr. Biggs in?"

"Yes Suh. He be finishin' his dinner."

"Tell him I'm here."

"Yes Suh," and stepping aside he motioned Henry into the foyer. He was unsure of what to do about the slave, Zeke, but finally stepped aside and waved him in, as well. "I'se go git' Massa Sam."

Entering the large dining room, he walked to the head of the table and bent to Sam's ear. "Massa Sam, dat Henry man be out front and he got one ah his field niggers wid him. Tole me he be ah needin' to talk to you'uns."

With a knowing contact of the eyes, Sam nodded at Buck and walked toward the front door.

Buck stood and turned to Rose. "Mighty fine meal, Miss Rose. Thank you kindly." He was anxious to join Sam and folding his napkin, placed it on the table. "Sorry ma'am," he said, secretly pleased there would be no further story-telling about his adventures on the road. For now, he was relieved he had only to offer Rose a smile—one ten years in the making.

"Evening Sam. Buck," said Henry.

"Yes?" Sam asked—no time for small talk.

"Ezekiel came up to the house about an hour ago," Henry answered. "Bear's back at the quarters with their women folk. Go on, Zeke. Tell Mr. Biggs what you were told to do."

"Well Suh. Just about dark, dat Mista' Graystone cum' up to the field where we was working and he tole me and Bear to git down to the dock tomorrow night. Said for us to be dare 'round midnight. He be drinking and was mad dat he had to come tell us he'self 'bout git'n down dare. He was real mad. Said when he see dat Mista' Johnson's overseer he gonna kill him. Said he gonna kill Mista' Johnson, too."

"Son of a bitch's got a lot of killing in mind, don't he?" Sam asked his friends, Buck and Henry.

They both declined to answer.

And back to Ezekiel, Sam asked, "What then?"

"He be ask'n if'n we knows where our womans an' chil'uns be. Said he be lookin' all ober dat Mista' Johnson's place, but dat Mista' Johnson weren't no where 'round. He say dat he was gonna tell him to hole our famblies up in a barn, but sum' ah de folks tole him our womans was gone. Sold off's what dey tole him. So he cum' stompin' all by he'self through the woods ah lookin' fer me an' Zeke. He acks us if we know'd ware dat Mista Johnson be off to and we tole him we don 't know nuff'n ."

***

The hour of reckoning was drawing near. Graystone's staggering bill for stealing was overdue, and the note had been called.

"Are their families protected? The women? The children?" Sam asked Henry, as he turned toward Zeke.

"Got 'em tucked away and I told some of the hired hands to keep an eye on them."

"Buck, this is not your fight, but will you ride over and tell Isaac that Henry and I need him? Tell him to bring someone with him he trusts. And guns."

"I'll ride with you, Sam," said Buck.

"Can't ask that of you," said Sam.

"Then don't."

***

"Isaac, Buck's coming with us." The others nodded their approval, glad to have Buck join them.

"First off, we need to face the facts. The last good crop of cotton we've made a dime off of was in sixty. Could have sold twice what we grew, what with our young men preparing for war. Not too bad in sixty-one, either. Our cotton, every boll of it went to the war effort. Sure, we made money, but this year's crop is sitting up in Brantley's warehouse. Davis won't let us sell any—not with the only markets for it being England or the North. There's nobody down these parts with money, anyway. A handful of blockade runners might be willing to take some of it, if the price is right, back to England . . . at least, that's what the papers said a few months ago. So anyway we look at it, this year's crops might be rotting away. Can't sell it. Can't give it away, but I'll be damned if I'll let anybody steal it from us."

Everyone agreed. Each had long suspected there was no way to sell their goods. The only alternative was to give it to the Cause.

The men looked dejected, but had known the chance of selling their cotton dwindled each day as the war progressed. The Confederacy was beginning to show wear and tear and the new money issued by the Southern states had quickly deflated to the point where one hundred dollars bought only a ten pound bag of flour.

"But all that aside, stealing is stealing. And I'll have none of that." The men seconded him. "Henry and I will go to the docks. We'll watch Graystone on that end."

"And no killing, either," he cautioned them. "We need to devise a strategy. Let somebody else take care of Adair and that other fellow—hang them, shoot them, do as they see fit. I'd just as soon let it be our government." His mind drifted to the upstairs bedroom where his son lay sleeping, and from there to the tales of the butchery of war he read in every daily he picked up. "I'm tired of blood."

The men were somber, each reliving the dark days of the past. None wanted to return to that time when, out of necessity, they had to become the law and do things in the dark of night.

Sam abruptly turned away and walked around the corner of the big house and shouted, "Willie, come up here."

Willie ran to Sam's side and waited his master's demand.

"Go get Hadley. That's Mr. Struthers to you. Tell him to come right away."

"Yas Suh," responded the man-child, happy as a lark that his beloved master trusted him for such important errands. He skipped as he ran toward the overseer's house.

"Here's my plan. We've done no wrong and need to steer away from us any blame which might result from what we have to do tonight. As always, no one will help us. But if we can paint Adair as the sorry piece of shit he is, we'll have all the help we need. Simply put, after we're through, I'll be in Fort Harwood early in the morning to send off a telegraph to Richmond, telling our President that the good people of Carlton County are sending supplies for the 'Cause.' And a surprise, to boot."

He told them the other things he knew, the layout of the warehouse, which direction the barges had to come from and how long it would take. And he told them the things he had seen or had been told by Ezekiel and Bear. And yet another thing they needed to know. "Graystone will be at the warehouse. He'll be drunk, he'll panic easily, and he'll be armed.

"From here on out, we got to play it by ear. I would appreciate it, Isaac, if you and Buck would ride hard over to Edenton, that little harbor town down on the Albemarle. The paper says General Harding and the Forty-seventh Infantry have been stationed there to keep an eye out for any Yankee warships trying to come up river."

"What do you want us to tell him?" asked Isaac.

"Tell him they got a blockade runner with a mess of barges coming at them, and all of them filled with cotton and tobacco that has been stolen from President Davis. And once done, come back to Weldon and meet up with us at Gentry's Stables. We'll take the back way into town. Henry, Hadley and I'll be waiting for you. Leave your horses and come down to the docks if we're not at the stables. Moon's half gone but there should be enough light to get around."

"Graystone will have men outside," stated Isaac.

"Reckon he will. We'll be careful. You, too," Sam answered. "But I want to get Adair at his worst. He'll be drinking, trying to calm his nerves. Sober won't matter much. He don't know the difference between drunk and calm anymore. Let him and that McDermott get everything loaded and on its way. Zeke said the barges should be loaded and floating before daybreak and General Harding needs a heads up."

"What about McDermott? Harding will kill him for sure," said Henry.

"I can't speak for you two, Henry, Isaac, but I hope we agree that Isaac can tell General Harding that if he has to kill those thieving bastards we would consider it a good thing for the Confederacy. But I got something different planned for Graystone. And it ain't going to be nice. I want that thieving son of a bitch alive and sweating."

Sam knew they would agree. Like him, they feared for the ability of the new country to survive. Each new edition of papers, once filled with glowing reports of Confederate battles fought and won, now the same paper had turned dark—the pages laced with words of a possible failure.

Hadley approached from the rear of the mansion. "Mr. Biggs?" he asked, knowing his boss never called for him after the day was finished. "Willie said you need me."

"Yes. Give me a minute."

"Isaac, General Harding might try to put you off, saying it's not his job to police the river for cotton runners. Remind the good man that we, the three of us, supplied the entirety of Company A with uniforms when they mustered up. Tell him those Enfield muskets we sent to Davis didn't come cheap, either. If that still doesn't get his attention, tell him I sent a wire to Richmond to tell President Davis to get ready for a free load of cotton, a lot of cotton. Tobacco, too. Harding will crap his pants if he lets Davis down. If nothing else, that fat little man is ambitious. He'll add a star to his others if he presents all that cotton and tobacco to Richmond. And Isaac, tell him not to let that river flooding towards the sound hold him up. The swamp always runs off fast. Always has. The tide will come back later tomorrow. And make sure he understands I've already told President Davis to be on the lookout for the train coming up from Weldon, so he needs to float those barges back up here for the Weldon-Petersburg train. Tell him he needs to be quick about it."

Sam then returned to Hadley Struthers. "I want you to go into Weldon with me and Henry tonight around ten," and briefly explained what was about to happen.

***

The warehouse was closed on three sides, only the front opened towards the Roanoke. Each end had wide doors tall enough to let the area's farm wagons pass through, unload, and leave through the far end. Along the back wall, windows—some boarded shut, and others, their panes either missing or the glass which had survived a long life of storms and vandalism and turned opaque from the passage of time—afforded tiny glimpses into the dark building. A yellow glow through the occasional window indicated where workmen toiled loading cotton.

In the dark, Henry, Sam, and Struthers hugged the rear wall, feeling their way through briars and brambles grown thick against the cypress-planked building.

Sam held his index finger to his lips. "Shhh," he said, and placed his ear against the dirty and mold-covered siding. Henry and Struthers pushed aside the weeds and pressed against the wall. The three stooped as they passed under a window.

The soft glow of a lamp filled with whale oil danced across the dirty and foggy panes. From inside, a shadow flitted across the window, and again, Sam's fingers crossed his lips.

Adair stood in the room, his back to the window.

Ezekiel thought he heard a shuffling noise beyond the wall and was frightened that Adair might hear it also. A quick glimpse into

Adair's drink-soaked face assured him that even if the man had heard the noise, the alcohol would have told him to ignore it.

Inside, his back still to the window, Adair slurred his commands. "Get to work, you sum'bitches," he said, as he pulled heavily from the bottle of whiskey he held. "Soon'r you damn fool darkies get done, the soon'r you can go looking for your women." Turning to Bear he said, "Go find McDermott. He was supposed to be here an hour ago. Zeke, how many more bales you got to load?"

"Yes suh, we'se 'bout through. One more ah dem big boats be cumin' up now. 'Bout ah nudder two hours, we be all dun'," the slave said as he glanced at the window again. He was beginning to worry if Massa Henry and Mista' Biggs had caused the noises outside.

Adair ignored the slave, waving him off with a shake of his hand. "Get after it. That goddamn cotton ain't gonna' jump on the barges all by itself. You still got the tobacco to get loaded, too."

"Yes Suh," answered Zeke, as he held a lantern over his head and pointed through the doorway of the room behind him. "Suh? Sum'body dun' chop a hole through the floor in de back room."

"Nobody chopped a hole in there," he said pointing at a dark room near the back of the warehouse. "It's rot. Wood rots, you damn fool. What business is it of yours anyway, Zeke? Speaking of which, you and Bear been acting kind of strange tonight. You and that goddamn Bear got to put your noses in everything. Something you want to tell me?"

"Nah Suh. We got the scares 'bout our famblies. Heard dat Mista' Johson dun' sole 'em off," he said, his heart racing.

Adair hoped the hole he'd spent an hour chopping through rock-hard cypress planking a few days before would go undiscovered until he needed it—again. The work had nearly caused him to have a heart attack, but once finished, he stepped back and admired his problem solving. He spent the day wondering who said wood rots. Whoever the hell it was, sure didn't know a thing about cypress. "Rot, my ass, not that stuff," Adair said, as his arms slowly stopped aching.

And now Ezekiel had questioned him about the hole. *So what?* he thought, *by early morning I'll be well on my way out of Weldon, fi-*

nally clear of Samuel Biggs—and my saddle bags stuffed with his money, his silver and his bars of gold.

He remembered the relief he'd felt, once the floor was broken through, with the creek below flowing deep enough and fast enough to dispose of the remaining threat to his life—Zeke and Bear. He reached inside his jacket to see if the Army Colt forty-four was still secure behind his belt. It was.

He thought of how anxious he was to be done with the last of his thieving. All that stood between him and Weldon was a half dozen or so of the new cone shaped chunks of lead Mr. Colt supplied with the nickel plated revolver—one each for that sorry-ass piece of work Samuel Elywn Biggs, the anchor he'd married twenty five years earlier, and of course, Zeke and Bear. Of his wife, he mused, *"I'll help you get on with your dying,"* while thinking of her constant complaining of how sick she was and how she just knew he'd be happy with her dead and gone.

The last thing he had done before he left home earlier was bid her goodnight, pull the shades down, place a jug of water on the night stand next to a loaf of bread, and lock the front door.

He'd tugged at the lapels of his jacket, snapped the collars tight to his neck, and stepped out onto the street leading down to Brantley's warehouses.

The lust for money and need to be free of Weldon had become a sickness. And of his wife, he thought, *A loaf of bread will hold you for a few days, you sack of shit. Why waste a perfectly good piece of lead? You can't get through the door. Next week this time, there'll be rats growing fat, gnawing your skinny ass. Hell yes, I'll be happy.* Too, he knew Brantley always hid out in his small office behind the warehouse every time he and McDermott told him to disappear. It would be a good time to solve yet another problem. And he now had an extra piece of lead. So on the way to the warehouse he stopped in to see the man.

Bear returned, following the man he'd been sent to find.

"Where the hell you been," Adair shouted at McDermott. "Where's that boy you brought with you?"

"You drunk already, asshole?" snapped McDermott. "Better put a cork in that bottle. We got business to see to. And while you're at it, you mousy little motherfucker, shove that goddamn bottle up your ass. That *boy*, as you call him, is my son, you damn fool. Best you leave him out of this fucking mess you made out of everything."

Adair was tired of the man and that snotty-acting son of his. He'd been paid, in advance, and had no further need of the two and did not hide the fact that he didn't give a damn what happened to them or the cotton. He wanted the bad memory of McDermott, his uppity-acting son, and the years of larceny behind him.

"You got six loads waiting on you. The Roanoke's damn near flooding and it's running fast. If you get going now, the last loads will be right behind you. You told them assholes you hired where you're heading, right? I'll see to it they leave soon as the boats are loaded. Then me and you are quits. Grab that boy of yours and get gone while the river's fast. The tide won't turn till you're down in the sound."

The end had arrived. McDermott stepped forward and shook Adair's hand. "Good run while it lasted, hey?" and without so much as a goodbye, McDermott turned to leave, joining his son as the younger man stood holding the reins of his father's horse.

"Yeah, yeah," said Adair just loud enough for his old partner to turn his head, not sure if Adair had spoken at all.

Adair nodded his head and turned away.

When I get back to Vermont, I'll find you. And when I do, do I ever have a surprise for you, he thought, as he rolled the forty-four caliber pieces of lead in his pocket.

Chapter Twenty-nine: Eighteen and sixty-five: January.

The job almost finished, Adair is anxious to flee. If only it were that simple.

"Mista' Graystone, Suh. We'se dun'. Can me an' Bear git on home? See if we can fine our famblies?"

"There's one last thing before you go. Follow me," said Adair, his eyes dancing around the interior of the now-empty warehouse. "Back in that room over there," he said pointing to the room with the hole in the floor.

Ezekiel's eyes shot to Bear's. He had shown Bear the room with the recently chopped hole and both had commented on how strange it was that the room was void of everything except the hole. There was no window to let the moonlight in and the door had a latch recently installed on the inside.

"Sum'body ought'a tell Mista Brantley 'bout that hole," Bear said to Ezekiel.

"Won't be you two," said Adair, his face dark and menacing.

They turned to Adair. In his hand he held a Colt Army revolver pointed level at their heads. "Stand by that hole. Both of you. Sorry boys," said Adair as he thumbed the hammer back. "End of the road."

Three more clicks sounded in the near dark of the room. "Whatever you're thinking of doing, Adair, don't do it." Sam said. "Hand me that Colt. What do you say we take a walk down to your office?" Adair dropped the revolver and it bounced off the cypress plank, through the hole, and splashed in the river racing past beneath.

Henry held his revolver inches from Adair's face as Sam turned to Hadley. "Mr. Struthers, I'd appreciate it if you would stop by the stables on your way over to Adair's office and bring those tongs hanging on the wall with you."

To Ezekiel, he said, "You and Bear come with me. Your families are safe. I might need your help in a bit."

***

"You want a drink, Adair?" Sam asked the man as he held a bottle out to him. "No? Not thirsty? Sit down."

Adair stepped behind his desk and sat in the heavily cushioned, leather covered chair. The chair had always been his throne and when in it he felt in control—but not this time. "What's this all about, Sam? You and your friends come at me with guns, and them cocked. What the fuck, Sam?"

"You weasel bastard," Sam spat the words at the man. "Where's the money you stole from me?"

"Stole?" the frightened man snorted. "I never stole nothing from nobody in my whole life. Did you ever think about going by the bank and ask them that question?" Caught red-handed, Adair still believed he could out-smart the man in front of him—the very man he'd always thought slow and often called a dullard.

"Did stop. There was some there, but not nearly enough to cover the load you and that other bastard took down river. All the cotton and tobacco's gone, but where is the rest of the money you bragged about cheating the three of us out of? You get paid for the extra?"

Somebody that shouldn't has been listening, was Adair's first thought. "That's it, Sam, all of it. Every dime. You know there's not a market for cotton now. Not with the war. Except England and they said they're through with it. I let it go for the best price I could get," his eyes pleading for understanding, his words saying he'd done his best by Sam.

"England, you say? Seems there's a market for cotton up in Vermont," answered Sam, sarcasm etching his voice. He closely watched Adair's face for a reaction. "I think that fellow McDermott called it Gordon Mills."

"No. It's on the way to England," stated Adair as his face drained of blood.

"Heard too, you and McDermott bragged about how long you and he have been at it—all that stealing you did, when you and him were standing on the back porch, drunker than mash-eating hogs and arguing. How long you been at it? I heard you bragged about doing it from day one."

A confused look clouded the man's eyes—a nervous tic pulled at his cheek. He was surprised to hear what only he and McDermott had discussed. Instantly he thought of the young man McDermott had brought with him. So McDermott and that Nathaniel fellow he seemed to be so fond of had set him up—tricked him, and now that they were out of harm's way while he sat surrounded with very upset men staring at him.

As Sam posted men at the two doors and each window, Adair's mind raced as he ran down the list of who in the outer office might have spied on him, while desperately trying to figure a way out of Weldon. *Alive would be nice*, he thought.

Slapping the desk to show how upset he was with whoever had betrayed him, he said, "Whoever told you that pack of lies is going to be fired first thing come tomorrow morning. Seems a decent person can't be found in all of Weldon."

"I said your back porch, asshole. That one out there," he pointed toward the rear door. "You got a surprise coming," thinking of the soon arrival of Isaac and Buck. "Now, I'm going to ask one more time. Where's my money?"

"Sam, there ain't none. I never took a damn cent from you. I don't give a flying dog fart what you think somebody told you. You'd believe a rumor before you'd believe me? You've known me for over twenty years, Sam."

"Like I said, Adair. Last time." He opened the door to the outer office and beckoned Ezekiel and Bear inside. "The two of you hold this piece of shit on top of that table." And then turned to Hadley Struthers while pointing at the tongs. "Clamp 'em hard," pointing at Adair's crotch. "Don't stop till he begs to talk to me. Then squeeze 'em harder so he doesn't go back on his word."

He walked from the office and stepped through the front door. He pulled two Carolina gold cigars from his vest, snipped the ends of both and handed one to Henry. "Smoke it fast. This won't take long."

***

Ezekiel opened the door, his face soaked with sweat, and held it open, an invitation for Sam and Henry to return to the office. Zeke sidestepped as the two men entered the room. He'd seen the bad things white men could do to black men, but never would he have ever believed what they were capable of doing to one of their own. Bear stood as far as he could get from Hadley, unable to take his eyes off of the tongs. Ezekiel joined him and both eased towards the door. Neither said a word.

"That whimpering piece of shit says he'll tell you anything and begged me to stop. He's a broken man, Mr. Biggs," Hadley added, as he stared menacingly at the man crumpled on the floor with both hands cupped around his crotch.

Sam stood towering over him. "Same question, Adair. Where's my money?"

"Sam, for Heaven's sake, you got to believe me. There is no money."

"Hadley," said Sam and pointed at the man on the floor. Hadley snapped the prongs of the tongs together. Adair pulled his knees up to his chest, assumed a fetal position, and whimpered.

"Alright. Alright. Pull back the rug under my desk."

Henry pushed the heavy chair aside. Beneath the desk, deep within a hole cut through the floor and covered with a plank and a throw rug, rested a strongbox plated with riveted sheets of steel, and padlocked with a jailers lock.

"The key." demanded Sam. "Give it to me."

"I don't have it," came the wrong answer.

"It's the key or I'll tear this whole building down. Give it to me," Sam said, extending his hand.

Key in hand he waited, thinking of problems which might come with his opening of the steel-plated strongbox. He was so close to regaining his lost fortune, a huge amount of money, some his, some Henry's, some Isaac's, that he felt it wise to do nothing outside the law.

He put the key in his vest pocket and stared at Adair.

"What am I going to find in that box?" Sam asked the man who lay drooling onto the floor.

"Everything, Sam. Everything. Just let me go. Please."

Sam ignored the sobbing man.

"Henry, we got to go slow. We make one mistake, that son of a bitch is liable to say we stole it *from* him." *"End up arrested for taking our own money. What a sweet revenge that would be for that piece of crap*, he thought, as he considered that with a careless mistake on his part, Adair could win the battle being played out. The irony made him laugh.

"Go down to the sheriff's house and get him out of bed, if you have to," he said. "We'll open the box after Adair tells us everything he's done."

"Okay," answered Henry.

Sam looked at Hadley and nodded his head. Hadley snapped the tongs again and Adair pulled himself into a tight ball and stared alternately at Sam and the tongs in Hadley's hands.

The sound of hobnail boots pounding loud and sharp in the early morning hours as the town slept, announced the arrival of Henry and the sheriff of Weldon.

"Tell the truth, Adair," Sam warned him and turning to Hadley, he said, "Throw those tongs out the back door." Hadley opened the door and tossed them into the alley by Adair's office building just as a big man, still in his nightshirt and slippers followed Henry into the room.

"Adair," said Weldon's sheriff, paying scant attention to Sam, Hadley, or the two very scared Negroes. "What you doing on the floor? These men beat you up?"

"No sir. I lied to him," he answered, pointing at Sam.

"What the hell's going on here, Mister Biggs?" the sheriff asked Sam.

"Ask him again," said Sam, seeing the man on the floor was anxious to cooperate.

"Nobody's leaving here until I know what happened. Everybody clear on that?" Weldon's sheriff and only peacekeeper warned.

Hadley, standing behind the sheriff and in view of Adair, dropped his hands below his waist, balled his fists, and scissored one across the other.

Adair's eyes grew large and as his face grew pale, said "Yes Sir, I stole him blind."

"I roughed that bastard up a bit," answered Sam. "Same as you would have if he'd been stealing from you twenty some years and bragging about it while he's doing it."

"So what did he steal from you and how come it took you so long to find out he was stealing?"

"Well, Sheriff. First things first. He stole a lot. Don't know how much and won't know 'til we open that box on his desk. Second thing is I trusted the sorry-ass bastard."

"So what's the need to get me a out of bed? Son of a bitch admits he's a thief."

"True, Sheriff. But he hasn't admitted nothing to you, yet. I want what he's saying on the record. There's some other things you need to hear, too."

"We'll get to that in a minute. But first," the Sheriff said, pointing at the box on the desk, "get on with it. Open that thing so I can see what all the fuss is about."

Sam turned the key, folded back the lid and stared at the contents for a long moment. "Son of a bitch," he swore as he stared daggers at Adair. "Take a look, Sheriff."

"Well. I'll be damned," said the Sheriff, struggling to tear his eyes off the contents of the box. "So, Adair? You're admitting on your own free will you stole all that from Mr. Biggs? That man over there, the big one," he said, pointing at Hadley Struthers, "make you say something what ain't true?"

"No Sir. Nothing."

"Them two darkies give you a good going over?"

"No Sir."

"Did Mr. Biggs hurt you?"

"My feelings a bit."

"Well. Did you take it or not?"

"Yes Sir and more. I need Doc Yardley real bad, Sheriff."

"I can see that. But that ain't gonna happen for a spell. Not 'til we count what's in that box. Maybe you ought'a hold your balls tighter . . . might keep 'em from swelling up some."

He turned to the men gathering around the desk. "Anybody know how much a bar of silver's worth? What about a bar of gold? Hell. Can anybody in here even count high enough for that load of money? No? I reckon we ought'a send for Mr. Wiggins, his accountant. You trust him, Mr. Biggs?"

"Sheriff, I'd prefer to hold off on that. Those other things I mentioned might require him to be here, too. But I don't think I trust anybody right now except those men with me. That fellow's Henry Atwell. He's one of my partners. Lives between here and my place." And pointing at Hadley Struthers, he added, "He's my overseer. I trust him. And those two over there, Ezekiel and Bear," as he pointed at the two black men. "Two more fellows I trust are coming into town. Another one of my partners and an old sheriffing friend from Fort Harwood'll be here soon. Might trust you some. But don't know yet."

"Mr. Biggs. I don't much appreciate you coming into our quiet little town and making statements that might be true, but might not be, too. Might be best to fetch the mayor, while we're at it but that ain't gonna happen 'til I decide one way or the other."

Strange thing how a badge pinned to the shirt and a gun stuck in a holster could give a man more confidence than anything else, Sam thought. But he'd seen such bravado before and found it foolish. He reasoned such things should help the man to at least think things through before he crossed his arms and spread his legs apart, to emphasize he was the boss in Weldon.

"Might as well get him, Sheriff. The Mayor's going to need to hear this, anyway. Did you know that sorry dog laying in his own piss is a spy for the Yankees?"

With that comment the sheriff hurried towards the door. "I'll be right back with Mayor Dutton, Mr. Biggs."

***

Half an hour later, the planks on the sidewalk once again announced the arrival of two men nearing the financial advisor's front door. In stepped the Sheriff and a short, fat man, wearing only a nightcap, a dark overcoat, and socks sagging around his thick ankles.

"Mr. Biggs, what's this you're saying about Adair being a traitor?" while pointing at the man still tightly holding himself in a protective ball.

"He's a Yankee spy," Sam answered.

"Have you lost your mind, man?" asked the mayor. "If you remember, he was in business, right here in this very building, when you and your folks come here from . . . ah, where was it? Petersburg? Was he a spy, then, Mr. Biggs?"

"Matter of fact, I believe he was. Son of a bitch made a point of telling me and everybody else how much he loved Vermont and hated slavery."

"Well, I ain't the biggest fan of slavery in Weldon, neither. That make me a spy? What's he doing laying down there holding his privates, anyway?"

"Reckon a mule kicked him."

"You saying a mule come traipsing in here and kicked him? Got to give me more than that," said Mayor Dutton, glaring at Sam.

"Okay," and Sam stepped closer to the man balled up on the floor. Behind the desk and out of sight of the mayor and the sheriff, he put his full weight on Adair's hands.

"I am a spy. I'm a spy," Adair yelped.

"What else you need?" asked Sam.

The sheriff turned to Weldon's short, and fat mayor and added, "He stole all that from Mr. Biggs, Sir. Done and 'fessed up to it, too," nodding his head while pointing at the box on top of the desk. "And his cotton, too. Said he sold it to a man out of Vermont. And that's against the law, Mayor Dutton. There ain't no trading allowed with the enemy."

"Shut up, you damn fool. Don't you be telling me the law," snapped the Mayor, puffing out his chest and stretching himself to be something he wished he were.

An hour later, Mayor Dutton instructed Weldon's sheriff to lock the so-called traitor up and ordered him to stay in the jail until the barges came back with the tide. "Meals will be brought to you.

You need an outhouse, the sheriff will fetch a slop jar," he said to a very sick-looking Adair.

"Who'da thought that mousy little man had so much larceny in him?" Mayor Dutton said to Sam, as the men left Adair Graystone's office. "And don't you fret none, Mr. Biggs. Me and him," meaning the sheriff, "will be with him every minute of the way to Richmond after they get all President Davis' cotton loaded up. And, oh yes. Before I forget, on behalf of all the citizens of Weldon, and those of Carlton County, I would like to thank you for including some of the good people of Weldon as donors of that train full of cotton and tobacco."

"You are more than welcome," Sam answered.

From an alley, Isaac and Buck stepped in front of Sam. "General Harding blew a hole in the side of the front-running barge, the one that McDermott fellow and his boy was on. Killed 'em both and some of the men helping him with the boats. He said to tell you the rest of the barges will be here late this afternoon, if there ain't no more rain. Funny, ain't it Sam? How things work out? We got most of our money and that general will get the credit for recovering President Davis' stolen supplies. But how did you know where Graystone's loyalty lay?"

"Told me enough over the years about his undying love for the North, especially his home state, Vermont. Vermont this, Vermont that. And here he was living with people he felt superior to. I got the feeling he was not the huge supporter of our new government he kept saying he was. Nor do I know if twisting the facts around like I did is right or wrong, but I do think in a round-about way he was helping the North more than the country he professed to love so much, our Confederacy," Sam said, his face that of a man rethinking what had happened.

"I'm not sure I follow you, Sam," responded Isaac.

"Think about it, Isaac. All that cotton was going to Vermont. Had to be. Nowhere else. England, my ass. Flat bottom barges crossing an ocean? Adair was a damn fool if he fell for that lie. Either that or he knew McDermott was taking it to Vermont. What's the difference anyway? Stealing is stealing."

Anyone could handle skimming along the coast line if there was a good boat captain leading them. Evidently McDermott was that. He'd done it enough. "McDermott got rich. Adair got rich, but they kept at it, getting richer and richer. The Army of the Potomac got new uniforms to wear. We lost money. Some. Not all. We'll make it through. Might have to punch new holes in our belts, now and then, but we'll be alright."

"You alright with what we did?" Isaac asked.

"Got to be. I wanted to kill him. That mad at first. But killing? No. That's not in me. Had my fill of righting wrongs that way. It's kind of like playing God. No. Let President Davis deal with it. We're through."

Sam put one arm on Isaac's shoulder and the other on Buck's. "Let's go join Henry and Hadley over at the Weldon for breakfast."

"Ain't no need to go looking for Brantley," Henry said as Sam pulled a chair from under the table.

"What about him?" asked Sam.

"The Sheriff found him dead in his office. A hole in his forehead."

"Town's sure gone to hell," said Sam.

the different masters she'd had. And how Tink Strickland had been the worse in the progression of owners.

"Damn. Sounds like if she had a hun'ert dollars in gold, she couldn't buy a minute's worth of luck. That sure 'counts for how skittish she is. Run off to her cabin when she seen me. You think maybe that fellow might be looking for her?" Buck asked.

"I doubt it. He's got bigger problems," and tapped his finger against his temple, an indication that Tink Strickland was not too well in the head. "But he could be. We used every trick we could think of to throw him off her track. If he ever does find out, it'd have to be by chance, and frankly, I don't think he'll live long enough to do much trying. He'll die from his drinking."

"And the slave thing. How's she feel about that?" Buck asked.

"She's no slave."

"So she's a free woman, huh?"

"She is if she wants to be. It's her choice. She knows it. I hold papers on her. They're just for show. She couldn't just come with us without some proof of ownership and when she finally saw there was no way she could stay there, not with that drunk bastard after her all the time, we had to account for her being with us in case we got stopped on the way back by any soldiers or lawmen. They'd be curious what with her being so light colored and all. We couldn't take a chance. So I took some of Tink's papers with his name on them and had a sales receipt made up."

"I ain't never seen nobody her color. Seen one or two what was darker, but still light enough to throw me off. Think they was called mulattos. Yeah, still plenty dark, just not nearly as much as the other Nigras," commented Buck. "She's almost white, though."

"True. Every man we passed on the way home with Tad, stared at her—even the ones with their wives staring at them. She is a fine looking woman, that's for sure."

"Some might'a thought she was your daughter," snickered Buck.

"Knowing her past, you'd think she'd take advantage of being as white looking as she is," said Sam. "Anyway, turned out we didn't need to worry none. Nobody ever asked about her. Probably didn't need the papers I had made up, but didn't want to chance it. Got ones showing me as her owner. I'll give them to her whenever she asks for them. That was part of the deal to get her to leave that place. She's a free woman—she knows it."

"Then why does she live in the quarters with the field hands, her being free and all?"

"That's where she feels the safest, I reckon."

"Well, that takes some figuring. Being more white than black, but pretending to be a Nigra."

"That's all she knows, Buck."

"What would you say, given the fact she is a free woman an' all, if I took to calling on her?"

"I'd say lots of luck. Her and men don't seem to get along none too well. Too bad, she's a fine woman. A heart as big as the sky. Loves Lillie and Billy as much as she loves her own boy. Just had a life filled with hard knocks."

"Pretty, though," smiled Buck.

"Buck, what the hell? She's half your age."

"True enough, but I ain't dead yet."

"No. I reckon not."

***

"You give any thought to what we talked about? You know, staying on? Working here?"

"Some. What you got in mind?" Buck asked.

"Well. The way I see it, there might be some folks in Weldon who might get an itching to come down here and pick a fight with me for getting rid of Adair that way—turning that little traitor bastard over to the army like we did. I imagine he cheated others same as he did us, but we got to what was due us first. I'd feel a whole lot better about things if I had someone I trust ride the upper part of the holdings. You know, keep an eye out for people thinking I took something of theirs. You see any, let me know. They want to fight, I'll accommodate 'em."

"Nope. Don't think so. Not interested in that line of work no more. Same as sheriffing to me. No guns. Through with 'em," answered Buck.

"So don't carry a gun, just watch over things. Hell. Take that fishing pole along. When you're not watching the road, fish. Do the watching as you see fit. You're the only person I trust, Buck."

"Fish, huh?"

"Set your own hours and go where you please. Kind'a like that walking you did and there's always the chance you might run into Miss Celine. Heard she likes fishing."

Buck liked the sound of that. The fishing part didn't bother him and the chance of seeing Celine, didn't either. "I'll give it a try. No guns, though."

***

Celine watched the man as he and a mangy flea bitten dog strolled casually past her cabin. Her first instinct was to flee through the back door, but the presence of a fishing pole in the man's one hand, a bucket of worms in the other, confused her. Suddenly her stomach knotted. It was possible the pole and bucket, even the ugly and smelly mutt, might be another of Tink's ruses. Outsiders seldom visited the quarters and those that did frightened her—especially if they were white. With the exception of Mister Biggs and the overseer, Mr. Struthers, the stranger was the first white man she had seen in the slave quarters since arriving.

From a distance the man by the far edge of her front yard had the build of Tink Strickland—tall and lanky, his age hard to determine. As he neared, she could see it wasn't Tink, her owner, as she had thought at first. But he could be. Stay on guard, she reminded herself, and wondered if Mister Biggs' counterfeit ownership papers could stand the test of an inspection.

Tink Strickland was a swarthy-skinned man. The meaty, purple, and swollen pouches that perpetually lived beneath his eyes said he'd long ago lost his direction in life, whereas the person on the path seemed to have a plan in his walking. He'd been marching through the quarters every morning for over a week now, on his way to do something unknown by those who lived in the slave shacks. He had the gait of a man looking for something. But again, her heart pounded at the possibility Tink would find her.

The rail-thin man continued his morning saunter past the caramel-colored woman's cabin, and as always he was careful not to let her see his eyes, slightly turned, enjoying his peripheral view. He never stopped during his walk through the quarters, but always slowed as he walked past her cabin.

Although confident it was not Tink, she dropped her arm to her hip, and felt the cold steel of the Army Colt she kept tucked into her belt. It gave her a sense of security. She'd taken to wearing it whenever she went outside her cabin—a habit born from earlier days and earlier problems. Holding the door ajar, she watched the man's eyes dart from one cabin to the next, searching.

A second week was spent strengthening his nerve, and as a third began, Buck had found the inner strength he needed. Still, he was cautious about approaching her—something he wanted to do more than anything. He was not familiar with the ways of women and believed she might shy away from any forwardness on his part.

"Hell, Dog," he said to the mangy one-eyed mutt which had tried to corner him in the barn on the day he arrived from Weldon, "I ain't getting no younger. Me and you'se gonna stop by and visit Miss Ceely this morning. Worse she can do is shoot me . . . and you."

With an abrupt right turn from his usual morning walk, one he never varied, he ambled toward the new cabin's porch and mounted the steps.

From the slit in the curtained window, the sun-tea-colored woman watched as he climbed the steps, removed his hat, and brushed the hair falling in his eyes. To Celine the nearer he came, the more he appeared rough and crusty, much like her former master Tink did—yet somehow softer, gentler. She saw eyes which seemed determined to absorb everything they saw, a thing he'd learned out of necessity during the past ten years. A moment's carelessness could be deadly on a strange road. On his face Buck wore an engaging smile. She judged his age at fifty-plus years. His hair was thinning and turning white, but hinted at the brown it must have been during an earlier time of his life. His mustache, full and thick, was all that remained of the nearly gone color. He was lean and worn, weary and washed-out looking, his skin sun-cooked and leathery. He had a halting gait to his step, one of a need to continue and one looking for rest.

He must have been a good-looking man, and as recently as the last few years. She thought him not hard to look at even now at his advanced age.

As he approached the porch, his steps firm of decision, Celine acknowledge she was more curious than frightened and let the curtain fall straight as she grabbed the latch of the door. Celine tugged at the rain-swollen door and stood to the side as it swung open. The stranger on the porch did something out of character of all the men she'd ever known—he smiled.

Buck stood with a fishing pole in his hand. The wreck of a bloodhound sniffed the bucket looking for worms.

"Morning, Ma'am" Buck said. "Pretty day, ain't it?"

"What do you want?" she answered aggressively.

"Name's Bucyrus Vance. Most folks call me Buck. You like to fish, Miss Celine?" he asked, his smile never wavering.

His question caught her off guard.

"How you know my name?"

"Asked Mr. Biggs," Buck answered.

"You work for him?"

"Ain't decided yet, but now, I think I'll take the job he offered."

That tidbit of information eased her apprehension. If Mister Sam liked the man enough to hire him, who was she to decide what kind of man stood before her.

"Do you?" Buck asked a second time.

"Do I what?"

"Like to fish?"

"Now and again," she answered, watching the roadway for people she did not know. With the exception of a few slave women grown too old for field work, standing in doorways or staring through windows, she saw no other strangers approaching, as she trained her eyes upon him, sizing him up from head to toe.

"Now seem like one of them times?" Buck asked, his smile expanding.

"I reckon now's fine, but I'm going to take Billy and Jacob with me. You got any ideas you don't need for fishing, you best leave 'em here on de porch. I'll get my pole. You got enough worms? An' duz you like eels?"

Buck's first answer was, "No, but I'll go dig some more." And the answer to her second question was, "Some. Like catfish more."

The awkward conversation continued. "We catch any eels, they's your'n," said Celine. "I'm sick to death of eels. You know that Willie fellow? He brings me eels nere' 'bout every single day."

The day passed quickly and the catfish were biting. So were the eels.

"Time to get home," Celine said, and rolled the string around her pole. "You clean dem fish, you can stay to dinner if'n you are of a mind to. Won't be nothing fancy. Collard greens, cornbread, catfish and all the eels you want."

***

Buck sat back in a well-crafted rocking chair and asked permission to smoke one of the cigars he'd bought from the tobacco shop in Rocky Mount and offered Celine one as well, which she took and joined him. He'd thought of asking her if they should smoke them on the porch but reasoned she might not want to give nosy neighbors anything to talk about. He rubbed his belly and smiling at the cook, said, "Mighty fine cooking, Miss Ceely."

The day had been enjoyable for both. And the night had taken possession of the quarters, as they talked of trivial matters.

"Miss Celine, Ma'am. You reckon it'd be alright if I stopped by again. Maybe we could go fishing again?"

"Mr. Vance, I think I'd like that."

"Just one thing, though Ma'am. Reckon we can throw away those eels next time? And I answers best to Buck."

Celine smiled. "We can, but Willie will only end up catching 'em and bringing 'em back here, anyway."

Buck, with a touch to the brim of his hat, said his good-byes and left for the solitude of the tack room.

Chapter Thirty-one: Eighteen and sixty-four. December. Winter's foothold on Swift Creek.

A strange union—that of Buck and Celine. She'd been a slave—born to it, for the full length of all her years and carried a list of ancestors as long as her arm, each and all slaves themselves. And he, a slave to his past, still wondering if he'd really killed that man or not. He was not necessarily a godly man, but after years spent being a sheriff he knew that all bad things eventually, like a boil, must come to a head. And that would be when his real pain would begin.

Of the two, Celine was the most forthcoming, willing to answer any questions put to her. She feared nothing any more. What could be worse than the life she'd led?

He guarded his life as if the rusting pieces of it was all that was left of him. Memories, mostly bad, held his tongue in check.

They lived their lives knowing others did not approve of their marriage. Neither cared.

A strange union, that of Buck and Celine.

"I'm glad you finally came for it. I was beginning to think you doubted your upcoming marriage to Buck would take," Sam said, smiling as he handed the sealed envelope to Celine. Inside, a faked certificate of ownership said to any who might inquire that Celine Strickland belonged to Samuel Elwyn Biggs. "It was starting to turn into an anchor. You and Buck need to get on with living, Miss Celine."

"What do I do with it, Mr. Biggs?' the woman asked.

"It's yours. That's up to you. If it was mine, I'd burn the damn thing." He blushed as he apologized, "Sorry, Ma'am. You've been your own person since you came here to live. You no longer belong to anyone," but pointing at Buck, "'Cept him. And that's a good thing. As ugly and old as he is, he might grow on you, " and then he chuckled.

She held the envelope to her bosom, afraid to open it, afraid not to. She was still called a Negro and would still be considered a slave by most, she knew.

"Help me, Buck," she said, taking her soon-to be husband's hand in her's.

"No," he said, holding up both hands, refusing Celine's request. "I think you ought to do it. It'll mean more to you."

She knew he was right. Such certificates had controlled every breath, every movement and every decision she'd ever made during her life—they, or the person holding the papers on her. And all the men she'd been bought by or traded to had used her and abused her. One of the bastards had even tried to kill her. A flash of Tink raising a hatchet above his head raced through her mind.

The burning of the cursed certificate would be the most momentous event of her entire life, something akin to giving birth to her two sons—Malcomb, now with the Lord, and little Jacob straddled across her hip.

"Buck," she said, "please take Jacob," as she handed her remaining child to the man she had finally agreed to marry.

Finished was that life of belonging to others. From now on she belonged to no man. But soon to be wed, she realized marriage was a form of ownership, as well. But that, in itself, was a trade off. In turn, she owned him. And she could live with that deal.

She held Buck and her son tightly, savoring the moment. *My family* she thought. *No one else's. Mine . . . all mine.*

"Why's you cryin', Mama?" asked Jacob.

"I'se free," she said. "We'se free."

"Ma'am," said Sam softly. "You've been free since the day we met." He stepped to her and circled her with his massive arms. "Now, don't forget, Rose and I are expecting the two of you for dinner. Lillie and Tad will be there. So will Samantha and Izzy. We'll drink a toast to your upcoming marriage."

From a slave to a plantation's formal dining room in less than a short day. Tears glistened in her eyes as Celine softly whispered, "Buck, I love you."

***

"But go where, Ceely?" asked Buck. "We have a home here. I have a good job with Sam. We have a little money put by. Not much. Enough for that dress you saw over in Rocky Mount, if you still want it. We got the little one on the way to think of, too. We need to stay put for a while. See what happens. The war's almost over." He reached under the blanket spread over them and rubbed her swollen stomach. "He needs a place to grow."

"She," Celine corrected her husband. "I don't mean now. After she gets to toddlin'. Maybe then. I want to see things, Buck. Go places. Get away from my upbringing. Here I'm a black woman in candy-colored skin. We go back to Louisiana, I could be a French lady."

"So today it's your color got you going?"

"Well, how would you feel if you was so dark they throw'd you behind a plow and tole you to git to plowin'? Make you work from sunup to dark just 'cause of the color of your skin? And you no more a Negro than a 'tater plant. All my life I've been looked down on 'cause I'se too white or not white enough."

"Ceely. We've been over this a hundred times. Who you are is not of your doing. It's you I love. Besides, have you ever thought of the possibility that maybe your great grandmother mighta' been French 'stead of black? Them French bastards done some low-down tricks back then. You know some of them brought their own slaves with them when they come here. And how is it I ain't nary never one time heard nobody ever call you a Negro. Never. Somewhere down the line somebody musta' been, but even if there was somebody way back, you ain't no more a Negro now than a Chine'r woman. Let it go," Buck pleaded.

"Well, you don't know how it feels to have people always staring at you."

"Of course I do. Just look at me," he said spreading his arms, cocking his head to the side and grinning. "Right handsome devil for forty five, huh?"

"Forty-five my foot. You look like an old worn out coon-dog. But," she hugged him, "you'se my coon-dog."

"So what if you have a drop or two of black in you. I still love you. Come to think of it, my bet would be there ain't no mor'n three people in all of the South what ain't got some Negro blood in them. Matter of fact, I think you're the only person I know who might not have none. What difference would it make to you, anyway? You're free."

"So can we go to Louisiana?"

Buck sat upright and turned to her, supporting himself with his arm. " Ceely. There ain't a chance in hell that'll happen."

"We got'ta stay here?"

"I thought you liked living here."

"I duz. It's jus' I ain't never seen nothing in my whole life."

"Okay. Someday. But let the little ones sprout a bit first."

She pouted. "Can't be no harm in going to Louisiana for a spell after the baby comes. We could go on the train out'ta Weldon." And with that, she rolled over to her side of the bed.

"War Department might not like that none too much. Too dangerous, anyway. Some folks in Louisiana might still be a bit upset with which side some of their neighbors took up with. Especially those goddamn Frenchmen. Onliest people I ever heard of what would determine if they was Confederate or Union depending on what color wagon was rolling by their houses. Them that ain't French are still determined to even the score with the Frenchies for trying to set up Louisiana as a sanctuary for Napoleon. A swamp kingdom. Yeah, right. Good place for that bastard. Anyway, we ain't going no where's 'til this war's done."

"How you know all that stuff 'bout Louisiana?"

"Read it. And one other thing. There ain't been so much as a Federal horse down this part of Carolina. Reckon our boys held the line each time they give it a try. This might be the safest place for us. Nothing for them to come here to revenge. Hope to hell it stays that way. But if any of them Yankees do come through here, they're gonna be a mite suspicious with two white folks living down here in the quarters. You need to stay inside if anybody you don't know comes riding up. I'll speak to Sam tomorrow and see if he'll give me some kind of an official name or maybe a title so I can put a sign over the front door of our cabin."

"You ashamed of me?"

"Never. Just scared. Scared they might try to steal you."

Chapter Thirty-two: Eighteen and sixty-four. A hard winter. But free at last.

Alcoholism has always existed, but has never been understood. There are men who can sip their alcohol and put it aside. Then, there are binge drinkers, men who drink only when the urge overrides good sense. They may spend days drowning themselves in alcohol and lose sense of who they are, and suddenly quit, their thirst sated. Reasoning and sanity return as the tranquilizing drug wears off, but always in lesser and lesser degrees, until that person can no longer live without alcohol. It may be months before they start eyeing the bottle again. Tink Strickland fought a long war with his binge drinking. Drunk and insane for long periods, clear-headed and recovering for long periods afterwards. But those periods of restoration of body and mind never lasted. He knew they wouldn't, but he didn't care after a while. That's one of the unknowns of alcohol—alcohol always wins the tug of war. Women can cause men to lose their way. It can happen. And does. But mostly, it's alcohol.

"You can't go to sleep?" Buck asked Celine. "It's past midnight. What's wrong?"

"Shh. Listen. I'm tellin' you, sumbody be outside the cabin. They keeps walkin' 'round an' 'round it . . . pullin' at the windows," she said, as she pushed herself up with her elbows.

"I don't hear nothing. You're just tired, Ceely. Cuddle up next to me. Go to sleep."

"It's not just now. I felt like when we's outside we's bein' watched. Didn't you feel sump'n?" she whispered, her voice edgy and apprehensive.

"No. What do you think you felt?"

"Eyes on me. Someone watchin' me . . . us. Sum'times while we'se fishing. It's the same feelin's I got from the woods back on the farm. That Tink Strickland feelin'," she added, and thought it foolish to try to explain something as vague as a feeling, or a sense of being watched. She'd told Buck of the irrational behavior of the man who had fathered the boy sleeping in the bed in the far corner of the room. But she didn't know how to put in words the things she meant. "I was skeered, Buck."

"Well. We'll find another place to fish." Buck said, as he put his arm protectively around her. "Try to go to sleep." In an effort to calm her, he chuckled. "Some place with no eels."

"You didn't see nothin' moving in the woods on the far bank of the creek?"

"Heard some things. Could'a been a deer. And don't forget, there's a boatload of wild hogs back in them woods. And the wind kicked up a few times."

"It weren't no deer nor no hogs and the wind weren't blowing when I saw them bushes moving, Buck, I'm tellin' you, I've felt that feelin' before."

The second step from the top always creaked whenever someone climbed the stairs to visit Celine and Buck. It had a distinct sound all its own. A stretched-out grinding squeak of weight on wood. The squeak sounded again, as if slow and carefully placed boots climbed the stringer of stairs. The front door rattled. The hard noise of boots receded as they headed back towards the steps. The squeak returned. A shuffle of feet crunched the gravel by the side of the house as a shadow of a person or some unknown thing passed the window. The grating of gravel grinding against gravel gave way to footsteps climbing the rear steps. And that, followed by the rattling of the rear door.

Buck reached over to the chair and pulled his D Square Bowie from its sheath. At the same time he threw the cover back and whispered to Celine, "What the hell was that? Be very quiet. I'm going out the front door and slip around back. It sure as hell better not be Willie. I'll skin his sorry ass and hang him in a tree for scaring us like that."

He slowly opened the door and barefooted, made little noise as he hugged the side of the house.

Celine reached under the bed and grabbing her Army Colt, thumbed the hammer to full cock and aimed it dead center of the rear door.

She jumped, startled by Buck's shouting, "Hey. Who the hell are you?" The soldered washtub leaning against the rear wall crashed to the porch floor. The clanging of the tub muffled an angry "Son of a bitch." She felt a fear she'd prayed she would never have to ever endure again—and the voice she feared was not Buck's.

"Where is she? It asked, and that followed with a man running towards the creek.

"You better run, you goddamn bastard," Buck shouted at the fading foot sets. "I get my hands on you, it'll take a week for ten people to pick up the fucking pieces, asshole. And don't come back, neither."

Two men, one fleeing, one chasing, ran towards the thick woods behind the rear of the house. "Git him, Dog," she heard Buck shouting at the blue tick hound.

The blue tick would return to its new home under Buck and Celine's cabin when it quit the chase.

Hearing the rear door open, Celine placed the Colt under the covers next to her.

"Willie?" she asked.

"No. Too tall. Too skinny."

"I know who it was, Buck," Celine said her eyes large with fright as she bit her lip and nervously wadded the sheet between her tiny hands

"Who?" he asked.

"Tink. My old massa."

"You must be wrong. Sam said he took care of that."

"Whatever he did didn't work," she said, her face strained with fear.

"Is that what you meant when you said you smelled a scent this morning?"

"Yes, Buck. You got'ta believe me. There's nothin' what smells like rottin' swamp trash, hickory smoke, and corn liquor all squished together. That's Tink Strickland's smell, I tell you."

"Well. He's skedaddled now. Ole Dog'll let us know if he comes back. Try to sleep, Celine. Come first light, I'll go looking for him. See if I can get a few men to go with me. There should still be fresh tracks or something," Buck said as he pulled her even closer. "Don't worry. I'll find that sorry-ass son of a bitch."

***

"That's him. Stay low. Get behind that tree, John. George, down below that log," ordered Buck, his finger pressed against his lips.

"Reach for the clouds, Mister. George get that cane hoe off his back. Be careful. He can take your head off with one quick pull of that hook blade. John, plug his ear with that squirrel rifle. Motherfucker so much as takes a deep breath, clean the wax out'ta both ears at one time."

As the cane hoe sank in the creek and the ear was plugged with a barrel, Buck said. "Mister, put your hands behind your back. Dog, bite his goddamn crotch if he so much as farts." And to the foul-smelling man, he added, "Dog'll do it, too. Bit my ass first time he ever seen me."

Buck grabbed the man's shoulder and spun him around. "You scared my wife, asshole. Now before I take you apart one piece at a time, tell me why."

"Your name Biggs?"

"Why, ain't you the cheeky one?" Buck spat. "Your name Tink?"

"Your name Biggs?" the stacked odor repeated.

"Nope. But you're going to meet him real quick," answered Buck, as he pointed to a windfall tree serving as a bridge across Swift Creek. "and you're probably going to wish you hadn't. Now Git."

***

"Throw some water on him. Better yet, stuff him in a tow sack and dunk his smelly ass in the creek. Something smells that bad might dissolve and float off on us," Sam said, nearly gagging. "Then bring him down to the barn."

"So you're that Tink Strickland fellow? Never did get to meet you. I thought I was through with you."

"Well, you ain't," snarled the rail-thin man, shriveled from the thorough soaking and the few months he'd survived without alcohol. You stole my slave woman."

"You're right. I did. So?"

"I come to get her."

"Won't happen. She's a free woman, now. Married to this man. Oh," Sam's voice filled with sarcasm, "you two already met. Right?"

"Got the law on my side."

"Put that aside for a bit. How'd you find her?"

"Had me a talk with Captain Tom. That barge fellow you paid to keep his trap shut," he said, smirking at Sam. "Remember him?"

"Oh yes. Captain Tom. Gave him two hundred American greenbacks to keep him quiet about us. Looks like it didn't work."

"He tole me you gave him the same in Confederate script for a busted-down mule," Tink said—still smirking, still thinking he held the upper hand.

"He lied to you. It was only a hundred. And that was script. Still a poor business decision, though" said Sam.

"Well, there you go. Can't trust nobody no more," smirked Tink.

"I was talking about the mule," answered Sam. "But it does look like Captain Tom never forgot me telling him where I was from. I lied to him, I admit it. Had me a reason to do it, though."

"And what reason you think you got to steal another man's woman?"

"Are you saying she was your wife, also? You married your slave woman? What did your neighbors think?"

"Fuck them neighbors," said Tink.

Turning to Buck, he asked. "She tell you she was married, Buck?"

"Told me as far as she knew this stupid son of a bitch was dead. Said he was her master, not her husband."

"Okay. Did you kill Captain Tom?" Sam abruptly asked Tink.

"After I got him to tell me all he knew about where you all went off to. Gave him a choice first. Told him I'd let him live if he told me the truth, but I reconsidered on that . . . went on and kilt him. Looks like he told me the truth, though," and the smirk on Tink's face began to border on a smile. "So what's it to you? I got you dead to rights on slave stealing."

"So which is it? They're going to hang me for the slave stealing or the wife stealing?" Sam said smiling at Tink.

Tink turned red with anger. He never liked being the punch line of a joke. "They'll hang you when I get you back to Hopewell."

The men laughed at the idiocy of the statement. Exaggerated glances around the barn should have explained why they laughed, but Tink couldn't see it was a convenient place to be hung.

"What will they do to a piece of shit like you for killing your wife and that baby you had with your slave girl? Bashed his head against a tree, was it?" Sam asked.

"You got Lillie and my boy Billie, and the young'un I had with her. I seen 'em." Tink said, sounding like he was preparing to return home with his possession and the three children he suddenly seemed to want near him.

"Yeah, I do," confirmed Sam.

The bar fell from the barn door catch and the heavy door groaned as it began to swing inward.

Tink's smirk disappeared. He pulled at the ropes holding his hands behind his back. As the squeaking grew louder, he strained to see who might be entering.

Celine let the door slam against the horse stall. The white dress she wore was accented by the early morning sun climbing the sky behind her. There was no emotion on her face. Her eyes sunken and dark, void of life, spoke of a weariness that was willing to settle for death. She walked straight towards Tink Strickland, never taking her eyes from him. As the men stepped aside, she walked up to her former master. From a pocket sewn into a fold of her pleated dress she pulled her Army Colt. As the revolver rose, a click said half cock.

At eye level, a second click announced it was ready to do its work. Tink stared at the hole in the end of the dark blue barrel. He never saw the gray piece of lead, nearly a half inch in diameter, explode from the depth of the black hole. A cannon ball cutting his legs from under him would have not made him collapse faster. Celine's arm sagged, her hand opened. The gun, a thin wisp of smoke drifting upwards from the end of the barrel, clattered on the barn floor.

The blue tick, startled by the sudden mass falling near him, spun and bit Tink Strickland's shoulder.

Tink's eyes stared, unseeing, at cotton weights hung from a beam above him.

"I'll be at the house whenever you need to come and get me," she said, her voice emotionless and hardly more than a whisper. She placed a palm against Buck's cheek, and said. "I love you, Buck."

Buck held her close, soothing her. His eyes begged understanding from the men standing before him. He whispered as he walked her to the door, "Wait outside the barn. I'll be there in a minute," he said.

"Don't seem like that dog likes him much, neither" said Henry pointing at the dog as it ripped at the dead man's shirt.

"Anybody got a problem with what just happened here?" asked Sam.

No one said anything. The matter was ended.

Chapter Thirty-three: The beginning of Eighteen and sixty-five. A white carriage and small pony for Lillie.

It doesn't happen often, but it does happen. Two people meet—brought together by fate, but an unexpected twist or turn can wreck their anticipated lives. One in need of help and care, and the other—the helper, the healer—provides an unselfish constancy of care. They merge, each interlaced into the heart of the other so solidly, so lovingly, their two hearts melt and become one. When two lovers share one heart, such mutual sharing must be a balanced thing.

Those that know them see striking opposites between the two who have chosen to live with that one heart. Each needs different things than the other. And it would seem those desires would harm the center of their being. But the one thing such love proves is true love provides all.

"Come with me. I want to show you something," Tad said as he reached for Lillie's hand. Together, they walked across the yard toward the barn.

"Close your eyes. It's a surprise." He pushed the barn door open and led her inside.

"Okay. Open them."

Before them stood a white buggy, freshly painted and mostly restored.

"That's the same buggy my father courted my mother in. It took a lot of work to clean it up. Needed a few repairs, still needs a few more, but it's in good enough shape to take you courting. That is, if you would so honor me," and with that said, Tad blushed.

His request was unexpected and took Lillie by surprise. She could not answer right away, her heart too busy pounding. A thousand thoughts raced through her. She needed to be cautious. He had finally shown an interest in her—something she had wanted and prayed for. But she was frightened at the suddenness of his question. To forestall an answer was to threaten her one chance at love.

At a loss of words, she thought diversion would be the best tack to take. She stared at the freshly cleaned and painted buggy and managed to ask, "When did you get it? It's beautiful. Whose is it?"

She had not answered his question. Tad looked confused, then embarrassed. He thought himself a fool for being so forward. What right did he have to pressure her? Or was his asking inappropriate?

Taken aback by her lack of an answer, he stuttered, "I'm . . . I'm . . . sorry. It's just that I . . . ."

She placed a finger on his lips. "Shhh," she whispered and, looking deep into his anxious blue eyes, answered, "Yes."

He smiled. The weight of the world had been removed with one simple word. "It's yours. There's more. Come," he said, his heart as light as a feather, and guided her toward the rear stall.

"She's yours, too," he said, pointing at a small white pony, its color and size matching the small buggy ladies preferred.

"I bought the pony from O'Day's Stable down in Fort Harwood. I kind of hoped I could take you for a ride." And with an exaggerated bow, his arm flaring outward and closing to his side, he asked, "May I?"

"Oh Tad. Of course. I would love to go riding with you," her heart still racing. *Do it. Do it*, her heart demanded.

So, it was not just her imagination. She had picked up a few indications he may be more interested in her than just as a nurse, and now her secret prayers had been answered. She wanted him to hug her, kiss her, say special words to her, but he didn't—or couldn't. That will come in time, she thought. Her face flushed, embarrassed at the nature of what she was thinking.

From his pocket Tad removed an apple and handed it to Lillie. "Mother said to tell you there's a secret to owning a pony such as this. Give her apples. Only you. Nobody else. Something to do with loyalty."

She laughed as the diminutive pony poked her head through the slats and nudged Tad's pocket. "Then how is it she knows where the apples are?"

As Lillie brushed the mare's mane, Tad watched Lillie. She liked his surprise. His plan was working.

"Toby," he shouted.

From the corral came, "Yas Suh?"

"Hitch the little one up to the buggy and bring it to the house. There's a new pony sized collar by her stall. Tell Annie I said for her to get a blanket and pack us a picnic. Fold the blanket and put it over the seat." He paused, and sheepishly said to Lillie, "The leather's in bad shape. It's one of the things needing fixing. You don't mind, do you?"

"No. Of course not, but I do need to change into something more fitting for a buggy ride."

***

Isaac waved from the front porch of The Ferns as a scene from the past unfolded. A white buggy pulled by a white pony turned into the plantation's drive.

"Morning, Isaac," greeted Tad. "Mind if we ride through?"

"Morning to you two, Tad, Miss Lillie. Course not. Where you two off to?"

"I thought I'd take Lillie to see the family park," said Tad.

Instantly, an old memory flashed across Isaac's mind. Many years earlier, when he had been the overseer on the same plantation he *now* managed, a man who looked much like the young man in the buggy before him, rode up in a similar buggy, that one white also. Beside that man sat a beautiful lady. And then as now, that man had stopped to greet him. The man from the past man was Tad's father—the beautiful lady beside him—his mother.

And on that long-ago day a huge thundercloud was threatening in the distance.

Isaac remembered saying the same words then as now, "Afraid that park needs a good going over. All grown up with brush, and vines. But the road running along the creek's still in pretty good shape. Might be best if you don't go in the front way, too much work for that little thing," he said nodding at the small pony. "Back road's not so bad. But the cemetery itself is seen to regularly. Your mother's always seen to that. I reckon you already know that."

Isaac looked to the west and shielded his eyes from the sun. "Don't let me hold the two of you up. Better keep an eye on that," he said, pointing at the far-away thunderhead. "They let loose, they'll wash the ugly off a billy goat, they will. You two have a good time." The same warning he'd given the man and woman so long ago.

"Charlie and Joe," said Tad, referring to Isaac's two sons, "should be home soon. Guess you heard Lee's holed up this side of Petersburg. There's talk he may surrender. Might have by now. 'Til then, may the Good Lord keep your boys from harm."

"Heard such things before. Me and the Missus pray every morning, every night, that each time it's true," answered Isaac. "Thanks for asking of our boys."

A fine young man Sam and Miss Rose got themselves, he thought. He struck a match against the porch column and leaning against it, lit a cigar. As the smoke curled upward he wondered how strange it was things always seemed to repeat themselves.

***

The dark sky rumbled in the far distance—but thankfully, the thunderhead was far enough away to be of little concern. Tad pulled the reins and the pony stopped, and turned its head back towards the couple.

"Your pony's looking at you. Better give her another apple," he said.

Lillie fed the apple to the pony. The apple disappeared quickly and she rubbed her nose against Lillie searching for yet another.

"Here, girl. You did a good job." The nose rubbing had worked. "Now be good and I'll see if I can find another one for you when we're ready to leave."

"This might seem a strange place to take you. When I was a boy, my mother and father brought us kids up here once or twice a year. Mother would lay out a picnic for us, then she and Father would stand by that crypt over yonder," he said, pointing at the steeple-like monolith. "Mother would read the names and rub her fingers across the letters, and all the while, she'd be crying. Father would stay with her and not say much until she'd run out of tears. I asked him about her crying every time. Never got the whole story. Just bits and pieces.

He said when I got old enough he'd tell me what happened to my mother's family. He always looked sad, telling me that. Almost twenty-seven years old and he still hasn't told me. But whatever it was that happened, it took Mother a long time to get over it. And Father told me not to worry about it. Said it was a long time ago and he'd make sure I knew everything before he left for his judging day. Called it his "judging," like he'd done some sort of bad things he needed to be judged for doing. Not that man. Bad has never been in him."

That was something Lillie could agree to. "He *is* a good man," she said as she read the names carved into the granite monolith. "Who's Emmett Detwyler? I've heard that name before."

"He was my grandfather. Mother's father. At least she called him her father. He was something else. Her uncle, I think. The two of them shared a secret. Whatever it was is still a secret. Regardless, she loved that old man more than life itself and the three of us children grew up calling him Grandfather."

"And this one?" She asked, pointing at the name *Abigail Detwyler Bailey* carved into the granite.

"That one, there is no mystery about. She was my mother's mother. My grandmother. Mother said when she was thirteen years old, her mother was killed down in Lumberton and that she witnessed the murder. But there really were secrets about her. I asked Father about them. Only answer I ever got was 'someday'."

He stood and took her hand, pulling her tight to his chest. "Enough of graveyards. I didn't bring you up here to look at names of dead people. This place used to be more of a park than what it's remembered for now." He clicked his tongue and taking the halter, guided the pony to the nearest tree and tied the reins to it. "Let's walk to the creek. We'll sit and have our picnic under the oak. The shade keeps the weeds from growing."

A deer snorted and dashed away as they neared the bank of the creek.

Tad had grabbed the blanket from the age-worn wagon seat and spread it out upon the edge of the creek. They sat together, both aware there was hardly any space between them. Neither was uncomfortable with the nearness of the other, each needing to be close.

"It's so quiet. I understand why you wanted to come here, but what made you bring me here?" she asked.

"I'm not sure. It's quiet and away from everyone. Even the slaves steer clear of the cemetery. Another reason, Lillie—is I never want to be far away from you. Never again. I have lost so many memories of things I must have done, that I hardly know who I am." He rambled for a bit longer, looking for just the right words. "It's hard to live with memories that come and go as they see fit. One day clear and alert—the next, I'm lost in a white cloud of fog. Seems I'm never quite sure of anything.

"There was a school at Fort Harwood. One through ten. Mother and Father swear I graduated from it. I don't remember doing it. And Thunder. They say I bought him. I remember bits and pieces of that, too. So it must be true. They told me they'd never been so mad at me for doing it. And now with you here, I need to know who I am. There's so much gone." He turned to her and grabbed both of her hands in his, "I'm so afraid you'll end up as a here some and gone some memory like all the rest." His voice caught and he looked away. He pointed at the pony by the hitch-rail, and said, "Your pony is one of the reasons I went to Fort Harwood. I figured it was time to try courting you, and the pony and carriage worked for my father. I bought her at O'Days, too," he added, not knowing why he told her that, but he knew his heart was pounding in his chest. If she was going to pull away from him, he felt it would be now and if she did all would be lost. But she didn't and the two sat quietly, each staring at their entwined hands.

His voice shaky, he added, "Mother and Father are always asking me if I remember this or that. I don't, but sometimes I tell them I do. I do recall that all in all we were a happy family, but for the sake of it, I don't know why."

"I do," Lillie answered. "Love. So much love in one family. Yours is what I wanted my family to be . . . happy. It was anything but." She was not sure of what or how much he might have been told about her own family by his father or Isaac and Henry, the men he called "uncle"—or if Celine had broken her trust and told Tad things best left untold.

"You asked me why I brought you here. It was wrong of me, I know, but I had to see the ghosts." His smile was whimsical, playful. "Heard tell I was close to joining them myself, and for a long time, at that. Figured they'd tell me how to get my life back to that good place. There's a lot of history buried back in here. There was so much love," he said, pointing at the cemetery. "And a lot of heartbreak. All the sadness is about gone. Mother still has her days. She still suffers her melancholy, but Father is always there for her. How did he do it? How could he hold us all together? Protect us. That's what I want to find out. That's the kind of man I want to be. I want to be that man for you. I want to be the kind of person you can depend on. Not just the blank sheet of paper I feel like."

She felt the void in which he lived, but could not feel the hollow left by his not knowing any of his past. But she could try and said, "I'll help you."

They kissed, each hungry for the other. A long kiss.

She felt as if Tad had stolen her breath, her very soul, and frightened by the power of the kiss. She felt the need to break their embrace. It alarmed her to know *such a* singular kind of love could be so demanding, so powerful, so consuming.

But she relished in the realization that he loved her, but hardly understood why it caused her breath to catch. She needed to slow down and think of the correct words to use, but managed only, "It must have been so beautiful here, back then. I can see you and your sisters chasing one another through the park," said Lillie.

"Not as beautiful as you." His words came easily. The door had been opened and he now needed to step through it.

A long anticipated dance of words was about to start. A never mentioned romance, two years long, had saturated every corner of their lives.

His participation in love's dance had been clearer than most of the things that ran through his mind. Perhaps it was as simple as the fact that they had shared no history, just the last two years. The word "love," with its thousands of meanings had never been uttered by either during that long, slow dance. Never spoken, but always present, the soul of the word flitted about the room whenever the two were alone in the presence of the other, waiting, hoping, for a chance to announce itself when the time was right. A curious thing, that unspoken *need* for them to come to terms with how they felt, one for the other, was now centered in their hearts. For two years, Tad had watched Lillie, unsure and afraid his wounds and inability to express himself to the woman caring for him, would drive her away, so he'd held his tongue. And she feared a misunderstood word, errantly said, would destroy the span of time in which she had felt the man was hers and hers alone. Each had been in love with the other for the entirety of those two years. Enough time had been wasted. And now their lifelong dance began in earnest.

"Lillie, I've grown very fond of you. I love you." There. It was said. *Why did that seem so hard?* he asked himself.

Lillie held her breath, trying not to say the same words to him, and failed, "I love you, too, Tad." She, too, thought the words sweet and easy to say, and once spoken, hard to retrieve.

Tad waited, afraid she might counter those beautiful words with a "but" or a "however." Time stood still and the words were not uttered. He believed what she said would always be what it had always been—unconditional.

"Are you sure, Tad?" she asked. "Or are you confusing the love you say you have for me as gratitude for me nursing you so long? Love's a cruel word when it's not meant."

"I do love you," answered Tad, daring to enclose her hand in his. "I fell in love with you the first time I saw your face. Or at least the first time I remember seeing your face," he chuckled, looking for a way to lighten the conversation. "You were standing above me holding something in your hand, wiping my face with cool water. There has never been enough fog to hide that memory from me."

"And that's love to you?" she laughed, in an effort to relieve the tension she felt. Although still not quite at ease, she playfully flapped a towel in his face. "Me patching you up, feeding you. You're suppose to say you heard bells ringing and doves singing."

His laughter eased a pressure so thick the air felt heavy.

"Heard the bells. Bells ringing everywhere, but especially in this ear," he smiled, pointing at the temple with the fading red scar. "But the doves sounded like chickens to me."

The tension between them began to ease.

She laughed again and bent to kiss him. "Might have been chickens. But the few we had then didn't last more than a day after the wounded started showing up. I do believe you love me. And I love you, but we need to go slowly."

"Will you marry me if I'm not too busted up for you?" he said, too anxious for more time to be wasted.

The question rocked her. She wanted to hear him ask it, but still the suddenness of it . . .

She knew the answer and had known it for a long time if he ever did ask.

"Seems you can't remember the definition of "slowly,'" she laughed. "Are you through with that going back to your old unit talk?"

"I think so."

"If you are, I will,' she answered, "even if the rest of my life is spent taking care of you. If anything, you're the finest specimen of man I've ever seen. But hear me, Thaddeus Samuel Biggs. I'll not be a war widow."

"Okay. Then those days are done. It's my time to take care of you."

They sealed their promises with yet another passionate kiss.

"When do we tell your mother and father?"

"I think they already know. When they see us together, they give us those little *know it* looks only parents can do. But now that it's official, we need to tell them."

Standing arm in arm, Lillie asked, "Do you think your father will let us build our home on that Slater's Corner. I love that piece of land," she said. "It's so peaceful there."

"No, I don't think he'll do that," Tad answered seriously. "First thing he'll say is it floods. Even though it never has. There's something about that place to him. He said someday I'd know."

He could have told Lillie the story his father had told him long ago. He was fond of the corner, also, but hardly would want to build a house over a place where another man had died such a violent death. He saw no reason to tell Lillie of what he had been told. But, still he thought his father had merely been trying to keep him away from the creek.

"Besides, he's already up to something. Clearing a parcel up the creek a ways. Still close to the creek. It's big enough for a house. Told me he was cutting down briars. Let's go tell them."

***

"Another daughter," said Sam as he hugged his future daughter-in-law. "That's wonderful news, isn't it, Mother?"

Feigning surprise, she hugged the young lady tightly to herself and said, "Oh Lillie. I'm so happy for the two of you. Have you two decided on a date?"

"We're thinking this coming spring. No date yet, though," answered Thaddeus. He retrieved Lillie and held her close.

"The war should be over by then," commented Sam.

"War or no war, we're getting married," furthered Thaddeus. He pressed his lips to Lillie's temple.

Taking Lillie's hand, Rose said, "If you'll pardon us, I want to take Lillie and break the news to her new sisters."

"Mother," said Sam. "Tell Holt to bring us brandy and cigars. This is a special occasion." He put his arm across his son's shoulders. "Son, I'm a very happy man today. Two years ago, your mother and I, would not have laid odds on this day ever happening. We prayed and prayed every day, and now here you are." He pulled his son close and hugged him again.

"Do you like her, Father? I mean really like her?" asked Tad.

"Your mother and I love her, son."

"She says I'm marrying her because I feel obligated to."

"If that's true, you need to tell her. If not, she'll realize it soon enough. First lesson, Tad. Never, never lie to a woman, especially your wife. Now, what are your plans after you two get hitched?"

"We haven't given it much thought."

"I have. Your mother and I want you to take over this place. Doc Yardley says I have to quit."

Chapter Thirty-four: Eighteen and sixty-four: Summer. A decision too late in the making.

A contrast of two worlds is about to collide. The war has raged across much of America but, finally a semblance of peace has come to Swift Creek. Sam is pleased Thaddeus has finally understood the degree of his injuries. Doc Yardley said it was something he would eventually, and, completely recover from, but it would take a long time. Maybe the war would be over soon, Sam has prayed. But people can change their minds and he feared Tad had lingering doubts about his decision to stay and serve the Confederacy from home.

The Sunday-after-church dinner was the largest and most lavish meal of the family. It was Annie's favorite meal to prepare—her weight proof enough that she tested and retested everything she cooked until she was satisfied with the quality, or stuffed from the tasting.

The family and guests were always dressed in their best Sunday go-to-meeting clothing and by mid morning Sam dressed for lunch, also. He'd never given in to Rose's constant request for him to attend church services, even if only once in a while. But each Sunday he replaced his comfortable everyday clothing with one of the three suits he owned. The suit of the day was removed from the cedar-lined closet in which it and the remaining two were stored for special occasions—weddings, funerals, and once for a Christmas affair which he'd found entertaining but no more informative than the family Bible. At first, he did it begrudgingly, but he had grown to enjoy the formality of the Sunday family dinner. Sunday dinners were always special and Sam always smelled faintly of cedar.

He was a spiritually inclined man, something born into him after decades of seeing the evil men did to one another. But instead of taking preacher-taught religion to heart, he found church services to be mostly showy events—the moaning and groaning of preachers in their pretend trances, nearing exhaustion after two hours spent sobbing, yelling and flapping arms in the air—and their insane claims of being able to talk in tongues. Mostly, to him, church seemed a grand opportunity for women to dress in their finest dresses and a chance for their fat husbands to fondle and twirl braided gold fobs attached to gold pocket watches—possessions with which to brag of their station in life

The walls of the church always pushed against him and made him feel like a hypocrite, considering the things he had been forced to do in the past. He believed in a higher power, but also, that he could worship his God in the church which he kept in his heart. But family was another matter. He felt even in the hard times the South had been steadily sliding into, there was a need to maintain the heady and dignified manner common to the wealthy owners of prosperous plantations.

The dinner exchange was lively and never limited to specific subjects, except when matters of great importance needed to be discussed. For the last three years the War of Northern Aggression dominated most of the conversations, to the point that Rose and his daughters were tired of "President Davis this" or "Confederate Army that", so Sam sought other things to discuss.

On Sundays, Samantha and her husband of two years were always present. And between them sat Rebecca, Robert's six year old daughter and the blossom of Sam's heart. Robert Earl McDaniel's came from down below Fort Harwood in a pleasant area known as Momeyer. His family had struggled for years, just as he and Rose had, to make something of their lives and now Robert Earl was the heir apparent of the thriving family plantation. He had courted Samantha for nearly two years before she finally agreed to accept his hand in marriage. Robert was a widower—his first wife died in childbirth, but Rebecca, the newborn daughter, had survived the heart-rending tragedy.

"Another fine meal," Sam said to Annie, and everyone agreed. "Thaddeus and I will take our leave. We have things of great importance to discuss."

And turning to his son-in-law, he said, "Robert. I have agreed to discuss some personal matters with Thaddeus, but before we get to it, come down to the library and enjoy a Carolina Gold and a glass of brandy with us."

"No. I'm stuffed. We can visit later, then. I promised Rebecca I would walk her down to the Slater corner," replied Robert.

Samantha led the way to the living room, Izzy, Lillie, and Rose following her. Izzy had accepted Bradley Smith's marriage proposal after he returned from his service with the Army of the Confederate States of America. With two brides-to-be, Izzy and now Lillie, the talk was that of weddings, bridal gowns, bridesmaids and marriage.

Night after night Izzy had cried herself to sleep, after Bradley had left. She feared for his life, as she had every day since he'd announced he was joining the infantry. They agreed to marry after he returned and soon he was mustered into the infantry near Samaria, a small crossroad village not far from Fort Harwood.

Before leaving, he'd jokingly told her he would rejoin for a second time if she would not marry him when he came home after his first year of voluntary duty and remembered her telling him she would not be blackmailed in such a manner.

When he did return, he returned a changed man. He was quiet, withdrawn, and spoke only when spoken to. She misunderstood his preoccupation with the things he had witnessed as a change of his feelings for her. She questioned him about his reluctance to communicate openly. Not knowing of war and the things which happened when men faced one another across a field, each desperate to kill the other before being killed themselves, he could hardly share such things with her, for fear that she would think him an evil man.

Yet, Bradley held a strong conviction to the idea of the Confederate States of America and was torn between enlisting for another year, but gave up that conviction after Izzy issued her own ultimatum,

"If you go back and get yourself killed, I'll never speak to you again, Bradley Smith."

***

"Thaddeus. You're about jumpy as a rabbit with buckshot tearing the ground up around it. What's going on?"

"I've been thinking. I've got'ta go back, Father," Thaddeus answered, matter-of-factly.

"You told Lillie?"

"Yes."

"What did she say?"

"She started crying."

"Only you can decide what you're going to do. If you go back, you'll lose her. You know that, don't you?"

"I'm confused. I feel I've let my friends down. Besides, it wouldn't be for long." Tad countered.

"I'll tell you this one last time, she won't be here when you get back, if you even get back. Don't do it. You've done enough."

"I have to go back. If I don't they'll write me up as a deserter. Now that I have healed, I have no say in it."

"Healed? You're some better, yes. But you're not healed. Not yet, Tad. That's what Lillie says. And what Doc Yardley says, too."

"But I am better. Besides, I'm still a Captain of Artillery."

"Then," Sam paused and pointed toward a row of books on a shelf across the room. "Can you read the spine of that book, top shelf, third from the right?"

Thaddeus strained his eyes. "It's The Iliad. It's a poem, a very long poem. And your favorite."

"Wrong. That book is the fifth from the right. I said third."

"It's ah . . . gilded . . . um, I can't make it out."

"That's the Bible, Thaddeus. You can't see like you used to, either."

"Some days I can't. Most I can."

"Does an artillery captain get to pick and choose which days he's willing to fight?"

"I'm serious, Father. It's time. Besides, there's plenty of fellows still fighting who were shot up bad. Worse than me. Some only got one arm, some one leg."

"But they're healed."

"No more than me."

Sam ignored the comment. "And your shoulder. You still can't stretch your arm out. Not full out. You still have the occasional catch in your walking, Son. Lillie says there's days, and more than one or two, when you forget things. You may think you have to go back. Might even want to, and I can't keep you here. But Son, you'll never lead artillery again. At best, you might be allowed to stay behind the lines doing paper work."

"But I served under General Jackson. That should go for something."

"He's dead, Thaddeus. I know you loved that man and he loved you, but that's no reason to go back. Stay here. Help me, Henry, and Isaac gather foodstuffs and supplies. Help us and serve from here. Wouldn't that be enough?"

"My mind's made up, Father."

"Change it. Listen to me. The army you remember does not exist anymore. They kept winning most of the battles after Malvern Hill, but Gettysburg ended that streak. Everybody knows that. There's some who say Lee should give it up. Quit."

"Is that what you think, Father?" Tad asked, his eyes questioning the man before him.

"It's not for me to decide. If it were, we would not be having this discussion. The entire South is in a state of denial. We're out of everything except hope. A war can't be won with hopes. Lee's retreating. Grant's got him on the run. That old man's trying to save Richmond and President Davis now. Papers say he's in a tangle with that murderer Grant in a place that doesn't even have a name. They call it the Wilderness or some such name. They are lost in the woods above and west of Richmond. You ask me, Lee doesn't have a fried dog-turd's chance of getting out of this mess alive. Grant's got three men to our one. He doesn't even need rifles, just marches his men out in front of our boys. If Lee puts more men in line, Grant stands twice as many up so the South will use up what little ammunition they have left. Grant's fighting a war of attrition—trading men for lead. You can do more good here, than there holding paper for some general to write orders on. Please, Son. Rethink this thing."

Thaddeus stood, ready to leave the room. "I won't sit here and listen to you talk like that. It's like you've given up, Father. What happened?"

"Yes you will. You're the one wanting to go and finish getting killed—I'm the one that wants you to stay. And I am offended that you think I am a traitor. I'm not. I'm a father."

"But . . ."

"No. You wait. I'm going to say something that might make you think even more lowly of me. But by God, it's the truth. Every person in this whole country, North and South combined, knows the war's already lost. It was lost before it started. And my heart is broken because of it. The South will bleed for years before we return to what we were, if we ever do. And we still won't be our own country. The Union is going to prevail. Son, there will be a price we have to pay for trying to leave the Union. Your grandchildren will still be paying for our stupidity in trying to break free from the United States when they're grown and old. That war should have never been fought."

"Pay how? Dying's not enough?"

"Dying's never been enough. 'To the victor goes the spoils.' Ever hear that?"

"Yes, who hasn't? But what does it mean when you use it with 'price'?"

"The South is broke . . . bankrupt, but the North is bad off, too. They'll be our kings and tax us so heavy we'll pray we were back in England."

"If we fail, can we survive?" Tad stood to leave.

"We'll make it. I've got a plan. You want to call me a traitor? Sit back down," Sam demanded. "I'm not, but I'll tell you why I think you want to go back. It's because of General Jackson."

"He's dead, Father. Dead."

"Yes. He is. But it's because he told you to, that you want to fight."

Thaddeus stood again his face turning red with anger.

"Did that man of higher education explain the reason for the South seceding?" asked Sam.

"Of course he did."

"Which version did he use? Was it States' rights? The Slavery issue? That the North was the aggressor? Or was it simply because the man loved the very thought of war? That's the only thing he ever knew, Tad—war and killing."

"He spoke of all those things," answered Thaddeus, and defended his hero with, "except what you call his love of killing."

"Is that why you volunteered, Tad?"

"Well . . .no. It's complicated."

"No it's not, Son. It's simple. Eating or starving. That's what started this war."

"What are you talking about?"

"I'm talking about growing fat from eating and starving from not eating. Food, Thaddeus. Food."

"Well. That makes it real clear," answered Tad, a touch of sarcasm staining his words.

With an exaggeration of placing food into his mouth, Sam said, "Try looking at it from where I do, but remember I'm a planter. That's what I am. That's what I do. Every person you talk to is going to give you a different opinion of why we went to war. I'll give you mine. Some are going to say the South had the right to secede from the Union. I tend to believe that myself. It's in the Constitution. Others are going to say it's because of the slaves. That's a load of bullshit. Even Lincoln knew how important slaves were to the welfare of those folks up north. He didn't give a rat's ass one way or the other about the slaves. He as much as said so himself. It was in the paper. And what he said proves that's how he felt about slavery. Said if he could save the Union without freeing the slaves, that's what he'd do. Then he turned right around and said if he had to free them all, he'd do that. And if that didn't work, and it came down to it, he'd free some of them and leave others be. Personally, I've always believed "Ole Massa Lincoln" didn't give a shit one way or the other. You following me?"

Tad did not answer.

"Those people up there will never say it, but deep down they know how important the slaves are, *especially* to them. And Lincoln knows it. And I know it. Like I said, I'm a planter."

Tad stood to leave.

"You sit and let me finish," Sam said sternly. "Think about this. We all have to eat. You've never been hungry a day in your life. Never had to fear starving, and hunger is not pleasant. Here in the South we are blessed with long growing seasons. The further south— the longer the season. Florida grows two, or more crops year round. Mississippi, Alabama, Georgia, Texas, all of them have long seasons. North Carolina, not so long, but we stay busy most of the year. The South always did grow more than it could use. So where did all of that surplus go? It went North, Son."

"Father what are you talking about?" irritation adding to Thaddeus' cynicism.

"I'm telling you why we're fighting. In return for selling our surplus to the North, for the most part, the South had grown wealthy. This is not the only plantation in the South. There's thousands of us all over. There was hordes of money to be made from selling our excess to the North, and guess what was done with the money they put in our hands. We decided to come of age. Recognized the benefits of being industrial like the North, so we put all that money that came from them into making things we had been buying from the North. We needed their money, they needed our crops. They bought everything. Cotton, corn, tobacco, you name it, they wanted it. Now you see a pattern developing, Thaddeus?

"No Sir. I'm still pondering fat and starving."

"The North doesn't grow nearly as much as the South and it has over twenty-two million people to feed. That's damn near three times the population of the South. They would starve without us feeding them. But we quit growing a surplus.

"So what's that got to do with anything?"

"It means they didn't like what we did with all that money we made off of them. It planted a fear in them. Little brother was getting too big and too big meant too strong, and that wouldn't do. And there's still more people than they can feed with their short growing seasons. We are no longer their food basket, but their industrial competitors. Especially with weapons of war. Do you remember the Tredegar Iron Works in Richmond? I took you there."

Tad nodded his head.

"They make, or did make, before the war started, farm implements, plows, axes, all kinds of equipment, anything made out of iron. Now it's cannon, guns, war machinery. Every single state in the South has its own foundries. Alabama's got the Montgomery Iron Works. Mississippi—one in Jackson and three in Vicksburg. Georgia. Tennessee. Virginia. Even North Carolina's got one in Beaufort and one in Greensboro. The South was about to become independent from the North, but would have been willing to remain in the Union before them uppity bastards said we had no rights. And there's one thing you don't say to a southerner—'you have no rights.'"

"And the North still needs enough food to feed twenty-two million people, is that what you're saying?" asked Tad.

"That's the irony of it all—us trying to be like those people up north. Like I said, this damn war's all about eating and starving, Son. The North thought of our industrial progress as a betrayal. So they found a way to teach us—the wayward sons—a lesson. For them, words like State's Rights, Slavery, Northern Aggression made war seem reasonable, and gave the South an excuse to secede. The South was happy. It'd grown rich and fat. We were full of ourselves. Kings of the world. We could take on anybody, any country. But we betrayed ourselves as much as those up there when we cut back with our farming. We can't even feed our own boys now. We produce only minimal clothing and most of that, shoddy at best. We have soldiers marching barefooted and wearing rags on their backs. They have no tents and those who have shoes are lucky. The few we do churn out are of such poor quality hogs would snout them out of their sties. All I heard for the last decade before that goddamn war started was how the South didn't need the North. But all them thought up words did was made it sound like there was something worth fighting for. They want—no, need—us back in the fields. Yes, I want the war over and I want our Confederacy to survive. But we can't survive killing one another, and we can't survive separated. Such fools we have been."

"Father, I see your point. I'm not sure I agree with it and, respectfully, I would suggest you keep your thoughts to yourself. They might get you hung."

"And who do you think would hang me, Tad? In the last two years, and you were here all that time, healing from your war, Henry,

Isaac and I have filled six trainloads with our own corn, wheat, vegetables, cotton, tobacco and anything else we could get our hands on to ship off to Richmond. And we were proud to do it. Too old to fight, but we helped. A traitor, you dare think of me. Were you aware we just sent another train-load of cotton and tobacco to the quartermaster in Richmond no more than two weeks ago?"

"Yes. Mother told me about it. And I am proud of you for doing that. I know you once, at least, hoped the South could make a go of it, Father."

"I still do. It would be a blessing from the Almighty if He would let us become such a country, but I fear it is not to be, Tad. There's simply nothing left."

"Mother said you sent Mr. Graystone with that load. Why'd you send him?"

"He was a spy."

Puzzled by the accusation, Thaddeus chose to not add to the tension in the room and remained quiet.

"Lets go down to the creek and visit with Robert and Rebecca," suggested Sam.

"I'll join you there with Lillie. And Father, I'll take you up on that offer to help with the sending of stuff to our men. Who would want a broken-down man like me anyway?"

"Lillie," answered Sam.

Chapter Thirty-five: Eighteen and sixty-five: A dynasty at the verge of imploding.

All may soon be lost. Sam introduces a plan to save Swift Creek. But to do so will require a great effort from him, Henry, Isaac, and most of all, Thaddeus. It is a bold plan and one never tried.

"Ezekiel and Bear told me their women are after them to 'Jump the broom,'" Henry announced to Sam. "I don't see no harm in it myself, but told them I'd talk to you about it."

He acknowledged Isaac standing inside the doorway. "Hey, Isaac," Sam said, waving him inside.

"Why now?" Sam asked, turning back to Henry. "They can do as they please soon enough . . . according to Lincoln."

"They said if they were turned out . . . their way of telling me they knew they were free, but not quite sure what "free" means to a Negro, they thought it might be easier to stay together as a family. I suppose it would make things seem more structured to them."

"Well, they will be free and not long from now," Sam said shaking his head at the turn of events. "Don't they know their new "Massa" Lincoln," his voice edgy with sarcasm, "freed them the first of January, back in 'sixty-three?"

"Well, it ain't took. Not yet, anyway. They was all happy about it when they first heard of it, but that was over a year ago. Nothing came of it so their excitement died off. Some of 'em got a mite uppity. But to most, all that talk about freedom was just a fairy tale. One or two of 'em told me they were going to lite out . . . head off to whatever their idea of paradise is. Couple of 'em got right in my face telling me they was free, so I kind'a had the field boss talk to them.

Show them the error with their thinking the South was finished," said Henry. "He got them to rethink things."

"You know how I feel about slave beating. He beat them?" asked Sam.

"Not that I know of. I told him not to. But nowadays none of them darkies say much about being free."

"Be best for all of us to say nothing about any of that to Rose," said Sam.

Each man remembered Sam's long-standing orders to never touch a slave, not in a way as to hurt or humiliate them, and how Rose had demanded such beatings be ended.

"What's done is done," said Sam." It's starting to turn cold . . . snow on the ground last week. They don't want to think about being free, not when they have no idea of what's coming with freedom," Sam continued. "Come spring and warmer days, that'll change."

Sam's face turned thoughtful. "You know they don't have a chance out there on their own. Don't you?"

Isaac was always the quietest of the men, but when he did say something it was well thought out and usually correct. "But it got him re-elected, didn't it? And that ain't all. From that day on our boys didn't know why they were fighting. Didn't know if it was for State's Rights or for the darkies. Him saying the darkies were free took the heart out of our boys. Most of our fighting men didn't have any slaves and if that was what they thought the war was about, no wonder so many deserted and lit out for home. They didn't have a dog in no fight over a Negro."

"True," answered Sam. "It did get him elected. But to free them? That's bullshit. They're like little children, even the old hunchbacked gray-haired ones. Can't feed themselves. Me, you, and Isaac have fed them all their lives. Had to tell them when to bathe, when to eat, when to go to the outhouse. Them going free is the same as killing them. They have any concept of money? None that I know of. All in all, I'd say if they do go free, it won't be long before they come back—begging for what they *had*. They'll want their cabins, ham on the table, collard greens and black-eyed peas on the stove. Hungry is not an easy way to live."

"But it's going to happen, Sam," said Henry.

"I know," and dropping his head, he stared at the ground. "You know, Rose and I have talked about that. She agrees if they are going to be set free, they need to start taking the Bible to heart. Give up that stuff they brought with them from Africa. Tell Zeke . . . and Bear I said to have a preacher there with a Bible to say a few words and if they have a broom handy, let 'em jump it afterwards."

"So a preacher and jump the broom? I'll see they'll do it both ways."

Sam, not quite ready to drop the thought, added, "You realize, don't you, they might not go free. The war's going badly but we're not out of it yet. Things could swing back our way. Who knows? Lincoln might have to back off that promise he made them."

"Hope's fading for that. We're beat," countered Henry.

"I agree. Just thinking. It could be the death of all of us if we lose. They will tax us until we hemorrhage blood. That's what victors do . . . punish the losers. How's that for fair? They start the damn war and we get to pay them for all they tore to hell and back. They'll suck us dry. That's the way of politicians"

"So what are we to do with all this?" asked Henry as he pointed in all directions. Each man took in the vast land that was their home.

"We're going to keep it, that's what. Let's meet this coming Saturday. Here in my office. Thaddeus will be there, also. One o'clock."

Walking them to their horses, Sam asked of Isaac and Henry, "Either of you heard from your boys?"

Isaac answered first. "Me and their mother got a letter two weeks gone. Short one. Joe said Charlie's been taken prisoner. Said he don't know where but would ask around. He said he and his unit are starving, damn near out of everything—food, clothes, gunpowder, lead. One unit hadn't shot a bullet in the last two battles. No firing caps for their guns. Now that's something, ain't it?" he said, shaking his head. "What are they suppose to do. Throw rocks at 'em. Anyway, without saying it in so many words, he hinted they was on the run."

Henry looked haggard. His face drawn. "Been two months since our boy wrote us. We both want the mail to come but we're afraid it will," he choked.

Sam understood their grief. He and Rose had suffered greatly when they heard of Tad's being wounded. His heart went out to his two best friends.

"The two of you know I'm not much for church ways, but I do know what's in my heart. Would you mind if I said a few words, you know, kind of a prayer for your boys?"

Henry and Isaac shook their heads.

"Be obliged," they answered, almost in unison.

***

One o'clock, Henry and Isaac entered the dark mahogany office, soon to be followed by Thaddeus. Sam called for Holt and directed him to pour his guests a brandy and to snip the ends off the cigars each held. The office had always been the center of decision making for the three different plantations. Sam was always in charge.

"And Holt," said Sam sternly to the long time house servant as he pointed at the door. "See no gets past you. Bring us extra cigars and another bottle of brandy. We'll be here for a while.

"Then sit by the stairs. Anybody comes this way, you tell them not now. If I catch you trying to listen to what we're talking about, I'll sell you tomorrow," and waved him away.

Holt was caught off guard. Sam had never spoken to him so sternly. "Yas Suh," the dark-skinned man answered, and with his eyes bulging, he hurriedly left to get the brandy and cigars. Returning, his hands shook as he poured the brandy and lit the smokes. Finished, he rushed to his post by the stairs.

The men sucked heavily on their expensive Carolina cigars and felt the calming effect of the nicotine. The brandy burned the throats scorched by the hot smoke.

"Gentlemen, we have a problem coming down the pike. Charging straight at us. There's no other way I can say this. I do not think President Davis, even with General Lee, is going to keep their promise to establish a new country for those of us in the South."

Uncomfortably, Henry and Isaac repositioned themselves in the heavy oxblood, maroon leather-covered chairs. Neither nodded their heads in agreement, although each knew what he said was true. But only Sam had the strength, or the misfortune, to do that which he saw as his duty—to make such a bold statement.

Thaddeus stared through the floor-to-ceiling window separating the men from the cold and blustery day waging its own war with the back wall of the mansion.

"Father," he said, "you talk as if the war is already ended. Lee's just had some set backs. They always do during the winter."

He and his father had discussed the coming war's end many times, and both had agreed to disagree. Now, that a year had passed, Thaddeus could see the wisdom of his father, but felt it was important for him to voice his halfhearted objection.

"Son, it's hardly something I want either. I have prayed and prayed for a turn of events. I believe if we lose Petersburg, it's over. The city and the Army of Northern Virginia has been holed up there since mid summer last year. Outside, Grant and his men are dug in, waiting them out. Our men are waiting, too. Remember what I said about the eating and starving of war? Grant and his men are eating. Lee and his are not eating. They're starving. And here it is, nearing the end of the fourth year of fighting. Bragg's off ripping around Tennessee. And he's not getting much done, either. Atlanta's burnt to the ground and Sherman's marching straight north at us. We're outnumbered, outgunned, and surrounded."

Thaddeus felt defeated and unable to bring himself to admit it, said, "I just don't think things are as desperate as you, Father." Sounding irritated, he asked, "So what's this meeting about?"

"It's about us not losing more than we've already lost. The Confederate States of America will never happen. Even right now, it's good as gone. But for them, those men who someday we'll have to call our brothers again, killing our dream is not enough. No. Not for those people. Next they'll want revenge. The Union will beat us down . . . take everything away from us, and give it to the wealthy of the North. They will tax us and call it "penalties." They will pillage and steal, and claim it as a right of victory. There's already talk of how our farms are going to be strangled with penalties. Penalties, my ass," he spat. "Just another way of saying they'll tax us to death."

Henry's face was etched with concern. Isaac's too.

"How much taxes you thinking, Sam?"

"More than most folks got put away," Sam said, staring at the floor. "But more than they think we got. It'll still be high and they'll keep figuring out new ways to beat us down. That's Washington for you. The crooks will stay in power. But we'll make it. They will not destroy what the four of us have built," Sam said, slamming his fist upon the desk.

"They're not going to let us off easy," said Isaac.

"I know," answered Sam. "But I do believe if we're careful, we'll make it through. They get to pushing hard at us, we give them some of what we have in order to stave them off. Stretch it out, tell them we need a first crop before we can settle up. Tell them maybe two crops, three. Stall at every turn. It'll work at least the first year. If we do what I'm proposing we do, we'll keep our places and I think most of our slaves—although they'll be free men—will end up staying here with us. Yes, some, thinking freedom is more than it is, will leave, but they'll come back. And therein lies my plan."

"Sam?" asked Henry and Isaac, each needing to ask the obvious question. Henry nodded to Isaac.

"How are we going to pay penalties or taxes? And with what?" asked Isaac. "The last two years have been a disaster for us. Shit, what we managed to get out of the ground, we couldn't get to market. Nobody to sell to. There's no money. We gave it all for the Cause and I think we did a lot of good with it. It woulda' only rotted away in the barns."

"If we do what we have to do close to the bone," answered Sam, "and watch everything, trim back our expenses, we can make it through. But our lives *are* going to change. We have enough money put by for a couple years. Two at best. Our plantations have done well by us. And don't forget how much we recovered from that thieving bastard Graystone. Son of a bitch stole a lot from us in twenty years."

He held the cigar, its smoke swirling toward the ceiling, and said. "Finish your brandy and enjoy another cigar. It might be the last for a long, long time."

"Okay. Now let's get down to it. Let's take inventory of what we have and what we don't have. Because what we have is going to get us what we don't have."

"And that is?" asked Thaddeus. He could hardly have lived with the man for the better part of his life without knowing his father would gamble everything he had on his statements.

"We have manpower."

"What are you saying, Sam. The slaves are going to stay?"

"Yes, Henry. That's exactly what I'm saying. Some will go but they won't go far. Then they'll come back. You might disagree, but think of human nature. Like I told Thaddeus, think about the basics of living, think about eating and starving—life's greatest teachers. Think about the things we've begun to take for granted. It's all around us," and he swung his arm outward, and pointed to the far reaches. "You ever sleep in the rain? Ever need a fireplace to warm by on a cold winter night? Like I said, some will leave, but first day out they'll be hungry. First rainy night and the women and babies start bawling, they'll start thinking and turning their heads, trying to catch a glimpse at what they left behind. It hasn't rained for a while, but as sure as I'm sitting here the weather will turn. Every try to start a fire with wet wood? Without an Axe? Those cabins are going to become *the* paradise they set out looking for." He watched the other men to see if they understood.

"Let's put it to the pencil," he said, as he touched the pressed-graphite lead to his tongue. "How many slaves down at The Ferns, Isaac?"

"Last count three hundred eighty-six."

"And cabins? The slaves and those the hired families live in?"

"Nigh on eighty."

"Up at The Meadows, Henry. Slaves?"

"Near 'bout the same. A few less, I reckon Three-forty. Three-fifty."

"Cabins? Counting the hired-on families', too."

"That I know. Seventy-six."

"Okay. Here on Swift Creek we got just shy of four hundred slaves and ninety-four cabins. What about out-buildings? Mules?

Hogs? Plows? Are the barns filled with last year's crops? The smoke houses filled with meat?"

Each answered in the affirmative. "This coming week, we'll take a complete inventory."

Looking from man to man, Sam saw worried faces. "We'll survive," he said, a smile breaking across his face.

"Holt," he said, opening the door. With a flourish of his hand, he ordered more cigars. "No more brandy, not just yet," he added. "Bring us coffee."

He returned to his desk and settled into the comfort of the massive chair. "Gentlemen. We are about to change professions. The North's not going to look kindly on us if we keep calling ourselves plantation owners. Too uppity for us *losers*. From now on we're calling ourselves landowners—just plain old landowners."

The room became quiet. Something momentous was about to be said.

"Between our three plantations . . . I mean 'farms,' we're holding almost twenty thousand acres. And it's damn good land, at that. The best the Piedmont's got to offer. Half of it's woods, the rest, broke to the plow. But if we can't farm it, and get that timber cut and sold, it might as well be nothing but red clay. And Gentlemen, the dirt and timber will be our salvation. Maybe we can use our timber for leverage. The south's rail systems have to be rebuilt. We can barter lumber for taxes.

"Many of our darkies are going to be pushing at the doors to get gone from here. Most, at first, I'd say. But they won't go for long. None of them's ever been out of sight of our places. Sure, they'll hoot and holler, even swear at us when freedom comes. Expect it—they will. They'll head north. Maybe make it to Weldon before reality sets in. Half of them will be hungry and all of 'em weary, worn out, and scared to death. And believe it or not, homesick. Three, four day's, most all of 'em will be slinking back to the quarters."

Sam was setting the stage for what human nature would require.

"Then what, Father?" asked Thaddeus. "They can't stay here."

"But that's where you're wrong. They'll be free. They can stay wherever they want. And what the four of us do will determine if they want to stay here or not."

"What are we going to do?" asked Henry.

"We're going to welcome them back. Feed them. Clothe them. I propose we divide our farms into small sections, small farms, say a hundred to two hundred acres each and tell them they can stay on it as long as they like, and leave when they want, but if they're willing to stay they got to work the land. And we've got to explain right up front we can't afford to pay them, not in cash money. But we'll share everything in halves. Half for us, half for them. We'll foot all the bills for the first year. The first year only. The next, all the expenses related to farming, and by that I mean the fertilizer and seeds, anything that cost money, will be split half and half. If they think half is not fair, turn them away. They'll be back. Half is a hell of a lot more than the nothing they got waiting for them. We'll stock a store where they can trade and run everything they need on the books. Make sure you explain that to each of them good. Explain how they'll have a roof over their heads to keep the rain out, and a fireplace to keep them warm in the winter. Point out the things they'll have and compare it to life on the road with nothing but the shirts on their backs and their little ones, crying from hunger. Tell them over and over they're their own men, free to do whatever they decide. Make sure they understand if they leave, they leave with nothing. Stay or go. Tell 'em it's Lincoln's doing. Not ours. They *have* to know the decision is theirs. That's important. Make them say it. That way they can't blame us if things go bad. It'll be a new kind of farming. Might call it '*sharecropping*.'"

Chapter Thirty-six: Eighteen and sixty-five: April. The great man is gone.

It has been a good life. There has been problems, but they are small in comparison to the joys the Biggs family has been blessed with. The father will be missed. The son, once selfish and egotistical, must now take the reins of Swift Creek Plantation and all that remains of the family. Can he do what is expected of him?

With the arrival of April the cold spring brought with it disheartening news from Petersburg. The war between the North and South had continued for four long years. It had taken a heavy toll of the soldiers from the South, as well as those of a Northern calling. The early spring of eighteen and sixty-five was not going well for the South. The South's once burning desire to be a government unto itself was fading and seemed more of a folly with each new day.

Running short of money and men to throw into battle, the Confederate States of America started dying. Daily, countless numbers of the dead fueled the doubts of the South's chance of victory, and thus the urgency to win at any cost began to falter. Many, those who had lost no son or husband, held tight to their dreams, still thinking the impossible—possible. Others wished for the killing to be done, but to say so publicly would be considered traitorous.

Those same preachers, who for four long years had pounded the ears of their congregants that the war was part of God's plan for a new nation, a righteous and God-fearing nation, now preached ser-

sermons as defeated as they. Every Sunday sermon was more apology than hope.

Indeed, until Gettysburg, the South had won more battles than it lost, but, too, there had been dreadful exceptions. After Gettysburg, the pews were less filled, and those still attending, sat on hard plank benches, and sweltering in the summer heat, began to wonder why God had forsaken them.

Sam always thought it the height of hypocrisy for those self-anointed holy men to pray for victory for the South and death for the North. He, too, had fallen for the promises of the preachers and the soon-to-be established Confederation Of the Southern States of America, one of the many names bandied about by which the new country should be called, but the trip to Malvern Hill put an end to his expectations and the desire for a new government. He understood no government could long survive with dried and hard blood being the pedestal upon which it was established.

As the war dragged relentlessly toward its inevitable end, the few papers—when found—were filled with horrific numbers of how many Southern men had died and how many were being slaughtered daily. They had died and were dying for naught. The cry from diminished families evolved from, "We must keep fighting," to "When will this ever end?"

Now, only the foolish held to their dream, and Sam wondered if the land would ever smell of plowed earth and not of blood.

During the first week of April, eighteen and sixty-five, although vastly outmanned, the Confederate Army fought diligently to hold on to Petersburg. Outnumbered, and imprisoned behind redoubts of poorly constructed forts and a maze of ditches miles long, they were desperately hungry with no foodstuffs to be found. As the cannon roared, stores of gunpowder, shot, and shell, each fired gun dwindled their supplies.

Within a few short days, General Lee would give the command to start a long walk. The march would end for the Army of Northern Virginia at Appomattox Court House, a nondescript building, some sixty miles west of Petersburg.

Sam held Rebecca's tiny hand and the two walked along the creek bank. Sam adored his new granddaughter, a surprise gift that came with Samantha's marriage to Robert. And one had only to look at Rebecca to know she was obviously loved by her new mother. Samantha fussed over the child as if she were her own.

Rebecca's face was angular and strikingly beautiful, her hair blond, long and curly to a fault. She wore it hanging down her back and tied with three blue bows. Her eyes were hazel, a gift from her birth mother.

That smile will break a million hearts, Sam thought.

His new granddaughter was good for Sam. Her presence calmed him. How he wished the plantation had allowed him more time to enjoy his own children.

The hot searing pain, once well on its way up his arm, eased and soon disappeared. Again, a pinch of nitrate forestalled the striations stinging across his chest. He was tired and stressed—worried, but the child had such a soothing effect on him.

"Grandpa, where's my daddy?" Rebecca asked.

"He went back to the house to see your mother. Do you want to see how I made sailboats for Uncle Tad and his sisters when they were about your age?" he asked the adorable little girl.

"Yes, yes, show me," she answered, clapping her hands together and gleefully hopping in excitement.

"Well. Help me find the things we need."

"What are sailboats made out of, Grandpa?"

"Now, they're made out of trees. Some of the big warships our navy built were wrapped in iron plates." He wondered why he'd told the child that. "But long ago, they were made out of reeds."

"Oh, Grandpa," she giggled. "Nuh uh. People can't float on weeds."

"Oh, but yes they did. I'll show you a picture of a reed boat when we go back to the house. There's some in one of my books about Egypt."

"What's Egypt?"

"It's a far away country. Across a big ocean. I'll show you that, too," he laughed, and ruffled her curls.

He stooped to the edge of the creek and with a pocket knife cut a sturdy cat-tail near its roots, and a lily frond from a plant floating in the slow-moving water.

"You know what they call these ship parts?"

"Daddy calls them bad words when he's cutting them down."

He laughed, he too, knew some of those words. "But let's pretend. This long one is called a cattail. In the late fall this thing on top turns fluffy, like your grandmother's cat's tail. So the name. Now watch." He slipped the knife into the stem, twisted it sideways and pried out a fibrous string. He pulled the string from the stem. Next, he bent the long stem of the frond back over the leaf and tied the pointed tip of the fan shaped leaf to the stem. Two gentle wraps of the stringy fiber pulled the sides up and into a round boat shape.

"There's your boat" he said to the wide-eyed child.

"Can we watch it float?" Rebecca asked.

"What about some rock people to put in it? One or two should be enough to make it sit upright."

"Here's one. Can I name this one Aunt Lillie," and laughing, "and this one Uncle Tad?"

"Sounds like a fine idea to me. They can go see the world. Stand here. I'll put it in the water," he said. "You want to name your boat? Your Uncle Tad always named his."

"Yes, Grandpa. Can I name it Rebecca Lynn?"

"Prettiest name I've ever heard," he said and bending gave the lily frond boat a gentle push. A needle of fire, the hottest ever, raced across his chest. The nitrate had only slowed the inevitable burn. But he showed no pain, afraid it would frighten his granddaughter. He stood slowly, hiding the pain in his chest. He held the beloved child's hand as they walked along the bank and back towards the Slater Corner.

"Look, Rebecca. There they are. Uncle Tad and Aunt Lillie," he said trying to not sound as short of breath as he felt.

Breaking free from his hand, Rebecca raced towards her Uncle. "Come, Uncle Tad," and tugged at his hand. "Come watch as you and Aunt Lillie go to Egypt."

The three walked to the bank of Swift Creek as Sam was emerging from the tree-shaded footpath, his skin, now chalky white. A stumble to his steps threatened to give way. Sweat stood in large drops upon his forehead. The grimace he tried to hide spoke of a chest tearing itself apart.

Tad rushed to him and helped him to the wrought iron bench.

"Father. What's wrong?" he asked.

"I don't feel so well right now. I . . .I . . . I'll be fine. Just let me rest a bit."

"It's your heart, isn't it? Mother told me," and turning to Lillie, he said. "Run to the house. Quick. Get Mother. Find Willie and another one of the slaves. And send Hadley, or Buck for Doc Yardley. Tell Willie to get up here fast with help."

Lillie left with a very confused and frightened Rebecca in hand. The last thing Sam heard before he fell sideways on the bench was Rebecca crying out, "Grandpa. Grandpa."

***

Willie and a brute of a man, a slave named Junior, struggled to get Sam up the curving stairs. The walk to the master bedroom was crowded with his daughters, his son, and his wife. But Sam knew nothing of their presence or of their concerns. In bed, he remained in a deep sleep.

Hadley returned from Weldon with Doc Yardley in tow. The doctor reached to the floor of his buggy and retrieved his medicine bag.

"In heah," said Holt, holding the massive mahogany doors open. He pointed towards the second floor. "He be up dare."

"Step aside," Doc Yardley demanded as he pushed through the gathering crowd and climbed the curving stairs to the bedroom. "Out of the way. Out of the way."

Turning right at the upper landing, the elderly physician hardly had to be told where the bedroom was—he'd been there before to visit Thaddeus, and now to see to Sam.

He rushed the family, with the exception of Rose, from the room, sat the bag upon a nightstand and removed the stethoscope. He placed the cold metal disk upon Sam's chest and listened.

"A bit ragged," he said to Rose, "but still strong. When did this happen?"

"Less than two hours ago. Is he going to be . . .," she choked, "is he alright, Doc?" begging for an answer.

"Has he been using his powders?"

"I always check to see if he needs a new paper filled with it every morning. Sometimes he still has the powder from the day before. But more and more, it's been empty by nighttime."

Doc circled his arthritic hand around Sam's wrist a second time. As he did he scolded Sam quietly for keeping himself moving with the help of the powder.

Without realizing he was speaking aloud, he said, "Oh, Sam. I told you to rest."

Sleeping, although fitfully, Sam's color had begun to return to the former red-brown of his sun-cooked skin.

He looks so old, Rose thought, *so used up,* and caught a sob welling up within her throat.

"Miss Rose. I'll stay for a while. Watch how things go. Will you ask Miss Lillie to come up here? And maybe some tea, if you don't mind. Damn near choked to death running my horse that fast on those dirt roads," said Doc Yardley.

Rose entered the living room where the three young ladies, Samantha, Izzy and Lillie crowded their mother, awaiting news of their father and father-in-law. Rebecca, thankfully had been gathered by Celine to her and Buck's cabin.

"He looks better," said Rose, as she stared blankly at the far wall and wrung her hands. And turning to Lillie, added, "He wants you to come upstairs, Doc does. I'll be up as soon as I tell Annie to make some tea.

***

"Doctor Yardley? Miss Rose said you asked for me."

"Yes, yes. Come in, come in" said the elderly Doctor. " Close the door," and waited for her to turn back toward him. In a low voice so as not to heard by any person chancing by in the hallway, he asked,

"Can you help the family again? I fear there's heartbreak on the way. Sam's fading, Miss Lillie. And your mother-in-law won't be able to handle it. She's about to fall apart as it is. Give him as much of this powder as he needs, but don't let him out of the bed. Get Willie to help you if he tries. And Lillie, look at me. Your father-in-law is very, very sick. Keep that to yourself for now. Miss Rose can't handle the truth, not just yet. Understand?"

"Yes Sir." Lillie answered, her heart thumping in her own chest. "I'll do my best."

"When I go down, I'll send someone for your husband. Tell Tad what I said. Tell him it might be a good idea to get the family together. Now, listen, child. I've got to get over to the Hickerman's. They got another young'un on the way. Number ten. You'd think them two would quit doing what it is they like doing so much, wouldn't you?" he smiled at young lady. "Speaking of which," as he pointed at her swollen belly, and asked, "How's the little one doing?"

Lillie blushed. "She started kicking."

"She?" he asked, not expecting or needing an explanation. "Well, that's good. I'll be back as soon as Hickerman Number Ten shows up. I won't be long"

Doc gathered his satchel and walked down the stairs and unseen, let himself out.

***

Lillie held tight to the hand railing as she descended the stairs. Her face was ashen, pale and a painter's portrait of unbearable grief.

Rose, without looking up the stairs, placed a foot upon the lower tread and sure her footing was solid and that she would not spill the tray, looked towards the upper landing. As she took another step, the tray fell from her hands. She ignored the tea staining her flowing gown and the carpet beneath her. She, too, grabbed the hand railing.

Lillie rushed to her, remembering Doc's warning of how fragile Rose was. She extended her arms, blocking Rose's ascent.

"No, Miss Rose. No. It's too late," she said. "He's gone."

She caught her mother-in-law as the shattered woman sagged upon the stairs.

Samantha and Izzy rushed from the living room into the foyer, each fearing the meaning of the commotion they'd heard. As they stood, one hugging the other, Tad came through the front doors. It took a moment for what had happened to register. And then Samuel Elywn Biggs' children raced up the stairs to comfort their mother . . . and each other.

Surrounded by those who loved her, a heart-rending moan unlike any her children had ever heard, escaped Rose's throat, and her body convulsed with sobs.

Epilogue: Eighteen and sixty-five. Late April. "Read his memoirs, Tad."

And so another page falls from the book of life and blows away. That's all we are—each merely a page in a huge book. Some pages, once read are more interesting than others, but taken as a whole, the book we are all part of is exciting, joyful, and hard to put aside.

"Yes, Mother. You wanted to see me?" Thaddeus asked, as he opened the door to the library-office that had been his father's private sanctuary and only escape from the pressures of running Swift Creek Plantation. He pushed the heavy door inward far enough to see the empty, elaborately hand carved chair behind the equally beautifully carved desk. With a trick of light, or perhaps the shadow of a curtain fluttering in the breeze, he saw his father sitting in the desk smoking a Carolina Gold. Tad had expected his mother to be occupying the chair, but as suddenly seen, the vision disappeared. The chair was empty.

Instead, she sat quietly in one of the two matching chairs placed in front of the desk. Her eyes were puffy, but thankfully, he saw they were closed. She looked so exhausted he feared for her well-being and prayed she had drifted off to sleep. She was thin and drawn—her hair whiter with each passing day. Covering her with the blanket from the back of the sofa, he would leave her to her much needed rest and return later, if finally she was taking Doc Yardley's advice and resting when and where she could.

He turned to leave. A soft voice from behind, said, "It took me three weeks to come in here. He read all those books, you know . . . every one of them, from front to back. Then he'd tell me wondrous stories of the things he read. Something I doubt he would have ever admitted to you or your sisters, was . . . he loved love stories." A tear squeezed past the eyelashes of her still closed eyes.

Thaddeus removed his hat and bent to slip his boots off. He felt the power of the sanctuary. His father had loved the dark and polished sheen of the waxed oak floors. And the son wanted to show the father the respect he so deserved.

"Mother, let's go to the living room . . . the porch."

"It's alright, Tad. You're thinking of your hob-nail boots. If you wear those in here, I do believe he'll stop in to speak to you. Don't you?" And finally she smiled. "I can hear him now. 'Get those boots off my floor right now, young man. Remember?' "

"I do. I still smell his cigars. Can you?"

The mother's smile grew and, tilting her face to the space above, she answered. "Yes, I do smell cigar smoke and the brandy he drank."

"Sometimes at night I hear him walking around down here. At least I think I do. Have you heard him? God! Mother. I miss him," he said, his voice cracking from grief.

"I know." She reached to comfort her son.

And there the two lost souls sat, each staring at the walls, the rows upon rows of books, the door, the window, framed pictures hanging on the wall—everything and anything—but each other. Mother ready to cry and son knowing he would if she did.

"It's time, Son," she said.

"Time?" he asked.

"Yes. Time to take your rightful place in this family. That chair," pointing at the chair covered in oxblood maroon leather behind the desk, "is yours."

"But Mother . . ."

"That's what he wanted . . . what we wanted. You're the head of the family now. He told me you'd do a fine job of taking care of us."

Thaddeus stood. He turned from his mother and walked to the far edge of the desk and stopped. "Will you tell me about my father?"

"I can only tell you things you already know. The rest of his life, our life before you came along . . . well, some of those are private, personal. Not even he would tell you of them. But the things you need to know, he's going to tell you," she said pointing at a large binder on the desk. "Don't be premature in judging him. Read it all before you decide who your father was."

"Will you tell me what you can? I spent my whole life with him and know so little. What was he like? Who was he?"

"I will tell you this. He was born poor and that he was a gambler before he came to this part of North Carolina. He was never ashamed of his past. This life he planned never did let him break free of the need to gamble. But not the kind you think I mean. Not cards and poker. No. And I'll leave it at that. He'll tell you what you need to know."

"Anything else?"

"Read his memoirs, Tad," she repeated.

Tad opened the binder, apprehension tearing at him.

He smiled and looked at his mother as he turned the loosely stacked pages toward her. "He always did have a way with words. Look."

Across the cover sheet of the stacked, hand written pages, and printed in red ink were the words,

For my children. My life. My Carolina gamble.
Samuel Elywn Biggs.

the end

CPSIA information can be obtained at www.ICGtesting.com
Printed in the USA
BVOW04s1216021114

373334BV00001B/82/P